Python Digital Forensics Cookbook

Effective Python recipes for digital investigations

Preston Miller
Chapin Bryce

BIRMINGHAM - MUMBAI

Python Digital Forensics Cookbook

First published: September 2017

Production reference: 1220917

Published by Packt Publishing Ltd.
Livery Place
35 Livery Street
Birmingham
B3 2PB, UK.

ISBN 978-1-78398-746-7

www.packtpub.com

Credits

Authors
Preston Miller
Chapin Bryce

Reviewer
Dr. Michael Spreitzenbarth

Commissioning Editor
Kartikey Pandey

Acquisition Editor
Rahul Nair

Content Development Editor
Sharon Raj

Technical Editor
Prashant Chaudhari

Copy Editor
Stuti Srivastava

Project Coordinator
Virginia Dias

Proofreader
Safis Editing

Indexer
Aishwarya Gangawane

Graphics
Kirk D'Penha

Production Coordinator
Aparna Bhagat

About the Authors

Preston Miller is a consultant at an internationally recognized risk management firm. He holds an undergraduate degree from Vassar College and a master's degree in Digital Forensics from Marshall University. While at Marshall, Preston unanimously received the prestigious J. Edgar Hoover Foundation's Scientific Scholarship. He is a published author, recently of Learning Python for Forensics, an introductory Python Forensics textbook. Preston is also a member of the GIAC advisory board and holds multiple industry-recognized certifications in his field.

Chapin Bryce works as a consultant in digital forensics, focusing on litigation support, incident response, and intellectual property investigations. After studying computer and digital forensics at Champlain College, he joined a firm leading the field of digital forensics and investigations. In his downtime, Chapin enjoys working on side projects, hiking, and skiing (if the weather permits). As a member of multiple ongoing research and development projects, he has authored several articles in professional and academic publications.

About the Reviewer

Dr. Michael Spreitzenbarth, after finishing his diploma thesis with the major topic of mobile phone forensics, worked as a freelancer in the IT security sectorfor several years. In 2013, he finished his PhD at the University of Erlangen-Nuremberg in the field of Android forensics and mobile malware analysis. Since then, he has been working as a team lead in an internationally operating CERT.

Dr. Michael Spreitzenbarth's daily work deals with the security of mobile systems, forensic analysis of smartphones and suspicious mobile applications, as well as the investigation of security-related incidents within ICS environments. At the same time he is working on the improvement of mobile malware analysis techniques and research in the field of Android and iOS forensics as well as mobile application testing.

www.PacktPub.com

For support files and downloads related to your book, please visit www.PacktPub.com.

Did you know that Packt offers eBook versions of every book published, with PDF and ePub files available? You can upgrade to the eBook version at www.PacktPub.com and as a print book customer, you are entitled to a discount on the eBook copy. Get in touch with us at service@packtpub.com for more details.

At www.PacktPub.com, you can also read a collection of free technical articles, sign up for a range of free newsletters and receive exclusive discounts and offers on Packt books and eBooks.

https://www.packtpub.com/mapt

Get the most in-demand software skills with Mapt. Mapt gives you full access to all Packt books and video courses, as well as industry-leading tools to help you plan your personal development and advance your career.

Why subscribe?

- Fully searchable across every book published by Packt
- Copy and paste, print, and bookmark content
- On demand and accessible via a web browser

Customer Feedback

Thanks for purchasing this Packt book. At Packt, quality is at the heart of our editorial process. To help us improve, please leave us an honest review on this book's Amazon page at `https://www.amazon.com/dp/1783987464`.

If you'd like to join our team of regular reviewers, you can email us at `customerreviews@packtpub.com`. We award our regular reviewers with free eBooks and videos in exchange for their valuable feedback. Help us be relentless in improving our products!

To my mother, Mary, whose love, courage, and guidance have had an indelible impact on me.
I love you very much.

Preston Miller

This book is dedicated to the love of my life and my best friend, Alexa.
Thank you for all of the love, support, and laughter.

Chapin Bryce

Table of Contents

Preface

At the outset of this book, we strove to demonstrate a nearly endless corpus of use cases for Python in today's digital investigations. Technology plays an increasingly large role in our daily life and shows no signs of stopping. Now, more than ever, it is paramount that an investigator develop programming expertise to work with increasingly large datasets. By leveraging the Python recipes explored throughout this book, we make the complex simple, efficiently extracting relevant information from large data sets. You will explore, develop, and deploy Python code and libraries to provide meaningful results that can be immediately applied to your investigations.

Throughout the book, recipes include topics such as working with forensic evidence containers, parsing mobile and desktop operating system artifacts, extracting embedded metadata from documents and executables, and identifying indicators of compromise. You will also learn how to integrate scripts with Application Program Interfaces (APIs) such as VirusTotal and PassiveTotal, and tools, such as Axiom, Cellebrite, and EnCase. By the end of the book, you will have a sound understanding of Python and will know how you can use it to process artifacts in your investigations.

What this book covers

Chapter 1, *Essential Scripting and File Information Recipes*, introduces you to the conventions and basic features of Python used throughout the book. By the end of the chapter, you will create a robust and useful data and metadata preservation script.

Chapter 2, *Creating Artifact Report Recipes*, demonstrates practical methods of creating reports with forensic artifacts. From spreadsheets to web-based dashboards, we show the flexibility and utility of various reporting formats.

Chapter 3, *A Deep Dive into Mobile Forensic Recipes*, features iTunes' backup processing, deleted SQLite database record recovery, and mapping Wi-Fi access point MAC addresses from Cellebrite XML reports.

Chapter 4, *Extracting Embedded Metadata Recipes*, exposes common file types containing embedded metadata and how to extract it. We also provide you with knowledge of how to integrate Python scripts with the popular forensic software, EnCase.

`Chapter` 5, *Networking and Indicators of Compromise Recipes*, focuses on network and web-based artifacts and how to extract more information from them. You will learn how to preserve data from websites, interact with processed IEF results, create hash sets for X-Ways, and identify bad domains or IP addresses.

`Chapter` 6, *Reading Emails and Taking Names Recipes*, explores the many file types for both individual e-mail messages and entire mailboxes, including Google Takeout MBox, and how to use Python for extraction and analysis.

`Chapter` 7, *Log-Based Artifact Recipes*, illustrates how to process artifacts from several log formats, such as IIS, and ingest them with Python info reports or other industry tools, such as Splunk. You will also learn how to develop and use Python recipes to parse files and create artifacts within Axiom.

`Chapter` 8,*Working with Forensic Evidence Container Recipes*, shows off the basic forensic libraries required to interact and process forensic evidence containers, including EWF and raw formats. You will learn how to access data from forensic containers, identify disk partition information, and iterate through filesystems.

`Chapter` 9, *Exploring Windows Forensic Artifacts Recipes Part I*, leverages the framework developed in `Chapter` 8,*Working with Forensic Evidence Container Recipes*, to process various Windows artifacts within forensic evidence containers. These artifacts include$I Recycle Bin files, various Registry artifacts, LNK files, and the Windows.edb index.

`Chapter` 10, *Exploring Windows Forensic Artifacts Recipes Part II*, continues to leverage the framework developed in `Chapter` 8,*Working with Forensic Evidence Container Recipes*, to process more Windows artifacts within forensic evidence containers. These artifacts include Prefetch files, Event logs, `Index.dat`, Volume Shadow Copies, and the Windows 10 SRUM database.

What you need for this book

In order to follow along with and execute the recipes within this cookbook, use a computer with an Internet connection and the latest Python 2.7 and Python 3.5 installations. Recipes may require additional third-party libraries to be installed; instructions for doing that are provided in the recipe.

For ease of development and implementation of these recipes, it is recommended that you set up and configure an Ubuntu virtual machine for development. These recipes, unless otherwise noted, were built and tested within an Ubuntu 16.04 environment with both Python 2.7 and 3.5. Several recipes will require the use of a Windows operating system, as many forensic tools operate onlyon this platform.

Who this book is for

If you are a digital forensics examiner, cyber security specialist, or analyst at heart that understands the basics of Python and want to take it to the next level, this is the book for you. Along the way, you will be introduced to a number of libraries suited for parsing forensic artifacts. You will be able to use and build upon the scripts we develop in order to elevate their analysis

Sections

In this book, you will find several headings that appear frequently (Getting ready, How to do it…, How it works…, There's more…, and See also).

To give clear instructions on how to complete a recipe, we use these sections as follows:

Getting ready

This section tells you what to expect in the recipe, and describes how to set up any software or any preliminary settings required for the recipe.

How to do it…

This section contains the steps required to follow the recipe.

How it works…

This section usually consists of a detailed explanation of what happened in the previous section.

There's more...

This section consists of additional information about the recipe in order to make the reader more knowledgeable about the recipe.

See also

This section provides helpful links to other useful information for the recipe.

Conventions

In this book, you will find a number of text styles that distinguish between different kinds of information. Here are some examples of these styles and an explanation of their meaning.

Code words in text, database table names, folder names, filenames, file extensions, pathnames, dummy URLs, user input, and Twitter handles are shown as follows: "We can gather the required information by calling the get_data() function."

A block of code is set as follows:

```
def hello_world():
    print("Hello World!")
hello_world()
```

When we wish to draw your attention to a particular part of a code block, the relevant lines or items are set in bold:

```
def hello_world():
    print("Hello World!")
hello_world()
```

Any command-line input or output is written as follows:

```
# pip install tqdm==4.11.2
```

New terms and **important words** are shown in bold. Words that you see on the screen, for example, in menus or dialog boxes, appear in the text like this: "Select **System info** from the **Administration** panel."

Warnings or important notes appear like this.

Tips and tricks appear like this.

Reader feedback

Feedback from our readers is always welcome. Let us know what you think about this book-what you liked or disliked. Reader feedback is important for us as it helps us develop titles that you will really get the most out of.

To send us general feedback, simply email `feedback@packtpub.com`, and mention the book's title in the subject of your message.

If there is a topic that you have expertise in and you are interested in either writing or contributing to a book, see our author guide at `www.packtpub.com/authors`.

Customer support

Now that you are the proud owner of a Packt book, we have a number of things to help you to get the most from your purchase.

Downloading the example code

You can download the example code files for this book from your account at `http://www.packtpub.com`. If you purchased this book elsewhere, you can visit `http://www.packtpub.com/support` and register to have the files e-mailed directly to you. You can download the code files by following these steps:

1. Log in or register to our website using your e-mail address and password.
2. Hover the mouse pointer on the **SUPPORT** tab at the top.
3. Click on **Code Downloads & Errata**.
4. Enter the name of the book in the **Search** box.

5. Select the book for which you're looking to download the code files.
6. Choose from the drop-down menu where you purchased this book from.
7. Click on **Code Download**.

You can also download the code files by clicking on the **Code Files** button on the book's webpage at the Packt Publishing website. This page can be accessed by entering the book's name in the **Search** box. Please note that you need to be logged in to your Packt account. Once the file is downloaded, please make sure that you unzip or extract the folder using the latest version of:

- WinRAR / 7-Zip for Windows
- Zipeg / iZip / UnRarX for Mac
- 7-Zip / PeaZip for Linux

The code bundle for the book is also hosted on GitHub at `https://github.com/PacktPublishing/Python-Digital-Forensics-Cookbook`. We also have other code bundles from our rich catalog of books and videos available at `https://github.com/PacktPublishing/`. Check them out!

Downloading the color images of this book

We also provide you with a PDF file that has color images of the screenshots/diagrams used in this book. The color images will help you better understand the changes in the output. You can download this file from `https://www.packtpub.com/sites/default/files/downloads/PythonDigitalForensicsCookbook_ColorImages.pdf`.

Errata

Although we have taken every care to ensure the accuracy of our content, mistakes do happen. If you find a mistake in one of our books-maybe a mistake in the text or the code-we would be grateful if you could report this to us. By doing so, you can save other readers from frustration and help us improve subsequent versions of this book. If you find any errata, please report them by visiting `http://www.packtpub.com/submit-errata`, selecting your book, clicking on the **Errata Submission Form** link, and entering the details of your errata. Once your errata are verified, your submission will be accepted and the errata will be uploaded to our website or added to any list of existing errata under the Errata section of that title.

To view the previously submitted errata, go to
https://www.packtpub.com/books/content/support and enter the name of the book in the
search field. The required information will appear under the **Errata** section.

Piracy

Piracy of copyrighted material on the Internet is an ongoing problem across all media. At
Packt, we take the protection of our copyright and licenses very seriously.

If you come across any illegal copies of our works in any form on the Internet, please
provide us with the location address or website name immediately so that we can pursue a
remedy.

Please contact us at copyright@packtpub.com with a link to the suspected pirated
material. We appreciate your help in protecting our authors and our ability to bring you
valuable content.

Questions

If you have a problem with any aspect of this book, you can contact us at
questions@packtpub.com, and we will do our best to address the problem.

1
Essential Scripting and File Information Recipes

The following recipes are covered in this chapter:

- Handling arguments like an adult
- Iterating over loose files
- Recording file attributes
- Copying files, attributes, and timestamps
- Hashing files and data streams
- Keeping track with a progress bar
- Logging results
- Multiple hands make light work

Introduction

Digital forensics involves the identification and analysis of digital media to assist in legal, business, and other types of investigations. Oftentimes, results stemming from our analysis have a major impact on the direction of an investigation. With *Moore's law* more or less holding true, the amount of data we are expected to review is steadily growing. Given this, it's a foregone conclusion that an investigator must rely on some level of automation to effectively review evidence. Automation, much like a theory, must be thoroughly vetted and validated so as not to allow for falsely drawn conclusions. Unfortunately, investigators may use a tool to automate some process but not fully understand the tool, the underlying forensic artifact, or the output's significance. This is where Python comes into play.

In *Python Digital Forensics Cookbook*, we develop and detail recipes covering a number of typical scenarios. The purpose is to not only demonstrate Python features and libraries for those learning the language but to also illustrate one of its great benefits: namely, a forced basic understanding of the artifact. Without this understanding, it is impossible to develop the code in the first place, thereby forcing you to understand the artifact at a deeper level. Add to that the relative ease of Python and the obvious benefits of automation, and it is easy to see why this language has been adapted so readily by the community.

One method of ensuring that investigators understand the product of our scripts is to provide meaningful documentation and explanation of the code. Hence the purpose of this book. The recipes demonstrated throughout show how to configure argument parsing that is both easy to develop and simple for the user to understand. To add to the script's documentation, we will cover techniques to effectively log the process that was taken and any errors encountered by the script.

Another unique feature of scripts designed for digital forensics is the interaction with files and their associated metadata. Forensic scripts and applications require the accurate retrieval and preservation of file attributes, including dates, permissions, and file hashes. This chapter will cover methods to extract and present this data to the examiner.

Interaction with the operating system and files found on attached volumes are at the core of any script designed for use in digital forensics. During analysis, we need to access and parse files with a wide variety of structures and formats. For this reason, it's important to accurately and properly handle and interact with files. The recipes presented in this chapter cover common libraries and techniques that will continue to be used throughout the book:

- Parsing command-line arguments
- Recursively iterating over files and folders
- Recording and preserving file and folder metadata
- Generating hash values of files and other content
- Monitoring code with progress bars
- Logging recipe execution information and errors
- Improving performance with multiprocessing

 Visit `www.packtpub.com/books/content/support` to download the code bundle for this chapter.

Handling arguments like an adult

Recipe Difficulty: Easy

Python Version: 2.7 or 3.5

Operating System: Any

> *Person A: I came here for a good argument!*
> *Person B: Ah, no you didn't, you came here for an argument!*
> *Person A: An argument isn't just contradiction.*
> *Person B: Well! it can be!*
> *Person A: No it can't! An argument is a connected series of statements*
> *intended to establish a proposition.*
> *Person B: No it isn't!*
> *Person A: Yes it is! It isn't just contradiction.*

Monty Python (http://www.montypython.net/scripts/argument.php) aside, arguments are an integral part of any script. Arguments allow us to provide an interface for users to specify options and configurations that change the way the code behaves. Effective use of arguments, not just contradictions, can make a tool more versatile and a favorite among examiners.

Getting started

All libraries used in this script are present in Python's standard library. While there are other argument-handling libraries available, such as optparse and ConfigParser, our scripts will leverage argparse as our de facto command-line handler. While optparse was the library to use in prior versions of Python, argparse has served as the replacement for creating argument handling code. The ConfigParser library parses arguments from a configuration file instead of the command line. This is useful for code that requires a large number of arguments or has a significant number of options. We will not cover ConfigParser in this book, though it is worth exploring if you find your argparse configuration becomes difficult to maintain.

 To learn more about the argparse library, visit https://docs.python. org/3/library/argparse.html.

How to do it...

In this script, we perform the following steps:

1. Create positional and optional arguments.
2. Add descriptions to arguments.
3. Configure arguments with select choices.

How it works...

To begin, we import `print_function` and the `argparse` module. By importing the `print_function` from the `__future__` library we can write print statements as they are written in Python 3.X but still run them in Python 2.X. This allows us to make recipes compatible with both Python 2.X and 3.X. Where possible, we carry this through with most recipes in the book.

After creating a few descriptive variables about the recipe, we initialize our `ArgumentParser` instance. Within the constructor, we define the `description` and `epilog` keyword arguments. This data will display when the user specifies the `-h` argument and can give the user additional context about the script being run. The `argparse` library is very flexible and can scale in complexity if required for a script. Throughout this book, we cover many of the library's different features, which are detailed on its document page:

```
from __future__ import print_function
import argparse

__authors__ = ["Chapin Bryce", "Preston Miller"]
__date__ = 20170815
__description__ = 'A simple argparse example'

parser = argparse.ArgumentParser(
    description=__description__,
    epilog="Developed by {} on {}".format(
        ", ".join(__authors__), __date__)
)
```

With the parser instance created, we can now begin adding arguments to our command-line handler. There are two types of arguments: positional and optional. Positional arguments start with an alphabetic character, unlike optional arguments, which start with a dash, and are required to execute the script. Optional arguments start with a single or double dash character and are non-positional (that is, the order does not matter). These characteristics can be manually specified to overwrite the default behavior we've described if desired. The following code block illustrates how to create two positional arguments:

```
# Add Positional Arguments
parser.add_argument("INPUT_FILE", help="Path to input file")
parser.add_argument("OUTPUT_FILE", help="Path to output file")
```

In addition to changing whether an argument is required, we can specify help information, create default values, and other actions. The `help` parameter is useful in conveying what the user should provide. Other important parameters are `default`, `type`, `choices`, and `action`. The `default` parameter allows us to set a default value, while `type` converts the type of the input, which is a string by default, to the specified Python object type. The `choices` parameter uses a defined list, dictionary, or set to create valid options the user can select from.

The `action` parameter specifies the type of action that should be applied to a given argument. Some common actions include `store`, which is the default and stores the passed value associated with the argument; `store_true`, which assigns `True` to the argument; and `version`, which prints the version of the code specified by the version parameter:

```
# Optional Arguments
parser.add_argument("--hash", help="Hash the files", action="store_true")

parser.add_argument("--hash-algorithm",
                    help="Hash algorithm to use. ie md5, sha1, sha256",
                    choices=['md5', 'sha1', 'sha256'], default="sha256"
                    )

parser.add_argument("-v", "--version", "--script-version",
                    help="Displays script version information",
                    action="version", version=str(__date__)
                    )

parser.add_argument('-l', '--log', help="Path to log file", required=True)
```

With our arguments defined and configured, we can now parse them and use the provided inputs in our code. The following snippet shows how we can access the values and test whether the user specified an optional argument. Notice how we refer to arguments by the name we assign them. If we specify a short and long argument name, we must use the long name:

```python
# Parsing and using the arguments
args = parser.parse_args()

input_file = args.INPUT_FILE
output_file = args.OUTPUT_FILE

if args.hash:
    ha = args.hash_algorithm
    print("File hashing enabled with {} algorithm".format(ha))
if not args.log:
    print("Log file not defined. Will write to stdout")
```

When combined into a script and executed at the command line with the -h argument, the preceding code will provide the following output:

```
(venv3) pyforcookbook@dev-vm$ python simple_arguments.py --help
usage: simple_arguments.py [-h] [--hash] [--hash-algorithm {md5,sha1,sha256}]
                           [-v] -l LOG
                           INPUT_FILE OUTPUT_FILE

A simple argparse example

positional arguments:
  INPUT_FILE            Path to input file
  OUTPUT_FILE           Path to output file

optional arguments:
  -h, --help            show this help message and exit
  --hash                Hash the files
  --hash-algorithm {md5,sha1,sha256}
                        Hash algorithm to use. ie md5, sha1, sha256
  -v, --version, --script-version
                        Displays script version information
  -l LOG, --log LOG     Path to log file

Developed by Chapin Bryce, Preston Miller on 20170815
```

As seen here, the -h flag displays the script help information, automatically created by argparse, along with the valid options for the --hash-algorithm argument. We can also use the -v option to display the version information. The --script-version argument displays the version in the same manner as the -v or -version arguments as shown here:

```
(venv3) pyforcookbook@dev-vm$ python simple_arguments.py -v
20170815
(venv3) pyforcookbook@dev-vm$ python simple_arguments.py --version
20170815
(venv3) pyforcookbook@dev-vm$ python simple_arguments.py --script-version
20170815
```

The following screenshot shows the message printed to the console when we select one of our valid hashing algorithms:

```
(venv3) pyforcookbook@dev-vm$ python simple_arguments.py input.file output.file
 --hash --hash-algorithm sha1 -l log.txt
File hashing enabled with sha1_algorithm
```

There's more...

This script can be further improved. We have provided a couple of recommendations here:

- Explore additional argparse functionality. For example, the argparse.FileType object can be used to accept a File object as an input.
- We can also use the argparse.ArgumentDefaultsHelpFormatter class to show defaults we set to the user. This is helpful when combined with optional arguments to show the user what will be used if nothing is specified.

Iterating over loose files

Recipe Difficulty: Easy

Python Version: 2.7 or 3.5

Operating System: Any

Often it is necessary to iterate over a directory and its subdirectories to recursively process all files. In this recipe, we will illustrate how to use Python to walk through directories and access files within them. Understanding how you can recursively navigate a given input directory is key as we frequently perform this exercise in our scripts.

Getting started

All libraries used in this script are present in Python's standard library. The preferred library, in most situations, for handling file and folder iteration is the built-in `os` library. While this library supports many useful operations, we will focus on the `os.path()` and `os.walk()` functions. Let's use the following folder hierarchy as an example to demonstrate how directory iteration works in Python:

```
SecretDocs/
|-- key.txt
|-- Plans
|   |-- plans_0012b.txt
|   |-- plans_0016.txt
|   `-- Successful_Plans
|       |-- plan_0001.txt
|       |-- plan_0427.txt
|       `-- plan_0630.txt
|-- Spreadsheets
|   |-- costs.csv
|   `-- profit.csv
`-- Team
    |-- Contact18.vcf
    |-- Contact1.vcf
    `-- Contact6.vcf

4 directories, 11 files
```

How to do it...

The following steps are performed in this recipe:

1. Create a positional argument for the input directory to scan.
2. Iterate over all subdirectories and print file paths to the console.

How it works...

We create a very basic argument handler that accepts one positional input, DIR_PATH, the path of the input directory to iterate. As an example, we will use the ~/Desktop path, the parent of SecretDocs, as the input argument for the script. We parse the command-line arguments and assign the input directory to a local variable. We're now ready to begin iterating over this input directory:

```
from __future__ import print_function
import argparse
import os

__authors__ = ["Chapin Bryce", "Preston Miller"]
__date__ = 20170815
__description__ = "Directory tree walker"

parser = argparse.ArgumentParser(
    description=__description__,
    epilog="Developed by {} on {}".format(
        ", ".join(__authors__), __date__)
)
parser.add_argument("DIR_PATH", help="Path to directory")
args = parser.parse_args()
path_to_scan = args.DIR_PATH
```

To iterate over a directory, we need to provide a string representing its path to os.walk(). This method returns three objects in each iteration, which we have captured in the root, directories, and files variables:

- root: This value provides the relative path to the current directory as a string. Using the example directory structure, root would start as SecretDocs and eventually become SecretDocs/Team and SecretDocs/Plans/SuccessfulPlans.
- directories: This value is a list of sub-directories located within the current root location. We can iterate through this list of directories, although the entries in this list will become part of the root value during successive os.walk() calls. For this reason, the value is not frequently used.
- files: This value is a list of files in the current root location.

Be careful in naming the directory and file variables. In Python the `dir` and `file` names are reserved for other uses and should not be used as variable names.

```
# Iterate over the path_to_scan
for root, directories, files in os.walk(path_to_scan):
```

It is common to create a second for loop, as shown in the following code, to step through each of the files located in that directory and perform some action on them. Using the `os.path.join()` method, we can join the root and `file_entry` variables to obtain the file's path. We then print this file path to the console. We may also, for example, append this file path to a list that we later iterate over to process each of the files:

```
# Iterate over the files in the current "root"
for file_entry in files:
    # create the relative path to the file
    file_path = os.path.join(root, file_entry)
    print(file_path)
```

We can also use `root + os.sep() + file_entry` to achieve the same effect, but it is not as Pythonic as the method we're using to join paths. Using `os.path.join()`, we can pass two or more strings to form a single path, such as directories, subdirectories, and files.

When we run the preceding script with our example input directory, we see the following output:

```
(venv3) pyforcookbook@dev-vm$ python os_walk.py ~/Desktop/
/home/pyforcookbook/Desktop/SecretDocs/key.txt
/home/pyforcookbook/Desktop/SecretDocs/Spreadsheets/profit.csv
/home/pyforcookbook/Desktop/SecretDocs/Spreadsheets/costs.csv
/home/pyforcookbook/Desktop/SecretDocs/Team/Contact6.vcf
/home/pyforcookbook/Desktop/SecretDocs/Team/Contact1.vcf
/home/pyforcookbook/Desktop/SecretDocs/Team/Contact18.vcf
/home/pyforcookbook/Desktop/SecretDocs/Plans/plans_0012b.txt
/home/pyforcookbook/Desktop/SecretDocs/Plans/plans_0016.txt
/home/pyforcookbook/Desktop/SecretDocs/Plans/Successful_Plans/plan_0427.txt
/home/pyforcookbook/Desktop/SecretDocs/Plans/Successful_Plans/plan_0630.txt
/home/pyforcookbook/Desktop/SecretDocs/Plans/Successful_Plans/plan_0001.txt
```

As seen, the `os.walk()` method iterates through a directory, then will descend into any discovered sub-directories, thereby scanning the entire directory tree.

There's more...

This script can be further improved. Here's a recommendation:

- Check out and implement similar functionality using the `glob` library which, unlike the `os` module, allows for wildcard pattern recursive searches for files and directories

Recording file attributes

Recipe Difficulty: Easy

Python Version: 2.7 or 3.5

Operating System: Any

Now that we can iterate over files and folders, let's learn to record metadata about these objects. File metadata plays an important role in forensics, as collecting and reviewing this information is a basic task during most investigations. Using a single Python library, we can gather some of the most important attributes of files across platforms.

Getting started

All libraries used in this script are present in Python's standard library. The `os` library, once again, can be used here to gather file metadata. One of the most helpful methods for gathering file metadata is the `os.stat()` function. It's important to note that the `stat()` call only provides information available with the current operating system and the filesystem of the mounted volume. Most forensic suites allow an examiner to mount a forensic image as a volume on a system and generally preserve the `file` attributes available to the stat call. In `Chapter 8`, *Working with Forensic Evidence Containers Recipes*, we will demonstrate how to open forensic acquisitions to directly extract file information.

 To learn more about the `os` library, visit `https://docs.python.org/3/library/os.html`.

How to do it...

We will record file attributes using the following steps:

1. Obtain the input file to process.
2. Print various metadata: MAC times, file size, group and owner ID, and so on.

How it works...

To begin, we import the required libraries: `argparse` for argument handling, `datetime` for interpretation of timestamps, and `os` to access the `stat()` method. The `sys` module is used to identify the platform (operating system) the script is running on. Next, we create our command-line handler, which accepts one argument, `FILE_PATH`, a string representing the path to the file we will extract metadata from. We assign this input to a local variable before continuing execution of the script:

```
from __future__ import print_function
import argparse
from datetime import datetime as dt
import os
import sys


__authors__ = ["Chapin Bryce", "Preston Miller"]
__date__ = 20170815
__description__ = "Gather filesystem metadata of provided file"

parser = argparse.ArgumentParser(
    description=__description__,
    epilog="Developed by {} on {}".format(", ".join(__authors__), __date__)
)
parser.add_argument("FILE_PATH",
                    help="Path to file to gather metadata for")
args = parser.parse_args()
file_path = args.FILE_PATH
```

Timestamps are one of the most common file metadata attributes collected. We can access the creation, modification, and access timestamps using the `os.stat()` method. The timestamps are returned as a float representing the seconds since 1970-01-01. Using the `datetime.fromtimestamp()` method, we convert this value into a readable format.

The `os.stat()` module interprets timestamps differently depending on the platform. For example, the `st_ctime` value on Windows displays the file's creation time, while on macOS and UNIX this same attribute displays the last modification of the file's metadata, similar to the NTFS entry modified time. This is not the only part of `os.stat()` that varies by platform, though the remainder of this recipe uses items that are common across platforms.

```
stat_info = os.stat(file_path)
if "linux" in sys.platform or "darwin" in sys.platform:
    print("Change time: ", dt.fromtimestamp(stat_info.st_ctime))
elif "win" in sys.platform:
    print("Creation time: ", dt.fromtimestamp(stat_info.st_ctime))
else:
    print("[-] Unsupported platform {} detected. Cannot interpret "
          "creation/change timestamp.".format(sys.platform)
          )
print("Modification time: ", dt.fromtimestamp(stat_info.st_mtime))
print("Access time: ", dt.fromtimestamp(stat_info.st_atime))
```

We continue printing file metadata following the timestamps. The file mode and `inode` properties return the file permissions and `inode` as an integer, respectively. The device ID refers to the device the file resides on. We can convert this integer into major and minor device identifiers using the `os.major()` and `os.minor()` methods:

```
print("File mode: ", stat_info.st_mode)
print("File inode: ", stat_info.st_ino)
major = os.major(stat_info.st_dev)
minor = os.minor(stat_info.st_dev)
print("Device ID: ", stat_info.st_dev)
print("\tMajor: ", major)
print("\tMinor: ", minor)
```

The `st_nlink` property returns a count of the number of hard links to the file. We can print the owner and group information using the `st_uid` and `st_gid` properties, respectively. Lastly, we can gather file size using `st_size`, which returns an integer representing the file's size in bytes.

Be aware that if the file is a symbolic link, the `st_size` property reflects the length of the path to the target file rather than the target file's size.

```
print("Number of hard links: ", stat_info.st_nlink)
print("Owner User ID: ", stat_info.st_uid)
print("Group ID: ", stat_info.st_gid)
print("File Size: ", stat_info.st_size)
```

But wait, that's not all! We can use the `os.path()` module to extract a few more pieces of metadata. For example, we can use it to determine whether a file is a symbolic link, as shown below with the `os.islink()` method. With this, we could alert the user if the `st_size` attribute is not equivalent to the target file's size. The `os.path()` module can also gather the absolute path, check whether it exists, and get the parent directory. We can also gather the parent directory using the `os.path.dirname()` function or by accessing the first element of the `os.path.split()` function. The `split()` method is more commonly used to acquire the filename from a path:

```
# Gather other properties
print("Is a symlink: ", os.path.islink(file_path))
print("Absolute Path: ", os.path.abspath(file_path))
print("File exists: ", os.path.exists(file_path))
print("Parent directory: ", os.path.dirname(file_path))
print("Parent directory: {} | File name: {}".format(
    *os.path.split(file_path)))
```

By running the script, we can relevant metadata about the file. Notice how the `format()` method allows us to print values without concern for their data types. Normally, we would have to convert integers and other data types to strings first if we were to try printing the variable directly without string formatting:

```
(venv3) pyforcookbook@dev-vm$ python file_metadata.py /var/log/syslog
Change time:  2017-08-28 08:17:01.767046
Modification time:  2017-08-28 08:17:01.767046
Access time:  2017-08-28 07:36:03.099046
File mode:  33184
File inode:  1050884
Device ID:  2049
        Major:  8
        Minor:  1
Number of hard links:  1
Owner User ID:  104
Group ID:  4
File Size:  725
Is a symlink:  False
Absolute Path:  /var/log/syslog
File exists:  True
Parent directory:  /var/log
Parent directory: /var/log | File name: syslog
```

There's more...

This script can be further improved. We have provided a couple of recommendations here:

- Integrate this recipe with the *Iterating over loose files* recipe to recursively extract metadata for files in a given series of directories
- Implement logic to filter by file extension, date modified, or even file size to only collect metadata information on files matching the desired criteria

Copying files, attributes, and timestamps

Recipe Difficulty: Easy

Python Version: 2.7 or 3.5

Operating System: Windows

Preserving files is a fundamental task in digital forensics. It is often preferable to containerize files in a format that can store hashes and other metadata of loose files. However, sometimes we need to copy files in a forensic manner from one location to another. Using this recipe, we will demonstrate some of the methods available to copy files while preserving common metadata fields.

Getting started

This recipe requires the installation of two third-party modules `pywin32` and `pytz`. All other libraries used in this script are present in Python's standard library. This recipe will primarily use two libraries, the built-in `shutil` and a third-party library, `pywin32`. The `shutil` library is our go-to for copying files within Python, and we can use it to preserve most of the timestamps and other file attributes. The `shutil` module, however, is unable to preserve the creation time of files it copies. Rather, we must rely on the Windows-specific `pywin32` library to preserve it. While the `pywin32` library is platform specific, it is incredibly useful to interact with the Windows operating system.

 To learn more about the `shutil` library, visit `https://docs.python.org/3/library/shutil.html`.

To install `pywin32`, we need to access its SourceForge page at `https://sourceforge.net/projects/pywin32/` and download the version that matches our Python installation. To check our Python version, we can import the `sys` module and call `sys.version` within an interpreter. Both the version and the architecture are important when selecting the correct `pywin32` installer.

 To learn more about the `sys` library, visit `https://docs.python.org/3/library/sys.html`.

In addition to the installation of the `pywin32` library, we need to install `pytz`, a third-party library used to manage time zones in Python. We can install this library using the `pip` command:

```
pip install pytz==2017.2
```

How to do it...

We perform the following steps to forensically copy files on a Windows system:

1. Gather source file and destination arguments.
2. Use `shutil` to copy and preserve most file metadata.
3. Manually set timestamp attributes with `win32file`.

How it works...

Let's now dive into copying files and preserving their attributes and timestamps. We use some familiar libraries to assist us in the execution of this recipe. Some of the libraries, such as `pytz`, `win32file`, and `pywintypes` are new. Let's briefly discuss their purpose here. The `pytz` module allows us to work with time zones more granularly and allows us to initialize dates for the `pywin32` library.

To allow us to pass timestamps in the correct format, we must also import `pywintypes`. Lastly, the `win32file` library, available through our installation of `pywin32`, provides various methods and constants for file manipulation in Windows:

```
from __future__ import print_function
import argparse
from datetime import datetime as dt
import os
import pytz
from pywintypes import Time
import shutil
from win32file import SetFileTime, CreateFile, CloseHandle
from win32file import GENERIC_WRITE, FILE_SHARE_WRITE
from win32file import OPEN_EXISTING, FILE_ATTRIBUTE_NORMAL

__authors__ = ["Chapin Bryce", "Preston Miller"]
__date__ = 20170815
__description__ = "Gather filesystem metadata of provided file"
```

This recipe's command-line handler takes two positional arguments, `source` and `dest`, which represent the source file to copy and the output directory, respectively. This recipe has an optional argument, `timezone`, which allows the user to specify a time zone.

To prepare the source file, we store the absolute path and split the filename from the rest of the path, which we may need to use later if the destination is a directory. Our last bit of preparation involves reading the timezone input from the user, one of the four common US time zones, and UTC. This allows us to initialize the `pytz` time zone object for later use in the recipe:

```
parser = argparse.ArgumentParser(
    description=__description__,
    epilog="Developed by {} on {}".format(
        ", ".join(__authors__), __date__)
)
parser.add_argument("source", help="Source file")
parser.add_argument("dest", help="Destination directory or file")
parser.add_argument("--timezone", help="Timezone of the file's timestamp",
                    choices=['EST5EDT', 'CST6CDT', 'MST7MDT', 'PST8PDT'],
                    required=True)
args = parser.parse_args()

source = os.path.abspath(args.source)
if os.sep in args.source:
    src_file_name = args.source.split(os.sep, 1)[1]
else:
    src_file_name = args.source
```

```
dest = os.path.abspath(args.dest)
tz = pytz.timezone(args.timezone)
```

At this point, we can copy the source file to the destination using the `shutil.copy2()` method. This method accepts either a directory or file as the destination. The major difference between the `shutil copy()` and `copy2()` methods is that the `copy2()` method also preserves file attributes, including the last written time and permissions. This method does not preserve file creation times on Windows, for that we need to leverage the `pywin32` bindings.

To that end, we must build the destination path for the file copied by the `copy2()` call by using the following `if` statement to join the correct path if the user provided a directory at the command line:

```
shutil.copy2(source, dest)
if os.path.isdir(dest):
    dest_file = os.path.join(dest, src_file_name)
else:
    dest_file = dest
```

Next, we prepare the timestamps for the `pywin32` library. We use the `os.path.getctime()` methods to gather the respective Windows creation times, and convert the integer value into a date using the `datetime.fromtimestamp()` method. With our `datetime` object ready, we can make the value time zone-aware by using the specified `timezone` and providing it to the `pywintype.Time()` function before printing the timestamps to the console:

```
created = dt.fromtimestamp(os.path.getctime(source))
created = Time(tz.localize(created))
modified = dt.fromtimestamp(os.path.getmtime(source))
modified = Time(tz.localize(modified))
accessed = dt.fromtimestamp(os.path.getatime(source))
accessed = Time(tz.localize(accessed))

print("Source\n======")
print("Created: {}\nModified: {}\nAccessed: {}".format(
    created, modified, accessed))
```

With the preparation complete, we can open the file with the `CreateFile()` method and pass the string path, representing the copied file, followed by arguments specified by the Windows API for accessing the file. Details of these arguments and their meanings can be reviewed at https://msdn.microsoft.com/en-us/library/windows/desktop/aa363858(v=vs.85).aspx:

```
handle = CreateFile(dest_file, GENERIC_WRITE, FILE_SHARE_WRITE,
                    None, OPEN_EXISTING, FILE_ATTRIBUTE_NORMAL, None)
SetFileTime(handle, created, accessed, modified)
CloseHandle(handle)
```

Once we have an open file handle, we can call the `SetFileTime()` function to update, in order, the file's created, accessed, and modified timestamps. With the destination file's timestamps set, we need to close the file handle using the `CloseHandle()` method. To confirm to the user that the copying of the file's timestamps was successful, we print the destination file's created, modified, and accessed times:

```
created = tz.localize(dt.fromtimestamp(os.path.getctime(dest_file)))
modified = tz.localize(dt.fromtimestamp(os.path.getmtime(dest_file)))
accessed = tz.localize(dt.fromtimestamp(os.path.getatime(dest_file)))
print("\nDestination\n===========")
print("Created: {}\nModified: {}\nAccessed: {}".format(
    created, modified, accessed))
```

The script output shows copying a file from the source to the destination with timestamps successfully preserved:

```
(venv3) C:\pyforcookbook>python copy_metadata.py --timezone EST5EDT wallpapers\gorilla.jpg new_wallpaper.jpg
Source
======
Created:  2017-09-02 09:38:30.980457-04:00
Modified: 2017-09-02 09:29:54.526623-04:00
Accessed: 2017-09-02 09:38:30.980457-04:00

Destination
===========
Created:  2017-09-02 09:38:30.980000-04:00
Modified: 2017-09-02 09:29:54.526000-04:00
Accessed: 2017-09-02 09:38:30.980000-04:00
```

There's more...

This script can be further improved. We have provided a couple of recommendations here:

- Hash the source and destination files to ensure they were copied successfully. Hashing files are introduced in the hashing files and data streams recipe in the next section.
- Output a log of the files copied and any exceptions encountered during the copying process.

Hashing files and data streams

Recipe Difficulty: Easy

Python Version: 2.7 or 3.5

Operating System: Any

File hashes are a widely accepted identifier for determining file integrity and authenticity. While some algorithms have become vulnerable to collision attacks, the process is still important in the field. In this recipe, we will cover the process of hashing a string of characters and a stream of file content.

Getting started

All libraries used in this script are present in Python's standard library. For generating hashes of files and other data sources, we implement the `hashlib` library. This built-in library has support for common algorithms, such as MD5, SHA-1, SHA-256, and more. As of the writing of this book, many tools still leverage the MD5 and SHA-1 algorithms, though the current recommendation is to use SHA-256 at a minimum. Alternatively, one could use multiple hashes of a file to further decrease the odds of a hash collision. While we'll showcase a few of these algorithms, there are other, less commonly used, algorithms available.

 To learn more about the `hashlib` library, visit `https://docs.python.org/3/library/hashlib.html`.

How to do it...

We hash files with the following steps:

1. Print hashed filename using the specified input file and algorithm.
2. Print hashed file data using the specified input file and algorithm.

How it works...

To begin, we must import `hashlib` as shown in the following. For ease of use, we have defined a dictionary of algorithms that our script can use: MD5, SHA-1, SHA-256 and SHA-512. By updating this dictionary, we can support other hash functions that have `update()` and `hexdigest()` methods, including some from libraries other than `hashlib`:

```python
from __future__ import print_function
import argparse
import hashlib
import os

__authors__ = ["Chapin Bryce", "Preston Miller"]
__date__ = 20170815
__description__ = "Script to hash a file's name and contents"

available_algorithms = {
    "md5": hashlib.md5,
    "sha1": hashlib.sha1,
    "sha256": hashlib.sha256,
    "sha512": hashlib.sha512
}

parser = argparse.ArgumentParser(
    description=__description__,
    epilog="Developed by {} on {}".format(", ".join(__authors__), __date__)
)
parser.add_argument("FILE_NAME", help="Path of file to hash")
parser.add_argument("ALGORITHM", help="Hash algorithm to use",
                    choices=sorted(available_algorithms.keys()))
args = parser.parse_args()

input_file = args.FILE_NAME
hash_alg = args.ALGORITHM
```

Notice how we define our hashing algorithm object using our dictionary and the argument provided at the command line, followed by open and close parentheses to initiate the object. This provides additional flexibility when adding new hashing algorithms.

With our hash algorithms defined, we now can hash the file's absolute path, a similar method employed during file naming for iTunes backups of an iOS device, by passing the string into the `update()` method. When we are ready to display the hex value of the calculated hash, we can call the `hexdigest()` method on our `file_name` object:

```
file_name = available_algorithms[hash_alg]()
abs_path = os.path.abspath(input_file)
file_name.update(abs_path.encode())

print("The {} of the filename is: {}".format(
    hash_alg, file_name.hexdigest()))
```

Let's move onto opening the file and hashing its contents. While we can read the entire file and pass it to the `hash` function, not all files are small enough to fit in memory. To ensure our code works on larger files, we will use the technique in the following example to read a file in a piecemeal fashion and hash it in chunks.

By opening the file as `rb`, we will ensure that we are reading the binary contents of the file, not the string content that may exist. With the file open, we will define the buffer size to read in content and then read the first chunk of data in.

Entering a while loop, we will update our hashing object with the new content for as long as there is content in the file. This is possible as the `read()` method allows us to pass an integer of the number of bytes to read and, if the integer is larger than the number of bytes remaining in the file, will simply pass us the remaining bytes.

Once the entire file is read, we call the `hexdigest()` method of our object to display the file hash to the examiner:

```
file_content = available_algorithms[hash_alg]()
with open(input_file, 'rb') as open_file:
    buff_size = 1024
    buff = open_file.read(buff_size)

    while buff:
        file_content.update(buff)
        buff = open_file.read(buff_size)

print("The {} of the content is: {}".format(
    hash_alg, file_content.hexdigest()))
```

When we execute the code, we see the output from the two print statements revealing the hash value of the file's absolute path and content. We can generate additional hashes for the file by changing the algorithm at the command line:

```
(venv3) pyforcookbook@dev-vm$ python hashing.py /var/log/auth.log sha256
The sha256 of the filename is: 0d1af57f863ec17d744cbcc9efb1a12eb58daceea0bcd978
c0cb0f8b01755122
The sha256 of the content is: c7c94388e7cb35927ff14b481bce86c5aeb08423b6cab9884
026c728b45a8089
```

There's more...

This script can be further improved. Here's a recommendation:

- Add support for additional hashing algorithms and create the appropriate entry within the `available_algorithms` global variable

Keeping track with a progress bar

Recipe Difficulty: Easy

Python Version: 2.7 or 3.5

Operating System: Any

Long-running scripts are unfortunately commonplace when processing data measured in gigabytes or terabytes. While your script may be processing this data smoothly, a user may think it's frozen after three hours with no indication of progress. Luckily, several developers have built an incredibly simple progress bar library, giving us little excuse for not incorporating this into our code.

Getting started

This recipe requires the installation of the third-party module `tqdm`. All other libraries used in this script are present in Python's standard library. The `tqdm` library, pronounced taqadum, can be installed via `pip` or downloaded from GitHub at `https://github.com/tqdm/tqdm`. To use all of the features shown in this recipe, ensure you are using release 4.11.2, available on the `tqdm` GitHub page or with `pip` using the following command:

```
pip install tqdm==4.11.2
```

How to do it...

To create a simple progress bar, we follow these steps:

1. Import `tqdm` and `time`.
2. Create multiple examples with `tqdm` and loops.

How it works...

As with all other recipes, we begin with the imports. While we only need the `tqdm` import to enable the progress bars, we will use the time module to slow down our script to better visualize the progress bar. We use a list of fruits as our sample data and identify which fruits containing "berry" or "berries" in their name:

```
from __future__ import print_function
from time import sleep
import tqdm

fruits = [
    "Acai", "Apple", "Apricots", "Avocado", "Banana", "Blackberry",
    "Blueberries", "Cherries", "Coconut", "Cranberry", "Cucumber",
    "Durian", "Fig", "Grapefruit", "Grapes", "Kiwi", "Lemon", "Lime",
    "Mango", "Melon", "Orange", "Papaya", "Peach", "Pear", "Pineapple",
    "Pomegranate", "Raspberries", "Strawberries", "Watermelon"
]
```

The following for loop is very straightforward and iterates through our list of fruits, checking for the substring `berr` is within the fruit's name before sleeping for one-tenth of a second. By wrapping the `tqdm()` method around the iterator, we automatically have a nice-looking progress bar giving us the percentage complete, elapsed time, remaining time, the number of iterations complete, and total iterations.

These display options are the defaults for tqdm and gather all of the necessary information using properties of our list object. For example, the library knows almost all of these details for the progress bar just by gathering the length and calculating the rest based on the amount of time per iteration and the number elapsed:

```
contains_berry = 0
for fruit in tqdm.tqdm(fruits):
    if "berr" in fruit.lower():
        contains_berry += 1
    sleep(.1)
print("{} fruit names contain 'berry' or 'berries'".format(contains_berry))
```

Extending the progress bar beyond the default configuration is as easy as specifying keyword arguments. The progress bar object can also be created prior to the start of the loop and using the list object, fruits, as the iterable argument. The following code exhibits how we can define our progress bar with our list, a description, and providing the unit name.

If we were not using a list but another iterator type that does not have a __len__ attribute defined, we would need to manually supply a total with the total keyword. Only basic statistics about elapsed time and iterations per second display if the total number of iterations is unavailable.

Once we are in the loop, we can display the number of results discovered using the set_postfix() method. Each iteration will provide an update of the number of hits we have found to the right of the progress bar:

```
contains_berry = 0
pbar = tqdm.tqdm(fruits, desc="Reviewing names", unit="fruits")
for fruit in pbar:
    if "berr" in fruit.lower():
        contains_berry += 1
    pbar.set_postfix(hits=contains_berry)
    sleep(.1)
print("{} fruit names contain 'berry' or 'berries'".format(contains_berry))
```

One other common use case for progress bars is to measure execution in a range of integers. Since this is a common use of the library the developers built a range call into the library, called trange(). Notice how we can specify the same arguments here as before. One new argument that we will use here, due to the larger numbers, is the unit_scale argument, which simplifies large numbers into a small number with a letter to designate the magnitude:

```
for i in tqdm.trange(10000000, unit_scale=True, desc="Trange: "):
    pass
```

When we execute the code, the following output is visible. Our first progress bar displays the default format, while the second and third show the customizations we have added:

```
(venv3) pyforcookbook@dev-vm$ python progressbars.py
100%|██████████████████████████| 29/29 [00:02<00:00,  9.94it/s]
5 fruit names contain 'berry' or 'berries'
Reviewing names: 100%|██████████| 29/29 [00:02<00:00,  9.92fruits/s, hits=5]
5 fruit names contain 'berry' or 'berries'
Trange: : 100%|██████████████| 10.0M/10.0M [00:03<00:00, 2.89Mit/s]
```

There's more...

This script can be further improved. Here's a recommendation:

- Further explore the capabilities the `tqdm` library affords developers. Consider using the `tqdm.write()` method to print status messages without breaking the progress bar.

Logging results

Recipe Difficulty: Easy

Python Version: 2.7 or 3.5

Operating System: Any

Outside of progress bars, we generally need to provide messages to the user to describe any exceptions, errors, warnings, or other information that has occurred during execution. With logging, we can provide this information at execution and in a text file for future reference.

Getting started

All libraries used in this script are present in Python's standard library. This recipe will use the built-in `logging` library to generate status messages to the console and a text file.

> To learn more about the `logging` library, visit https://docs.python.org/3/library/logging.html.

How to do it...

The following steps can be used to effectively log program execution data:

1. Create a log formatting string.
2. Log various message types during script execution.

How it works...

Let's now learn to log results. After our imports, we create our `logger` object by initializing an instance using the script's name represented by the __file__ attribute. With our `logging` object initiated, we will set the level and specify various formatters and handlers for this script. The formatters provide the flexibility to define what fields will be displayed for each message, including timestamps, function name, and the message level. The format strings follow the standards of Python string formatting, meaning we can specify padding for the following strings:

```
from __future__ import print_function
import logging
import sys

logger = logging.getLogger(__file__)
logger.setLevel(logging.DEBUG)

msg_fmt = logging.Formatter("%(asctime)-15s %(funcName)-20s"
                            "%(levelname)-8s %(message)s")
```

The handlers allow us to specify where the log message should be recorded, including a log file, standard output (console), or standard error. In the following example, we use the standard output for our stream handler and the script's name with the `.log` extension for the file handler. Lastly, we register these handlers with our logger object:

```
strhndl = logging.StreamHandler(sys.stdout)
strhndl.setFormatter(fmt=msg_fmt)

fhndl = logging.FileHandler(__file__ + ".log", mode='a')
fhndl.setFormatter(fmt=msg_fmt)

logger.addHandler(strhndl)
logger.addHandler(fhndl)
```

The logging library by default uses the following levels in increasing order of severity: NOTSET, DEBUG, INFORMATION, WARNING, ERROR, and CRITICAL. To showcase some of the features of the format string, we will log a few types of messages from functions:

```python
logger.info("information message")
logger.debug("debug message")


def function_one():
    logger.warning("warning message")


def function_two():
    logger.error("error message")


function_one()
function_two()
```

When we execute this code, we can see the following message information from the invocation of the script. Inspection of the generated log file matches what was recorded in the console:

```
(venv3) pyforcookbook@dev-vm$ python logging_recipe.py
2017-08-28 09:24:02,005 <module>          INFO     information message
2017-08-28 09:24:02,007 <module>          DEBUG    debug message
2017-08-28 09:24:02,007 function_one      WARNING  warning message
2017-08-28 09:24:02,007 function_two      ERROR    error message
(venv3) pyforcookbook@dev-vm$ cat logging_recipe.py.log
2017-08-28 09:24:02,005 <module>          INFO     information message
2017-08-28 09:24:02,007 <module>          DEBUG    debug message
2017-08-28 09:24:02,007 function_one      WARNING  warning message
2017-08-28 09:24:02,007 function_two      ERROR    error message
```

There's more...

This script can be further improved. Here's a recommendation:

- It is often important to provide as much information as possible to the user in the event of an error in the script or for a user's validation of the process. Therefore, we recommend implementing additional formatters and logging levels. Using the stderr stream is best practice for logging, as we can provide the output at the console while not disrupting stdout.

Multiple hands make light work

Recipe Difficulty: Medium

Python Version: 2.7 or 3.5

Operating System: Any

While Python is known for being single threaded, we can use built-in libraries to spin up new processes to handle tasks. Generally, this is preferred when there are a series of tasks that can be run simultaneously and the processing is not already bound by hardware limits, such as network bandwidth or disk speed.

Getting started

All libraries used in this script are present in Python's standard library. Using the built-in `multiprocessing` library, we can handle the majority of situations where we would need multiple processes to efficiently tackle a problem.

 To learn more about the `multiprocessing` library, visit `https://docs.python.org/3/library/multiprocessing.html`.

How to do it...

With the following steps, we showcase basic multiprocessing support in Python:

1. Set up a log to record `multiprocessing` activity.
2. Append data to a list using `multiprocessing`.

How it works...

Let's now look at how we can achieve multiprocessing in Python. Our imports include the `multiprocessing` library, shortened to `mp`, as it is quite lengthy otherwise; the `logging` and `sys` libraries for thread status messages; the `time` library to slow down execution for our example; and the `randint` method to generate times that each thread should wait for:

```
from __future__ import print_function
import logging
import multiprocessing as mp
from random import randint
import sys
import time
```

Before creating our processes, we set up a function that they will execute. This is where we put the task each process should execute before returning to the main thread. In this case, we take a number of seconds for the thread to sleep as our only argument. To print a status message that allows us to differentiate between the processes, we use the `current_process()` method to access the name property for each thread:

```
def sleepy(seconds):
    proc_name = mp.current_process().name
    logger.info("{} is sleeping for {} seconds.".format(
        proc_name, seconds))
    time.sleep(seconds)
```

With our worker function defined, we create our `logger` instance, borrowing code from the previous recipe, and set it to only record to the console.

```
logger = logging.getLogger(__file__)
logger.setLevel(logging.DEBUG)
msg_fmt = logging.Formatter("%(asctime)-15s %(funcName)-7s "
                            "%(levelname)-8s %(message)s")
strhndl = logging.StreamHandler(sys.stdout)
strhndl.setFormatter(fmt=msg_fmt)
logger.addHandler(strhndl)
```

We now define the number of workers we want to spawn and create them in a for loop. Using this technique, we can easily adjust the number of processes we have running. Inside of our loop, we define each `worker` using the `Process` class and set our target function and the required arguments. Once the process instance is defined, we start it and append the object to a list for later use:

```
num_workers = 5
workers = []
for w in range(num_workers):
```

```
p = mp.Process(target=sleepy, args=(randint(1, 20),))
p.start()
workers.append(p)
```

By appending the `workers` to a list, we can join them in sequential order. Joining, in this context, is the process of waiting for a process to complete before execution continues. If we do not join our process, one of them could continue to the end of the script and complete the code before other processes complete. While that wouldn't cause huge problems in our example, it can cause the next snippet of code to start too early:

```
for worker in workers:
    worker.join()
    logger.info("Joined process {}".format(worker.name))
```

When we execute the script, we can see the processes start and join over time. Since we stored these items in a list, they will join in an ordered fashion, regardless of the time it takes for one worker to finish. This is visible below as `Process-5` slept for 14 seconds before completing, and meanwhile, `Process-4` and `Process-3` had already completed:

```
(venv3) pyforcookbook@dev-vm$ python multiproc_example.py
2017-08-28 09:28:24,621 sleepy    INFO       Process-1 is sleeping for 14 seconds.
2017-08-28 09:28:24,622 sleepy    INFO       Process-2 is sleeping for 11 seconds.
2017-08-28 09:28:24,634 sleepy    INFO       Process-5 is sleeping for 14 seconds.
2017-08-28 09:28:24,623 sleepy    INFO       Process-4 is sleeping for 1 seconds.
2017-08-28 09:28:24,633 sleepy    INFO       Process-3 is sleeping for 12 seconds.
2017-08-28 09:28:38,649 <module>  INFO        Joined process Process-1
2017-08-28 09:28:38,650 <module>  INFO        Joined process Process-2
2017-08-28 09:28:38,650 <module>  INFO        Joined process Process-3
2017-08-28 09:28:38,651 <module>  INFO        Joined process Process-4
2017-08-28 09:28:38,652 <module>  INFO        Joined process Process-5
```

There's more...

This script can be further improved. We have provided a recommendation here:

- Rather than using function arguments to pass data between threads, review pipes and queues as alternatives to sharing data. Additional information about these objects can be found at https://docs.python.org/3/library/multiprocessing.html#exchanging-objects-between-processes.

2
Creating Artifact Report Recipes

In this chapter, we will cover the following recipes:

- Using HTML templates
- Creating a paper trail
- Working with CSVs
- Visualizing events with Excel
- Auditing your work

Introduction

Probably within the first few hours of starting your career in cyber security, you were already hunched over a screen, feverishly scanning a spreadsheet for clues. This sounds familiar because it is true and part of the daily process for most investigations. Spreadsheets are the bread and butter of cyber security. Within them are details of various processes and specific information extracted from valuable artifacts. In this cookbook, we will frequently output parsed artifact data into a spreadsheet due to its portability and ease of use. However, considering that at one time or another every cyber security professional has created a technical report for a nontechnical audience, a spreadsheet may not be the best option.

Why create reports at all? I think I've heard that muttered by stressed examiners before. Today, everything is built on information interchange and people want to know things as soon as you do. But that doesn't necessarily mean they want a technical spreadsheet and to figure it out themselves. Examiners must be able to effectively distill technical knowledge to laymen audiences in order to properly do their job. As good as an artifact may be, even if it is the proverbial smoking gun for a given case, it will likely require detailed explanation to nontechnical individuals for them to fully understand the meaning and ramifications. Give up; reports are here to stay and there's nothing that can be done about that.

In this chapter, you will learn how to create a number of different types of reports and a script to automatically audit our investigation. We will create HTML, XLSX, and CSV reports to summarize data in a meaningful manner:

- Developing an HTML dashboard template
- Parsing FTK Imager acquisition logs
- Building a robust CSV writer
- Plotting charts and data with Microsoft Excel
- Creating an audit trail of screenshots throughout an investigation

 Visit `www.packtpub.com/books/content/support` to download the code bundle for this chapter.

Using HTML templates

Recipe Difficulty: Easy

Python Version: 2.7 or 3.5

Operating System: Any

HTML can be an effective medium for a report. There are a great number of snazzy templates out there that can make even technical reports look appealing. That's the first step towards hooking the audience. Or, at the very least, a preventative measure to forestall the audience from instantly nodding off. This recipe uses one such template and some test data to create a visually compelling example of acquisition details. We really have our work cut out for us here.

Getting started

This recipe introduces HTML templating with the `jinja2` module. The `jinja2` library is a very powerful tool and has a number of different documented features. We will be using it in a rather simple scenario. All other libraries used in this script are present in Python's standard library. We can use pip to install `jinja2`:

```
pip install jinja2==2.9.6
```

In addition to `jinja2`, we will also be using a slightly modified template, called light bootstrap dashboard. This slightly modified dashboard has been provided with the recipe's code bundle.

 To learn more about the `jinja2` library, visit
`http://jinja.pocoo.org/docs/2.9/`.
To download the light bootstrap dashboard, visit `https://www.creative-tim.com/product/light-bootstrap-dashboard`.

How to do it...

We deploy an HTML dashboard following these principles:

1. Design HTML template global variables.
2. Process the test acquisition metadata.
3. Render the HTML templates with the inserted acquisition metadata.
4. Create a report in the desired output directory.

How it works...

First, we import the required libraries to handle argument parsing, creating counts of objects, and copying files:

```
from __future__ import print_function
import argparse
from collections import Counter
import shutil
import os
import sys
```

This recipe's command-line handler takes one positional argument, OUTPUT_DIR, which represents the desired output path for the HTML dashboard. After checking whether the directory exists, and creating it if it doesn't, we call the main() function and pass the output directory to it:

```
if __name__ == "__main__":
    # Command-line Argument Parser
    parser = argparse.ArgumentParser(
        description=__description__,
        epilog="Developed by {} on {}".format(
            ", ".join(__authors__), __date__)
    )
    parser.add_argument("OUTPUT_DIR", help="Desired Output Path")
    args = parser.parse_args()

    main(args.OUTPUT_DIR)
```

Defined at the top of the script are a number of global variables: DASH, TABLE, and DEMO. These variables represent the various HTML and JavaScript files we create as a product of the script. This is a book about Python, so we will not get into the details of how these files are structured and how they work. However, let's look at an example to showcase how jinja2 bridges the gap between these types of files and Python.

A portion of the global variable DEMO is captured in the following snippet. Note that the string block is passed to the jinja2.Template() method. This allows us to create an object for which we can use jinja2 to interact with and dynamically insert data into the JavaScript file. Specifically, the following code block shows two locations where we can use jinja2 to insert data. These are denoted by the double curly braces and the keywords we will refer to them by in the Python code - pi_labels and pi_series, respectively:

```
DEMO = Template("""type = ['','info','success','warning','danger'];
[snip]
        Chartist.Pie('#chartPreferences', dataPreferences,
          optionsPreferences);

        Chartist.Pie('#chartPreferences', {
          labels: [{{pi_labels}}],
          series: [{{pi_series}}]
        });
[snip]
""")
```

Let's now turn our attention to the `main()` function. This function is really quite simple for reasons you will understand in the second recipe. This function creates a list of lists containing sample acquisition data, prints a status message to the console, and sends that data to the `process_data()` method:

```
def main(output_dir):
    acquisition_data = [
        ["001", "Debbie Downer", "Mobile", "08/05/2017 13:05:21", "32"],
        ["002", "Debbie Downer", "Mobile", "08/05/2017 13:11:24", "16"],
        ["003", "Debbie Downer", "External", "08/05/2017 13:34:16", "128"],
        ["004", "Debbie Downer", "Computer", "08/05/2017 14:23:43", "320"],
        ["005", "Debbie Downer", "Mobile", "08/05/2017 15:35:01", "16"],
        ["006", "Debbie Downer", "External", "08/05/2017 15:54:54", "8"],
        ["007", "Even Steven", "Computer", "08/07/2017 10:11:32", "256"],
        ["008", "Even Steven", "Mobile", "08/07/2017 10:40:32", "32"],
        ["009", "Debbie Downer", "External", "08/10/2017 12:03:42", "64"],
        ["010", "Debbie Downer", "External", "08/10/2017 12:43:27", "64"]
    ]
    print("[+] Processing acquisition data")
    process_data(acquisition_data, output_dir)
```

The purpose of the `process_data()` method is to get the sample acquisition data into an HTML or JavaScript format that we can drop in place within the `jinja2` templates. This dashboard is going to have two components: a series of charts visualizing the data and a table of the raw data. The following code block deals with the latter. We accomplish this by iterating through the acquisition list and adding each element of the table to the `html_table` string with the appropriate HTML tags:

```
def process_data(data, output_dir):
    html_table = ""
    for acq in data:
        html_table += "<tr><td>{}</td><td>{}</td><td>{}</td><td>{}</td>" \
            "<td>{}</td></tr>\n".format(
                acq[0], acq[1], acq[2], acq[3], acq[4])
```

Next, we use the `Counter()` method from the `collections` library to quickly generate a dictionary-like object of the number of occurrences of each item in the sample data. For example, the first `Counter` object, `device_types`, creates a dictionary-like object where each key is a different device type (for example, mobile, external, and computer) and the value represents the number of occurrences of each key. This allows us to quickly summarize data across the data set and cuts down on the legwork required before we can plot this information.

Once we have created the `Counter` objects, we again iterate through each acquisition to perform a more manual summation of acquisition date information. This `date_dict` object maintains keys for all the acquisition data and adds the size of all acquisitions made on that day as the key's value. We specifically split on a space to isolate just the date value from the date-time string (for example, `08/15/2017`). If the specific date is already in the dictionary, we add the acquisition size directly to the key. Otherwise, we create the key and assign its value to the acquisition size. Once we have created the various summarizing objects, we call the `output_html()` method to populate the HTML dashboard with this information:

```
device_types = Counter([x[2] for x in data])
custodian_devices = Counter([x[1] for x in data])

date_dict = {}
for acq in data:
    date = acq[3].split(" ")[0]
    if date in date_dict:
        date_dict[date] += int(acq[4])
    else:
        date_dict[date] = int(acq[4])
output_html(output_dir, len(data), html_table,
        device_types, custodian_devices, date_dict)
```

The `output_html()` method starts by printing a status message to the console and storing the current working directory to a variable. We append the folder path to light-bootstrap-dashboard and use `shutil.copytree()` to copy the bootstrap files to the output directory. Following that, we create three file paths representing the output locations and names of the three `jinja2` templates:

```
def output_html(output, num_devices, table, devices, custodians, dates):
    print("[+] Rendering HTML and copy files to {}".format(output))
    cwd = os.getcwd()
    bootstrap = os.path.join(cwd, "light-bootstrap-dashboard")
    shutil.copytree(bootstrap, output)

    dashboard_output = os.path.join(output, "dashboard.html")
    table_output = os.path.join(output, "table.html")
    demo_output = os.path.join(output, "assets", "js", "demo.js")
```

Let's start by looking at the two HTML files, as these are relatively simple. After opening file objects for the two HTML files, we use the `jinja2.render()` method and use keyword arguments to refer to the placeholders in the curly brackets from the `Template` objects. With the file rendered with the Python data, we write the data to the file. Simple, right? The JavaScript file, thankfully, is not much more difficult:

```
with open(dashboard_output, "w") as outfile:
```

```
outfile.write(DASH.render(num_custodians=len(custodians.keys()),
                          num_devices=num_devices,
                          data=calculate_size(dates)))

with open(table_output, "w") as outfile:
    outfile.write(TABLE.render(table_body=table))
```

While syntactically similar to the previous code block, when we render the data this time, we feed the data to the `return_labels()` and `return_series()` methods. These methods take the key and values from the `Counter` objects and format them appropriately to work with the JavaScript file. You may have also noticed a call to the `calculate_size()` method in the previous code block called on the `dates` dictionary. Let's explore these three supporting functions now:

```
with open(demo_output, "w") as outfile:
    outfile.write(
        DEMO.render(bar_labels=return_labels(dates.keys()),
                    bar_series=return_series(dates.values()),
                    pi_labels=return_labels(devices.keys()),
                    pi_series=return_series(devices.values()),
                    pi_2_labels=return_labels(custodians.keys()),
                    pi_2_series=return_series(custodians.values())))
```

The `calculate_size()` method simply uses the built-in `sum()` method to return each date key's total size collected. The `return_labels()` and `return_series()` methods use string methods to format the data appropriately. Essentially, the JavaScript file expects the labels to be within single quotes, which is accomplished with the `format()` method, and both labels and series must be comma-delimited:

```
def calculate_size(sizes):
    return sum(sizes.values())


def return_labels(list_object):
    return ", ".join("'{}'".format(x) for x in list_object)


def return_series(list_object):
    return ", ".join(str(x) for x in list_object)
```

When we run this script, we receive a copy of the report in the specified output directory along with the required assets for loading and rendering the page. We can zip up this folder and provide it to team members, as it is designed to be portable. Viewing this dashboard shows us the first page with the chart information:

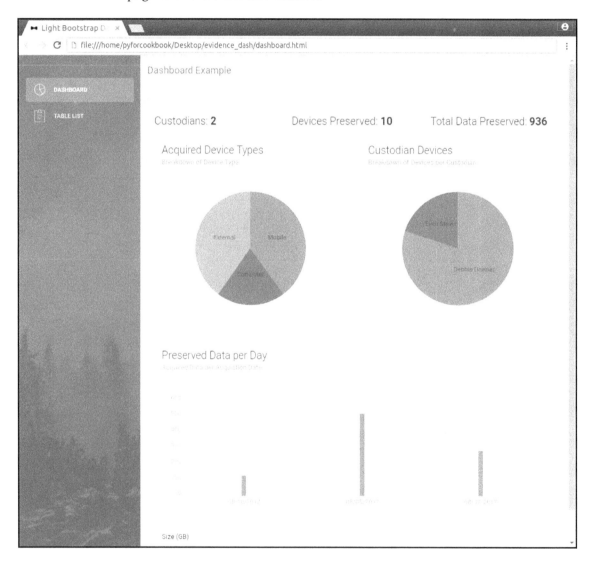

And the second page as the table of acquisition information:

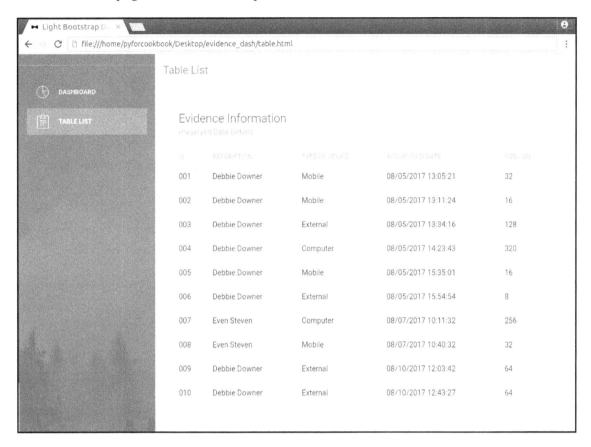

There's more...

This script can be further improved. We have provided a couple of recommendations here:

- Add support for additional types of reports to better highlight the data
- Include the ability to export the tables and charts for printing and sharing through additional javascript

Creating a paper trail

Recipe Difficulty: Medium

Python Version: 2.7 or 3.5

Operating System: Any

Most imaging utilities create audit logs recording the details of the acquisition media and other available metadata. Admit it; unless something goes horribly wrong, these logs are mostly untouched if the evidence verifies. Let's change that and leverage the newly created HTML dashboard from the previous recipe and make better use of this acquisition data.

Getting started

All libraries used in this script are present in Python's standard library or functions imported from the prior script.

How to do it...

We parse acquisition logs with these steps:

1. Identify and validate FTK logs.
2. Parse the log to extract relevant fields.
3. Create a dashboard with the acquisition data.

How it works...

First, we import the required libraries to handle argument parsing, parsing dates, and the `html_dashboard` script we created in the previous recipe:

```
from __future__ import print_function
import argparse
from datetime import datetime
import os
import sys
import html_dashboard
```

This recipe's command-line handler takes two positional arguments, `INPUT_DIR` and `OUTPUT_DIR`, which represent the path to the directory containing acquisition logs and the desired output path, respectively. After creating the output directory, if necessary, and validating that the input directory exists, we call the `main()` method and pass these two variables to it:

```
if __name__ == "__main__":
    # Command-line Argument Parser
    parser = argparse.ArgumentParser(
        description=__description__,
        epilog="Developed by {} on {}".format(
            ", ".join(__authors__), __date__)
    )
    parser.add_argument("INPUT_DIR", help="Input Directory of Logs")
    parser.add_argument("OUTPUT_DIR", help="Desired Output Path")
    args = parser.parse_args()

    if os.path.exists(args.INPUT_DIR) and os.path.isdir(args.INPUT_DIR):
        main(args.INPUT_DIR, args.OUTPUT_DIR)
    else:
        print("[-] Supplied input directory {} does not exist or is not "
              "a file".format(args.INPUT_DIR))
        sys.exit(1)
```

In the `main()` function, we use the `os.listdir()` function to get a directory listing of the input directory and identify only those files with a `.txt` file extension. This is important, as FTK Imager creates acquisition logs with the `.txt` extension. This helps us avoid some files that should not be processed by the extension alone. We will, however, take it one step further. After we create a list of the possible FTK logs, we create a placeholder list, `ftk_data`, to store the processed acquisition data. Next, we iterate through each potential log and set up a dictionary with the desired keys we will extract. To further eliminate false positives, we call the `validate_ftk()` method, which returns either a `True` or `False` Boolean value depending on the results of its inspection. Let's take a quick look at how it works:

```
def main(in_dir, out_dir):
    ftk_logs = [x for x in os.listdir(in_dir)
                if x.lower().endswith(".txt")]
    print("[+] Processing {} potential FTK Imager Logs found in {} "
          "directory".format(len(ftk_logs), in_dir))
    ftk_data = []
    for log in ftk_logs:
        log_data = {"e_numb": "", "custodian": "", "type": "",
                    "date": "", "size": ""}
        log_name = os.path.join(in_dir, log)
        if validate_ftk(log_name):
```

Thankfully, each FTK Imager log contains the words "`Created by AccessData`" on the first line. We can rely on this to be the case to verify that the log is likely a valid FTK Imager log. With the input `log_file` path, we open the file object and read the first line using the `readline()` method. With the first line extracted, we check whether the phrase is present and return `True` if it is or `False` otherwise:

```
def validate_ftk(log_file):
    with open(log_file) as log:
        first_line = log.readline()
        if "Created By AccessData" not in first_line:
            return False
        else:
            return True
```

Back in the `main()` method, after having validated the FTK Imager log, we open the file, set a few variables to `None`, and begin iterating through each line in the file. Based on the dependable layout of these logs, we can use specific keywords to identify whether the current line is one we are interested in. For example, if the line contains the phrase "`Evidence Number:`", we can be sure that this line contains the evidence number value. And in fact, we split the phrase and take the value to the right of the colon and associate it with the dictionary `e_numb` key. This type of logic can be applied to most of the desired values, with a few exceptions.

For the acquisition time, we must use the `datetime.strptime()` method to convert the string into an actual `datetime` object. We must do this to store it in the format that the HTML dashboard is expecting. We use the `strftime()` method on the `datetime` object and associate it with the `date` key in the dictionary:

```
with open(log_name) as log_file:
    bps, sec_count = (None, None)
    for line in log_file:
        if "Evidence Number:" in line:
            log_data["e_numb"] = line.split(
                "Number:")[1].strip()
        elif "Notes:" in line:
            log_data["custodian"] = line.split(
                "Notes:")[1].strip()
        elif "Image Type:" in line:
            log_data["type"] = line.split("Type:")[1].strip()
        elif "Acquisition started:" in line:
            acq = line.split("started:")[1].strip()
            date = datetime.strptime(
                acq, "%a %b %d %H:%M:%S %Y")
            log_data["date"] = date.strftime(
                "%M/%d/%Y %H:%M:%S")
```

The bytes per sector and sector count are handled a little differently from the rest. Due to the fact that the HTML dashboard script is expecting to receive the data size (in GB), we need to extract these values and calculate the acquired media size. To do this, once identified, we convert each value into an integer and assign it to the two local variables that were originally None. Once we finish iterating through all lines, we check whether these variables are no longer None, and if they are not, we send them to the calculate_size() method. This method performs the necessary calculation and stores the media size within the dictionary:

```
def calculate_size(bytes, sectors):
    return (bytes * sectors) / (1024**3)
```

Once the file has been processed, the dictionary with the extracted acquisition data is appended to the ftk_data list. After all the logs have been processed, we call the html_dashboard.process_data() method and supply it with the acquisition data and output directory. The process_data() function is, of course, the exact same as the previous recipe. Therefore, you know that this acquisition data replaces the sample acquisition data of the previous recipe and populates the HTML dashboard with real data:

```
            elif "Bytes per Sector:" in line:
                bps = int(line.split("Sector:")[1].strip())
            elif "Sector Count:" in line:
                sec_count = int(
                    line.split("Count:")[1].strip().replace(
                        ",", ""))
                )
        if bps is not None and sec_count is not None:
            log_data["size"] = calculate_size(bps, sec_count)

        ftk_data.append(
            [log_data["e_numb"], log_data["custodian"],
             log_data["type"], log_data["date"], log_data["size"]]
        )

    print("[+] Creating HTML dashboard based acquisition logs "
          "in {}".format(out_dir))
    html_dashboard.process_data(ftk_data, out_dir)
```

When we run this tool, we can see the acquisition log information, as shown in the following two screenshots:

There's more...

This script can be further improved. Here's a recommendation:

- Create additional scripts to support logs from other acquisition tools, such as **Guymager**, **Cellebrite**, **MacQuisition**, and so on

Working with CSVs

Recipe Difficulty: Easy

Python Version: 2.7 or 3.5

Operating System: Any

Everyone has reviewed data in a CSV spreadsheet at some point. They are pervasive and a common output format for most applications. Writing CSVs with Python is one of the easiest methods to create a report of processed data. In this recipe, we will demonstrate how you can use the csv and unicodecsv libraries to create quick reports with Python.

Getting started

Part of this recipe uses the unicodecsv module. This module replaces the built-in Python 2 csv module and adds Unicode support. Python 3's csv module does not have this limitation and can be used without the support of any additional library. All other libraries used in this script are present in Python's standard library. The unicodecsv library can be installed with pip:

```
pip install unicodecsv==0.14.1
```

To learn more about the unicodecsv library, visit https://github.com/jdunck/python-unicodecsv.

How to do it...

We follow these steps to create CSV spreadsheets:

1. Identify the version of Python that invoked the script.
2. Output a list of lists and a list of dictionaries using Python 2 and Python 3 conventions to spreadsheets in the current working directory.

How it works...

First, we import the required libraries to write spreadsheets. Later on in this recipe, we also import the `unicodecsv` module:

```
from __future__ import print_function
import csv
import os
import sys
```

This recipe does not use `argparse` as a command-line handler. Instead, we directly call the desired functions based on the version of Python. We can determine the version of Python running with the `sys.version_info` attribute. If the user is using Python 2.X, we call both the `csv_writer_py2()` and `unicode_csv_dict_writer_py2()` methods. Both of these methods take four arguments, where the last argument is optional: these are the data to write, a list of headers, the desired output directory, and, optionally, the name of the output CSV spreadsheet. Alternatively, if Python 3.X is being used, we call the `csv_writer_py3()` method. While similar, CSV writing is handled a little differently between the two versions of Python, and the `unicodecsv` module is applicable only to Python 2:

```
if sys.version_info < (3, 0):
    csv_writer_py2(TEST_DATA_LIST, ["Name", "Age", "Cool Factor"],
                   os.getcwd())
    unicode_csv_dict_writer_py2(
        TEST_DATA_DICT, ["Name", "Age", "Cool Factor"], os.getcwd(),
        "dict_output.csv")

elif sys.version_info >= (3, 0):
    csv_writer_py3(TEST_DATA_LIST, ["Name", "Age", "Cool Factor"],
                   os.getcwd())
```

This recipe has two global variables that represent sample data types. The first of these, TEST_DATA_LIST, is a nested list structure containing strings and integers. The second, TEST_DATA_DICT, is another representation of this data but stored as a list of dictionaries. Let's look at how the various functions write this sample data to the output CSV file:

```
TEST_DATA_LIST = [["Bill", 53, 0], ["Alice", 42, 5],
                  ["Zane", 33, -1], ["Theodore", 72, 9001]]

TEST_DATA_DICT = [{"Name": "Bill", "Age": 53, "Cool Factor": 0},
                  {"Name": "Alice", "Age": 42, "Cool Factor": 5},
                  {"Name": "Zane", "Age": 33, "Cool Factor": -1},
                  {"Name": "Theodore", "Age": 72, "Cool Factor": 9001}]
```

The csv_writer_py2() method first checks whether the name input was provided. If it is still the default value of None, we simply assign the output name ourselves. Next, after printing a status message to the console, we open a File object in the "wb" mode in the desired output directory. Note that it is important to open CSV files in the "wb" mode in Python 2 to prevent intervening gaps between rows in the resulting spreadsheet. Once we have the File object, we use the csv.writer() method to convert this into a writer object. With this, we can use the writerow() and writerows() methods to write a single list of data and a nested list structure, respectively. Now, let's look at how unicodecsv works with lists of dictionaries:

```
def csv_writer_py2(data, header, output_directory, name=None):
    if name is None:
        name = "output.csv"

    print("[+] Writing {} to {}".format(name, output_directory))

    with open(os.path.join(output_directory, name), "wb") as csvfile:
        writer = csv.writer(csvfile)
        writer.writerow(header)

        writer.writerows(data)
```

The unicodecsv module is a drop in for the built-in csv module and can be used interchangeably. The difference, and it's a big one, is that unicodecsv automatically handles Unicode strings in a way that the built-in csv module in Python 2 does not. This was addressed in Python 3.

First, we attempt to import the `unicodecsv` module and print a status message to the console if the import fails before exiting the script. If we are able to import the library, we check whether the name input was supplied and create a name if it wasn't, before opening a `File` object. With this `File` object, we use the `unicodecsv.DictWriter` class and supply it with the list of headers. This object, by default, expects the keys present in the supplied `fieldnames` list to represent all of the keys in each dictionary. If this behavior is not desired or if this is not the case, it can be ignored by setting the extrasaction keyword argument to the string `ignore`. Doing so will result in all additional dictionary keys not specified in the `fieldnames` list being ignored and not added to the CSV spreadsheet.

After the `DictWriter` object is set up, we use the `writerheader()` method to write the field names and `writerows()` to, this time, write the list of dictionaries to the CSV file. Another important thing to note is that the columns will be in the order of the elements in the supplied `fieldnames` list:

```
def unicode_csv_dict_writer_py2(data, header, output_directory, name=None):
    try:
        import unicodecsv
    except ImportError:
        print("[+] Install unicodecsv module before executing this"
            " function")
        sys.exit(1)

    if name is None:
        name = "output.csv"

    print("[+] Writing {} to {}".format(name, output_directory))
    with open(os.path.join(output_directory, name), "wb") as csvfile:
        writer = unicodecsv.DictWriter(csvfile, fieldnames=header)
        writer.writeheader()

        writer.writerows(data)
```

Lastly, the `csv_writer_py3()` method operates in mostly the same fashion. However, note the difference in how the `File` object is created. Rather than opening a file in the `"wb"` mode, with Python 3, we open the file in the `"w"` mode and set the newline keyword argument to an empty string. After doing that, the rest of the operations proceed in the same manner as previously described:

```
def csv_writer_py3(data, header, output_directory, name=None):
    if name is None:
        name = "output.csv"

    print("[+] Writing {} to {}".format(name, output_directory))
```

```
with open(os.path.join(output_directory, name), "w", newline="") as \
        csvfile:
    writer = csv.writer(csvfile)
    writer.writerow(header)

    writer.writerows(data)
```

When we run this code, we can look at either of the two newly generated CSV files and see the same information, as in the following screenshot:

Name	Age	Cool Factor
Bill	53	0
Alice	42	5
Zane	33	-1
Theodore	72	9001

There's more...

This script can be further improved. Here's a recommendation:

- Create more robust CSV writers with additional feature sets and options. The idea here is that you could supply data of different types and have a method to handle them equivalently.

Visualizing events with Excel

Recipe Difficulty: Easy

Python Version: 2.7 or 3.5

Operating System: Any

Let's take it one step further from the previous recipe with Excel. Excel is a very robust spreadsheet application and we can do a lot with it. We will use Excel to create a table and plot graphs of the data.

Getting started

There are a number of different Python libraries with varying support for Excel and its many features. In this recipe, we use the `xlsxwriter` module to create a table and graph of the data. This module can be used for much more than that. This module can be installed by `pip` using the following command:

```
pip install xlsxwriter==0.9.9
```

 To learn more about the `xlsxwriter` library, visit `https://xlsxwriter.readthedocs.io/`.

We also use a custom `utilcsv` module that we wrote based on the previous recipe to handle interactions with CSVs. All other libraries used in this script are present in Python's standard library.

How to do it...

We create an Excel spreadsheet via the following steps:

1. Create a workbook and worksheet objects.
2. Create a table of spreadsheet data.
3. Create a chart of the event log data.

How it works...

First, we import the required libraries to handle argument parsing, creating counts of objects, parsing dates, writing XLSX spreadsheets, and our custom `utilcsv` module, which handles CSV reading and writing in this recipe:

```
from __future__ import print_function
import argparse
from collections import Counter
from datetime import datetime
import os
import sys
from utility import utilcsv

try:
    import xlsxwriter
```

```
except ImportError:
    print("[-] Install required third-party module xlsxwriter")
    sys.exit(1)
```

This recipe's command-line handler takes one positional argument: OUTPUT_DIR. This represents the desired output path for the XLSX file. Before calling the main() method, we check whether the output directory exists and create it if it does not:

```
if __name__ == "__main__":
    # Command-line Argument Parser
    parser = argparse.ArgumentParser(
        description=__description__,
        epilog="Developed by {} on {}".format(
            ", ".join(__authors__), __date__)
    )
    parser.add_argument("OUTPUT_DIR", help="Desired Output Path")
    args = parser.parse_args()

    if not os.path.exists(args.OUTPUT_DIR):
        os.makedirs(args.OUTPUT_DIR)

    main(args.OUTPUT_DIR)
```

The main() function is really quite simple; its job is to print a status message to the console, use the csv_reader() method, which is a slightly modified function from the previous recipe, and then write the resulting data to the output directory with the xlsx_writer() method:

```
def main(output_directory):
    print("[+] Reading in sample data set")
    # Skip first row of headers
    data = utilcsv.csv_reader("redacted_sample_event_log.csv")[1:]
    xlsx_writer(data, output_directory)
```

The xlsx_writer() starts by printing a status message and creating the workbook object in the output directory. Next, we create two worksheet objects for the dashboard and data worksheets. The dashboard worksheet will contain a graph summarizing the raw data on the data worksheet:

```
def xlsx_writer(data, output_directory):
    print("[+] Writing output.xlsx file to {}".format(output_directory))
    workbook = xlsxwriter.Workbook(
        os.path.join(output_directory, "output.xlsx"))
    dashboard = workbook.add_worksheet("Dashboard")
    data_sheet = workbook.add_worksheet("Data")
```

We use the `add_format()` method on the `workbook` object to create customized formats for the spreadsheet. These formats are dictionaries with key-value pairs configuring the format. Most of these keys are self-explanatory based on the key name. A description of the various format options and features can be found at `http://xlsxwriter.readthedocs.io/format.html`:

```
title_format = workbook.add_format({
    'bold': True, 'font_color': 'white', 'bg_color': 'black',
    'font_size': 30, 'font_name': 'Calibri', 'align': 'center'
})
date_format = workbook.add_format(
    {'num_format': 'mm/dd/yy hh:mm:ss AM/PM'})
```

With the formats set, we can enumerate through the list of lists and write each using the `write()` method. This method takes a few inputs; the first and second arguments are the row and column followed by the value to write. Note that in addition to the `write()` method, we also use the `write_number()` and `write_datetime()` methods. These preserve the data type within the XLSX spreadsheet. Specifically, with the `write_datetime()` method, we supply it with the `date_format` variable to appropriately format the date object. After looping through all of the data, we have successfully stored the data within the spreadsheet and retained its value types. However, we can do much more than that with an XLSX spreadsheet.

We use the `add_table()` method to create a table of the data we just wrote. To accomplish this, we must supply the function using the Excel notation to denote the top-left and bottom-right columns of the table. Beyond that, we can also provide a dictionary of objects to further configure the table. In this case, the dictionary only contains the header names for each column of the table:

```
for i, record in enumerate(data):
    data_sheet.write_number(i, 0, int(record[0]))
    data_sheet.write(i, 1, record[1])
    data_sheet.write(i, 2, record[2])
    dt = datetime.strptime(record[3], "%m/%d/%Y %H:%M:%S %p")
    data_sheet.write_datetime(i, 3, dt, date_format)
    data_sheet.write_number(i, 4, int(record[4]))
    data_sheet.write(i, 5, record[5])
    data_sheet.write_number(i, 6, int(record[6]))
    data_sheet.write(i, 7, record[7])

data_length = len(data) + 1
data_sheet.add_table(
    "A1:H{}".format(data_length),
    {"columns": [
        {"header": "Index"},
```

```
                    {"header": "File Name"},
                    {"header": "Computer Name"},
                    {"header": "Written Date"},
                    {"header": "Event Level"},
                    {"header": "Event Source"},
                    {"header": "Event ID"},
                    {"header": "File Path"}
             ]}
      )
```

With the data worksheet complete, let's now turn our focus on the dashboard worksheet. We will create a graph on this dashboard, breaking down the event IDs by frequency. First, we calculate this frequency using a `Counter` object, as shown in the HTML dashboard recipe. Next, we set a title for this page by merging a number of columns and setting the title text and format.

Once that is complete, we iterate through the frequency of event IDs `Counter` object and write them to the worksheet. We write them starting at row `100` to make sure the data is out of the way and not at the forefront. Once this data is written, we convert it into a table using the same method discussed previously:

```
event_ids = Counter([x[6] for x in data])
dashboard.merge_range('A1:Q1', 'Event Log Dashboard', title_format)
for i, record in enumerate(event_ids):
    dashboard.write(100 + i, 0, record)
    dashboard.write(100 + i, 1, event_ids[record])

dashboard.add_table("A100:B{}".format(
    100 + len(event_ids)),
    {"columns": [{"header": "Event ID"}, {"header": "Occurrence"}]}
)
```

Finally, we can plot this chart we keep talking about. We use the `add_chart()` method and specify the type as a bar chart. Next, we use the `set_title()` and `set_size()` methods to properly configure this graph. All that is left is to use the `add_series()` method to add the data to the chart. This method takes a dictionary with a category and values key. In a bar chart, the categories values represent the *x* axis and the values represent the *y* axis. Note the use of Excel notation to designate the range of cells that make up the categories and values keys. Once the data has been selected, we use the `insert_chart()` method on the `worksheet` object to display it before closing the `workbook` object:

```
event_chart = workbook.add_chart({'type': 'bar'})
event_chart.set_title({'name': 'Event ID Breakdown'})
event_chart.set_size({'x_scale': 2, 'y_scale': 5})

event_chart.add_series(
```

```
        {'categories': '=Dashboard!$A$101:$A${}'.format(
            100 + len(event_ids)),
         'values': '=Dashboard!$B$101:$B${}'.format(
            100 + len(event_ids))})
    dashboard.insert_chart('C5', event_chart)

    workbook.close()
```

When we run this script, we can review the data in an XLSX spreadsheet and the chart we created summarizing Event IDs:

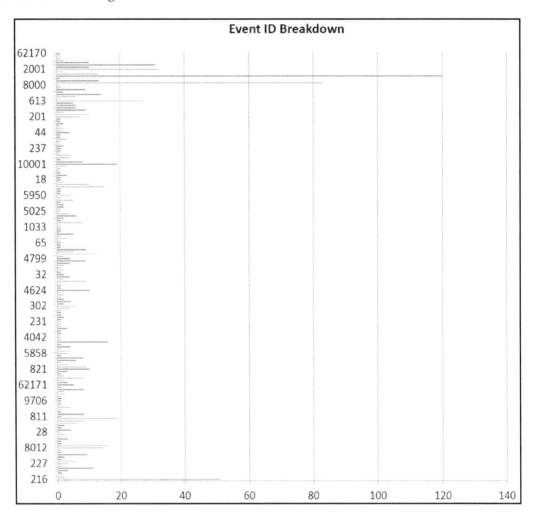

Auditing your work

Recipe Difficulty: Easy

Python Version: 2.7 or 3.5

Operating System: Any

Keeping detailed investigative notes is a key to any investigation. Without this, it can be difficult to put all of the pieces together or accurately recall findings. Sometimes, it can be helpful to have a screenshot or a series of them to remind you of the various steps you took during your review.

Getting started

In order to create a recipe with cross-platform support, we have elected to use the `pyscreenshot` module. This module relies on a few dependencies, specifically the **Python Imaging Library** (**PIL**), and one or more backends. The backend used here is the WX GUI library. All three of these modules can be installed with `pip`:

```
pip install pyscreenshot==0.4.2
pip install Pillow==4.2.1
pip install wxpython==4.0.0b1
```

 To learn more about the pyscreenshot library, visit `https://pypi.python.org/pypi/pyscreenshot`.

All other libraries used in this script are present in Python's standard library.

How to do it...

We use the following methodology to accomplish our objective:

1. Process user-supplied arguments.
2. Take screenshots based on user-supplied inputs.
3. Save screenshots to the specified output folder.

How it works...

First, we import the required libraries to handle argument parsing, sleeping the script, and taking screenshots:

```
from __future__ import print_function
import argparse
from multiprocessing import freeze_support
import os
import sys
import time

try:
    import pyscreenshot
    import wx
except ImportError:
    print("[-] Install wx and pyscreenshot to use this script")
    sys.exit(1)
```

This recipe's command-line handler takes two positional arguments, OUTPUT_DIR and INTERVAL, which represent the desired output path and the interval between screenshots, respectively. The optional total argument can be used to impose an upper limit on the number of screenshots that should be taken. Note that we specify the type for both INTERVAL and total arguments as integers. After validating that the output directory exists, we pass these inputs to the main() method:

```
if __name__ == "__main__":
    # Command-line Argument Parser
    parser = argparse.ArgumentParser(
        description=__description__,
        epilog="Developed by {} on {}".format(
            ", ".join(__authors__), __date__)
    )
    parser.add_argument("OUTPUT_DIR", help="Desired Output Path")
    parser.add_argument(
        "INTERVAL", help="Screenshot interval (seconds)", type=int)
    parser.add_argument(
        "-total", help="Total number of screenshots to take", type=int)
    args = parser.parse_args()

    if not os.path.exists(args.OUTPUT_DIR):
        os.makedirs(args.OUTPUT_DIR)

    main(args.OUTPUT_DIR, args.INTERVAL, args.total)
```

The `main()` function creates an infinite `while` loop and starts incrementing a counter by one for each screenshot taken. Following that, the script sleeps for the provided interval before using the `pyscreenshot.grab()` method to capture a screenshot. With the screenshot captured, we create the output filename and use the screenshot object's `save()` method to save it to the output location. That's really it. We print a status message notifying the user about this and then check whether the `total` argument was provided and whether the counter is equal to it. If it is, the `while` loop is exited, but otherwise, it continues forever. As a word of caution/wisdom, if you choose not to provide a `total` limit, make sure to stop the script manually once you have completed your review. Otherwise, you may come back to an ominous blue screen and full hard drive:

```
def main(output_dir, interval, total):
    i = 0
    while True:
        i += 1
        time.sleep(interval)
        image = pyscreenshot.grab()
        output = os.path.join(output_dir, "screenshot_{}.png").format(i)
        image.save(output)
        print("[+] Took screenshot {} and saved it to {}".format(
            i, output_dir))
        if total is not None and i == total:
            print("[+] Finished taking {} screenshots every {} "
                "seconds".format(total, interval))
            sys.exit(0)
```

With the screenshotting script running every five seconds and storing the pictures in the folder of our choice, we can see the following output, as captured in the following screenshot:

There's more...

This script can be further improved. We have provided a couple of recommendations here:

- Add video recording support to the script
- Add the functionality to automatically create archives of the screenshots with the date as the archive name

3
A Deep Dive into Mobile Forensic Recipes

The following recipes are covered in this chapter:

- Parsing PLIST files
- Handling SQLite databases
- Identifying gaps in SQLite databases
- Processing iTunes backups
- Putting Wi-Fi on the map
- Digging deep to recover messages

Introduction

Perhaps it is becoming a bit of a cliché, but it remains true that as technology evolves it continues to become more integrated with our lives. Never has this been so apparent as with the development of the first smartphone. These precious devices seemingly never leave the possession of their owners and often receive more interaction than human companions. It should be no surprise then that a smartphone can supply investigators with lots of insight into their owner. For example, messages may provide insight into the state of mind of the owner or knowledge of particular facts. They may even shed light on previously unknown information. Location history is another useful artifact we can extract from these devices and can be helpful to validate an individual's alibi. We will learn to extract this information and more.

A common source of evidentiary value on smartphones are SQLite databases. These databases serve as the de facto storage for applications in most smartphone operating systems. For this reason, many scripts in this chapter will focus on teasing out data and drawing inferences from these databases. In addition to that, we will also learn how to process PLIST files, commonly used with Apple operating systems, including iOS, and extract relevant data. The scripts in this chapter focus on solving specific problems and are ordered by complexity:

- Learning to process XML and binary PLIST files
- Using Python to interact with SQLite databases
- Identifying missing gaps in SQLite databases
- Converting an iOS backup into a human-readable format
- Processing output from Cellebrite and performing Wi-Fi MAC address geolocation lookups with WiGLE
- Identifying potentially intact deleted content from SQLite databases

Visit `www.packtpub.com/books/content/support` to download the code bundle for this chapter.

Parsing PLIST files

Recipe Difficulty: Easy

Python Version: 2.7 or 3.5

Operating System: Any

This recipe will process the `Info.plist` file present in every iOS backup and extract device-specific information such as the device name, IMEI, serial number, product make, model, and iOS version, and the last backup date. Property lists, or PLISTs, come in two different formats: XML or binary. Typically, when dealing with binary PLISTs, one will need to use the plutil utility on a macOS platform to convert it to a readable XML format. However, we will introduce a Python library that handles both types readily and easily. Once we extract the relevant data elements from the `Info.plist` file, we will print this data to the console.

Getting started

This recipe requires the installation of the third-party library `biplist`. All other libraries used in this script are present in Python's standard library. The `biplist` module provides a means of processing both XML and binary PLIST files.

 To learn more about the `biplist` library, visit `https://github.com/wooster/biplist`.

Python has a built-in PLIST library, `plistlib`; however, this library was found to not support binary PLIST files as extensively as `biplist` does.

 To learn more about the `plistlib` library, visit `https://docs.python.org/3/library/plistlib.html`.

Installing `biplist` can be accomplished using `pip`:

```
pip install biplist==1.0.2
```

Be sure to grab your own `Info.plist` file to process with this script. If you cannot find an `Info.plist` file, any PLIST file should be suitable. Our script is not so specific and should technically work with any PLIST file.

How to do it...

We will employ the following steps to process the PLIST file:

1. Open the input PLIST file.
2. Read PLIST data into a variable.
3. Print formatted PLIST data to the console.

How it works...

First, we import the required libraries to handle argument parsing and processing PLISTs:

```
from __future__ import print_function
import argparse
import biplist
import os
import sys
```

This recipe's command-line handler accepts one positional argument, PLIST_FILE, which represents the path to the PLIST file we will process:

```
if __name__ == "__main__":
    parser = argparse.ArgumentParser(
        description=__description__,
        epilog="Developed by {} on {}".format(
            ", ".join(__authors__), __date__)
    )
    parser.add_argument("PLIST_FILE", help="Input PList File")
    args = parser.parse_args()
```

We use the os.exists() and os.path.isfile() functions to validate that the input file exists and is a file, as opposed to a directory. We do not perform any further validation on this file, such as confirming whether it is a PLIST file rather than a text file and instead rely on the biplist library (and common sense) to catch such errors. If the input file passes our tests, we call the main() function and pass it the PLIST file path:

```
    if not os.path.exists(args.PLIST_FILE) or \
            not os.path.isfile(args.PLIST_FILE):
        print("[-] {} does not exist or is not a file".format(
            args.PLIST_FILE))
        sys.exit(1)

    main(args.PLIST_FILE)
```

The main() function is relatively straightforward and accomplishes the goal of reading the PLIST file and then printing the data to the console. First, we print an update to the console that we are attempting to open the file. Then, we use the biplist.readPlist() method to open and read the PLIST into our plist_data variable. If the PLIST is corrupt or otherwise inaccessible, biplist will raise an InvalidPlistException or NotBinaryPlistException error. We catch both of these in a try and except block and exit the script accordingly:

```
def main(plist):
    print("[+] Opening {} file".format(plist))
```

```
try:
    plist_data = biplist.readPlist(plist)
except (biplist.InvalidPlistException,
        biplist.NotBinaryPlistException) as e:
    print("[-] Invalid PLIST file - unable to be opened by biplist")
    sys.exit(2)
```

Once we have successfully read in the PLIST data, we iterate through the keys in the resulting `plist_data` dictionary and print them to the console. Notice that we print all keys in the `Info.plist` file with the exception of the `Applications` and `iTunes Files` keys. Both of these keys contain a great deal of data that floods the console and therefore are not desirable for this type of output. We use the format method to help create legible console output:

```
print("[+] Printing Info.plist Device "
      "and User Information to Console\n")
for k in plist_data:
    if k != 'Applications' and k != 'iTunes Files':
        print("{:<25s} - {}".format(k, plist_data[k]))
```

Notice the additional formatting characters in the first curly brackets. We are specifying here to left-align the input string with a static width of 25 characters. As you can see in the following screenshot, this ensures the data is presented in an orderly and structured format:

```
(venv3) pyforcookbook@dev-vm$ python plist_parser.py ~/Desktop/Info.plist
[+] Opening /home/pyforcookbook/Desktop/Info.plist file
[+] Printing Info.plist Device and User Information to Console

Target Type               - Device
Installed Applications    - ['com.amazon.Amazon', 'com.facebook.Messenger', 'co
m.google.photos', 'com.google.Sheets', 'com.google.Maps']
Product Version           - 10.2.1
Target Identifier         - 925f63da60ab18face38417fb8fb80ad3109a23a
Device Name               - Testing iPad
Build Version             - 14D27
GUID                      - 24437EEE990B55C92F52E69A575B71D3
Product Name              - iPad Air 2
Product Type              - iPad5,3
Serial Number             - DWRS8GHUG5GY
iTunes Settings           - {'DeletedApplications': ['com.google.Drive', 'com.s
martthings', 'com.citrixonline.iOS.GoToMeeting', 'com.move.Realtor']}
Unique Identifier         - 925F63DA60AB18FACE38417FB8FB80AD3109A23A
Last Backup Date          - 2017-08-28 14:18:12
iTunes Version            - 12.6.2.20
Display Name              - Testing iPad
```

There's more...

This script can be further improved. We have provided a couple of recommendations here:

- Rather than printing data to the console, add a CSV function to write the data to a CSV file
- Add support for processing a directory full of PLIST files

Handling SQLite databases

Recipe Difficulty: Easy

Python Version: 3.5

Operating System: Any

As discussed, SQLite databases serve as the primary data repository on mobile devices. Python has a built-in library, `sqlite3`, which can be used to interface with these databases. In this script, we will interact with the iPhone `sms.db` file and extract data from the `message` table. We will also use this script as an opportunity to introduce the `csv` library and write the message data to a spreadsheet.

> To learn more about the `sqlite3` library, visit `https://docs.python.org/3/library/sqlite3.html`.

Getting started

All libraries used in this script are present in Python's standard library. For this script, make sure to have an `sms.db` file from which to query. With some minor modification, you can use this script with any database; however, we will specifically be talking about it with respect to the iPhone SMS database from an iOS 10.0.1 device.

How to do it...

The recipe follows these basic principles:

1. Connect to the input database.
2. Query table PRAGMA to extract column names.
3. Fetch all table content.
4. Write all table content to CSV.

How it works...

First, we import the required libraries to handle argument parsing, writing spreadsheets, and interacting with SQLite databases:

```
from __future__ import print_function
import argparse
import csv
import os
import sqlite3
import sys
```

This recipe's command-line handler accepts two positional arguments, SQLITE_DATABASE and OUTPUT_CSV, which represent the file paths for the input database and the desired CSV output, respectively:

```
if __name__ == '__main__':
    # Command-line Argument Parser
    parser = argparse.ArgumentParser(
        description=__description__,
        epilog="Developed by {} on {}".format(
            ", ".join(__authors__), __date__)
    )
    parser.add_argument("SQLITE_DATABASE", help="Input SQLite database")
    parser.add_argument("OUTPUT_CSV", help="Output CSV File")
    args = parser.parse_args()
```

Next, we use the `os.dirname()` method to extract just the directory path of the output file. We do this to check if the output directory already exists. If it does not, we use the `os.makedirs()` method to create each directory in the output path that does not already exist. This avoids issues later on if we were to try to write the output CSV to a directory that does not exist:

```
directory = os.path.dirname(args.OUTPUT_CSV)
if directory != '' and not os.path.exists(directory):
    os.makedirs(directory)
```

Once we have verified that the output directory exists, we pass the supplied arguments to the `main()` function:

```
main(args.SQLITE_DATABASE, args.OUTPUT_CSV)
```

The `main()` function prints a status update for the user to the console and then checks if the input file exists and is a file. If it does not exist, we use the `sys.exit()` method to exit the script using a value greater than 0 to indicate the script exited due to an error:

```
def main(database, out_csv):
    print("[+] Attempting connection to {} database".format(database))
    if not os.path.exists(database) or not os.path.isfile(database):
        print("[-] Database does not exist or is not a file")
        sys.exit(1)
```

Next, we use the `sqlite3.conn()` method to connect to the input database. It is important to note that the `sqlite3.conn()` method opens a database of the supplied name regardless of whether it exists or not. Therefore, it is vital to check that the file exists before trying to open a connection to it. Otherwise, we could create an empty database, which would likely cause issues in the script when we interact with it. Once we have a connection, we need to create a `Cursor` object to interact with the database:

```
# Connect to SQLite Database
conn = sqlite3.connect(database)
c = conn.cursor()
```

We can now perform queries against the database using the `Cursor` object's `execute()` command. At this point, the strings we pass into the execute function are just standard SQLlite queries. For the most part, you can run any query that you normally would when interacting with an SQLite database. The results returned from a given command are stored in the `Cursor` object. We need to use the `fetchall()` method to dump the results into a variable we can manipulate:

```
# Query DB for Column Names and Data of Message Table
c.execute("pragma table_info(message)")
```

```
table_data = c.fetchall()
columns = [x[1] for x in table_data]
```

The `fetchall()` method returns a tuple of results. Each column's name is stored in the first index of each tuple. By using list comprehension, we store the column names for the `message` table into a list. This comes into play later when we write the results of the data to a CSV file. After we obtain the column names for the `message` table, we directly query that table for all of its data and store it in the `message_data` variable:

```
c.execute("select * from message")
message_data = c.fetchall()
```

With the data extracted, we print a status message to the console and pass the output CSV and the message table columns and data to the `write_csv()` method:

```
print("[+] Writing Message Content to {}".format(out_csv))
write_csv(out_csv, columns, message_data)
```

You'll find that most of the scripts end with writing data to a CSV file. There are a few reasons for that. Writing CSVs in Python is very straightforward and can be accomplished in a few lines of code for most datasets. Additionally, having data in a spreadsheet allows one to sort and filter on columns to help summarize and understand large datasets.

Before we begin to write to the CSV file, we use the `open()` method to create a file object and its alias, `csvfile`. The way in which you open this file changes depending on if you are using Python 2.x or Python 3.x. For Python 2.x, you open the file in `wb` mode and without the newline keyword argument. With Python 3.x, you instead open the file in `w` mode and with the newline keyword set to an empty string. Where possible the code is written for Python 3.x, so we use the latter. Failing to open the file object in this manner results in the output CSV file containing an empty row between each row that is written.

After opening the file object, we pass it to the `csv.writer()` method. We can use the `writerow()` and `writerows()` methods from this object to write the column header list and the list of tuples, respectively. As an aside, we could iterate through each tuple in the `msgs` list and call `writerow()` for each tuple. The `writerows()` method eliminates the need for the unnecessary loop and is used here:

```
def write_csv(output, cols, msgs):
    with open(output, "w", newline="") as csvfile:
        csv_writer = csv.writer(csvfile)
        csv_writer.writerow(cols)
        csv_writer.writerows(msgs)
```

When we run this script, we see the following console message. Within the CSV we can gather in-depth details about the messages sent and received, along with interesting metadata including dates, errors, the source, and so on:

ROWID	text	handle_id	service	account	date	date_read	date_delivered
1	G-571235 is your Google verification code.	1	SMS	e:	494382482	494382486	494382486
2	I miss you!	2	iMessage	e: pyforcookbook@gmail.com	494436707	494437117	494437117
3	Chipotle: Chiptopia FREE rewards are only around until Sept. 30th. Make sure you get them while you can.	3	SMS	e:	494437008	494437128	494437128
4	I miss you too	2	iMessage	e: pyforcookbook@gmail.com	494437123	0	494437124
5	Chipotle: Kids and parents rejoice-kids eat free every Sunday in September with the purchase of a regular entree.	3	SMS	e:	494525250	494526218	494526218
6	G-702892 is your Google verification code.	1	SMS	e:	494527143	494527152	494527152

is_delivered	is_finished	is_emote	is_from_me	is_empty	is_delayed	is_auto_reply	is_prepared	is_read	is_system_message	is_sent
1	1	0	0	0	0	0	0	1	0	0
1	1	0	0	0	0	0	0	1	0	0
1	1	0	0	0	0	0	0	1	0	0
1	1	0	1	0	0	0	0	0	0	1
1	1	0	0	0	0	0	0	1	0	0
1	1	0	0	0	0	0	0	1	0	0

Identifying gaps in SQLite databases

Recipe Difficulty: Easy

Python Version: 2.7 or 3.5

Operating System: Any

This recipe will demonstrate how to programmatically identify missing entries for a given table by using its primary key. This technique allows us to identify records that are no longer active in the database. We will use this to identify which and how many messages have been deleted from an iPhone SMS database. This, however, will work with any table that uses an auto-incrementing primary key.

 To learn more about SQLite tables and primary keys, visit `https://www.sqlite.org/lang_createtable.html`.

One fundamental idea governing SQLite databases and their tables are primary keys. A primary key is typically a column that serves as a unique integer for a particular row in the table. A common implementation is the auto-incrementing primary key, starting typically at 1 for the first row, and incrementing by 1 for each successive row. When rows are removed from the table, the primary key does not change to account for that or reorder the table.

For example, if we had a database with 10 messages and deleted messages 4 through 6, we would have a gap in the primary key column from 3 to 7. With our understanding of auto-incrementing primary keys, we can make the inference that messages 4 through 6, at one point present, are no longer active entries in the database. In this manner, we can quantify the number of messages no longer active in the database and the primary key value associated with them. We will use this in a later recipe, *Digging deep to recover messages*, to then go hunt for those entries in an effort to determine if they are intact and recoverable.

Getting started

All libraries used in this script are present in Python's standard library. This recipe does require a database to run against. For this example, we will use the iPhone `sms.db` database.

How to do it...

We will perform the following steps in this recipe:

1. Connect to the input database.
2. Query table PRAGMA to identify a table's primary key(s).
3. Fetch all primary key values.
4. Calculate and display gaps in the table to the console.

How it works...

First, we import the required libraries to handle argument parsing and interacting with SQLite databases:

```
from __future__ import print_function
import argparse
import os
import sqlite3
import sys
```

This recipe's command-line handler accepts two positional arguments, SQLITE_DATABASE and TABLE, which represents the path of the input database and the name of the table to review, respectively. An optional argument, column, indicated by the dash, can be used to manually supply the primary key column if it is known:

```
if __name__ == "__main__":
    # Command-line Argument Parser
    parser = argparse.ArgumentParser(
        description=__description__,
        epilog="Developed by {} on {}".format(
            ", ".join(__authors__), __date__)
    )
    parser.add_argument("SQLITE_DATABASE", help="Input SQLite database")
    parser.add_argument("TABLE", help="Table to query from")
    parser.add_argument("--column", help="Optional column argument")
    args = parser.parse_args()
```

If the optional column argument is supplied, we pass it to the main() function as a keyword argument along with the database and table name. Otherwise, we just pass the database and table name to the main() function without the col keyword argument:

```
if args.column is not None:
    main(args.SQLITE_DATABASE, args.TABLE, col=args.column)
else:
    main(args.SQLITE_DATABASE, args.TABLE)
```

The main() function, like the previous recipe, first performs some validation that the input database exists and is a file. Because we are using keyword arguments with this function, we must indicate this with the **kwargs argument in the function definition. This argument serves as a dictionary that stores all provided keyword arguments. In this case, if the optional column argument were supplied, this dictionary would contain a col key/value pair:

```
def main(database, table, **kwargs):
    print("[+] Attempting connection to {} database".format(database))
    if not os.path.exists(database) or not os.path.isfile(database):
        print("[-] Database does not exist or is not a file")
        sys.exit(1)
```

After validating the input file, we use `sqlite3` to connect to this database and create the `Cursor` object we use to interact with it:

```
# Connect to SQLite Database
conn = sqlite3.connect(database)
c = conn.cursor()
```

In order to identify the primary key for the desired table, we run the `pragma table_info` command with the table name inserted in parentheses. We use the `format()` method to dynamically insert the name of the table into the otherwise static string. After we store the command's results in the `table_data` variable, we perform validation on the table name input. If the user supplied a table name that does not exist, we will have an empty list as the result. We check for this and exit the script if the table does not exist:

```
# Query Table for Primary Key
c.execute("pragma table_info({})".format(table))
table_data = c.fetchall()
if table_data == []:
    print("[-] Check spelling of table name - '{}' did not return "
        "any results".format(table))
    sys.exit(2)
```

At this point, we create an `if-else` statement for the remainder of the script, depending on whether the optional column argument was supplied by the user. If `col` is a key in the `kwargs` dictionary, we immediately call the `find_gaps()` function and pass it the `Cursor` object, `c`, the table name, and the user-specified primary key column name. Otherwise, we try to identify the primary key(s) in the `table_data` variable.

The command previously executed and stored in the `table_data` variable returns a tuple for each column in the given table. The last element of each tuple is a binary option between 1 or 0, where 1 indicates that the column is a primary key. We iterate through each of the last elements in the returned tuples and, if they are equal to 1, the column name, stored in index one of the tuple, is appended to the `potential_pks` list:

```
if "col" in kwargs:
    find_gaps(c, table, kwargs["col"])

else:
    # Add Primary Keys to List
    potential_pks = []
    for row in table_data:
        if row[-1] == 1:
            potential_pks.append(row[1])
```

Once we have identified all primary keys, we check the list to determine if there are zero or more than one keys present. If either of these cases exists, we alert the user and exit the script. In these scenarios, the user would need to specify which column should be treated as the primary key column. If the list contains a single primary key, we pass the name of that column along with the database cursor and table name to the `find_gaps()` function:

```
if len(potential_pks) != 1:
    print("[-] None or multiple primary keys found -- please "
            "check if there is a primary key or specify a specific "
            "key using the --column argument")
    sys.exit(3)

find_gaps(c, table, potential_pks[0])
```

The `find_gaps()` method starts by displaying a message to the console, alerting the user of the current execution status of the script. We attempt the database query in a `try` and `except` block. If the user-specified column does not exist or was misspelled, we will receive an `OperationalError` from the `sqlite3` library. This is the last validation step of user-supplied arguments and will exit the script if the except block is triggered. If the query executes successfully, we fetch all of the data and store it in the `results` variable:

```
def find_gaps(db_conn, table, pk):
    print("[+] Identifying missing ROWIDs for {} column".format(pk))
    try:
        db_conn.execute("select {} from {}".format(pk, table))
    except sqlite3.OperationalError:
        print("[-] '{}' column does not exist -- "
                "please check spelling".format(pk))
        sys.exit(4)
    results = db_conn.fetchall()
```

We use list comprehension and the built-in `sorted()` function to create a list of sorted primary keys. The `results` list contains tuples with one element at index 0, the primary key, which for the `sms.db message` table is the column named ROWID. With the sorted list of ROWIDs, we can quickly calculate the number of entries missing from the table. This would be the most recent ROWID minus the number of ROWIDs present in the list. If all entries were active in the database, this value would be zero.

 We are working under the assumption that the most recent ROWID is the actual most recent ROWID. It is possible that one could delete the last few entries and the recipe would only detect the most recent active entry as the highest ROWID.

```
rowids = sorted([x[0] for x in results])
total_missing = rowids[-1] - len(rowids)
```

If we are not missing any values from the list, we print this fortuitous message to the console and exit with 0, indicating a successful termination. On the other hand, if we are missing entries, we print that to the console along with the count of the missing entries:

```
if total_missing == 0:
    print("[*] No missing ROWIDs from {} column".format(pk))
    sys.exit(0)
else:
    print("[+] {} missing ROWID(s) from {} column".format(
        total_missing, pk))
```

To calculate the missing gaps, we generate a set of all ROWIDs between the first ROWID and the last using the `range()` method and then compare that against the sorted list that we have. The `difference()` function can be used with a set to return a new set with elements in the first set that are not present in the object in parentheses. We then print the identified gaps to the console, which completes the execution of the script:

```
# Find Missing ROWIDs
gaps = set(range(rowids[0], rowids[-1] + 1)).difference(rowids)
print("[*] Missing ROWIDS: {}".format(gaps))
```

An example of the output of this script may look like the following screenshot. Note how quickly the console can become cluttered based on the number of deleted messages. This, however, is not the intended end of this recipe. We will use the logic from this script in a more advanced recipe, *Digging deep to recover messages*, later in the chapter to identify and then attempt to locate potentially recoverable messages:

```
(venv3) pyforcookbook@dev-vm$ python sqlite_gaps.py ~/Desktop/iOS-sms/sms.db \
> message
[+] Attempting connection to /home/pyforcookbook/Desktop/iOS-sms/sms.db database
[+] Identifying missing ROWIDs for ROWID column
[+] 15 missing ROWID(s) from ROWID column
[*] Missing ROWIDS: {450, 3394, 6019, 4678, 7879, 3280, 467, 5651, 7641, 4444, 21
44, 7141, 2989, 5879, 6520}
```

See also

For more on SQLite database structure and primary keys, refer to their extensive documentation at https://www.sqlite.org/.

Processing iTunes backups

Recipe Difficulty: Easy

Python Version: 2.7 or 3.5

Operating System: Any

In this recipe, we will convert unencrypted iTunes backups into a human-readable format, allowing us to easily explore its contents without any third-party tools. Backups can be found in the `MobileSync\Backup` folder on the host computer.

 For details on default iTunes backup locations for Windows and OS X, visit `https://support.apple.com/en-us/HT204215`.

If an Apple product has been backed up to the machine, there will be a number of folders whose name is a GUID representing a specific device within the backup folder. These folders contain differential backups for each device over a period of time.

With the new backup format introduced in iOS 10, files are stored in subfolders containing the first two hexadecimal characters of the file name. Each file's name is a `SHA-1` hash of its path on the device. In the root of the device's backup folder, there are a few files of interest, such as the `Info.plist` file we discussed earlier and the `Manifest.db` database. This database stores details on each backed up file, including its `SHA-1` hash, file path, and name. We will use this information to recreate the native backup folder structure with human-friendly names.

Getting started

All libraries used in this script are present in Python's standard library. To follow along, you will need to procure an unencrypted iTunes backup to work with. Make sure the backup is of the newer iTunes backup format (iOS 10+) matching what was described previously.

How to do it...

We will use these steps to process the iTunes backup in this recipe:

1. Identify all backups in the `MobileSync\Backup folder`.
2. Iterate through each backup.
3. Read the Manifest.db file and associate `SHA-1` hash names with filenames.
4. Copy and rename backed-up files to the output folder with the appropriate file path and name.

How it works...

First, we import the required libraries to handle argument parsing, logging, copying files, and interacting with SQLite databases. We also set up a variable used to later construct the recipe's logging component:

```
from __future__ import print_function
import argparse
import logging
import os
from shutil import copyfile
import sqlite3
import sys

logger = logging.getLogger(__name__)
```

This recipe's command-line handler accepts two positional arguments, `INPUT_DIR` and `OUTPUT_DIR`, which represent the iTunes backup folder and the desired output folder, respectively. An optional argument can be supplied to specify the location of the log file and the verbosity for the log messages:

```
if __name__ == "__main__":
    # Command-line Argument Parser
    parser = argparse.ArgumentParser(
        description=__description__,
        epilog="Developed by {} on {}".format(
            ", ".join(__authors__), __date__)
    )
    parser.add_argument(
        "INPUT_DIR",
        help="Location of folder containing iOS backups, "
        "e.g. ~\Library\Application Support\MobileSync\Backup folder"
    )
    parser.add_argument("OUTPUT_DIR", help="Output Directory")
```

```
parser.add_argument("-l", help="Log file path",
                    default=__file__[:-2] + "log")
parser.add_argument("-v", help="Increase verbosity",
                    action="store_true")
args = parser.parse_args()
```

Next, we begin to set up the log for this recipe. We check if the optional verbosity argument was supplied by the user, and if it has been, we increase the level from INFO to DEBUG:

```
if args.v:
    logger.setLevel(logging.DEBUG)
else:
    logger.setLevel(logging.INFO)
```

For this log, we set up the message format and configure handlers for the console and file output, attaching them to our defined logger:

```
msg_fmt = logging.Formatter("%(asctime)-15s %(funcName)-13s"
                            "%(levelname)-8s %(message)s")
strhndl = logging.StreamHandler(sys.stderr)
strhndl.setFormatter(fmt=msg_fmt)
fhndl = logging.FileHandler(args.l, mode='a')
fhndl.setFormatter(fmt=msg_fmt)

logger.addHandler(strhndl)
logger.addHandler(fhndl)
```

With the log file set up, we log a few debug details to the log, including the arguments supplied to this script and details about the host and Python version. We exclude the first element of the sys.argv list, which is the name of the script and not one of the supplied arguments:

```
logger.info("Starting iBackup Visualizer")
logger.debug("Supplied arguments: {}".format(" ".join(sys.argv[1:])))
logger.debug("System: " + sys.platform)
logger.debug("Python Version: " + sys.version)
```

Using the os.makedirs() function, we create any necessary folders for the desired output directory if they do not already exist:

```
if not os.path.exists(args.OUTPUT_DIR):
    os.makedirs(args.OUTPUT_DIR)
```

Lastly, if the input directory exists and is actually a directory, we pass the supplied input and output directories to the `main()` function. If the input directory fails validation, we print an error to the console and log before exiting the script:

```
if os.path.exists(args.INPUT_DIR) and os.path.isdir(args.INPUT_DIR):
    main(args.INPUT_DIR, args.OUTPUT_DIR)
else:
    logger.error("Supplied input directory does not exist or is not "
                 "a directory")
    sys.exit(1)
```

The `main()` function starts by calling the `backup_summary()` function to identify all backups present in the input folder. Let's first look at the `backup_summary()` function and understand what it does before continuing on with the `main()` function:

```
def main(in_dir, out_dir):
    backups = backup_summary(in_dir)
```

The `backup_summary()` function uses the `os.listdir()` method to list the contents of the input directory. We also instantiate the `backups` dictionary, which stores details for each discovered backup:

```
def backup_summary(in_dir):
    logger.info("Identifying all iOS backups in {}".format(in_dir))
    root = os.listdir(in_dir)
    backups = {}
```

For each item in the input directory, we use the `os.path.join()` method with the input directory and item. We then check if this is a directory, rather than a file and if the name of the directory is 40 characters long. If the directory passes these checks, this is likely a backup directory and so we instantiate two variables to keep track of the number of files within the backup and the total size of those files:

```
for x in root:
    temp_dir = os.path.join(in_dir, x)
    if os.path.isdir(temp_dir) and len(x) == 40:
        num_files = 0
        size = 0
```

We use the `os.walk()` method discussed in Chapter 1, *Essential Scripting and File Information Recipes*, and create lists for the root, subdirectories, and files under the backup folder. We can, therefore, use the length of the files list and continue to add it to the `num_files` variable as we iterate through the backup folder. In a similar manner, we use a nifty one-liner to add each file's size to the `size` variable:

```
for root, subdir, files in os.walk(temp_dir):
    num_files += len(files)
    size += sum(os.path.getsize(os.path.join(root, name))
                for name in files)
```

After we finish iterating through the backup, we add the backup to the `backups` dictionary using its name as the key and store the backup folder path, file count, and size as values. Once we complete iteration of all backups, we return this dictionary to the `main()` function. Let's pick it back up there:

```
backups[x] = [temp_dir, num_files, size]

return backups
```

Back in the `main()` function, we print a summary of each backup to the console if any were found. For each backup, we print an arbitrary number identifying the backup, the name of the backup, the number of files, and the size. We use the `format()` method and manually specify newlines (\n) to ensure the console remains legible:

```
print("Backup Summary")
print("=" * 20)
if len(backups) > 0:
    for i, b in enumerate(backups):
        print("Backup No.: {} \n"
              "Backup Dev. Name: {} \n"
              "# Files: {} \n"
              "Backup Size (Bytes): {}\n".format(
                  i, b, backups[b][1], backups[b][2])
              )
```

Next, we use a `try-except` block to dump the contents of the `Manifest.db` file to the `db_items` variable. If the `Manifest.db` file is not found, the identified backup folder is either of an older format or invalid and so we skip it with the `continue` command. Let's briefly discuss the `process_manifest()` function, which uses `sqlite3` to connect to and extract all data in the `Manifest.db` files table:

```
try:
    db_items = process_manifest(backups[b][0])
except IOError:
```

```
logger.warn("Non-iOS 10 backup encountered or "
            "invalid backup. Continuing to next backup.")
continue
```

The `process_manifest()` method takes the directory path of the backup as its only input. To this input, we join the `Manifest.db` string, to represent the location where this database should exist in a valid backup. If it is found that this file does not exist, we log that error and raise an `IOError` to the `main()` function, which as we just discussed will cause a message to be printed to the console and continue on to the next backup:

```
def process_manifest(backup):
    manifest = os.path.join(backup, "Manifest.db")

    if not os.path.exists(manifest):
        logger.error("Manifest DB not found in {}".format(manifest))
        raise IOError
```

If the file does exist, we connect to it and create the `Cursor` object using `sqlite3`. The `items` dictionary stores each entry in the `Files` table using the item's `SHA-1` hash as the key and storing all other data as values in a list. Notice here an alternative method of accessing the results of the query rather than the `fetchall()` function used in previous recipes. After we have extracted all of the data from the `Files` table, we return the dictionary back to the `main()` function:

```
conn = sqlite3.connect(manifest)
c = conn.cursor()
items = {}
for row in c.execute("SELECT * from Files;"):
    items[row[0]] = [row[2], row[1], row[3]]

return items
```

Back in the `main()` function, we immediately pass the returned dictionary, now referred to as `db_items`, to the `create_files()` method. The dictionary we just created is going to be used by the next function to perform lookups on the file `SHA-1` hash and determine its real filename, extension, and native file path. The `create_files()` function performs these lookups and copies the backed-up file to the output folder with the appropriate path, name, and extension.

The `else` statement handles situations where there were no backups found by the `backup_summary()` function. We remind the user of what the appropriate input folder should be and exit the script. This completes the `main()` function; now let's move onto the `create_files()` method:

```
                create_files(in_dir, out_dir, b, db_items)
        print("=" * 20)

    else:
        logger.warning(
            "No valid backups found. The input directory should be "
            "the parent-directory immediately above the SHA-1 hash "
            "iOS device backups")
        sys.exit(2)
```

We start the `create_files()` method by printing a status message to the log:

```
    def create_files(in_dir, out_dir, b, db_items):
        msg = "Copying Files for backup {} to {}".format(
            b, os.path.join(out_dir, b))
        logger.info(msg)
```

Next, we create a counter to track the number of files found in the manifest but not within the backup. We then iterate through each key in the `db_items` dictionary generated from the `process_manifest()` function. We first check if the associated file name is `None` or an empty string and continue onto the next SHA-1 hash item otherwise:

```
        files_not_found = 0
        for x, key in enumerate(db_items):
            if db_items[key][0] is None or db_items[key][0] == "":
                continue
```

If the associated file name is present, we create a few variables representing the output directory path and the output file path. Notice the output path is appended to the name of the backup, `b`, to mimic the backup folder structure in the input directory. We use the output directory path, `dirpath`, to first check if it exists and create it otherwise:

```
            else:
                dirpath = os.path.join(
                    out_dir, b, os.path.dirname(db_items[key][0]))
                filepath = os.path.join(out_dir, b, db_items[key][0])
                if not os.path.exists(dirpath):
                    os.makedirs(dirpath)
```

We create a few more path variables, including the location of the backed-up file in the input directory. We do this by creating a string with the backup name, the first two characters of the SHA-1 hash key, and the SHA-1 key itself separated by forward slashes. We then join this to the input directory:

```
original_dir = b + "/" + key[0:2] + "/" + key
path = os.path.join(in_dir, original_dir)
```

With all of these paths created, we can now begin to perform a few more validation steps and then copy files over to the new output destination. First, we check if the output file already exists in the output folder. During development of this script, we noticed some files had the same name and were stored in the same folder in the output. This caused data to be overwritten and file counts to not match up between the backup folder and the output folder. To remedy this, if the file already exists in the backup, we append an underscore and an integer, x, which represents the loop iteration number, which serves as a unique value for our purposes:

```
if os.path.exists(filepath):
    filepath = filepath + "_{}".format(x)
```

With filename collisions sorted out, we use the `shutil.copyfile()` method to copy the backed-up file, represented by the path variable, and rename it and store it in the output folder, represented by the `filepath` variable. If the path variable refers to a file that is not in the backup folder, it will raise an IOError, which we catch and log to the log file and add to our counter:

```
try:
    copyfile(path, filepath)
except IOError:
    logger.debug("File not found in backup: {}".format(path))
    files_not_found += 1
```

We then provide a warning to the user about the number of files that were not found in the Manifest.db, just in case the user did not enable verbose logging. Once we have copied all files in the backup directory, we use the `shutil.copyfile()` method to individually copy the non-obfuscated PLIST and database files present in the backup folder to the output folder:

```
if files_not_found > 0:
    logger.warning("{} files listed in the Manifest.db not"
                   "found in backup".format(files_not_found))

copyfile(os.path.join(in_dir, b, "Info.plist"),
         os.path.join(out_dir, b, "Info.plist"))
copyfile(os.path.join(in_dir, b, "Manifest.db"),
```

```
                        os.path.join(out_dir, b, "Manifest.db"))
        copyfile(os.path.join(in_dir, b, "Manifest.plist"),
                 os.path.join(out_dir, b, "Manifest.plist"))
        copyfile(os.path.join(in_dir, b, "Status.plist"),
                 os.path.join(out_dir, b, "Status.plist"))
```

When we run this code, we can see the following updated file structure in our output:

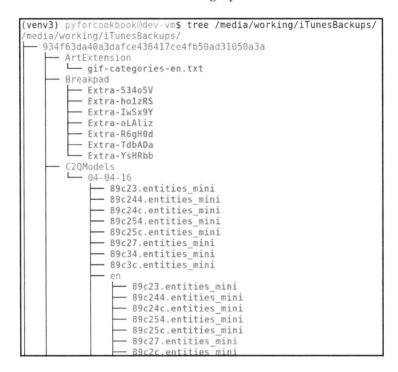

There's more...

This script can be further improved. We have provided a recommendation here:

- Add functionality to convert encrypted iTunes backups. Using a third-party library, such as `pycrypto`, one can decrypt the backups by supplying the correct password.

Putting Wi-Fi on the map

Recipe Difficulty: Medium

Python Version: 3.5

Operating System: Any

Without a connection to the outside world, mobile devices are little more than an expensive paperweight. Fortunately, open Wi-Fi networks are everywhere, and sometimes a mobile device will connect to them automatically. On the iPhone, a list of Wi-Fi networks the device has connected to is stored in a binary PLIST named `com.apple.wifi.plist`. This PLIST records, among other things, the Wi-Fi SSID, BSSID, and connection time. In this recipe, we will show how to extract Wi-Fi details from a standard Cellebrite XML report or supply Wi-Fi MAC addresses in a newline-delimited file. As the Cellebrite report formats may evolve over time, we are basing our XML parsing on a report generated with UFED Physical Analyzer version 6.1.6.19.

WiGLE is an online searchable repository of, at the time of writing, over 300 million Wi-Fi networks. We will use the Python `requests` library to access the API for WiGLE, to perform automated searches based on Wi-Fi MAC addresses. To install the `requests` library, we can use `pip`, as shown here:

```
pip install requests==2.18.4
```

If a network is found in the WiGLE repository, we can obtain a great deal of data about it, including its latitude and longitude coordinates. With this information, we can understand where a user's device, and presumably the user itself, has been and when that connection was made.

 To learn more about and use WiGLE, visit the website `https://wigle.net/`.

Getting started

This recipe requires an API key from the WiGLE website. To register for a free API key, visit `https://wigle.net/account` and follow the instructions to display your API key. There are two API values, the name and key. For this recipe, please create a file with a single line where the API name value is first, followed by a colon (no spaces), and then the API key. This format will be read by the script to authenticate you to the WiGLE API.

At the time of writing, in order to query the WiGLE API you must contribute data to the service. This is because the whole site is built on community sourced data and this encourages users to share information with others. There are many ways to contribute data, as documented on `https://wigle.net`.

How to do it...

This recipe follows the following steps to accomplish the goal:

1. Identify input as either a Cellebrite XML report or a line-separated text file of MAC addresses.
2. Process either type of input into a Python dataset.
3. Query the WiGLE API using `requests`.
4. Optimize the returned WiGLE results into a more convenient format.
5. Write the processed output to a CSV file.

How it works...

First, we import the required libraries to handle argument parsing, writing spreadsheets, processing XML data, and interacting with the WiGLE API:

```
from __future__ import print_function
import argparse
import csv
import os
import sys
import xml.etree.ElementTree as ET
import requests
```

This recipe's command-line handler accepts two positional arguments, INPUT_FILE and OUTPUT_CSV, representing the input file with Wi-Fi MAC addresses and the desired output CSV, respectively. By default, the script assumes the input file is a Cellebrite XML report. The user can specify the type of the input file using the optional -t flag and choose between xml or txt. Additionally, we can set the path of the file containing our API key. By default, this is set in the base of the user's directory and named .wigle_api, though you can update this value to reflect what is easiest in your environment.

> This file holding your API key should have additional protections, through file permissions or otherwise, to prevent theft of your key.

```
if __name__ == "__main__":
    # Command-line Argument Parser
    parser = argparse.ArgumentParser(
        description=__description__,
        epilog="Developed by {} on {}".format(
            ", ".join(__authors__), __date__),
        formatter_class=argparse.ArgumentDefaultsHelpFormatter
    )
    parser.add_argument("INPUT_FILE", help="INPUT FILE with MAC Addresses")
    parser.add_argument("OUTPUT_CSV", help="Output CSV File")
    parser.add_argument(
        "-t", help="Input type: Cellebrite XML report or TXT file",
        choices=('xml', 'txt'), default="xml")
    parser.add_argument('--api', help="Path to API key file",
                        default=os.path.expanduser("~/.wigle_api"),
                        type=argparse.FileType('r'))
    args = parser.parse_args()
```

We perform the standard data validation steps and check that the input file exists and is a file, exiting the script otherwise. We use os.path.dirname() to extract the directory path and check if it exists. If it does not already exist, we use the os.makedirs() function to create the directory. We also read in and split the API name and key before calling the main() function:

```
    if not os.path.exists(args.INPUT_FILE) or \
            not os.path.isfile(args.INPUT_FILE):
        print("[-] {} does not exist or is not a file".format(
            args.INPUT_FILE))
        sys.exit(1)

    directory = os.path.dirname(args.OUTPUT_CSV)
    if directory != '' and not os.path.exists(directory):
        os.makedirs(directory)
```

```
api_key = args.api.readline().strip().split(":")
```

After we perform argument validation, we pass all arguments to the `main()` function:

```
main(args.INPUT_FILE, args.OUTPUT_CSV, args.t, api_key)
```

In the `main()` function, we first determine the type of input we are working with. By default, the `type` variable is `"xml"` unless otherwise specified by the user. Depending on the file type, we send it to the appropriate parser, which returns the extracted Wi-Fi data elements in a dictionary. This dictionary is then passed, along with the output CSV, to the `query_wigle()` function. This function is responsible for querying, processing, and writing the query results to a CSV file. First, let's take a look at the parsers, starting with the `parse_xml()` function:

```
def main(in_file, out_csv, type, api_key):
    if type == 'xml':
        wifi = parse_xml(in_file)
    else:
        wifi = parse_txt(in_file)

    query_wigle(wifi, out_csv, api_key)
```

We parse the Cellebrite XML report using `xml.etree.ElementTree`, which we have imported as `ET`.

 To learn more about the `xml` library, visit `https://docs.python.org/3/library/xml.etree.elementtree.html`.

Parsing a report generated by a forensic tool can be tricky business. These reports may change in format and break your script. Therefore, we cannot assume that this script will continue to function with future iterations of Cellebrite's Physical Analyzer software. And it is for that reason that we've included an option to use this script with a text file containing MAC addresses instead.

As with any XML file, we need to first access the file and parse it using the `ET.parse()` function. We then use the `getroot()` method to return the root element of the XML file. We use this root as the initial foothold in the file as we search for the Wi-Fi data tags within the report:

```
def parse_xml(xml_file):
    wifi = {}
    xmlns = "{http://pa.cellebrite.com/report/2.0}"
    print("[+] Opening {} report".format(xml_file))
```

```
xml_tree = ET.parse(xml_file)
print("[+] Parsing report for all connected WiFi addresses")
root = xml_tree.getroot()
```

We use the `iter()` method to iterate through the child elements of the root. We check the tag for each child looking for the model tag. If found, we check if it has a location type attribute:

```
for child in root.iter():
    if child.tag == xmlns + "model":
        if child.get("type") == "Location":
```

For each location model found, we iterate through each of its field elements using the `findall()` method. This element contains metadata about the location artifact, such as the timestamp, BSSID, and SSID, of the network. We can check if the field has a name attribute with the value of `"Timestamp"` and store its value in the `ts` variable. If the value does not have any text content, we continue on to the next field:

```
for field in child.findall(xmlns + "field"):
    if field.get("name") == "TimeStamp":
        ts_value = field.find(xmlns + "value")
        try:
            ts = ts_value.text
        except AttributeError:
            continue
```

In a similar fashion, we check if the field's name matches `"Description"`. This field contains the BSSID and SSID of the Wi-Fi network in a tab-delimited string. We attempt to access the text of this value and except an `AttributeError` if there is no text:

```
if field.get("name") == "Description":
    value = field.find(xmlns + "value")
    try:
        value_text = value.text
    except AttributeError:
        continue
```

Because there may be other types of "Location" artifacts in the Cellebrite report, we check that the string "SSID" is present in the value's text. If so, we split the string using the tab special character into two variables. These strings we extracted from the value's text contain some unnecessary characters, which we remove from the string using string slicing:

```
if "SSID" in value.text:
    bssid, ssid = value.text.split("\t")
    bssid = bssid[7:]
    ssid = ssid[6:]
```

After we extract the timestamp, BSSID, and SSID from the report, we can add them to the wifi dictionary. If the Wi-Fi BSSID is already stored as one of the keys, we append the timestamp and SSID to the list. This is so that we can capture all historical connections to this Wi-Fi network and any changes to the name of the network. If we have not yet added this MAC address to the wifi dictionary, we create the key/value pairs including the WiGLE dictionary that stores API call results. After we have parsed all Location model artifacts, we return the wifi dictionary to the main() function:

```
if bssid in wifi.keys():
    wifi[bssid]["Timestamps"].append(ts)
    wifi[bssid]["SSID"].append(ssid)
else:
    wifi[bssid] = {
        "Timestamps": [ts], "SSID": [ssid],
        "Wigle": {}}

    return wifi
```

In contrast to the XML parser, the TXT parser is much more straightforward. We iterate through each line of the text file and set up each line, which should be one MAC address, as a key to an empty dictionary. After we have processed all lines in the file, we return the dictionary to the main() function:

```
def parse_txt(txt_file):
    wifi = {}
    print("[+] Extracting MAC addresses from {}".format(txt_file))
    with open(txt_file) as mac_file:
        for line in mac_file:
            wifi[line.strip()] = {"Timestamps": ["N/A"], "SSID": ["N/A"],
                                  "Wigle": {}}
    return wifi
```

With the dictionary of MAC addresses, we can now move onto the `query_wigle()` function and use `requests` to make WiGLE API calls. First, we print a message to the console informing the user of the current execution status. Next, we iterate through each MAC address in the dictionary and use the `query_mac_addr()` function to query the site for the BSSID:

```
def query_wigle(wifi_dictionary, out_csv, api_key):
    print("[+] Querying Wigle.net through Python API for {} "
        "APs".format(len(wifi_dictionary)))
    for mac in wifi_dictionary:
        wigle_results = query_mac_addr(mac, api_key)
```

The `query_mac_addr()` function takes our MAC address and API key and constructs the URL for the request. We use the base URL for the API and insert the MAC address at the end of it. This URL is then provided to the `requests.get()` method, along with an `auth` kwarg to provide the API name and key. The `requests` library handles forming and sending the packet to the API with the correct HTTP basic authentication. The `req` object is now ready for us to interpret, so we can call the `json()` method to return the data as a dictionary:

```
def query_mac_addr(mac_addr, api_key):
    query_url = "https://api.wigle.net/api/v2/network/search?" \
        "onlymine=false&freenet=false&paynet=false" \
        "&netid={}".format(mac_addr)
    req = requests.get(query_url, auth=(api_key[0], api_key[1]))
    return req.json()
```

With the returned `wigle_results` dictionary, we check the `resultCount` key to determine how many results were found in the `Wigle` database. If there are no results, we append an empty list to the results key in the `Wigle` dictionary. Likewise, if there are results, we directly append the returned `wigle_results` dictionary to the dataset. The API does have limits to a number of calls you can execute per day. When you reach that limit, a `KeyError` will be generated, which we catch and print to the console. We also provide reporting for other errors identified in a run, as the API may grow to expand the error reporting. After searching for each address and adding the results to the dictionary, we pass it, along with the output CSV, to the `prep_output()` method:

```
    try:
        if wigle_results["resultCount"] == 0:
            wifi_dictionary[mac]["Wigle"]["results"] = []
            continue
        else:
            wifi_dictionary[mac]["Wigle"] = wigle_results
    except KeyError:
        if wigle_results["error"] == "too many queries today":
```

```
            print("[-] Wigle daily query limit exceeded")
            wifi_dictionary[mac]["Wigle"]["results"] = []
            continue
        else:
            print("[-] Other error encountered for "
                  "address {}: {}".format(mac, wigle_results['error']))
            wifi_dictionary[mac]["Wigle"]["results"] = []
            continue
    prep_output(out_csv, wifi_dictionary)
```

If you haven't noticed, the data is becoming increasingly complicated, which makes writing it and working with it a bit more complicated. The `prep_output()` method essentially flattens the dictionary into easily writable chunks. The other reason we need this function is that we need to create separate rows for each instance a particular Wi-Fi network was connected to. While the WiGLE results for that network will be the same, the connection timestamp and the network SSID may be different.

To accomplish this, we start by creating a dictionary for the final processed results and a Google Maps-related string. We use this string to create a query with the latitude and longitude so the user can easily paste the URL into their browser to view geolocation details in Google Maps:

```
def prep_output(output, data):
    csv_data = {}
    google_map = "https://www.google.com/maps/search/"
```

We iterate through each MAC address in the dictionary and create two additional loops to iterate through all timestamps and all WiGLE results for the MAC address. With these loops, we can now access all of the data we have collected thus far and begin to add the data to the new output dictionary.

Due to the complexity of the initial dictionary, we create a variable called `shortres` to act as a shortcut to a deeper part of the output dictionary. This prevents us from unnecessarily writing the entire directory structure each and every time we need to access that part of the dictionary. The first use of the `shortres` variable can be seen as we extract the latitude and longitude of this network from the WiGLE results and append it to the Google Maps query:

```
for x, mac in enumerate(data):
    for y, ts in enumerate(data[mac]["Timestamps"]):
        for z, result in enumerate(data[mac]["Wigle"]["results"]):
            shortres = data[mac]["Wigle"]["results"][z]
            g_map_url = "{}{},{}".format(
                google_map, shortres["trilat"], shortres["trilong"])
```

In one (rather complicated) line, we add a key and value pair where the key is unique based on loop iteration counters and the value is the flattened dictionary. We do this by first creating a new dictionary containing the BSSID, SSID, timestamp, and the newly created Google Maps URL. Because we want to simplify the output, we need to merge the new dictionary and the WiGLE results, stored in the `shortres` variable, together.

We could iterate through each key in the second dictionary and add its key and value pairs one by one. However, it is much quicker to use a feature introduced in Python 3.5 whereby we can merge the two dictionaries by placing two `*` symbols before each dictionary. This will combine both dictionaries and, if there are any keys with the same name, overwrite data from the first dictionary with the second one. In this case, we do not have any key overlap, so this will simply combine the dictionaries as desired.

See the following StackOverflow post to learn more about dictionary merging:
`https://stackoverflow.com/questions/38987/how-to-merge-two-python-dictionaries-in-a-single-expression.`

After all of the dictionaries have been merged, we proceed to the `write_csv()` function to finally write the output:

```
csv_data["{}-{}-{}".format(x, y, z)] = {
    **{
        "BSSID": mac, "SSID": data[mac]["SSID"][y],
        "Cellebrite Connection Time": ts,
        "Google Map URL": g_map_url},
    **shortres
}

write_csv(output, csv_data)
```

In this recipe, we reintroduce the `csv.DictWriter` class, which allows us to easily write dictionaries to a CSV file. This is preferable over the `csv.writer` class we have used previously as it provides us a few benefits, including ordering the columns. To take advantage of that, we need to know all of the fields we use. Because WiGLE is dynamic and the reported results may change, we elected to dynamically find the names of all keys in the output dictionary. By adding them to a set, we ensure we only have unique keys:

```
def write_csv(output, data):
    print("[+] Writing data to {}".format(output))
    field_list = set()
    for row in data:
        for field in data[row]:
            field_list.add(field)
```

Once we have identified all of the keys we have in the output, we can create the CSV object. Notice how with the `csv.DictWriter` object we use two keyword arguments. The first, as mentioned previously, is a list of all the keys in the dictionary that we have sorted. This sorted list is the order of the columns in the resulting CSV. If the `csv.DictWriter` encounters a key that is not in the supplied `field_list`, which shouldn't happen in this case due to our precautions, it will ignore the error rather than raise an exception due to the configuration in the `extrasaction kwarg`:

```
with open(output, "w", newline="") as csvfile:
    csv_writer = csv.DictWriter(csvfile, fieldnames=sorted(
        field_list), extrasaction='ignore')
```

Once we have the writer set up, we can use the `writeheader()` method to automatically write the columns based on the supplied field names. After that, it's a simple matter of iterating through each dictionary in the data and writing it to the CSV file with the `writerow()` function. While this function is simple, imagine the headache we would have if we did not simplify the original data structure first:

```
csv_writer.writeheader()
for csv_row in data:
    csv_writer.writerow(data[csv_row])
```

After running this script, we can see all sorts of useful information in our CSV report. The first few columns include the BSSID, Google Maps URL, City and County:

BSSID	Google Map URL	channel	city	country	firsttime	freenet
88:75:56:14:D2:85	https://www.google.com/maps/search/42.93465805,-78.73145294	1			2016-06-25T16:01:51.000Z	?
84:18:3A:0D:73:78	https://www.google.com/maps/search/40.90498352,-74.10243988	6	Saddle Brook	US	2014-09-06T03:06:39.000Z	?
00:02:6F:D6:22:BA	https://www.google.com/maps/search/18.33517838,-64.97145844	6		US	2012-09-27T19:26:16.000Z	?
DC:9F:DB:58:AE:B3	https://www.google.com/maps/search/18.33928299,-64.92727661	8			2014-11-05T23:42:26.000Z	?
06:18:0A:79:58:8C	https://www.google.com/maps/search/40.99767685,-74.10984039	1	Ho-Ho-Kus	US	2016-04-08T17:17:45.000Z	?
C0:C5:20:34:C3:88	https://www.google.com/maps/search/42.88834763,-78.87303162	6			2015-06-17T00:43:41.000Z	?
6C:AA:B3:09:08:28	https://www.google.com/maps/search/42.87720108,-78.87604523	1			2015-06-23T22:57:32.000Z	?
AC:16:2D:DA:2E:C0	https://www.google.com/maps/search/42.88530731,-78.87268066	44		US	2013-01-24T19:04:01.000Z	?
00:14:F2:27:92:D0	https://www.google.com/maps/search/41.02758408,-74.2399292	6		US	2001-01-01T08:00:00.000Z	?

We then see several timestamps such as the first time seen, most recent time seen, and more specific locations such as the region and road:

lasttime	lastupdt	paynet	qos	region	road
2016-07-29T23:01:21.000Z	2016-07-29T23:01:38.000Z	Y		0	
2017-09-10T20:14:32.000Z	2017-09-10T20:15:10.000Z	?		7 NJ	Pehle Avenue
2013-11-25T22:04:02.000Z	2013-11-25T20:04:12.000Z	?		2 Virgin Islands of the United States	
2015-03-20T11:42:13.000Z	2015-03-20T09:42:31.000Z	?		2	
2017-09-05T17:55:29.000Z	2017-09-05T17:56:25.000Z	?		7 NJ	North Franklin Turnpike
2015-06-17T01:16:04.000Z	2015-06-17T01:16:12.000Z	?		0	
2016-07-23T01:19:04.000Z	2016-07-23T01:19:17.000Z	?		4	
2015-08-24T16:13:36.000Z	2015-08-24T16:13:41.000Z	?		7 NY	
2015-06-26T12:13:03.000Z	2015-06-26T12:13:08.000Z	Y		7 NJ	

And finally, we can learn the SSID, coordinates, and type of network and authentication used:

ssid	transid	trilat	trilong	type	wep
Boingo Hotspot	20160729-00787	42.9346581	-78.7314529	infra	?
Marriott_GUEST	20140907-00383	40.9049835	-74.1024399	infra	?
TravelerAccess	20120927-00220	18.3351784	-64.9714584	infra	?
FREE_WIFI	20141105-00289	18.339283	-64.9272766	infra	?
Innkeeper	20160408-00269	40.9976769	-74.1098404	infra	2
HyattRegencyBuffalo	20150616-00420	42.8883476	-78.8730316	infra	?
Courtyard_Guest	20150710-00199	42.8772011	-78.8760452	infra	?
Lafayette Hotel	20130124-00211	42.8853073	-78.8726807	infra	N
attwifi	20090302-00030	41.0275841	-74.2399292	infra	N

Digging deep to recover messages

Recipe Difficulty: Hard

Python Version: 3.5

Operating System: Any

Earlier in this chapter, we developed a recipe to identify missing records from a database. In this recipe, we will leverage the output from that recipe and identify recoverable records and their offset within a database. This is accomplished by understanding some internals of SQLite databases and leveraging that understanding to our advantage.

For a detailed description of the SQLite file internals, review `https://www.sqlite.org/fileformat.html`.

With this technique, we will be able to quickly triage a database and identify recoverable messages.

When a row from a database is deleted, similar to a file, the entry is not necessarily overwritten. This entry can still persist for some time based on database activity and its allocation algorithms. Our chances for data recovery decrease when, for example, a `vacuum` command is triggered.

We will not get into the weeds discussing SQLite structure; suffice to say that each entry is made up of four elements: payload length, the ROWID, the payload header, and the payload itself. The previous recipe identifies missing ROWID values, which we will use here to find all such occurrences of the ROWID across the database. We will use other data, such as known standard payload header values, with the iPhone SMS database to validate any hits. While this recipe is focused on extracting data from the iPhone SMS database, it can be modified to work for any database. We will later point out the few lines of code one would need to change to use it for other databases.

Getting started

All libraries used in this script are present in Python's standard library. If you would like to follow along, obtain an iPhone SMS database. If the database does not contain any deleted entries, open it with an SQLite connection and delete a few. This is a good test to confirm the script works as intended on your dataset.

How to do it...

This recipe is made up of the following steps:

1. Connect to the input database.
2. Query table PRAGMA and identify active entry gaps.
3. Convert ROWID gaps into their varint representation.
4. Search the raw hex of the database for missing entries.
5. Output results to a CSV file.

How it works...

First, we import the required libraries to handle argument parsing, manipulating hex and binary data, writing spreadsheets, creating tuples of cartesian products, searching with regular expression, and interacting with SQLite databases:

```
from __future__ import print_function
import argparse
import binascii
import csv
from itertools import product
import os
import re
import sqlite3
import sys
```

This recipe's command-line handler takes three positional and one optional argument. This is largely the same as the *Identifying gaps in SQLite databases* recipe earlier in this chapter; however, we have also added an argument for the output CSV file:

```
if __name__ == "__main__":
    # Command-line Argument Parser
    parser = argparse.ArgumentParser(
        description=__description__,
        epilog="Developed by {} on {}".format(
            ", ".join(__authors__), __date__)
    )
    parser.add_argument("SQLITE_DATABASE", help="Input SQLite database")
    parser.add_argument("TABLE", help="Table to query from")
    parser.add_argument("OUTPUT_CSV", help="Output CSV File")
    parser.add_argument("--column", help="Optional column argument")
    args = parser.parse_args()
```

After we parse the arguments, we pass the supplied arguments to the `main()` function. If the optional column argument was supplied by the user, we pass it to the `main()` function using the `col` keyword argument:

```
    if args.column is not None:
        main(args.SQLITE_DATABASE, args.TABLE,
            args.OUTPUT_CSV, col=args.column)
    else:
        main(args.SQLITE_DATABASE, args.TABLE, args.OUTPUT_CSV)
```

Because this script leverages what we have previously built, the `main()` function is largely duplicative of what we have already shown. Rather than repeating the comments about the code (there's only so much one can say about a line of code) we refer you to the *Identifying gaps in SQLite databases* recipe for an explanation of that portion of the code.

To refresh everyone's collective memory, see the following summary of that recipe: the `main()` function performs basic input validation, identifies potential primary keys from a given table (unless the column was supplied by the user), and calls the `find_gaps()` function. The `find_gaps()` function is another holdover from the previous script and is almost identical to the previous with the exception of one line. Rather than printing all of the identified gaps, this function now returns the identified gaps back to the `main()` function. The remainder of the `main()` function and all other code covered here on out is new. This is where we pick back up the thread as we continue to understand this recipe.

With gaps identified, we call a function called `varint_converter()` to process each gap into its varint counterpart. Varints, also known as variable-length integers, are big-endian integers between one and nine bytes in size. Varints are used by SQLite because they can take up less space than actually storing the ROWID integer itself. Therefore, in order to search for the deleted ROWID effectively, we must first convert it to a varint as we must search for that instead:

```
print("[+] Carving for missing ROWIDs")
varints = varint_converter(list(gaps))
```

For ROWIDs less than or equal to 127, their varint equivalent is simply the hex representation of the integer. We use the built-in `hex()` method to convert the integer into a hex string and use string slicing to remove the prepended `0x`. For example, executing `hex(42)` returns the string `0x2a`; in this case, we remove the leading `0x` hex designator as we are only interested in the value:

```
def varint_converter(rows):
    varints = {}
    varint_combos = []
    for i, row in enumerate(rows):
        if row <= 127:
            varints[hex(row)[2:]] = row
```

If the missing ROWID is `128` or greater, we start an infinite `while` loop to find the relevant varint. Before starting the loop, we use list comprehension to create a list containing numbers `0` through `255`. We also instantiate a counter variable with a value of `1`. The first part of the `while` loop creates a list of tuples, whose number of elements equals to the `counter` variable, containing every combination of the `combos` list. For example, if counter is equal to `2`, we see a list of tuples representing all possible 2-byte varints as `[(0, 0), (0, 1), (0, 2), ..., (255, 255)]`. After that process completes, we use list comprehension again to remove all tuples whose first element is less than or equal to `127`. Due to the fact that this part of the `if-else` loop deals with rows greater than or equal to `128`, we know the varint cannot be equal to or less than `127` and so those values are eliminated from consideration:

```
else:
    combos = [x for x in range(0, 256)]
    counter = 1
    while True:
        counter += 1
        print("[+] Generating and finding all {} byte "
            "varints..".format(counter))
        varint_combos = list(product(combos, repeat=counter))
        varint_combos = [x for x in varint_combos if x[0] >= 128]
```

After creating the list of n-byte varints, we loop through each combination and pass it to the `integer_converter()` function. This function treats these numbers as part of a varint and decodes them into the corresponding ROWID. We can then check the returned ROWID against the missing ROWID. If it matches, we add a key and value pair to the `varints` dictionary where the key is the hexadecimal representation of the varint and the value is the missing ROWID. At this point, we increment the `i` variable by `1` and try to fetch the next row element. If successful, we process that ROWID and so on until we have reached the end of the ROWIDs that will generate an `IndexError`. We catch such an error and return the `varints` dictionary back to the `main()` function.

One important thing to note about this function, because the input was a sorted list of ROWIDs, we only need to calculate the n-byte varint combinations once as the next ROWID in line can only be bigger not smaller. Additionally, due to the fact that we know the next ROWID is at least one greater than the previous, we continue looping through the varint combinations we created without restarting as it would be impossible for the next ROWID to be smaller. These techniques show a great use case for `while` loops as they vastly improve the execution speed of the recipe:

```
for varint_combo in varint_combos:
    varint = integer_converter(varint_combo)
    if varint == row:
```

```
            varints["".join([hex(v)[2:].zfill(2) for v in
                            varint_combo])] = row
        i += 1
        try:
            row = rows[i]
        except IndexError:
            return varints
```

The `integer_converter()` function is relatively straightforward. This function makes use of the built-in `bin()` method, similar to the `hex()` method already discussed, to convert an integer into its binary equivalent. We iterate through each value in the proposed varint, first converting each using `bin()`. This returns a string, this time with the binary prefix value `0b` prepended, which we remove using string slicing. We again use `zfill()` to ensure the bytes have all bits intact as the `bin()` method removes leading `0` bits by default. After that, we remove the first bit from every byte. As we iterate through each number of our varint, we add the resulting processed bits to a variable called `binary`.

This process may sound a little confusing; however, this is the manual process of decoding varints.

 Refer to this blog post on *Forensics from the sausage factory* for more details about how to manually convert varints to integers and other SQLite internals:
`https://forensicsfromthesausagefactory.blogspot.com/2011/05/analysis-of-record-structure-within.html`.

After we finish iterating through the list of numbers, we use `lstrip()` to strip out any leftmost zero values in the binary string. If the resulting string is empty, we return `0`; otherwise, we convert and then return the processed binary data back into an integer from the base-2 binary representation:

```
def integer_converter(numbs):
    binary = ""
    for numb in numbs:
        binary += bin(numb)[2:].zfill(8)[1:]
    binvar = binary.lstrip("0")
    if binvar != '':
        return int(binvar, 2)
    else:
        return 0
```

Back in the `main()` function, we pass the `varints` dictionary and the path to the database file to the `find_candidates()` function:

```
search_results = find_candidates(database, varints)
```

The two candidates we search for are `"350055"` and `"360055"`. As discussed before, in a database, following the ROWID for a cell is the payload header length. This payload header length is typically one of two values in the iPhone SMS database: either `0x35` or `0x36`. Following the payload header length is the payload header itself. The first serial type of the payload header will be `0x00` and represents a `NULL` value, which the primary key of the database--the first column and hence the first serial type--will always be recorded as. Next is the serial type `0x55` corresponding to the second column in the table, the message GUID, which is always a `21` byte string and therefore will always be represented by the serial type `0x55`. Any validated hits are appended to the results list.

By searching for the ROWID varint and these three additional bytes, we can greatly reduce the number of false positives. Note that if you are working on a database other than the iPhone SMS database, you need to change the value of these candidates to reflect any static content proceeding the ROWID in your table:

```
def find_candidates(database, varints):
    results = []
    candidate_a = "350055"
    candidate_b = "360055"
```

We open the database in `rb` mode to search its binary content. In order to do so, we must first read in the entire database and, using the `binascii.hexlify()` function, convert this data into hex. As we have already stored the varints as hex, we can now easily search this dataset for the varint and other surrounding data. We begin the search process by looping through each varint and creating two different search strings to account for either of the two static footholds in the iPhone SMS database:

```
with open(database, "rb") as infile:
    hex_data = str(binascii.hexlify(infile.read()))
for varint in varints:
    search_a = varint + candidate_a
    search_b = varint + candidate_b
```

We then use the `re.finditer()` method to iterate through each hit based on the `search_a` and `search_b` keywords. For each result, we append a list with the ROWID, the search term used, and the offset within the file. We must divide by 2 to accurately report the number of bytes rather than the number of hex digits. After we finish searching the data, we return the results to the `main()` function:

```
for result in re.finditer(search_a, hex_data):
    results.append([varints[varint], search_a, result.start() / 2])

for result in re.finditer(search_b, hex_data):
    results.append([varints[varint], search_b, result.start() / 2])

return results
```

For the last time, we are back in the `main()` function. This time we check if there are any search results. If there are, we pass them along with the CSV output to the `csvWriter()` method. Otherwise, we print a status message to the console notifying the user that there were no intact recoverable ROWIDs identified:

```
if search_results != []:
    print("[+] Writing {} potential candidates to {}".format(
        len(search_results), out_csv))
    write_csv(out_csv, ["ROWID", "Search Term", "Offset"],
            search_results)
else:
    print("[-] No search results found for missing ROWIDs")
```

The `write_csv()` method is true to form and simple as always. We open a new CSV file and create three columns for the three elements stored in the nested list structure. We then use the `writerows()` method to write all rows in the results data list to the file:

```
def write_csv(output, cols, msgs):
    with open(output, "w", newline="") as csvfile:
        csv_writer = csv.writer(csvfile)
        csv_writer.writerow(cols)
        csv_writer.writerows(msgs)
```

When we look at the exported report we can clearly see our row ID, the searched hex value, and the offset within the database the record was found:

ROWID	Search Term	Offset
1645	8c6d360055	16760179
1651	8c73350055	16764554
1665	8d01360055	16782042
1667	8d03360055	16787789
1668	8d04360055	16787196
1669	8d05350055	16785934
1670	8d06360055	16792125
1672	8d08360055	16796341
2040	8f78350055	17152861
2438	9306360055	17622679
2440	9308350055	17621500
2545	9371350055	17707805
2568	9408360055	17729297

There's more...

This script can be further improved. We have provided a recommendation here:

- Rather than hard-coding the candidates, accept a text file of such candidates or command-line entries to increase the recipe's flexibility

4
Extracting Embedded Metadata Recipes

This chapter covers the following recipes:

- Extracting audio and video metadata
- The big picture
- Mining for PDF metadata
- Reviewing executable metadata
- Reading office document metadata
- Integrating our metadata extractor with EnCase

Introduction

When an investigation comes down to just a few files of interest, it is critical to extract every piece of available information about the file. Embedded metadata, often overlooked, can provide us with crucial information that solidifies the evidentiary value of a given file. Whether it is gathering authorship information from Microsoft Office files, mapping GPS coordinates from pictures, or extracting compilation information from executables, we can learn a lot more about files we are investigating. In this chapter, we will develop scripts to examine these file formats, and others, to extract key information for our review. We will illustrate how to integrate these recipes with EnCase, the popular forensic suite, and add them to your investigative workflow.

In particular, we will develop code that highlights the following:

- Parsing ID3 and QuickTime-formatted metadata from audio and video formats
- Revealing GPS coordinates embedded within images
- Identifying authorship and lineage information from PDF files
- Extracting embedded names, compilation dates, and other attributes of Windows executable files
- Reporting on document creation and source of Microsoft Office files
- Launching Python scripts from EnCase

 Visit `www.packtpub.com/books/content/support` to download the code bundle for this chapter.

Extracting audio and video metadata

Recipe Difficulty: Easy

Python Version: 2.7 or 3.5

Operating System: Any

Audio and video files are common file formats that make use of embedded metadata. This information, for example, is used by your preferred media player to show the artist, album, and track name information of the content you import. Though the majority of this information is standard and focused on providing information to the listener, we sometimes find important details in this area of the file. We begin our exploration of embedded metadata with the extraction of the common attributes from audio and video files.

Getting started

This recipe requires the installation of the third-party library `mutagen`. All other libraries used in this script are present in Python's standard library. This library allows us to extract metadata from audio and video files. This library can be installed using `pip`:

```
pip install mutagen==1.38
```

To learn more about the `mutagen` library, visit `https://mutagen.readthedocs.io/en/latest`.

How to do it...

In this script, we perform the following steps:

1. Identify the input file type.
2. Extract embedded metadata from the file type processor.

How it works...

To extract information from a sample MP3 or MP4 file, we first import the three libraries needed for this recipe: `argparse`, `json`, and `mutagen`. The `json` library allows us to load definitions for the QuickTime MP4 metadata format used later in this recipe.

```
from __future__ import print_function
import argparse
import json
import mutagen
```

This recipe's command-line handler takes one positional argument, `AV_FILE`, which represents the path to the MP3 or MP4 file to process. After parsing the user-supplied arguments, we use the `mutagen.File()` method to open a handle to the file. Depending on the extension of the input file, we send this handle to the appropriate function: `handle_id3()` or `handle_mp4()`.

```
if __name__ == '__main__':
    parser = argparse.ArgumentParser(
        description=__description__,
        epilog="Developed by {} on {}".format(
            ", ".join(__authors__), __date__)
    )
    parser.add_argument("AV_FILE", help="File to extract metadata from")
    args = parser.parse_args()
    av_file = mutagen.File(args.AV_FILE)

    file_ext = args.AV_FILE.rsplit('.', 1)[-1]
    if file_ext.lower() == 'mp3':
        handle_id3(av_file)
```

```
    elif file_ext.lower() == 'mp4':
        handle_mp4(av_file)
```

The `handle_id3()` function is responsible for extracting metadata from MP3 files. The MP3 format uses the ID3 standard for storing its metadata. In our ID3 parsing function, we first create a dictionary, called `id3_frames`, mapping the ID3 fields, as they are represented in the raw file, to human-readable strings. We can add more fields to this definition to extend the information we extract. Before we extract the embedded metadata, we print appropriate column headers to the console.

```python
def handle_id3(id3_file):
    # Definitions from http://id3.org/id3v2.4.0-frames
    id3_frames = {
        'TIT2': 'Title', 'TPE1': 'Artist', 'TALB': 'Album',
        'TXXX': 'Custom', 'TCON': 'Content Type', 'TDRL': 'Date released',
        'COMM': 'Comments', 'TDRC': 'Recording Date'}
    print("{:15} | {:15} | {:38} | {}".format("Frame", "Description",
                                                "Text", "Value"))
    print("-" * 85)
```

Next, we use a loop to extract the names and various values of each `id3` frame. We query the name of the frame against the `id3_frames` dictionary to extract the human-readable version of it. Additionally, from each of the frames, we extract the description, text, and value(s) (if they are present) using the `getattr()` method. Finally, we print the pipe-delimited text to the console for review. That takes care of MP3 files, now let's move onto MP4 files.

```python
    for frames in id3_file.tags.values():
        frame_name = id3_frames.get(frames.FrameID, frames.FrameID)
        desc = getattr(frames, 'desc', "N/A")
        text = getattr(frames, 'text', ["N/A"])[0]
        value = getattr(frames, 'value', "N/A")
        if "date" in frame_name.lower():
            text = str(text)

        print("{:15} | {:15} | {:38} | {}".format(
            frame_name, desc, text, value))
```

The `handle_mp4()` function is responsible for processing MP4 files and follows a similar workflow to the previous function. We begin by setting up the metadata mappings in a dictionary, called `qt_tag`, using the Unicode value for the copyright symbol (`u"\u00A9"`) as a prepended character to the field names. This mapping dictionary is designed so the tag name is the key and the human-readable string is the value. We then use the `json.load()` method to bring in a large list of definitions for types of media genres (Comedy, Podcasts, Country, and so on). By storing the JSON data to the `genre_ids` variable, in this case, we have a dictionary with genre look up values where keys are integers and their values are different genres. These definitions are from `http://www.sno.phy.queensu.ca/~phil/exiftool/TagNames/QuickTime.html#GenreID`.

```
def handle_mp4(mp4_file):
    cp_sym = u"\u00A9"
    qt_tag = {
        cp_sym + 'nam': 'Title', cp_sym + 'art': 'Artist',
        cp_sym + 'alb': 'Album', cp_sym + 'gen': 'Genre',
        'cpil': 'Compilation', cp_sym + 'day': 'Creation Date',
        'cnID': 'Apple Store Content ID', 'atID': 'Album Title ID',
        'plID': 'Playlist ID', 'geID': 'Genre ID', 'pcst': 'Podcast',
        'purl': 'Podcast URL', 'egid': 'Episode Global ID',
        'cmID': 'Camera ID', 'sfID': 'Apple Store Country',
        'desc': 'Description', 'ldes': 'Long Description'}
    genre_ids = json.load(open('apple_genres.json'))
```

Next, we iterate through the MP4 file's embedded metadata key-value pairs. For each key, we use the `qt_tag` dictionary to look up the human-readable version of the key. If the value is a list, we join all of its elements into a semi-colon separated string. Alternatively, if the value is "`geID`", we use the `genre_ids` dictionary to look up the integer and print the mapped genre for the user.

```
    print("{:22} | {}".format('Name', 'Value'))
    print("-" * 40)
    for name, value in mp4_file.tags.items():
        tag_name = qt_tag.get(name, name)
        if isinstance(value, list):
            value = "; ".join([str(x) for x in value])
        if name == 'geID':
            value = "{}: {}".format(
                value, genre_ids[str(value)].replace("|", " - "))
        print("{:22} | {}".format(tag_name, value))
```

Using a MP3 podcast as an example, the script shows additional details otherwise unavailable. We now know the release date, what appears to be the software used, and several identifiers that we can use for keywords to try and identify the file elsewhere.

```
(venv3) pyforcookbook@dev-vm$ python av_metadata.py ~/Desktop/765_\ The\ Holiday\ I
ndustrial\ Complex.mp3
Frame            | Description    | Text                                    | Value
------------------------------------------------------------------------------------
TGID             | N/A            | d4825239-caf9-448f-b17a-029f1028a8f8    | N/A
Custom           | OrigTime       | 17:42:56                                | N/A
Custom           | TimeReference  | 0                                       | N/A
Title            | N/A            | #765: The Holiday Industrial Complex    | N/A
Comments         | iTunPGAP       | 0                                       | N/A
Artist           | N/A            | NPR                                     | N/A
WFED             | N/A            | N/A                                     | N/A
Recording Date   | N/A            | 2017                                    | N/A
Custom           | OrigReference  | #GZHrunh4aoaaaGk                        | N/A
Date released    | N/A            | 2017-04-18 12:00                        | N/A
Custom           | OrigDate       | 2017-04-1                               | N/A
Content Type     | N/A            | Business                                | N/A
PCST             | N/A            | N/A                                     | 0
Custom           | Originator     | Pro Tools                               | N/A
Album            | N/A            | Planet Money                            | N/A
```

Let's look at another podcast, but this time, one that is an MP4. After running the script, we are presenting with a great deal of information about the MP4 file's source and type of content. Again, we have several interesting identifiers, source URLs, and other attribution details available to us due to this exercise.

```
(venv3) pyforcookbook@dev-vm$ python av_metadata.py \
> ~/Desktop/tiny_desk_concert_alt-j.mp4
Name                       | Value
- - - - - - - - - - - - - - - - - - - - - - - - - - - - - - - - - - - - - -
Apple Store Country        | 0
Podcast URL                | https://www.npr.org/rss/podcast.php?id=510292
Camera ID                  | 0
Long Description           | I have a self-imposed rule for Tiny Desk Concerts: No arti
st can visit twice unless there's something wholly different about what they're doi
ng. alt-J was happy to oblige.
stik                       | 0
Title                      | alt-J
Description                | I have a self-imposed rule for Tiny Desk Concerts: No arti
st can visit twice unless there's something wholly different about what they're doi
ng. alt-J was happy to oblige.
Podcast                    | True
rtng                       | 0
tmpo                       | 0
©mvi                       | 0
Creation Date              | 2017-04-24T12:00:00Z
pgap                       | False
tves                       | 0
Album Title ID             | 125443881
Playlist ID                | 362115318
Genre ID                   | 1310: Podcasts - Music
tvsn                       | 0
©ART                       | NPR
Genre                      | Music
Compilation                | False
Album                      | Tiny Desk Concerts - Video
Apple Store Content ID     | 1000384721776
©mvc                       | 0
Episode Global ID          | d28ed53a-68ac-47b6-b9a1-87d496b3269e
```

There's more...

This script can be further improved. here's a recommendation:

- Add additional support for other multimedia formats using the `mutagen` library.

The big picture

Recipe Difficulty: Easy

Python Version: 2.7 or 3.5

Operating System: Any

Images can contain many metadata attributes, depending on the file format and the device that was used to capture the image. Fortunately, most devices will embed GPS information within the photos they take. Using third-party libraries, we will extract GPS coordinates and plot them with Google Earth. This script focuses exclusively on this task, however, the recipe can be easily tweaked to extract all embedded **Exchangeable Image File Format** (**EXIF**) metadata in JPEG and TIFF images as well.

Getting started

This recipe requires the installation of two third-party libraries: `pillow` and `simplekml`. All other libraries used in this script are present in Python's standard library. The `pillow` library provides a clean interface to the **Python Imaging Library** (**PIL**) and can be used to extract embedded metadata from images:

```
pip install pillow==4.2.1
```

 To learn more about the `pillow` library, visit `https://pillow.readthedocs.io/en/4.2.x/`.

To add some extra flair to this recipe, we will be writing the GPS details to a KML file, for use in a program like Google Earth. To handle this, we will use the `simplekml` library, available for installation by executing the following command:

```
pip install simplekml==1.3.0
```

 To learn more about the `simplekml` library, visit `http://www.simplekml.com/en/latest/`.

How to do it...

We extract metadata from image files in the following steps:

1. Open the input photo with PIL.
2. Use PIL to extract all EXIF tags.
3. If GPS coordinates are found, create a Google Earth KML file.
4. Print the Google Maps URL to view the GPS data in the browser.

How it works...

We begin by importing argparse along with the newly installed simplekml and PIL libraries. For this example, we will only need the Image and ExifTags.Tags classes from PIL.

```
from __future__ import print_function
import argparse
from PIL import Image
from PIL.ExifTags import TAGS
import simplekml
import sys
```

This recipe's command-line handler accepts one positional argument, PICTURE_FILE, which represents the file path to the photo to process.

```
parser = argparse.ArgumentParser(
    description=__description__,
    epilog="Developed by {} on {}".format(", ".join(__authors__), __date__)
)
parser.add_argument('PICTURE_FILE', help="Path to picture")
args = parser.parse_args()
```

After configuring these arguments, we specify two URLs, gmaps and open_maps, that we will populate with coordinate information. Since the PIL library provides coordinates as a tuple of tuples in the **degrees minutes seconds** (**DMS**) format, we will need a function to convert them into decimal, which is another commonly used format for expressing coordinates. Each of the three elements in the provided tuple represents a different component of the coordinate. Additionally, within each tuple, there are two elements: the first element represents the value and the second is the scale that must be used to convert the value into an integer.

For each component of the coordinate, we need to divide the first value in the nested tuple by the second value. This structure is used for the second and third tuple, which describe the minute and second values of the DMS coordinate. Additionally, we need to ensure that the minutes and seconds are added together properly by dividing each by the product of 60 to the power of the current iteration count (which will be 1 and 2). While this won't change the first value (as enumeration begins at zero), it will ensure the second and third values are properly expressed.

The following code block highlights an example of the coordinate format provided by the PIL library. Notice how the degree, minute, and second values are grouped into their own tuples. The first element represents the value of the coordinate and the second represents the scale. For example, for the seconds element (the third tuple), we need to divide the integer by 1000 before performing our other operations to ensure the value is represented correctly:

- **Latitude**: ((41 , 1), (53 , 1), (23487 , 1000))
- **Longitude**: ((12 , 1), (29 , 1), (10362 , 1000))
- **GPS coordinates**: 41.8898575 , 12.486211666666666

```
gmaps = "https://www.google.com/maps?q={},{}"
open_maps = "http://www.openstreetmap.org/?mlat={}&mlon={}"


def process_coords(coord):
    coord_deg = 0
    for count, values in enumerate(coord):
        coord_deg += (float(values[0]) / values[1]) / 60**count
    return coord_deg
```

With the DMS to decimal coordinate conversion process configured, we open the image using the Image.open() method to open a file by path as a PIL object. We then use the _getexif() method to extract a dictionary containing EXIF data. If PIL is unable to extract metadata from the photo, this variable will be None.

With the EXIF dictionary, we iterate through the keys and values to convert the numeric value to a human-readable name. This uses the TAGS dictionary from PIL, which maps the numeric value to a string representing the tag. The TAGS object acts in a similar manner to the manually specified mappings in the prior recipe.

```
img_file = Image.open(args.PICTURE_FILE)
exif_data = img_file._getexif()

if exif_data is None:
    print("No EXIF data found")
```

```
        sys.exit()

    for name, value in exif_data.items():
        gps_tag = TAGS.get(name, name)
        if gps_tag is not 'GPSInfo':
            continue
```

Once the `GPSInfo` tag is found, we extract four values of interest, found within the dictionary keys 1 through 4. In pairs, we store the GPS reference and process the coordinates with the `process_coords()` method previously described. By storing the reference as a Boolean, we can easily use an `if` statement to determine whether the GPS decimal coordinates should be positive or negative.

```
        lat_ref = value[1] == u'N'
        lat = process_coords(value[2])
        if not lat_ref:
            lat = lat * -1

        lon_ref = value[3] == u'E'
        lon = process_coords(value[4])
        if not lon_ref:
            lon = lon * -1
```

To add our KML support, we initiate a `kml` object from the `simplekml` library. From there, we add a new point with a name and the coordinates. For the name, we simply use the file's name. The coordinates are provided as a tuple within a list where the first element is the longitude and the second is the latitude. We could also provide a third element in this tuple to specify the zoom level, though we omit it in this instance. To produce our KML file, we call the `save()` method and write it to a `.kml` file with the same name as the input file.

```
        kml = simplekml.Kml()
        kml.newpoint(name=args.PICTURE_FILE, coords=[(lon, lat)])
        kml.save(args.PICTURE_FILE + ".kml")
```

With the processed GPS information, we can print the coordinates, KML file, and URLs to the console. Notice how we nest the format strings, allowing us to print a basic message along with the URL.

```
        print("GPS Coordinates: {}, {}".format(lat, lon))
        print("Google Maps URL: {}".format(gmaps.format(lat, lon)))
        print("OpenStreetMap URL: {}".format(open_maps.format(lat, lon)))
        print("KML File {} created".format(args.PICTURE_FILE + ".kml"))
```

When we run this script at the command line, we quickly see the coordinates, two links to view the location on a map, and the path to the KML file.

```
(venv3) pyforcookbook@dev-vm$ python pic_metadata.py ~/Desktop/art.jpg
GPS Coordinates: 30.260602777777777, -97.74109166666666
Google Maps URL: https://www.google.com/maps?q=30.260602777777777,-97.741091666
66666
OpenStreetMap URL: http://www.openstreetmap.org/?mlat=30.260602777777777&mlon=-
97.74109166666666
KML File /home/pyforcookbook/Desktop/art.jpg.kml created
```

Following the two links we generated, we can see the pins on the two maps and share these links with others if so desired.

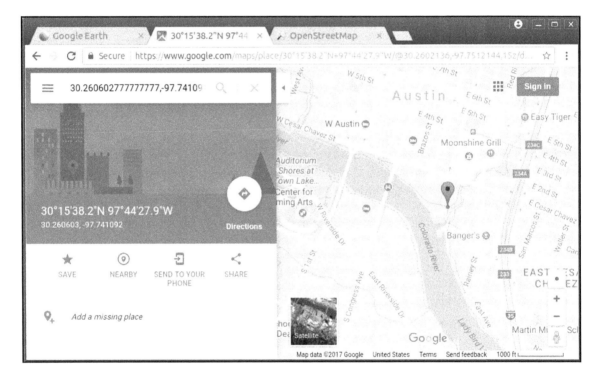

Lastly, we can use the KML file to store and reference the location found within the image. Google Earth allows this file to be viewed through both the web and desktop clients.

There's more...

This script can be further improved. We have provided one or more recommendations as follows:

- Integrate file recursion to process multiple photos to create larger KML files that map many GPS coordinates.
- Experiment with the `simplekml` library to add additional detail to each point, such as a description, timestamp, coloring, and more.

Mining for PDF metadata

Recipe Difficulty: Easy

Python Version: 2.7 or 3.5

Operating System: Any

While PDF documents can represent a wide variety of media, including images, text, and forms, they contain structured embedded metadata in the **Extensible Metadata Platform** (**XMP**) format that can provide us with some additional information. Through this recipe, we access a PDF using Python and extract metadata describing the creation and lineage of the document.

Getting started

This recipe requires the installation of the third-party library `PyPDF2`. All other libraries used in this script are present in Python's standard library. The `PyPDF2` module provides us with bindings to read and write PDF files. In our case, we will only use this library to read the metadata stored in the XMP format. To install this library, run the following command:

```
pip install PyPDF2==1.26.0
```

 To learn more about the `PyPDF2` library, visit `http://mstamy2.github.io/PyPDF2/`.

How to do it...

To handle PDFs for this recipe, we follow these steps:

1. Open the PDF file with `PyPDF2` and extract embedded metadata.
2. Define a custom print function for different Python object types.
3. Print various embedded metadata properties.

How it works...

First, we import the `argparse`, `datetime`, and `sys` libraries along with the newly installed `PyPDF2` module.

```
from __future__ import print_function
from argparse import ArgumentParser, FileType
import datetime
from PyPDF2 import PdfFileReader
import sys
```

This recipe's command-line handler accepts one positional argument, `PDF_FILE`, which represents the file path to the PDF to process. For this script, we need to pass an open file object to the `PdfFileReader` class, so we use the `argparse.FileType` handler to open the file for us.

```
parser = ArgumentParser(
    description=__description__,
    epilog="Developed by {} on {}".format(", ".join(__authors__), __date__)
)
parser.add_argument('PDF_FILE', help='Path to PDF file',
                    type=FileType('rb'))
args = parser.parse_args()
```

After providing the open file to the `PdfFileReader` class, we call the `getXmpMetadata()` method to provide an object containing the available XMP metadata. If this method returns `None`, we print a succinct message to the user before exiting.

```
pdf_file = PdfFileReader(args.PDF_FILE)

xmpm = pdf_file.getXmpMetadata()
if xmpm is None:
    print("No XMP metadata found in document.")
    sys.exit()
```

With the `xmpm` object ready, we begin extracting and printing relevant values. We extract a number of different values including the title, creator, contributor, description, creation, and modification dates. These value definitions are from `http://wwwimages.adobe.com/content/dam/Adobe/en/devnet/xmp/pdfs/XMP%20SDK%20Release%20cc-2016-08/XMPSpecificationPart1.pdf`. Even though many of these elements are different data types, we pass them to the `custom_print()` method in the same manner. Let's take a look at how this function works.

```
custom_print("Title: {}", xmpm.dc_title)
custom_print("Creator(s): {}", xmpm.dc_creator)
custom_print("Contributors: {}", xmpm.dc_contributor)
custom_print("Subject: {}", xmpm.dc_subject)
custom_print("Description: {}", xmpm.dc_description)
custom_print("Created: {}", xmpm.xmp_createDate)
custom_print("Modified: {}", xmpm.xmp_modifyDate)
custom_print("Event Dates: {}", xmpm.dc_date)
```

Since the XMP values stored may differ based on the software used to generate the PDF, we use a custom print handling function, creatively called `custom_print()`. This allows us, as presented here, to handle the conversion of lists, dictionaries, dates, and other values into a readable format. This function is portable and can be brought into other scripts as needed. The function, through a series of `if-elif-else` statements, checks if the input `value` is a supported object type using the built-in `isinstance()` method and handles them appropriately. If the input `value` is an unsupported type, this is printed to the console instead.

```
def custom_print(fmt_str, value):
    if isinstance(value, list):
        print(fmt_str.format(", ".join(value)))
    elif isinstance(value, dict):
        fmt_value = [":".join((k, v)) for k, v in value.items()]
        print(fmt_str.format(", ".join(value)))
    elif isinstance(value, str) or isinstance(value, bool):
        print(fmt_str.format(value))
    elif isinstance(value, bytes):
        print(fmt_str.format(value.decode()))
    elif isinstance(value, datetime.datetime):
        print(fmt_str.format(value.isoformat()))
    elif value is None:
        print(fmt_str.format("N/A"))
    else:
        print("warn: unhandled type {} found".format(type(value)))
```

Our next set of metadata includes more details about the document's lineage and creation. The `xmp_creatorTool` attribute stores information about the software used to create the resource. Separately, we can also deduce additional lineage information based on the following two IDs:

- The `Document ID` represents an identifier, usually stored as a GUID, that is generally assigned when the resource is saved to a new file. For example, if we create `DocA.pdf` and then save it as `DocB.pdf`, we would have two different `Document IDs`.
- Following the `Document ID` is the second identifier, `Instance ID`. This `Instance ID` is usually generated once per save. An example of this identifier updating is when we update `DocA.pdf` with a new paragraph of text and save it with the same filename.

When editing the same PDF, you would expect the `Document ID` to remain the same while the `Instance ID` would likely update, though this behavior can vary depending on the software used.

```
custom_print("Created With: {}", xmpm.xmp_creatorTool)
custom_print("Document ID: {}", xmpm.xmpmm_documentId)
custom_print("Instance ID: {}", xmpm.xmpmm_instanceId)
```

Following this, we continue extracting other common XMP metadata, including the language, publisher, resource type, and type. The resource type field should represent a **Multipurpose Internet Mail Extensions** (**MIME**) value and the type field should store a **Dublin Core Metadata Initiative** (**DCMI**) value.

```
custom_print("Language: {}", xmpm.dc_language)
custom_print("Publisher: {}", xmpm.dc_publisher)
custom_print("Resource Type: {}", xmpm.dc_format)
custom_print("Type: {}", xmpm.dc_type)
```

Lastly, we extract any custom properties saved by the software. Since this should be a dictionary, we can print it without our `custom_print()` function.

```
if xmpm.custom_properties:
    print("Custom Properties:")
    for k, v in xmpm.custom_properties.items():
        print("\t{}: {}".format(k, v))
```

When we execute the script, we can quickly see many of the attributes stored within the PDF. Notice how the `Document ID` does not match the `Instance ID`, this suggests this document may have been modified from the original PDF.

```
(venv3) pyforcookbook@dev-vm$ python pdf_metadata.py ~/Desktop/paper_database_ima
ge_content_explorer_-_carving_data_that_does_not_officially_exist.pdf
PdfReadWarning: Xref table not zero-indexed. ID numbers for objects will be corre
cted. [pdf.py:1736]
Title: x-default
Creator(s): James Wagner, Alexander Rasin, Jonathan Grier
Contributors:
Subject: Database forensics, File carving, Data recovery, Memory analysis, Stocha
stic analysis
Description: x-default
Created: 2016-07-15T18:01:25
Modified: 2016-07-16T07:35:46
Event Dates:
Created With: Elsevier
Document ID: uuid:b1bb5cd5-ae18-4cfb-b351-0a7fcb2c8516
Instance ID: uuid:5175c232-ada5-4848-b65d-5f89db3a1388
Language:
Publisher: Elsevier Ltd
Resource Type: application/pdf
Type:
Custom Properties:
        CrossmarkMajorVersionDate: 2010-04-23
        ElsevierWebPDFSpecifications: 6.5
        robots: noindex
        doi: 10.1016/j.diin.2016.04.015
        CrossMarkDomains[2]: elsevier.com
        CrossMarkDomains:


        CrossMarkDomains[1]: sciencedirect.com
        CrossmarkDomainExclusive: true
```

There's more...

This script can be further improved. We have provided one or more recommendations as follows:

- Explore and integrate other PDF-related libraries, such as `slate` and `pyocr`:
    - The `slate` module, `https://github.com/timClicks/slate`, can extract text from a PDF file.
    - The `pyocr` module, `https://github.com/openpaperwork/pyocr`, can be used to OCR a PDF to capture handwritten text.

Reviewing executable metadata

Recipe Difficulty: Easy

Python Version: 2.7 or 3.5

Operating System: Any

During the course of an investigation, we may identify a potentially suspicious or unauthorized portable executable file. This executable may be interesting because of the time it was used on the system, its location on the system, or other attributes specific to the investigation. Whether we are investigating it as malicious software or an unauthorized utility, we need to have the capability to learn more about it.

By extracting embedded metadata from Windows executable files, we can learn about the components that make up the file. In this recipe, we will expose the compilation date, useful **Indicator of Compromise** (**IOC**) data from the section headers, and the imported and exported symbols.

Getting started

This recipe requires the installation of the third-party library `pefile`. All other libraries used in this script are present in Python's standard library. The `pefile` module saves us from needing to specify all of the structures of Windows executable files. The `pefile` library can be installed like so:

```
pip install pefile==2017.8.1
```

 To learn more about the `pefile` library, visit `https://github.com/erocarrera/pefile`.

How to do it...

We extract metadata from executable files via the following steps:

1. Open the executable and dump the metadata with `pefile`.
2. If present, dynamically print metadata to the console.

How it works...

We begin by importing libraries to handle arguments, parsing dates, and interacting with executable files. Notice that we specifically import the `PE` class from `pefile`, allowing us to invoke the `PE` class attributes and methods directly later in the recipe.

```
from __future__ import print_function
import argparse
from datetime import datetime
from pefile import PE
```

This recipe's command-line handler takes one positional argument, `EXE_FILE`, the path to the executable file we will be extracting metadata from. We will also take one optional argument, `v`, to allow the user to decide if they would like verbose or simplified output.

```
parser = argparse.ArgumentParser(
    description=__description__,
    epilog="Developed by {} on {}".format(
        ", ".join(__authors__), __date__)
)
parser.add_argument("EXE_FILE", help="Path to exe file")
parser.add_argument("-v", "--verbose", help="Increase verbosity of output",
                    action='store_true', default=False)
args = parser.parse_args()
```

Using the `PE` class, we load the input executable file simply by providing it the file's path. Using the `dump_dict()` method, we dump the executable data to a dictionary object. This library allows us to explore the key-value pairs through this `ped` dictionary or as properties of the `pe` object. We will demonstrate how to extract embedded metadata using both techniques.

```
pe = PE(args.EXE_FILE)
ped = pe.dump_dict()
```

Let's start by extracting basic file metadata, such as the embedded authorship, version, and compilation time. This metadata is stored within the `StringTable` in the `FileInfo` object. Using `for` loops and `if` statements, we ensure the correct values are extracted and assign the string `"Unknown"` to values that are `None` or whose length is zero to better accommodate printing this data to the console. With all key-value pairs extracted and printed to the console, we move onto processing the executable's embedded compilation time, which is stored elsewhere.

```
file_info = {}
for structure in pe.FileInfo:
    if structure.Key == b'StringFileInfo':
```

```
                for s_table in structure.StringTable:
                    for key, value in s_table.entries.items():
                        if value is None or len(value) == 0:
                            value = "Unknown"
                        file_info[key] = value
    print("File Information: ")
    print("==================")
    for k, v in file_info.items():
        if isinstance(k, bytes):
            k = k.decode()
        if isinstance(v, bytes):
            v = v.decode()
        print("{}: {}".format(k, v))
```

The compilation timestamp is stored within the file and shows the date the executable was compiled. The `pefile` library interprets the raw data for us, whereas the `Value` key stores both the original hex value and an interpreted date within square brackets. We can either interpret the hex value ourselves or, more simply, convert the timestamp from the parsed date string into a `datetime` object.

We extract the parsed date string in square brackets using the `split()` and `strip()` methods to extract only the string contained within the brackets. An abbreviated time zone (for example, UTC, EST, or PST) must also be separated from the parsed date string prior to its conversion. Once the date string is isolated, we use the `datetime.strptime()` method with `datetime` formatters to properly convert and print the executable's embedded compilation date.

```
# Compile time
comp_time = ped['FILE_HEADER']['TimeDateStamp']['Value']
comp_time = comp_time.split("[")[-1].strip("]")
time_stamp, timezone = comp_time.rsplit(" ", 1)
comp_time = datetime.strptime(time_stamp, "%a %b %d %H:%M:%S %Y")
print("Compiled on {} {}".format(comp_time, timezone.strip()))
```

The next element we extract is metadata about the executable's sections. This time, rather than using the `pe` object and its attributes, we use the dictionary object we created, `ped`, to iterate through the sections and display the section name, address, sizes, and MD5 hash of its content. This data can be added to your IOCs to assist with the identification of other malicious files on this and other hosts in the environment.

```
# Extract IOCs from PE Sections
print("\nSections: ")
print("==========")
for section in ped['PE Sections']:
    print("Section '{}' at {}: {}/{} {}".format(
        section['Name']['Value'], hex(section['VirtualAddress']['Value']),
```

```
            section['Misc_VirtualSize']['Value'],
            section['SizeOfRawData']['Value'], section['MD5'])
    )
```

Another set of metadata within a portable executable file is a listing of its imports and exports. Let's start with the import entries. First, we ensure that the attribute exists before attempting to access this attribute of the pe variable. If it is present, we use two for loops to step through the imported DLLs and, if the user specified verbose output, each of the imports within the DLLs. If the user did not specify verbose output, the innermost loop is skipped and only the DLL names are presented to the console. From these loops, we extract the DLL names, addresses, and import names. We can use the getattr() built-in function to ensure we don't receive any errors in the instance where the attribute is not present.

```
if hasattr(pe, 'DIRECTORY_ENTRY_IMPORT'):
    print("\nImports: ")
    print("=========")
    for dir_entry in pe.DIRECTORY_ENTRY_IMPORT:
        dll = dir_entry.dll
        if not args.verbose:
            print(dll.decode(), end=", ")
            continue

        name_list = []
        for impts in dir_entry.imports:
            if getattr(impts, "name", b"Unknown") is None:
                name = b"Unknown"
            else:
                name = getattr(impts, "name", b"Unknown")
            name_list.append([name.decode(), hex(impts.address)])
        name_fmt = ["{} ({})".format(x[0], x[1]) for x in name_list]
        print('- {}: {}'.format(dll.decode(), ", ".join(name_fmt)))
    if not args.verbose:
        print()
```

Lastly, let's review the code block related to export metadata. Because some executable may not have exports, we use the hasattr() function to confirm the DIRECTORY_ENTRY_EXPORT attribute is present. If it is, we iterate through each symbol and print the names and addresses for each of the symbols in a bulleted list to better distinguish them in the console.

```
# Display Exports, Names, and Addresses
if hasattr(pe, 'DIRECTORY_ENTRY_EXPORT'):
    print("\nExports: ")
    print("=========")
    for sym in pe.DIRECTORY_ENTRY_EXPORT.symbols:
        print('- {}: {}'.format(sym.name.decode(), hex(sym.address)))
```

Using a Firefox installer as our example, we are able to extract a great deal of embedded metadata attributes from the executable. This information shows us a number of things, such as the compilation date; that this appears to be a packed executable, likely with 7-Zip; and the hash values for the different sections.

```
(venv3) pyforcookbook@dev-vm$ python exe_metadata.py ~/Desktop/Firefox%20Insta
ller.exe -v
File Information:
==================
FileVersion: 4.42
InternalName: 7zS.sfx
ProductName: Firefox
OriginalFilename: 7zS.sfx.exe
LegalCopyright: Mozilla
FileDescription: Firefox
CompanyName: Mozilla
ProductVersion: 4.42
Compiled on 2017-07-05 16:09:48 UTC

Sections:
==========
Section 'UPX0\x00\x00\x00\x00' at 0x1000: 139264/0 d41d8cd98f00b204e9800998ecf
8427e
Section 'UPX1\x00\x00\x00\x00' at 0x23000: 57344/57344 0aa6760f748bb6229f0b7e1
26860423c
Section '.rsrc\x00\x00\x00' at 0x31000: 36864/35328 51d888059c9199e109dfc744a7
0b87fd

Imports:
=========
- KERNEL32.DLL: LoadLibraryA (0x439808), GetProcAddress (0x43980c), VirtualPro
tect (0x439810), ExitProcess (0x439814)
- MSVCRT.dll: free (0x43981c)
```

When we run this same script against a DLL, we see many of the same fields from the executable run, in addition to the exports section. Due to the length of the output, we've omitted some of the text in the following screenshot:

```
(venv3) pyforcookbook@dev-vm$ python exe_metadata.py ~/Desktop/sqlite3.dll
File Information:
=================
LegalCopyright: http://www.sqlite.org/copyright.html
FileVersion: 3.20.0
FileDescription: SQLite is a software library that implements a self-contained, serverl
ess, zero-configuration, transactional SQL database engine.
InternalName: sqlite3
CompanyName: SQLite Development Team
ProductVersion: 3.20.0
ProductName: SQLite
SourceId: 2017-08-01 13:24:15 9501e22dfeebdcefa783575e47c60b514d7c2e0cad73b2a496c0bc4b6
80900a8
Compiled on 2017-08-01 14:25:20 UTC

Sections:
=========
Section '.text\x00\x00\x00' at 0x1000: 1407028/1407488 5d7884be21baaa19f1608a92d7b7cbe9
Section '.rdata\x00\x00' at 0x159000: 208551/208896 5aaef2806fdc92c2b370cc34043100bb
Section '.data\x00\x00\x00' at 0x18c000: 23289/16896 ab62a77533412c9b509c627cf0719f1a
Section '.pdata\x00\x00' at 0x192000: 67188/67584 564f0645b8c059b6824508a6b1380004
Section '.idata\x00\x00' at 0x1a3000: 5444/5632 0c1cc3c329676e04376f2e42d75ad2f4
Section 'text\x00\x00\x00\x00' at 0x1a5000: 1098/1536 965736a7e86d1e86d647d807665d32e9
Section 'data\x00\x00\x00\x00' at 0x1a6000: 8262/8704 068cf81c59967d5502aac5718f9060b2
Section '.rsrc\x00\x00\x00' at 0x1a9000: 4812/5120 2ca19ec6941d58fdddfbd9550e6a1f3d
Section '.reloc\x00\x00' at 0x1ab000: 8171/8192 74d86844545624dcf022fbe0ec7fd08b

Imports:
=========
KERNEL32.dll,

Exports:
=========
- sqlite3_aggregate_context: 0x1384
- sqlite3_aggregate_count: 0x102d
- sqlite3_auto_extension: 0x1104
- sqlite3_backup_finish: 0x10e1
- sqlite3_backup_init: 0x11a4
- sqlite3_backup_pagecount: 0x11b8
- sqlite3_backup_remaining: 0x1343
- sqlite3_backup_step: 0x10f5
```

There's more...

This script can be further improved. We have provided one or more recommendations as follows:

- Using recipes that we develop in Chapter 5, *Networking and Indicator of Compromise Recipes*, query the discovered hash values against online resources, such as VirusTotal, and report on any matches from other submissions.
- Integrate pytz to allow the user to interpret dates in a local or otherwise specified timezone

Reading office document metadata

Recipe Difficulty: Medium

Python Version: 2.7 or 3.5

Operating System: Any

Reading metadata from office documents can expose interesting information about the authorship and history of those files. Conveniently, the 2007 formatted .docx, .xlsx, and .pptx files store metadata in XML. The XML tags can be easily processed with Python.

Getting started

All libraries used in this script are present in Python's standard library. We use the built-in xml library and the zipfile library to allow us access to the XML documents within the ZIP container.

To learn more about the xml library, visit https://docs.python.org/3/library/xml.etree.elementtree.html.
To Learn more about the zipfile library, visit https://docs.python.org/3/library/zipfile.html.

How to do it...

We extract embedded Office metadata by performing the following steps:

1. Confirm that the input file is a valid ZIP file.
2. Extract the `core.xml` and `app.xml` files from Office file.
3. Parse XML data and print embedded metadata.

How it works...

First, we import the `argparse` and `datetime` libraries, followed by `xml.etree` and `zipfile` libraries. The `ElementTree` class allows us to read an XML string into an object that we can iterate through and interpret.

```
from __future__ import print_function
from argparse import ArgumentParser
from datetime import datetime as dt
from xml.etree import ElementTree as etree
import zipfile
```

This recipe's command-line handler takes one positional argument, `Office_File`, the path to the office file we will be extracting metadata from.

```
parser = argparse.ArgumentParser(
    description=__description__,
    epilog="Developed by {} on {}".format(", ".join(__authors__), __date__)
)
parser.add_argument("Office_File", help="Path to office file to read")
args = parser.parse_args()
```

Following our argument handling, we check to make sure the input file is a `zipfile` and raise an error if it is not. If it is, we open the valid ZIP file using the `ZipFile` class before accessing the two XML documents containing the metadata we are interested in. Though there are other XML files containing data describing the document, the two with the most metadata are named `core.xml` and `app.xml`. We will open the two XML files from the ZIP container with the `read()` method and send the returned string directly to the `etree.fromstring()` XML parsing method.

```
# Check if input file is a zipfile
zipfile.is_zipfile(args.Office_File)

# Open the file (MS Office 2007 or later)
zfile = zipfile.ZipFile(args.Office_File)
```

```
# Extract key elements for processing
core_xml = etree.fromstring(zfile.read('docProps/core.xml'))
app_xml = etree.fromstring(zfile.read('docProps/app.xml'))
```

With the prepared XML objects, we can start extracting data of interest. We set up a dictionary, called `core_mapping`, to specify the fields we want to extract, as key names, and the value we want to display them as. This method allows us to easily print only the values important to us, if present, with a friendly title. This XML file contains great information about the authorship of the file. For instance, the two authorship fields, `creator` and `lastModifiedBy`, can show scenarios where one account modified a document created by another user account. The date values show us information about creation and modification of the document. Additionally, metadata fields like `revision` can give some indication to the number of versions of this document.

```
# Core.xml tag mapping
core_mapping = {
    'title': 'Title',
    'subject': 'Subject',
    'creator': 'Author(s)',
    'keywords': 'Keywords',
    'description': 'Description',
    'lastModifiedBy': 'Last Modified By',
    'modified': 'Modified Date',
    'created': 'Created Date',
    'category': 'Category',
    'contentStatus': 'Status',
    'revision': 'Revision'
}
```

In our `for` loop, we iterate over the XML using the `iterchildren()` method to access each of the tags within the XML root of the `core.xml` file. Using the `core_mapping` dictionary, we can selectively output specific fields if they are found. We have also added logic to interpret date values using the `strptime()` method.

```
for element in core_xml.getchildren():
    for key, title in core_mapping.items():
        if key in element.tag:
            if 'date' in title.lower():
                text = dt.strptime(element.text, "%Y-%m-%dT%H:%M:%SZ")
            else:
                text = element.text
            print("{}: {}".format(title, text))
```

The next set of column mappings focuses on the `app.xml` file. This file contains statistical information about the contents of the document, including total edit time and counts of words, pages, and slides. It also contains information about the company name registered with the software and hidden elements. To print these values to the console, we use a similar set of `for` loops as we did with the `core.xml` file.

```python
app_mapping = {
    'TotalTime': 'Edit Time (minutes)',
    'Pages': 'Page Count',
    'Words': 'Word Count',
    'Characters': 'Character Count',
    'Lines': 'Line Count',
    'Paragraphs': 'Paragraph Count',
    'Company': 'Company',
    'HyperlinkBase': 'Hyperlink Base',
    'Slides': 'Slide count',
    'Notes': 'Note Count',
    'HiddenSlides': 'Hidden Slide Count',
}
for element in app_xml.getchildren():
    for key, title in app_mapping.items():
        if key in element.tag:
            if 'date' in title.lower():
                text = dt.strptime(element.text, "%Y-%m-%dT%H:%M:%SZ")
            else:
                text = element.text
            print("{}: {}".format(title, text))
```

When we run the script with a sample word document, as the following shows, a number of details about the document are in question.

```
(venv3) pyforcookbook@dev-vm$ python msoffice_metadata.py ~/Desktop/manual.docx
Title: XMLmind W2X Manual
Subject: Explains how to install and use XMLmind Word To XML (w2x for short),
how to customize the output of w2x and how to embed a w2x processor in a Java™
application.
Author(s): Hussein Shafie
Last Modified By: hussein
Revision: 65
Created Date: 2016-11-22 10:57:00
Modified Date: 2017-06-12 08:08:00
Edit Time (minutes): 117
Page Count: 63
Word Count: 16048
Character Count: 98381
Line Count: 2893
Paragraph Count: 2080
Company: XMLmind Software
Character Count: 112349
```

Separately, we can use the script on a PPTX document and review format-specific metadata associated with PPTX files:

```
(venv3) pyforcookbook@dev-vm$ python msoffice_metadata.py ~/Desktop/ehlingerpre
sentation.pptx
Title: PowerPoint Presentation
Author(s): Ed Ehlinger
Last Modified By: Ed Ehlinger
Revision: 61
Created Date: 2015-03-11 13:50:11
Modified Date: 2015-03-23 18:50:03
Edit Time (minutes): 1272
Word Count: 2067
Paragraph Count: 348
Slide count: 36
Note Count: 9
Hidden Slide Count: 0
Company: Minnesota Department of Health
```

Integrating our metadata extractor with EnCase

Recipe Difficulty: Medium

Python Version: 2.7 or 3.5

Operating System: Windows

The embedded metadata extracting recipes we have designed work against loose files, not with files found within a forensic image. Annoyingly, this adds an extra step in our process, requiring us to export the files of interest from the image for this type of review. We show in this recipe, how to connect our scripts to a forensic tool, EnCase, and execute them without needing to export the files from a forensic image.

Getting started

With EnCase installed, we need to create a case and add in the evidence file, as we would for any other case. This recipe demonstrates the steps required to perform this in EnCase V6, although the same techniques can be applied to later versions.

Before starting, we will also need to ensure Python 2.7 or 3.5, the script we wish to use, and the required dependencies are installed on the machine.

How to do it...

We integrate the metadata recipes with EnCase via the following steps:

1. Open EnCase V6 and add evidence to a case.
2. Use the **View** file viewer menu to configure a custom file viewer with the EXIF metadata extractor.
3. Extract embedded GPS coordinates from a photo within EnCase using the newly created file viewer.

How it works...

With the open case, we can look at the hex of a photo of interest to confirm we can see the EXIF header within the file. Following this header are the raw values processed by the script. With a good candidate identified, let's look at how we can configure EnCase to run the script.

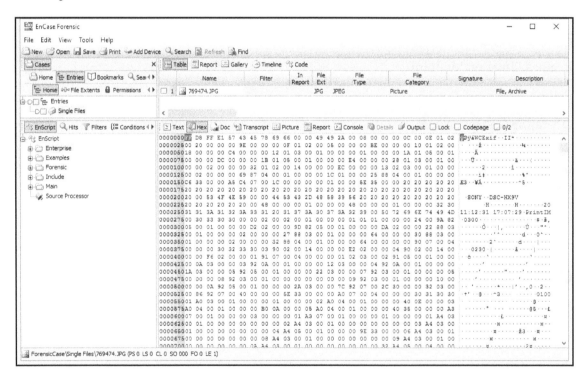

Under the **View** menu, we select the **File Viewers** option. This opens a tab listing the available viewers. The instance of EnCase we used does not have any viewers and so we must add any we wish to use first.

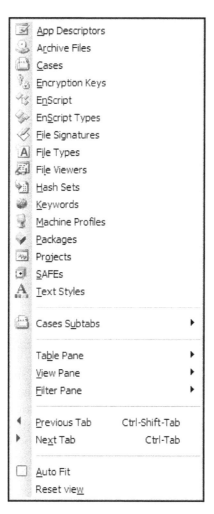

In this tab, right-click on the top-level `File Viewers` element and select **New...** to create our custom viewer.

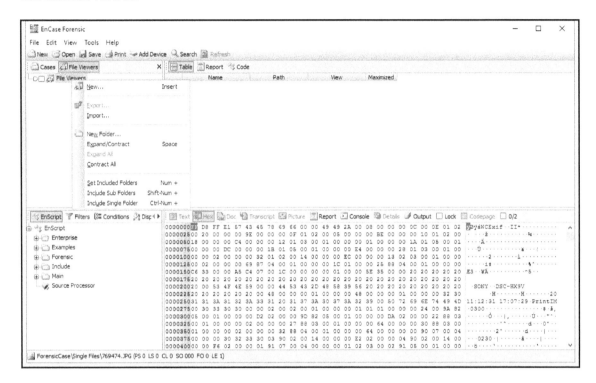

A new window, shown in the following screenshot, allows us to specify the parameters to execute the script. In this example, we are implementing the GPS extraction script, though we can add others in this same manner. The first line specifies the name of the viewer. We should name this something memorable as it will be the only description available to us when selecting the file viewer later. The second line is the path to the executable. In our instance, we will launch the Command Prompt, since our Python script is not a standalone executable. We need to provide the full path to `cmd.exe` for EnCase to accept this parameter.

The last line is where we add in the script. This line allows us to specify the arguments to pass to the Command Prompt. We start with /k to keep our Command Prompt open after our script completes. This isn't required; although if your code displays information to the console (as ours does), we should implement this feature. Otherwise, the Command Prompt will close as soon as the code completes. Following the /k argument, we provide the parameters to launch the code. As shown here, this includes the Python executable and full path to the script. The last element, [file], is a placeholder for EnCase that is replaced by the file we want to view when the file viewer is executed.

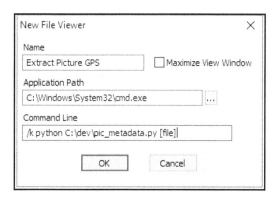

The new file viewer entry is now displayed within the File Viewer tab and shows us the name, executable, and arguments we specified. If everything looks right, we can return to the photo of interest in the file entry tab.

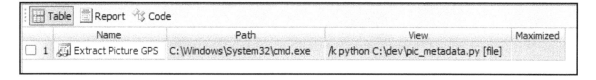

Back on the file entry view, we can right-click on the photo of interest and select the file viewer from the `Send To` submenu.

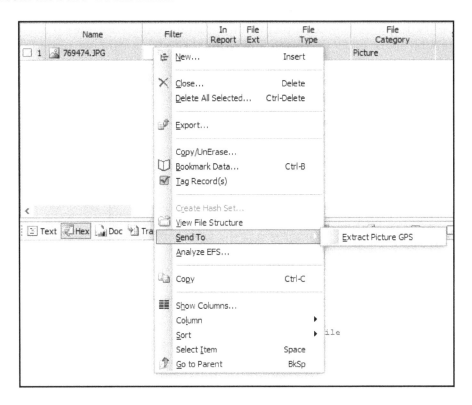

When we select this option, the command window appears and shows the output from the script. Notice that the KML file is automatically placed in the `Temp` directory for the case. This is because the file we are inspecting is cached in this directory during the script's execution.

There's more...

This process can be further improved. We have provided one or more recommendations as follows:

- While not Python-related, look into EnScripting as another option to automate and parse multiple files and display the output within the EnCase Console tab.
- Add the other recipes covered in this chapter to EnCase by following a similar method. Since the information for these scripts is printed to the console, we should use the /k argument or rework the logic to place the output in a directory for us.

5
Networking and Indicators of Compromise Recipes

The following recipes are covered in this chapter:

- Getting a jump start with IEF
- Coming into contact with IEF
- It's a beautiful soup
- Going hunting for viruses
- Gathering intel
- Totally passive

Introduction

Technology has come a long way and, with it, the extent to which tools are made widely available has changed too. As a matter of fact, being cognizant of the tools' existence is half the battle due to the sheer volume of tools available on the internet. Some of these tools are publicly available and can be bent toward forensic purposes. In this chapter, we will learn how to interact with websites and identify malware through Python, including an automated review of potentially malicious domains, IP addresses, or files.

We start out by taking a look at how to manipulate **Internet Evidence Finder** (**IEF**) results and perform additional processing outside of the context of the application. We also explore using services such as VirusShare, PassiveTotal, and VirusTotal to create HashSets of known malware, query suspicious domain resolutions, and identify known bad domains or files, respectively. Between these scripts, you will become familiar with using Python to interact with APIs.

The scripts in this chapter focus on solving particular problems and are ordered by complexity:

- Learning to extract data from IEF results
- Processing cached Yahoo contacts data from Google Chrome
- Preserving web pages with Beautiful Soup
- Creating an X-Ways-compatible HashSet from VirusShare
- Using PassiveTotal to automate the review of sketchy domains or IP addresses
- Automating identification of known bad files, domains, or IPs with VirusTotal

 Visit `www.packtpub.com/books/content/support` to download the code bundle for this chapter.

Getting a jump start with IEF

Recipe Difficulty: Easy

Python Version: 3.5

Operating System: Any

This recipe will act as a quick means of dumping all reports from IEF to a CSV file and an introduction to interacting with IEF results. IEF stores data in a SQLite database, which we explored rather thoroughly in `Chapter 3`, *A Deep Dive into Mobile Forensic Recipes*. As IEF can be configured to scan specific categories of information, it is not so simple as dumping out set tables for each IEF database. Instead, we must determine this information dynamically and then interact with said tables. This recipe will dynamically identify result tables within the IEF database and dump them to respective CSV files. This process can be performed on any SQLite database to quickly dump its contents to a CSV file for review.

Getting started

All libraries used in this script are present in Python's standard library. For this script, make sure to have an IEF results database generated after executing the program. We used IEF version 6.8.9.5774 to generate the database used to develop this recipe. After IEF finishes processing the forensic image, for example, you should see a file named `IEFv6.db`. This is the database we will interact with in this recipe.

How to do it...

We will employ the following steps to extract data from the IEF results database:

1. Connect to the database.
2. Query the database to identify all tables.
3. Write result tables to an individual CSV file.

How it works...

First, we import the required libraries to handle argument parsing, writing spreadsheets, and interacting with SQLite databases.

```python
from __future__ import print_function
import argparse
import csv
import os
import sqlite3
import sys
```

This recipe's command-line handler is relatively straightforward. It accepts two positional arguments, `IEF_DATABASE` and `OUTPUT_DIR`, representing the file path to the `IEFv6.db` file and the desired output location, respectively.

```python
if __name__ == '__main__':
    parser = argparse.ArgumentParser(
        description=__description__,
        epilog="Developed by {} on {}".format(
            ", ".join(__authors__), __date__)
    )
    parser.add_argument("IEF_DATABASE", help="Input IEF database")
    parser.add_argument("OUTPUT_DIR", help="Output DIR")
    args = parser.parse_args()
```

We perform the input validation steps as usual prior to calling the `main()` function of the script. First, we check the output directory and create it if it does not exist. Then, we confirm that the IEF database exists as expected. If all is as expected, we execute the `main()` function and supply it with the two user-supplied inputs:

```
if not os.path.exists(args.OUTPUT_DIR):
    os.makedirs(args.OUTPUT_DIR)

if os.path.exists(args.IEF_DATABASE) and \
        os.path.isfile(args.IEF_DATABASE):
    main(args.IEF_DATABASE, args.OUTPUT_DIR)
else:
    print("[-] Supplied input file {} does not exist or is not a "
        "file".format(args.IEF_DATABASE))
    sys.exit(1)
```

The `main()` function starts out simply enough. We print a status message to the console and create the `sqlite3` connection to the database to execute the necessary SQLite queries:

```
def main(database, out_directory):
    print("[+] Connecting to SQLite database")
    conn = sqlite3.connect(database)
    c = conn.cursor()
```

Next, we need to query the database to identify all tables present. Notice the rather complex query we execute to perform this. If you are familiar with SQLite, you may shake your head and wonder why we have not executed the `.table` command. Unfortunately, in Python, this cannot be done so easily. Rather, one must execute the following command to achieve the desired goal.

As we have seen previously, the `Cursor` returns results as a list of tuples. The command we have executed returns a number of details about each table in the database. In this case, we are only interested in extracting the name of the table. We accomplish this using list comprehension by first fetching all results from the cursor object and then appending the second element of each result to the tables list if the name matches certain criteria. We have elected to ignore table names that start with _ or end with _DATA. From a review of these tables, they contained actual cached file content rather than the metadata IEF presents for each record.

```
print("[+] Querying IEF database for list of all tables to extract")
c.execute("select * from sqlite_master where type='table'")
# Remove tables that start with "_" or end with "_DATA"
tables = [x[2] for x in c.fetchall() if not x[2].startswith('_') and
        not x[2].endswith('_DATA')]
```

With the list of table names in hand, we can now iterate through each one and extract their contents into a variable. Prior to that, we print an update status message to the console to inform the user of the current execution status of the script. In order to write the CSVs, we need to first determine the column names for a given table. This is performed, as we saw in Chapter 3, using the `pragma table_info` command. With some simple list comprehension, we extract just the names of the columns and store them in a variable for later.

With that accomplished, we execute the favorite and simplest SQL query and select all (*) data from each table. Using the `fetchall()` method on the cursor object, we store the list of tuples containing the table's data in its entirety in the `table_data` variable:

```
print("[+] Dumping {} tables to CSV files in {}".format(
    len(tables), out_directory))
for table in tables:
    c.execute("pragma table_info('{}')".format(table))
    table_columns = [x[1] for x in c.fetchall()]
    c.execute("select * from '{}'".format(table))
    table_data = c.fetchall()
```

We can now begin to write the data for each table to its appropriate CSV file. To keep things simple, the name of each CSV file is simply the table name and an appended `.csv` extension. We use `os.path.join()` to combine the output directory with the desired CSV name.

Next, we print a status update to the console and begin the process to write each CSV file. This is accomplished by first writing the table column names as the header of the spreadsheet followed by the contents of the table. We use the `writerows()` method to write the list of tuples in one line rather than create an unnecessary loop and execute `writerow()` repeatedly for each tuple.

```
csv_name = table + '.csv'
csv_path = os.path.join(out_directory, csv_name)
print('[+] Writing {} table to {} CSV file'.format(table,
                                                    csv_name))
with open(csv_path, "w", newline="") as csvfile:
    csv_writer = csv.writer(csvfile)
    csv_writer.writerow(table_columns)
    csv_writer.writerows(table_data)
```

When we run this script, we can see the discovered artifacts and extract CSV reports of the text information:

```
(venv3) pyforcookbook@dev-vm$ python ief_parser.py ~/Desktop/IEFv6.db ~/Desktop/
IEF_Reports
[+] Connecting to SQLite database
[+] Querying IEF database for list of all tables to extract
[+] Dumping 36 tables to CSV files in /home/pyforcookbook/Desktop/IEF_Reports
[+] Writing Chrome Bookmarks table to Chrome Bookmarks.csv CSV file
[+] Writing Chrome Cookies table to Chrome Cookies.csv CSV file
[+] Writing Google Analytics First Visit Cookies table to Google Analytics First
 Visit Cookies.csv CSV file
[+] Writing Google Analytics Referral Cookies table to Google Analytics Referral
 Cookies.csv CSV file
[+] Writing Chrome Current Session table to Chrome Current Session.csv CSV file
[+] Writing Chrome FavIcons table to Chrome FavIcons.csv CSV file
[+] Writing Chrome Current Tabs table to Chrome Current Tabs.csv CSV file
[+] Writing Google Searches table to Google Searches.csv CSV file
[+] Writing Cloud Services URLs table to Cloud Services URLs.csv CSV file
[+] Writing Pictures table to Pictures.csv CSV file
[+] Writing Social Media URLs table to Social Media URLs.csv CSV file
[+] Writing Chrome Web History table to Chrome Web History.csv CSV file
```

Once we have completed the script, we can see information about an artifact as seen in the following snippet of a report:

Site Name	URL	Located At	Date/Time - UTC (yyyy-mm-dd)	Artifact	Artifact ID	Source
Amazon	http://www.amazon.com/	Table: urls(id: 290)	04/22/17 05:20 PM	Chrome Web History	22	Entire Disk
Amazon	https://www.amazon.com/	Table: urls(id: 291)	04/22/17 05:20 PM	Chrome Web History	23	Entire Disk
Amazon	http://www.amazon.com/	Table: visits(id: 14058), Table: urls(id: 290)	04/22/17 05:20 PM	Chrome Web Visits	4961	Entire Disk
Amazon	https://www.amazon.com/	Table: visits(id: 14059), Table: urls(id: 291)	04/22/17 05:20 PM	Chrome Web Visits	4962	Entire Disk

Coming into contact with IEF

Recipe Difficulty: Medium

Python Version: 3.5

Operating System: Any

We can take further advantage of the IEF results in the SQLite database by manipulating and gleaning, even more, information from artifacts that IEF does not necessarily support. This can be particularly important when new artifacts are discovered and are unsupported. As the internet, and many businesses using the internet change constantly, it is unrealistic for software to keep up with every new artifact. In this case, we will look at cached Yahoo Mail contacts that get stored on the local system as a byproduct of using Yahoo Mail.

Getting started

All libraries used in this script are present in Python's standard library. Again, as in the previous recipe, if you would like to follow along, you will need an IEF results database. We used IEF version 6.8.9.5774 to generate the database used to develop this recipe. In addition to that, you will likely need to generate Yahoo Mail traffic to create the necessary situation where Yahoo Mail contacts are cached. In this example, we used the Google Chrome browser to use Yahoo Mail and will, therefore, be looking at Google Chrome cache data. This recipe, while specific to Yahoo, illustrates how you can use the IEF results database to further process artifacts and identify additional relevant information.

How to do it...

The recipe follows these basic principles:

1. Connect to the input database.
2. Query the Google Chrome cache table for Yahoo Mail contact records.
3. Process contact cache JSON data and metadata.
4. Write all relevant data to a CSV.

How it works...

First, we import the required libraries to handle argument parsing, writing spreadsheets, processing JSON data, and interacting with SQLite databases.

```
from __future__ import print_function
import argparse
import csv
import json
import os
import sqlite3
import sys
```

This recipe's command-line handler does not differ from the first recipe. It accepts two positional arguments, IEF_DATABASE and OUTPUT_DIR, representing the file paths to the IEFv6.db file and the desired output location, respectively.

```
if __name__ == '__main__':
    parser = argparse.ArgumentParser(
        description=__description__,
        epilog="Developed by {} on {}".format(
```

```
            ", ".join(__authors__), __date__)
    )
    parser.add_argument("IEF_DATABASE", help="Input IEF database")
    parser.add_argument("OUTPUT_CSV", help="Output CSV")
    args = parser.parse_args()
```

And again, we perform the same data validation steps as executed in the first recipe of this chapter. If it ain't broke, why fix it? After validation, we execute the `main()` function and supply it with the two validated inputs.

```
    directory = os.path.dirname(args.OUTPUT_CSV)
    if not os.path.exists(directory):
        os.makedirs(directory)

    if os.path.exists(args.IEF_DATABASE) and \
            os.path.isfile(args.IEF_DATABASE):
        main(args.IEF_DATABASE, args.OUTPUT_CSV)
    else:
        print(
            "[-] Supplied input file {} does not exist or is not a "
            "file".format(args.IEF_DATABASE))
        sys.exit(1)
```

The `main()` function starts again by creating a connection to the input SQLite database (we promise this recipe isn't identical to the first one: keep reading).

```
def main(database, out_csv):
    print("[+] Connecting to SQLite database")
    conn = sqlite3.connect(database)
    c = conn.cursor()
```

We can now begin scouring the database for all instances of Yahoo Mail contact cache records. Notice that the URL fragment we are looking for is rather specific to our purpose. This should ensure that we do not get any false positives. The percent sign (`%`) at the end of the URL is the SQLite wildcard equivalent character. We execute the query in a `try` and `except` statement in the event the input directory does not have the Chrome cache records table, is corrupt, or is encrypted.

```
    print("[+] Querying IEF database for Yahoo Contact Fragments from "
        "the Chrome Cache Records Table")
    try:
        c.execute(
            "select * from 'Chrome Cache Records' where URL like "
            "'https://data.mail.yahoo.com"
            "/classicab/v2/contacts/?format=json%'")
    except sqlite3.OperationalError:
        print("Received an error querying the database -- database may be"
```

```
            "corrupt or not have a Chrome Cache Records table")
        sys.exit(2)
```

If we were able to execute the query successfully, we store the returned list of tuples into the `contact_cache` variable. This variable serves as the only input to the `process_contacts()` function, which returns a nested list structure convenient for the CSV writer.

```
        contact_cache = c.fetchall()
        contact_data = process_contacts(contact_cache)
        write_csv(contact_data, out_csv)
```

The `process_contacts()` function starts by printing a status message to the console, setting up the `results` list, and iterating through each contact cache record. Each record has a number of metadata elements associated with it beyond the raw data. This includes the URL, the location of the cache on the filesystem, and the timestamps for the first visit, last visit, and last sync time.

We use the `json.loads()` method to store the JSON data extracted from the table into the `contact_json` variable for further manipulation. The `total` and `count` keys from the JSON data, store the total number of Yahoo Mail contacts and the count of them present in the JSON cache data.

```
def process_contacts(contact_cache):
    print("[+] Processing {} cache files matching Yahoo contact cache "
        " data".format(len(contact_cache)))
    results = []
    for contact in contact_cache:
        url = contact[0]
        first_visit = contact[1]
        last_visit = contact[2]
        last_sync = contact[3]
        loc = contact[8]
        contact_json = json.loads(contact[7].decode())
        total_contacts = contact_json["total"]
        total_count = contact_json["count"]
```

Before we extract contact data from contact JSON, we need to ensure that it has contacts in the first place. If it does not, we continue onto the next cache record in the hopes that we find contacts there. If on the other hand, we do have contacts, we initialize a number of variables to an empty string. This is achieved in one line by bulk-assigning variables to a tuple of empty strings:

```
if "contacts" not in contact_json:
    continue

for c in contact_json["contacts"]:
    name, anni, bday, emails, phones, links = (
        "", "", "", "", "", "")
```

With these variables initialized, we begin looking for each of them in each of the contacts. Sometimes the particular cache record will not retain full contact details such as the `"anniversary"` key. For this reason, we initialized these variables to avoid referring to variables that do not exist if that particular key isn't present in a given cache record.

For the `name`, `"anniversary"`, and `"birthday"` keys, we need to perform some string concatenation so that they are in a convenient format. The `emails`, `phones`, and `links` variables could have more than one result and we, therefore, use list comprehension and the `join()` method to create a comma-separated list of those respective elements. The great thing about that line of code is that if there is only one email, phone number, or link, it will not place a comma after that one element unnecessarily.

```
if "name" in c:
    name = c["name"]["givenName"] + " " + \
        c["name"]["middleName"] + " " + c["name"]["familyName"]
if "anniversary" in c:
    anni = c["anniversary"]["month"] + \
        "/" + c["anniversary"]["day"] + "/" + \
        c["anniversary"]["year"]
if "birthday" in c:
    bday = c["birthday"]["month"] + "/" + \
        c["birthday"]["day"] + "/" + c["birthday"]["year"]
if "emails" in c:
    emails = ', '.join([x["ep"] for x in c["emails"]])
if "phones" in c:
    phones = ', '.join([x["ep"] for x in c["phones"]])
if "links" in c:
    links = ', '.join([x["ep"] for x in c["links"]])
```

We handle the `company`, `jobTitle`, and `notes` sections differently by using the `get()` method instead. Because these are simple key and value pairs, we do not need to do any additional string processing on them. Instead, with the `get()` method, we can extract the key's value or, if it isn't present, set the default value to an empty string.

```
company = c.get("company", "")
title = c.get("jobTitle", "")
notes = c.get("notes", "")
```

After we have processed the contact data, we append a list of the metadata and extracted data elements to the `results` list. Once we have processed each contact and each cache record, we return the `results` list back to the `main()` function, which gets passed onto the CSV writer function.

```
results.append([
    url, first_visit, last_visit, last_sync, loc, name, bday,
    anni, emails, phones, links, company, title, notes,
    total_contacts, total_count])
return results
```

The `write_csv()` method takes the nested `results` list structure and the output file path as its inputs. After we print a status message to the console, we employ the usual strategy to write the results to the output file. Namely, we first write the headers of the CSV followed by the actual contact data. Thanks to the nested list structure, we can just use the `writerows()` method to write all of the results to the file in one line.

```
def write_csv(data, output):
    print("[+] Writing {} contacts to {}".format(len(data), output))
    with open(output, "w", newline="") as csvfile:
        csv_writer = csv.writer(csvfile)
        csv_writer.writerow([
            "URL", "First Visit (UTC)", "Last Visit (UTC)",
            "Last Sync (UTC)", "Location", "Contact Name", "Bday",
            "Anniversary", "Emails", "Phones", "Links", "Company", "Title",
            "Notes", "Total Contacts", "Count of Contacts in Cache"])
        csv_writer.writerows(data)
```

This screenshot illustrates an example of the type of data that this script can extract:

First Visit (UTC)	Last Visit (UTC)	Last Sync (UTC)	Contact Name	Bday	Anniversary	Emails	Phones
05/23/17 12:23 AM	05/23/17 12:23 AM	05/23/17 12:23 AM	Pulp Fiction	10/14/94		pulp@example.com	2545555666
05/23/17 12:23 AM	05/23/17 12:23 AM	05/23/17 12:23 AM	Usual Suspects	08/16/95		usualsusp@example.com	8595557887
05/23/17 12:23 AM	05/23/17 12:23 AM	05/23/17 12:23 AM	A hard day's night	05/04/17	07/10/64	beatles@example.com	3595554848

Beautiful Soup

Recipe Difficulty: Medium

Python Version: 3.5

Operating System: Any

In this recipe, we create a website preservation tool leveraging the **Beautiful Soup** library. This is a library meant to process markup languages, such as HTML or XML, and can be used to easily process these types of data structures. We will use it to identify and extract all links from a web page in a few lines of code. This script is meant to showcase a very simplistic example of a website preservation script; it is by no means intended to replace existing software out there on the market.

Getting started

This recipe requires the installation of the third-party library `bs4`. This module can be installed via the following command. All other libraries used in this script are present in Python's standard library.

```
pip install bs4==0.0.1
```

 Learn more about the `bs4` library; visit `https://www.crummy.com/software/BeautifulSoup/bs4/doc/`.

How to do it...

We will perform the following steps in this recipe:

1. Access index web page and identify all initial links.
2. Recurse through all known links to:
    1. Find additional links and add them to the queue.
    2. Generate `SHA-256` hash of each web page.
    3. Write and then verify web page output to the destination directory.
3. Log relevant activity and hash results.

How it works...

First, we import the required libraries to handle argument parsing, parsing HTML data, parsing dates, hashing files, logging data, and interacting with web pages. We also setup a variable used to later construct the recipe's logging component.

```
from __future__ import print_function
import argparse
from bs4 import BeautifulSoup, SoupStrainer
from datetime import datetime
import hashlib
import logging
import os
import ssl
import sys
from urllib.request import urlopen
import urllib.error

logger = logging.getLogger(__name__)
```

This recipe's command-line handler takes two positional inputs, DOMAIN and OUTPUT_DIR, which represent the website URL to preserve and the desired output directory, respectively. The optional -l argument can be used to specify the location of the log file path.

```
if __name__ == "__main__":
    parser = argparse.ArgumentParser(
        description=__description__,
        epilog="Developed by {} on {}".format(
            ", ".join(__authors__), __date__)
    )
    parser.add_argument("DOMAIN", help="Website Domain")
    parser.add_argument("OUTPUT_DIR", help="Preservation Output Directory")
    parser.add_argument("-l", help="Log file path",
                        default=__file__[:-3] + ".log")
    args = parser.parse_args()
```

We will now setup the logging for the script, using the default or user-specified path. Using the logging format in *Chapter 1*, we specify a file and stream handler to keep the user in the loop and document the acquisition process.

```
    logger.setLevel(logging.DEBUG)
    msg_fmt = logging.Formatter("%(asctime)-15s %(funcName)-10s"
                                "%(levelname)-8s %(message)s")
    strhndl = logging.StreamHandler(sys.stderr)
    strhndl.setFormatter(fmt=msg_fmt)
    fhndl = logging.FileHandler(args.l, mode='a')
    fhndl.setFormatter(fmt=msg_fmt)
```

```
logger.addHandler(strhndl)
logger.addHandler(fhndl)
```

After setting up the log, we log a few details about the execution context of the script, including the supplied arguments and OS details.

```
logger.info("Starting BS Preservation")
logger.debug("Supplied arguments: {}".format(sys.argv[1:]))
logger.debug("System " + sys.platform)
logger.debug("Version " + sys.version)
```

We perform some additional input validation on the desired output directory. After these steps, we call the `main()` function and pass it the website URL and the output directory.

```
if not os.path.exists(args.OUTPUT_DIR):
    os.makedirs(args.OUTPUT_DIR)

main(args.DOMAIN, args.OUTPUT_DIR)
```

The `main()` function is used to perform a few tasks. First, it extracts the base name of the website by removing any unnecessary elements before the actual name. For example, `https://google.com` becomes `google.com`. We also create the set, `link_queue`, which will hold all unique links found on the web page.

We perform some additional validation on the input URL. During development, we ran into some errors when URLs were not preceded by `https://` or `http://`, so we check whether that is the case here and exit the script and inform the user of the requirement if they are not present. If everything checks out, we are ready to access the base web page. To do that, we create the unverified SSL context to avoid errors when accessing the web page.

```
def main(website, output_dir):
    base_name = website.replace(
        "https://", "").replace("http://", "").replace("www.", "")
    link_queue = set()
    if "http://" not in website and "https://" not in website:
        logger.error(
            "Exiting preservation - invalid user input: {}".format(
                website))
        sys.exit(1)
    logger.info("Accessing {} webpage".format(website))
    context = ssl._create_unverified_context()
```

Next, in a `try-except` block, we open a connection to the website with the unverified SSL context using the `urlopen()` method and read in the web page data. If we receive an error when attempting to access the web page, we print and log a status message prior to exiting the script. If we are successful, we log a success message and continue script execution.

```
try:
    index = urlopen(website, context=context).read().decode("utf-8")
except urllib.error.HTTPError as e:
    logger.error(
        "Exiting preservation - unable to access page: {}".format(
            website))
    sys.exit(2)
logger.debug("Successfully accessed {}".format(website))
```

With this first web page, we call the `write_output()` function to write it to the output directory and the `find_links()` function to identify all links on the web page. Specifically, this function attempts to identify all internal links on the website. We will explore both of these functions momentarily.

After identifying links on the first page, we print two status messages to the console and then call the `recurse_pages()` method to iterate through and discover all links on the discovered web pages and add them to the queue set. That completes the `main()` function; let's now take a look at the supporting cast of functions, starting with the `write_output()` method.

```
write_output(website, index, output_dir)
link_queue = find_links(base_name, index, link_queue)
logger.info("Found {} initial links on webpage".format(
    len(link_queue)))
recurse_pages(website, link_queue, context, output_dir)
logger.info("Completed preservation of {}".format(website))
```

The `write_output()` method takes a few arguments: the URL of the web page, its page data, the output directory, and an optional counter argument. By default this argument is set to zero if it is not supplied in the function call. The counter argument is used to append a loop iteration number to the output file to avoid writing over identically named files. We start by removing some unnecessary characters in the name of the output file that may cause it to create unnecessary directories. We also join the output directory with the URL directories and create them with `os.makedirs()`.

```
def write_output(name, data, output_dir, counter=0):
    name = name.replace("http://", "").replace("https://", "").rstrip("//")
    directory = os.path.join(output_dir, os.path.dirname(name))
    if not os.path.exists(directory) and os.path.dirname(name) != "":
        os.makedirs(directory)
```

Now, we log a few details about the web page we are writing. First, we log the name and output destination for the file. Then, we log the hash of the data as it was read from the web page with the `hash_data()` method. We create the path variable for the output file and append the counter string to avoid overwriting resources. We then open the output file and write the web page content to it. Finally, we log the output file hash by calling the `hash_file()` method.

```
logger.debug("Writing {} to {}".format(name, output_dir))
logger.debug("Data Hash: {}".format(hash_data(data)))
path = os.path.join(output_dir, name)
path = path + "_" + str(counter)
with open(path, "w") as outfile:
    outfile.write(data)
logger.debug("Output File Hash: {}".format(hash_file(path)))
```

The `hash_data()` method is really quite simple. We read in the UTF-8 encoded data and then generate the `SHA-256` hash of it using the same methodology as seen in previous recipes.

```
def hash_data(data):
    sha256 = hashlib.sha256()
    sha256.update(data.encode("utf-8"))
    return sha256.hexdigest()
```

The `hash_file()` method is just a little more complicated. Before we can hash the data, we must first open the file and read its contents into the `SHA-256` algorithm. With this complete, we call the `hexdigest()` method and return the generated `SHA-256` hash. Let's now shift to the `find_links()` method and how we leverage `BeautifulSoup` to quickly find all relevant links.

```
def hash_file(file):
    sha256 = hashlib.sha256()
    with open(file, "rb") as in_file:
        sha256.update(in_file.read())
    return sha256.hexdigest()
```

The `find_links()` method accomplishes a few things in its initial `for` loop. First of all, we create a `BeautifulSoup` object out of the web page data. Secondly, while creating that object, we specify that we only want to process part of the document, specifically, `<a href>` tags. This helps limit CPU cycles and memory usage and allows us to focus on only what is relevant. The `SoupStrainer` object is a fancy name for a filter and, in this case, filters only `<a href>` tags.

With the list of links set up, we then create some logic to test whether they are part of this domain. In this case, we accomplish this by checking whether the website's URL is part of the link. Any link that passes that test must then not start with a "#" symbol. During testing, on one of the websites, we found this would cause internal page references, or named anchors, to get added as a separate page, which was not desirable. After a link passes those tests, it is added to the set queue (unless it is already present in the set object). After we process all such links, the queue is returned to the calling function. The recurse_pages() function makes multiple calls to this function to find all links in every page we index.

```
def find_links(website, page, queue):
    for link in BeautifulSoup(page, "html.parser",
                         parse_only=SoupStrainer("a", href=True)):
        if website in link.get("href"):
            if not os.path.basename(link.get("href")).startswith("#"):
                queue.add(link.get("href"))
    return queue
```

The recurse_pages() function takes as its inputs the website URL, current link queue, the unverified SSL context, and the output directory. We start by creating a processed list to keep track of the links we have already explored. We also set up the loop counter, which we later pass into the write_output() function to uniquely name the output files.

Next, we begin the dreaded while True loop, always a somewhat dangerous way of iteration, but it is used in this instance to continue iterating over the queue, which becomes progressively larger as we discover more pages. In this loop, we increment the counter by 1, but more importantly, check whether the processed list length matches the length of all found links. If that is the case, this loop will be broken. However, until that scenario is met, the script will continue iterating over all links, looking for more internal links and writing them to the output directory.

```
def recurse_pages(website, queue, context, output_dir):
    processed = []
    counter = 0
    while True:
        counter += 1
        if len(processed) == len(queue):
            break
```

We start iterating through a copy of the queue to process each link. We use the set `copy()` command so that we can update the queue without generating errors during its iterative loops. If the link has already been processed, we continue onto the next link to avoid performing redundant tasks. If this is the first time the link is being processed, the `continue` command is not executed, and instead, we append this link to the processed list so it will not be processed again in the future.

```
for link in queue.copy():
    if link in processed:
        continue
    processed.append(link)
```

We attempt to open and read in the data for each link. If we cannot access the web page, we print and log that and continue executing the script. This way, we preserve all of the pages that we can access and have a log with details on links we were unable to access and preserve.

```
try:
    page = urlopen(link, context=context).read().decode(
        "utf-8")
except urllib.error.HTTPError as e:
    msg = "Error accessing webpage: {}".format(link)
    logger.error(msg)
    continue
```

Finally, for each link we are able to access, we write its output to a file by passing the link name, page data, output directory, and the counter. We also set the `queue` object equal to the new set, which will have all elements from the old `queue` and any additional new links from the `find_links()` method. Eventually, and it may take some time based on the size of the website, we will have processed all items in the link queue and will exit the script after printing a status message to the console.

```
write_output(link, page, output_dir, counter)
queue = find_links(website, page, queue)
logger.info("Identified {} links throughout website".format(
    len(queue)))
```

When we execute this script, we provide the URL for the website, the output folder, and a path to the log file as seen here:

```
(venv3) pyforcookbook@dev-vm$ python beautiful_preservation.py http://facebook.com
~/Desktop/website-collection-0001 -l ~/Desktop/website-collection-0001.log
2017-09-02 15:51:58,533 <module>  INFO     Starting BS Preservation
2017-09-02 15:51:58,534 <module>  DEBUG    Supplied arguments: ['http://facebook.co
m', '/home/pyforcookbook/Desktop/website-collection-0001', '-l', '/home/pyforcookbo
ok/Desktop/website-collection-0001.log']
2017-09-02 15:51:58,534 <module>  DEBUG    System linux
2017-09-02 15:51:58,534 <module>  DEBUG    Version 3.5.2 (default, Nov 17 2016, 17:
05:23)
[GCC 5.4.0 20160609]
2017-09-02 15:51:58,565 main       INFO     Accessing http://facebook.com webpage
2017-09-02 15:51:59,596 main       DEBUG    Successfully accessed http://facebook.co
m
2017-09-02 15:51:59,596 write_outputDEBUG   Writing facebook.com to /home/pyforcoo
kbook/Desktop/website-collection-0001
2017-09-02 15:51:59,597 write_outputDEBUG   Data Hash: de601e54a61eec2325c4cc8f392
6f4a2640079488b98e03e6f3525eb16c824be
2017-09-02 15:51:59,598 write_outputDEBUG   Output File Hash: de601e54a61eec2325c4
cc8f3926f4a2640079488b98e03e6f3525eb16c824be
2017-09-02 15:51:59,656 main       INFO     Found 16 initial links on webpage
2017-09-02 15:52:00,576 write_outputDEBUG   Writing www.facebook.com/help/56813749
3302217 to /home/pyforcookbook/Desktop/website-collection-0001
2017-09-02 15:52:00,578 write_outputDEBUG   Data Hash: b5d8ec888ce778d791ad15c5d96
1ae86dd072290b2cdc20439969d010eaa634d
2017-09-02 15:52:00,579 write_outputDEBUG   Output File Hash: b5d8ec888ce778d791ad
15c5d961ae86dd072290b2cdc20439969d010eaa634d
2017-09-02 15:52:01,276 write_outputDEBUG   Writing zh-cn.facebook.com to /home/py
forcookbook/Desktop/website-collection-0001
2017-09-02 15:52:01,278 write_outputDEBUG   Data Hash: cc2c5d6847a7b6593ba042647af
164cef79856ca65af95626f2d72aad21e1523
2017-09-02 15:52:01,280 write_outputDEBUG   Output File Hash: cc2c5d6847a7b6593ba0
42647af164cef79856ca65af95626f2d72aad21e1523
```

We can then open the output file in a browser and view the preserved content:

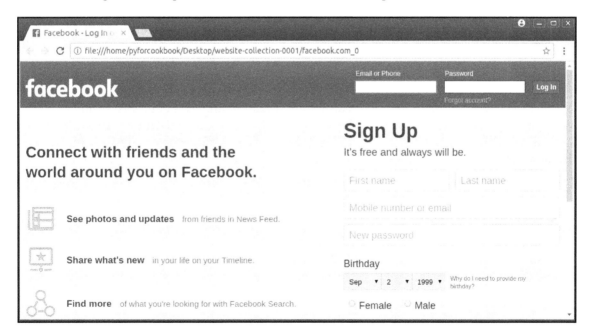

There's more...

We can extend this script in many ways, including:

- Collecting CSS, images, and other resources
- Screenshotting rendered pages in a browser with selenium
- Setting the user-agent to disguise collections

Going hunting for viruses

Recipe Difficulty: Medium

Python Version: 3.5

Operating System: Any

VirusShare is the largest privately owned collection of malware samples, with over 29.3 million samples and counting. One of the great benefits of VirusShare, besides the literal cornucopia of malware that is every malware researcher's dream, is the list of malware hashes which is made freely available. We can use these hashes to a create a very comprehensive hash set and leverage that in casework to identify potentially malicious files.

 To learn more about and use `VirusShare`, visit the website `https://virusshare.com/`.

In this recipe, we demonstrate how to automate downloading lists of hashes from VirusShare to create a newline-delimited hash list. This list can be used by forensic tools, such as X-Ways, to create a HashSet. Other forensic tools, EnCase, for example, can use this list as well but require the use of an EnScript to successfully import and create the HashSet.

Getting started

This recipe uses the `tqdm` third-party library to create an informative progress bar. The `tqdm` module can be installed via the following command. All other libraries used in this recipe are native to Python.

```
pip install tqdm==4.11.2
```

Learn more about the `tqdm` library; visit `https://github.com/noamraph/tqdm`.

How to do it...

We will perform the following steps in this recipe:

1. Read the VirusShare hashes page and dynamically identify the most recent hash list.
2. Initialize progress bar and download hash lists in the desired range.

How it works...

First, we import the required libraries to handle argument parsing, creating progress bars, and interacting with web pages.

```
from __future__ import print_function
import argparse
import os
import ssl
import sys
import tqdm
from urllib.request import urlopen
import urllib.error
```

This recipe's command-line handler takes one positional argument, OUTPUT_HASH, the desired file path for the hash set we will create. An optional argument, --start, captured as an integer, is the optional starting location for the hash lists. VirusShare maintains a page of links to malware hashes, where each link contains a list of between 65,536 and 131,072 MD5 hashes. Rather than downloading all hash lists (which can take some time), the user can specify the desired starting location. For example, this may come in handy if an individual has previously downloaded hashes from VirusShare and now wishes to download the latest few hash lists that have been released.

```
if __name__ == '__main__':
    parser = argparse.ArgumentParser(
        description=__description__,
        epilog="Developed by {} on {}".format(
            ", ".join(__authors__), __date__)
    )
```

```
parser.add_argument("OUTPUT_HASH", help="Output Hashset")
parser.add_argument("--start", type=int,
                    help="Optional starting location")
args = parser.parse_args()
```

We perform the standard input validation steps to ensure the supplied inputs will not cause any unexpected errors. We use the `os.path.dirname()` method to separate the directory path from the file path and check that it exists. If it doesn't, we create the directory now rather than encountering issues trying to write to a directory that does not exist. Lastly, we use an `if` statement and supply the `main()` function with the `start` argument as a keyword, if it was supplied.

```
directory = os.path.dirname(args.OUTPUT_HASH)
if not os.path.exists(directory):
    os.makedirs(directory)

if args.start:
    main(args.OUTPUT_HASH, start=args.start)
else:
    main(args.OUTPUT_HASH)
```

The `main()` function is the only function in this recipe. While it is long, the task is relatively straightforward, making additional functions somewhat unnecessary. Notice the `**kwargs` argument in the definition of the function. This creates a dictionary we can refer to support supplied keyword arguments. Prior to accessing the VirusShare website, we set up a few variables and print a status message to the console first. We use `ssl._create_unverified_context()` in order to bypass an SSL verification error received in Python 3.X.

```
def main(hashset, **kwargs):
    url = "https://virusshare.com/hashes.4n6"
    print("[+] Identifying hash set range from {}".format(url))
    context = ssl._create_unverified_context()
```

We use a `try` and `except` block to open the VirusShare hashes page using the `urllib.request.urlopen()` method with the unverified SSL context. We use the `read()` method to read the page data and decode it to UTF-8. If we receive an error attempting to access this page, we print a status message to the console and exit the script accordingly.

```
try:
    index = urlopen(url, context=context).read().decode("utf-8")
except urllib.error.HTTPError as e:
    print("[-] Error accessing webpage - exiting..")
    sys.exit(1)
```

The first task with the downloaded page data is to identify the latest hash list. We do this by looking for the last instance of an HTML `href` tag to a VirusShare hash list. For instance, an example link may look like "hashes/VirusShare_00288.md5". We use string slicing and methods to separate the hash number (288 in the previous example) from the link. We now check the `kwargs` dictionary to see whether the `start` argument was supplied. If it wasn't, we set the `start` variable to zero to download the first hash list and all intervening hash lists, up to and including the last one, to create the hash set.

```
tag = index.rfind(r'<a href="hashes/VirusShare_')
stop = int(index[tag + 27: tag + 27 + 5].lstrip("0"))

if "start" not in kwargs:
    start = 0
else:
    start = kwargs["start"]
```

Before we begin downloading the hash lists, we perform a sanity check and validate the `start` variable. Specifically, we check whether it is less than zero or greater than the latest hash list. We are using the `start` and `stop` variables to initialize the `for` loop and progress bar and therefore must validate the `start` variable to avoid unexpected outcomes. If the user supplied a bad `start` argument, we print a status message to the console and exit the script.

After the last sanity check, we print a status message to the console and set the `hashes_downloaded` counter to zero. We use this counter in a later status message to record how many hashes were downloaded and written to the hash list.

```
if start < 0 or start > stop:
    print("[-] Supplied start argument must be greater than or equal "
        "to zero but less than the latest hash list, "
        "currently: {}".format(stop))
    sys.exit(2)

print("[+] Creating a hashset from hash lists {} to {}".format(
    start, stop))
hashes_downloaded = 0
```

As discussed in Chapter 1, *Essential Scripting and File Information Recipes*, we can use the `tqdm.trange()` method as a substitute for the built-in `range()` method to create a loop and also a progress bar. We supply it with the desired `start` and `stop` integers and set a scale and a description for the progress bar. We must add 1 to the `stop` integer, due to the way `range()` works, to actually download the last hash list.

In the `for` loop, we create a base URL and insert a five-digit number to specify the appropriate hash list. We accomplish this by converting the integer to a string and using `zfill()` to ensure the digit has five characters by prepending zeroes to the front of the string until it is five digits long. Next, as before, we use a `try` and `except` to open, read, and decode the hash list. We split on any new line characters to quickly create a list of hashes. If we encounter an error accessing the web page, we print a status message to the console and continue executing rather than exiting from the script.

```
for x in tqdm.trange(start, stop + 1, unit_scale=True,
                     desc="Progress"):
    url_hash = "https://virusshare.com/hashes/VirusShare_"\
               "{}.md5".format(str(x).zfill(5))
    try:
        hashes = urlopen(
            url_hash, context=context).read().decode("utf-8")
        hashes_list = hashes.split("\n")
    except urllib.error.HTTPError as e:
        print("[-] Error accessing webpage for hash list {}"
              " - continuing..".format(x))
        continue
```

Once we have the hash list, we open the hash set text file in "a+" mode to append to the bottom of the text file and create the file if it does not already exist. Afterward, we only need to iterate through the downloaded hash list and write each hash to the file. Note that each hash list starts with a few commented lines (denoted by the # symbol) and so we implement logic to ignore those lines in addition to empty lines. After all hashes have been downloaded and written to the text file, we print a status message to the console and indicate the number of hashes downloaded.

```
with open(hashset, "a+") as hashfile:
    for line in hashes_list:
        if not line.startswith("#") and line != "":
            hashes_downloaded += 1
            hashfile.write(line + '\n')

print("[+] Finished downloading {} hashes into {}".format(
    hashes_downloaded, hashset))
```

When we run this script the hashes start downloading locally and are stored in the specified file as seen here:

```
(venv3) pyforcookbook@dev-vm$ python virus_hashset.py ~/Desktop/vsx_hashset.txt
[+] Identifying hash set range from https://virusshare.com/hashes.4n6
[+] Creating a hashset from hash lists 0 to 296
Progress: 100%|██████████████████████████| 297/297 [25:55<00:00, 3.82s/it]
[+] Finished downloading 29229054 hashes into /home/pyforcookbook/Desktop/vsx_hashs
et.txt
```

When previewing the output file, we can see the MD5 hash values saved as plain text. As previously mentioned, we can import this into the forensic tools either directly, as with X-Ways, or through a script, as with EnCase (http://www.forensickb.com/2014/02/enscript-to-create-encase-v7-hash-set.html).

```
(venv3) pyforcookbook@dev-vm$ head ~/Desktop/vsx_hashset.txt
2d75cc1bf8e57872781f9cd04a529256
00f538c3d410822e241486ca061a57ee
3f066dd1f1da052248aed5abc4a0c6a1
781770fda3bd3236d0ab8274577dddde
86b6c59aa48a69e16d3313d982791398
42914d6d213a20a2684064be5c80ffa9
10699ac57f1cf851ae144ebce42fa587
248338632580f9c018c4d8f8d9c6c408
999eb1840c209aa70a84c5cf64909e5f
12c4201fe1db96a1a1711790b52a3cf9
```

Gathering intel

Recipe Difficulty: Medium

Python Version: 3.5

Operating System: Any

In this recipe, we use **VirusTotal**, a free online virus, malware, and URL scanner, to automate the review of potentially malicious websites or files. VirusTotal maintains detailed documentation of their API on their website. We will demonstrate how to perform basic queries against their system using their documented API and store returned results into a CSV file.

Getting started

To follow this recipe, you need to first create an account with VirusTotal and decide between the free public API or the private API. The public API has request limitations, which the private API does not. For example, with the public API, we are limited to 4 requests per minute and 178,560 requests per month. More details about the different API types can be found on VirusTotal's website. We will make these API calls with the `requests` library. This library can be installed using:

```
pip install requests==2.18.4
```

To learn more about and use `VirusTotal`, visit the website at `https://www.virustotal.com/`.

Learn more about the `VirusTotal` Public API; visit `https://www.virustotal.com/en/documentation/public-api/`.

Learn more about the `VirusTotal` Private API; visit `https://www.virustotal.com/en/documentation/private-api/`.

To view your API key, which you will need for the script, click on your account name in the top-right corner and navigate to **My API key**. Here you can view details of your API key and request a private key. Take a look at the following screenshot for additional details. All libraries used in this script are present in Python's standard library.

How to do it...

We use the following methodology to accomplish our objective:

1. Read in the list of signatures, as either domains and IPs or file paths and hashes, to research.
2. Query VirusTotal using the API for domain and IPs or files.
3. Flatten results into a convenient format.
4. Write results to a CSV file.

How it works...

First, we import the required libraries to handle argument parsing, creating spreadsheets, hashing files, parsing JSON data, and interacting with web pages.

```
from __future__ import print_function
import argparse
import csv
import hashlib
```

```
import json
import os
import requests
import sys
import time
```

This recipe's command-line handler is a little more complicated than normal. It takes three positional arguments, INPUT_FILE, OUTPUT_CSV, and API_KEY, which represent the input text file of domains and IPs or file paths, the desired output CSV location, and a text file containing the API key to use, respectively. In addition to this, there are a few optional arguments, -t (or --type) and --limit, to specify the type of data in the input file and file paths or domains and to limit requests to comply with public API limitations. By default, the type argument is configured to the domain value. If the limit switch is added, it will have the Boolean value of True; otherwise, it will be False.

```
if __name__ == '__main__':
    parser = argparse.ArgumentParser(
        description=__description__,
        epilog="Developed by {} on {}".format(
            ", ".join(__authors__), __date__)
    )
    parser.add_argument("INPUT_FILE",
                        help="Text File containing list of file paths/"
                             "hashes or domains/IPs")
    parser.add_argument("OUTPUT_CSV",
                        help="Output CSV with lookup results")
    parser.add_argument("API_KEY", help="Text File containing API key")
    parser.add_argument("-t", "--type",
                        help="Type of data: file or domain",
                        choices=("file", "domain"), default="domain")
    parser.add_argument(
        "--limit", action="store_true",
        help="Limit requests to comply with public API key restrictions")
    args = parser.parse_args()
```

Next, we perform the standard data validation process on the input file and output CSV. If the inputs pass the data validation steps, we pass all arguments to the main() function or otherwise exit the script.

```
    directory = os.path.dirname(args.OUTPUT_CSV)
    if not os.path.exists(directory):
        os.makedirs(directory)

    if os.path.exists(args.INPUT_FILE) and os.path.isfile(args.INPUT_FILE):
        main(args.INPUT_FILE, args.OUTPUT_CSV,
             args.API_KEY, args.limit, args.type)
    else:
```

```
        print("[-] Supplied input file {} does not exist or is not a "
              "file".format(args.INPUT_FILE))
        sys.exit(1)
```

The `main()` function starts by reading the input file into a set called `objects`. A set was used here to cut down on duplicate lines and duplicate calls to the API. In this manner, we can try to prolong hitting the limitations of the public API unnecessarily.

```
def main(input_file, output, api, limit, type):
    objects = set()
    with open(input_file) as infile:
        for line in infile:
            if line.strip() != "":
                objects.add(line.strip())
```

After we have read in the data, we check whether the type of data we read in is in the domain and IP category or file paths. Depending on the type, we send the set of data to the appropriate function, which will return VirusTotal query results to the `main()` function. We will then send these results to the `write_csv()` method to write the output. Let's look at the `query_domain()` function first.

```
    if type == "domain":
        data = query_domain(objects, api, limit)
    else:
        data = query_file(objects, api, limit)
    write_csv(data, output)
```

This function first performs additional input validation, this time on the API key file, to ensure the file exists prior to trying to make calls with said key. If the file does exist, we read it into the `api` variable. The `json_data` list will store returned JSON data from the VirusTotal API calls.

```
def query_domain(domains, api, limit):
    if not os.path.exists(api) and os.path.isfile(api):
        print("[-] API key file {} does not exist or is not a file".format(
            api))
        sys.exit(2)

    with open(api) as infile:
        api = infile.read().strip()
    json_data = []
```

After we print a status message to the console, we begin to loop through each domain or IP address in the set. For each item, we increment `count` by one to keep track of how many API calls we have made. We create a parameter dictionary and store the domain or IP to search and API key and set `scan` to `1`. By setting `scan` to `1`, we will automatically submit the domain or IP for review if it is not already in the VirusTotal database.

We make the API call with the `requests.post()` method, querying the appropriate URL with the parameter dictionary to obtain the results. We use the `json()` method on the returned requests object to convert it into easily manipulated JSON data.

```
print("[+] Querying {} Domains / IPs using VirusTotal API".format(
    len(domains)))
count = 0
for domain in domains:
    count += 1
    params = {"resource": domain, "apikey": api, "scan": 1}
    response = requests.post(
        'https://www.virustotal.com/vtapi/v2/url/report',
        params=params)
    json_response = response.json()
```

If the API call was successful and the data was found in the VirusTotal database, we append the JSON data to the list. If the data was not present in the VirusTotal database, we can use the API to retrieve the report after it has been created. Here, for simplicity, we assume the data is already present in their database and only add results if they were found rather than waiting for the report to be generated if the item does not already exist.

```
if "Scan finished" in json_response["verbose_msg"]:
    json_data.append(json_response)
```

Next, we check whether `limit` is `True` and the `count` variable is equal to 3. If so, we need to wait a minute before continuing the queries to comply with the public API limitations. We print status messages to the console so the user is aware of what the script is doing and use the `time.sleep()` method to halt script execution for a minute. After we have waited a minute, we reset the count back to zero and begin querying the remaining domain or IPs in the list. Once we have finished this process, we return the list of JSON results back to the `main()` function.

```
if limit and count == 3:
    print("[+] Halting execution for a minute to comply with "
        "public API key restrictions")
    time.sleep(60)
    print("[+] Continuing execution of remaining Domains / IPs")
    count = 0
```

```
        return json_data
```

The `query_file()` method is similar to the `query_domain()` method we just explored. First, we validate that the API key file exists or exit the script otherwise. Once validated, we read in the API key and store it in the `api` variable and instantiate the `json_data` list to store the API JSON data.

```
def query_file(files, api, limit):
    if not os.path.exists(api) and os.path.isfile(api):
        print("[-] API key file {} does not exist or is not a file".format(
            api))
        sys.exit(3)

    with open(api) as infile:
        api = infile.read().strip()
    json_data = []
```

Unlike the `query_domain()` function, we need to perform some additional validation and processing on each file path before we can use it. Namely, we need to validate that each file path is valid and then we must hash each file, or use the hash provided in the signatures file. We hash these files as this is how we will look them up in the VirusTotal database. Recall that we are assuming the file is already present in the database. We can use the API to submit samples and retrieve reports after the file is scanned.

```
    print("[+] Hashing and Querying {} Files using VirusTotal API".format(
        len(files)))
    count = 0
    for file_entry in files:
        if os.path.exists(file_entry):
            file_hash = hash_file(file_entry)
        elif len(file_entry) == 32:
            file_hash = file_entry
        else:
            continue
        count += 1
```

Let's take a quick look at the `file_hash` function. The `hash_file()` method is relatively straightforward. This function takes a file path as its only input and returns the SHA-256 hash for the said file. We accomplish this, similar to how we did so in *Chapter 1, Essential Scripting and File Information Recipes*, by creating a `hashlib` algorithm object, reading the file data into it 1,024 bytes at a time, and then calling the `hexdigest()` method to return the calculated hashes. With that covered, let's look at the remainder of the `query_file()` method.

```
def hash_file(file_path):
    sha256 = hashlib.sha256()
```

```
    with open(file_path, 'rb') as open_file:
        buff_size = 1024
        buff = open_file.read(buff_size)

        while buff:
            sha256.update(buff)
            buff = open_file.read(buff_size)
    return sha256.hexdigest()
```

The `query_file()` method continues by creating a parameter dictionary with the API key and file hash to look up. Again, we use the `requests.post()` and `json()` methods to make the API call and convert it into JSON data, respectively.

```
        params = {"resource": file_hash, "apikey": api}
        response = requests.post(
            'https://www.virustotal.com/vtapi/v2/file/report',
            params=params)
        json_response = response.json()
```

If the API call was successful and the file was already present in the VirusTotal database, we append the JSON data to the list. Once more, we perform checks on the count and limit to ensure we comply with the public API limitations. After we have completed all of the API calls, we return the list of JSON data back to the `main()` function for output.

```
        if "Scan finished" in json_response["verbose_msg"]:
            json_data.append(json_response)

        if limit and count == 3:
            print("[+] Halting execution for a minute to comply with "
                "public API key restrictions")
            time.sleep(60)
            print("[+] Continuing execution of remaining files")
            count = 0


    return json_data
```

The `write_csv()` method first checks that the output data actually contains API results. If it does not, the script will exit rather than write an empty CSV file.

```
def write_csv(data, output):
    if data == []:
        print("[-] No output results to write")
        sys.exit(4)
```

If we do have results, we print a status message to the console and begin by flattening the JSON data into a convenient output format. We create a `flatten_data` list, which will store each flattened JSON dictionary. The field list maintains the list of keys in the flattened JSON dictionary and the desired column headers.

We use a few `for` loops to get to the JSON data and append a dictionary with this data to the list. After this process is completed, we will have a very simple list of dictionary structures to work with. We can use the `csv.DictWriter` class as we have previously to easily handle this type of data structure.

```
print("[+] Writing output for {} domains with results to {}".format(
    len(data), output))
flatten_data = []
field_list = ["URL", "Scan Date", "Service",
              "Detected", "Result", "VirusTotal Link"]
for result in data:
    for service in result["scans"]:
        flatten_data.append(
            {"URL": result.get("url", ""),
             "Scan Date": result.get("scan_date", ""),
             "VirusTotal Link": result.get("permalink", ""),
             "Service": service,
             "Detected": result["scans"][service]["detected"],
             "Result": result["scans"][service]["result"]})
```

With the data set ready for output, we open the CSV file and create the `DictWriter` class instance. We supply it the file object and the list of headers in the dictionary. We write the headers to the spreadsheet before writing each dictionary to a row.

```
with open(output, "w", newline="") as csvfile:
    csv_writer = csv.DictWriter(csvfile, fieldnames=field_list)
    csv_writer.writeheader()
    for result in flatten_data:
        csv_writer.writerow(result)
```

The following screenshot reflects when we run the script against files and hashes, and a second for running against domains and IPs:

```
(venv3) pyforcookbook@dev-vm$ python total_virus.py ~/Desktop/vx_file_sigs.txt ~
/Desktop/vt_lookup.csv ~/.vt_key -t file --limit
[+] Hashing and Querying 16 Files using VirusTotal API
[+] Halting execution for a minute to comply with public API key restrictions
[+] Continuing execution of remaining files
[+] Halting execution for a minute to comply with public API key restrictions
[+] Continuing execution of remaining files
[+] Halting execution for a minute to comply with public API key restrictions
[+] Continuing execution of remaining files
[+] Halting execution for a minute to comply with public API key restrictions
[+] Continuing execution of remaining files
[+] Halting execution for a minute to comply with public API key restrictions
[+] Continuing execution of remaining files
[+] Writing output for 16 domains with results to /home/pyforcookbook/Desktop/vt
_lookup.csv
```

```
(venv3) pyforcookbook@dev-vm$ python total_virus.py ~/Desktop/vx_ip_sigs.txt ~/D
esktop/vt_ip_lookup.csv ~/.vt_key -t domain --limit
[+] Querying 10 Domains / IPs using VirusTotal API
[+] Halting execution for a minute to comply with public API key restrictions
[+] Continuing execution of remaining Domains / IPs
[+] Halting execution for a minute to comply with public API key restrictions
[+] Continuing execution of remaining Domains / IPs
[+] Halting execution for a minute to comply with public API key restrictions
[+] Continuing execution of remaining Domains / IPs
[+] Writing output for 8 domains with results to /home/pyforcookbook/Desktop/vt_
ip_lookup.csv
```

Looking at the output, we can learn about the malware classifications for the files and hashes and the domain or IP ranking in CSV format:

Scan Date ▼	Service ▼	Detected ▼	Result ▼	VirusTotal Link ▼
2017-07-20 16:37:16	AegisLab	True	Malware.Gen!c	https://www.virustotal.com/file/321fc878239
2017-07-20 16:42:24	AegisLab	True	Malware.Gen!c	https://www.virustotal.com/file/5e1f857866c
2017-07-20 17:13:29	Panda	True	Trj/CI.A	https://www.virustotal.com/file/e04031a7c2
2017-07-20 17:13:29	BitDefender	True	Trojan.Generic.7656461	https://www.virustotal.com/file/e04031a7c2
2017-07-20 17:13:29	Tencent	True	Win32.Trojan-dropper.Injector.Hrfr	https://www.virustotal.com/file/e04031a7c2
2017-07-20 17:13:29	Webroot	True	W32.Trojan.Gen	https://www.virustotal.com/file/e04031a7c2
2017-07-20 17:13:29	ALYac	True	Trojan.Generic.7656461	https://www.virustotal.com/file/e04031a7c2
2017-07-20 17:13:29	ZoneAlarm	True	Trojan-Dropper.Win32.Injector.ckvw	https://www.virustotal.com/file/e04031a7c2
2017-07-20 17:13:29	Bkav	True	W32.Clod593.Trojan.aaee	https://www.virustotal.com/file/e04031a7c2
2017-07-20 17:13:29	Comodo	True	UnclassifiedMalware	https://www.virustotal.com/file/e04031a7c2
2017-07-20 17:13:29	ESET-NOD32	True	a variant of Win32/GameHack.AJR potentially unsafe	https://www.virustotal.com/file/e04031a7c2

URL	Scan Date ▼	Service ▼	Detecte ▼	Result ▼	VirusTotal Link ▼
http://oracljar.itsuport.org/	2016-10-07 11:46:47	Fortinet	True	malware site	https://www.virustotal.com/url/6e9d5d312b7965c0f
http://176.56.236.180/	2017-06-28 17:27:08	Sophos	True	malicious site	https://www.virustotal.com/url/635800178c3088d51
http://176.56.236.180/	2017-06-28 17:27:08	Fortinet	True	malware site	https://www.virustotal.com/url/635800178c3088d51
http://176.56.236.180/	2017-06-28 17:27:08	BitDefender	True	malware site	https://www.virustotal.com/url/635800178c3088d51
http://81.4.127.29/	2017-07-12 22:17:15	BitDefender	True	malware site	https://www.virustotal.com/url/7a28b95bbdd10d41e
http://176.56.237.58/	2017-02-17 16:34:31	Sophos	True	malicious site	https://www.virustotal.com/url/df69485dc95ae429b
http://176.56.237.58/	2017-02-17 16:34:31	Fortinet	True	malware site	https://www.virustotal.com/url/df69485dc95ae429b
http://176.56.237.58/	2017-02-17 16:34:31	BitDefender	True	malware site	https://www.virustotal.com/url/df69485dc95ae429b
http://chancetowin.quezknal.net/	2016-10-07 11:31:59	CLEAN MX	False	suspicious site	https://www.virustotal.com/url/10e042266bfe01bab
http://chancetowin.quezknal.net/	2016-10-07 11:31:59	Yandex Safebrowsing	True	malware site	https://www.virustotal.com/url/10e042266bfe01bab
http://chancetowin.quezknal.net/	2016-10-07 11:31:59	CRDF	True	malicious site	https://www.virustotal.com/url/10e042266bfe01bab

Totally passive

Recipe Difficulty: Medium

Python Version: 3.5

Operating System: Any

This recipe explores the PassiveTotal API and how to use it to automate the review of domains and IP addresses. This service is particularly useful in viewing historical resolution details for a given domain. For example, you may have a suspected phishing website and, based on historical resolution patterns, can identify how long it has been active and what other domains used to share that IP. This then gives you additional domains to review and search for, in your evidence as you identify the different means and methods of how the attackers maintained persistence as they compromised multiple users across the environment.

Getting started

To use the PassiveTotal API, you need to first create a free account on their website. Once you are logged in, you can view your API key by navigating to your account settings and clicking on the **User Show** button under the **API ACCESS** section. See the following screenshot for a visual representation of this page.

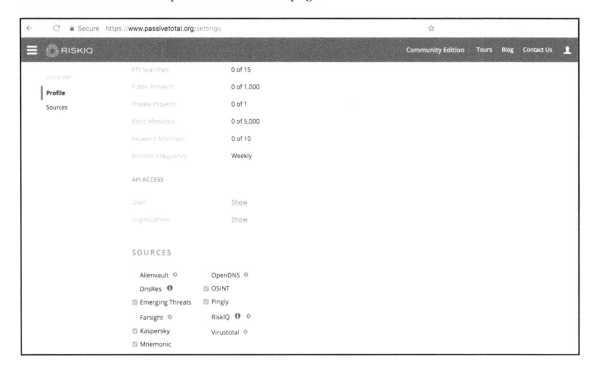

All libraries used in this script are present in Python's standard library. However, we do install the PassiveTotal Python API client and follow the installation and setup instructions in the README found at `https://github.com/passivetotal/python_api` or with `pip install passivetotal==1.0.30`. We do this to use the PassiveTotal command-line `pt-client` application. In this script, we make the API calls through this client rather than performing this at a more manual level as we did in the previous recipe. More details on the PassiveTotal API, especially if you are interested in developing something more advanced, can be found on their website.

To learn more about and use `PassiveTotal`, visit the website `https://www.passivetotal.org`.
Learn more about the `PassiveTotal` API; visit `https://api.passivetotal.org/api/docs`.
Learn more about the `PassiveTotal` Python API; visit `https://github.com/passivetotal/python_api`.

How to do it...

We use the following methodology to accomplish our objective:

1. Read in the list of domains to review.
2. Call the command-line `pt-client` using `subprocess` and return results to our script for each domain.
3. Write results to a CSV file.

How it works...

First, we import the required libraries to handle argument parsing, creating spreadsheets, parsing JSON data, and spawning subprocesses.

```
from __future__ import print_function
import argparse
import csv
import json
import os
import subprocess
import sys
```

This recipe's command-line handler takes two positional arguments, INPUT_DOMAINS and OUTPUT_CSV, for the input text file containing domains and/or IPs and the desired output CSV, respectively.

```
if __name__ == '__main__':
    parser = argparse.ArgumentParser(
        description=__description__,
        epilog="Developed by {} on {}".format(
            ", ".join(__authors__), __date__)
    )
    parser.add_argument("INPUT_DOMAINS",
                        help="Text File containing Domains and/or IPs")
    parser.add_argument("OUTPUT_CSV",
```

```
                    help="Output CSV with lookup results")
    args = parser.parse_args()
```

We perform the standard input validation steps on each of the inputs to avoid unexpected errors in the script. With the inputs validated, we called the `main()` function and pass it the two inputs.

```
    directory = os.path.dirname(args.OUTPUT_CSV)
    if not os.path.exists(directory):
        os.makedirs(directory)

    if os.path.exists(args.INPUT_DOMAINS) and \
            os.path.isfile(args.INPUT_DOMAINS):
        main(args.INPUT_DOMAINS, args.OUTPUT_CSV)
    else:
        print(
            "[-] Supplied input file {} does not exist or is not a "
            "file".format(args.INPUT_DOMAINS))
        sys.exit(1)
```

The `main()` function is rather straightforward, and similar, to that in the previous recipe. We again use a set to read in the objects in the input file. Once again, this is to avoid redundant API calls to the PassiveTotal API as there are daily limitations to the free API. After we read in these objects, we call the `query_domains()` function, which uses the `pt-client` application to make API calls. Once we have all of the returned JSON data from the API calls, we call the `write_csv()` method to write the data to the CSV file.

```
def main(domain_file, output):
    domains = set()
    with open(domain_file) as infile:
        for line in infile:
            domains.add(line.strip())
    json_data = query_domains(domains)
    write_csv(json_data, output)
```

The `query_domains()` function starts by creating a `json_data` list to store the returned JSON data and printing a status message to the console. We then begin to iterate through each object in the input file and remove any `"https://"` or `"http://"` substrings. While testing `pt-client`, it was observed to generate an internal server error if that substring was present. For example, instead of `https://www.google.com`, the query should just be `www.google.com`.

```
def query_domains(domains):
    json_data = []
    print("[+] Querying {} domains/IPs using PassiveTotal API".format(
        len(domains)))
```

```
for domain in domains:
    if "https://" in domain:
        domain = domain.replace("https://", "")
    elif "http://" in domain:
        domain = domain.replace("http://", "")
```

With the domain or IP address ready to be queried, we use the `subprocess.Popen()` method to open a new process and execute the `pt-client` application. Arguments to be executed in this process are in a list. The command that will be executed, if the domain is `www.google.com`, would look like `pt-client pdns -q www.gooogle.com`. Supplying the `stdout` keyword argument as `subprocess.PIPE` creates a new pipe for the process so that we can retrieve results from the query. We do exactly that in the following line by calling the `communicate()` method and then converting the returned data into a JSON structure that we can then store.

```
proc = subprocess.Popen(
    ["pt-client", "pdns", "-q", domain], stdout=subprocess.PIPE)
results, err = proc.communicate()
result_json = json.loads(results.decode())
```

If the `quota_exceeded` message is in the JSON results, then we have exceeded the daily API limit and print that to the console and continue executing. We continue executing rather than exiting so that we can write any results we did retrieve before exceeding the daily API quota.

```
if "message" in result_json:
    if "quota_exceeded" in result_json["message"]:
        print("[-] API Search Quota Exceeded")
        continue
```

Next, we set the `result_count` and check if it is equal to zero. If results were found for the query, we append the results to the JSON list. We return the JSON list, after performing this operation on all domains and/or IPs in the input file.

```
result_count = result_json["totalRecords"]

print("[+] {} results for {}".format(result_count, domain))
if result_count == 0:
    pass
else:
    json_data.append(result_json["results"])

return json_data
```

The `write_csv()` method is pretty straightforward. Here we first check that we have data to write to the output file. Then, we print a status message to the console and create the list of headers and the order in which they should be written.

```
def write_csv(data, output):
    if data == []:
        print("[-] No output results to write")
        sys.exit(2)

    print("[+] Writing output for {} domains/IPs with "
          "results to {}".format(len(data), output))
    field_list = ["value", "firstSeen", "lastSeen", "collected",
                  "resolve", "resolveType", "source", "recordType",
                  "recordHash"]
```

After we have created the list of headers, we use the `csv.DictWriter` class to set up the output CSV file, write the header row, and iterate through each dictionary in the JSON results and write them to their respective rows.

```
    with open(output, "w", newline="") as csvfile:
        csv_writer = csv.DictWriter(csvfile, fieldnames=field_list)
        csv_writer.writeheader()
        for result in data:
            for dictionary in result:
                csv_writer.writerow(dictionary)
```

Running the script provides insight to the number of responses per item in the PassiveTotal lookup:

```
(venv3) pyforcookbook@dev-vm$ python passive_lookup.py ~/Desktop/vx_ip_sigs.txt
~/Desktop/pt_lookup.csv
[+] Querying 10 domains/IPs using PassiveTotal API
[+] 9 results for 81.4.127.29
[+] 1 results for oracljar.itsuport.org
[+] 11 results for 185.109.146.75
[+] 4 results for 176.56.237.58
[+] 28 results for 176.56.236.180
[+] 99 results for 37.48.103.240
[+] 1 results for conf.serviceupdateres.com
[+] 5 results for chancetowin.quezknal.net
[+] 7 results for 89.46.222.126
[+] 4 results for 185.109.144.102
[+] Writing output for 10 domains/IPs with results to /home/pyforcookbook/Deskto
p/pt_lookup.csv
```

The CSV report displays the collected information as seen here:

value	firstSeen	lastSeen	collected	resolve	resolveType	source	recordType
81.4.127.29	2016-12-18 00:00:00	2017-08-27 21:59:49	2017-09-02 22:59:44	rychlewski.org	domain	['kaspersky', 'riskiq', 'virustotal']	A
81.4.127.29	2017-03-30 00:00:00	2017-03-30 10:21:55	2017-09-02 22:59:44	www.garbas.si	domain	['kaspersky', 'virustotal']	A
81.4.127.29	2014-03-17 06:03:32	2015-07-10 10:56:14	2017-09-02 22:59:44	bakke.co	domain	['kaspersky', 'riskiq', 'virustotal']	A
81.4.127.29	2016-07-25 07:20:57	2017-09-02 12:46:13	2017-09-02 22:59:44	garbas.si	domain	['riskiq', 'virustotal']	A
81.4.127.29	2014-01-15 14:51:25	2014-01-15 16:23:23	2017-09-02 22:59:44	bradescoinforma.strangled.net	domain	['riskiq']	A
81.4.127.29	2014-08-19 19:26:56	2015-06-03 07:09:19	2017-09-02 22:59:44	bifrost.bakke.co	domain	['kaspersky', 'riskiq', 'virustotal']	A
81.4.127.29	2014-05-11 00:00:00	2015-06-15 16:50:01	2017-09-02 22:59:44	www.bakke.co	domain	['riskiq', 'virustotal']	A
81.4.127.29	2014-05-11 00:00:00	2014-09-06 23:39:25	2017-09-02 22:59:43	secure.bakke.co	domain	['riskiq', 'virustotal']	A
81.4.127.29	2015-03-03 19:39:18	2015-06-11 06:09:19	2017-09-02 22:59:44	sirius.bakke.co	domain	['riskiq']	A
oracljar.itsuport.org	2015-11-11 00:00:00	2017-09-02 22:59:50	2017-09-02 22:59:51	81.17.28.123	ip	['emerging_threats', 'kaspersky', 'mnemonic', 'pingly', 'riskiq', 'virustotal']	A
185.109.146.75	2010-03-07 08:03:46	2010-03-07 08:03:46	2017-09-02 22:59:55	b81cf676eee2d78857e434 28edf344e1f2d3.1.ziyoufor ever.com	domain	['riskiq']	A
185.109.146.75	2015-09-10 13:04:16	2015-09-10 23:41:47	2017-09-02 22:59:55	www.akbnulasut.space	domain	['riskiq']	A
185.109.146.75	2015-09-10 13:03:39	2015-09-10 13:27:09	2017-09-02 22:59:55	akbnulasut.space	domain	['riskiq']	A
185.109.146.75	2015-07-24 12:33:50	2016-07-23 15:47:22	2017-09-02 22:59:55	ns2.Interiorpaintpainting.p arty	domain	['riskiq']	A
185.109.146.75	2015-07-24 12:33:50	2015-08-03 16:17:50	2017-09-02 22:59:55	www.interiorpaintpainting.p arty	domain	['riskiq']	A
185.109.146.75	2015-07-24 12:33:58	2015-07-28 10:05:05	2017-09-02 22:59:55	zl3cv3hb.interiorpaintpaint ing.party	domain	['riskiq']	A
185.109.146.75	2016-01-09 12:05:02	2017-01-08 01:15:14	2017-09-02 22:59:55	1lavsma.top	domain	['kaspersky', 'riskiq']	A
185.109.146.75	2015-07-24 12:33:50	2016-07-23 15:47:22	2017-09-02 22:59:55	ns1.interiorpaintpainting.p arty	domain	['riskiq']	A
185.109.146.75	2015-07-24 12:33:57	2015-07-28 10:12:25	2017-09-02 22:59:55	interiorpaintpainting.party	domain	['kaspersky', 'riskiq']	A
185.109.146.75	2015-09-10 13:03:40	2015-09-11 05:24:29	2017-09-02 22:59:55	jrwpo.akbnulasut.space	domain	['riskiq']	A
185.109.146.75	2016-01-09 12:04:51	2016-01-13 06:13:16	2017-09-02 22:59:55	wo6y7f.1lavsma.top	domain	['riskiq']	A
176.56.237.58	2015-04-07 16:54:48	2015-12-17 10:40:11	2017-09-02 22:59:59	prezident.se	domain	['kaspersky', 'riskiq']	A
176.56.237.58	2017-03-02 00:13:34	2017-03-14 23:50:06	2017-09-02 22:59:59	www.tennisgudarna.se	domain	['riskiq']	A
176.56.237.58	2014-08-29 22:45:15	2015-07-12 20:51:20	2017-09-02 22:59:59	node.jtwe.co	domain	['kaspersky', 'riskiq']	A
176.56.237.58	2014-08-27 09:28:55	2014-09-02 12:12:00	2017-09-02 22:59:59	penguinspromall.com	domain	['riskiq']	A

6
Reading Emails and Taking Names Recipes

The following recipes are covered in this chapter:

- Parsing EML files
- Viewing MSG files
- Ordering Takeout
- What's in the box?
- Parsing PST and OST mailboxes

Introduction

The he-said-she-said game is often thrown out the window once computer evidence is added to the fray. The email plays a major role in most types of investigations. The email evidence extends to both business and personal devices, as it is widely used to send files, communicate with peers, and to receive notifications from online services. By examining email, we can learn what social media, cloud storage, or other sites are used by the custodian. We can also look for data exfiltration outside of an organization or investigate the source of a phishing scheme.

This chapter will cover recipes that expose this information for investigations, including:

- Reading the EML format using built-in libraries
- Leveraging the `win32com` library to extract information from Outlook MSG files
- Preserving Google Gmail with Takeouts and parsing the preservation
- Using built-in libraries to read from MBOX containers
- Reading PST files with `libpff`

 Visit `www.packtpub.com/books/content/support` to download the code bundle for this chapter.

Parsing EML files

Recipe Difficulty: Easy

Python Version: 2.7 or 3.5

Operating System: Any

The EML file format is widely used for storing email messages, as it is a structured text file that is compatible across multiple email clients. This text file stores email headers, body content, and attachment data as plain text, using `base64` to encode binary data and the **Quoted-Printable** (**QP**) encoding to store content information.

Getting started

All libraries used in this script are present in Python's standard library. We will use the built-in `email` library to read and extract key information from the EML files.

 To learn more about the `email` library, visit `https://docs.python.org/3/library/email.html`.

How to do it...

To create an EML parser, we must:

1. Accept an argument for an EML file.
2. Read values from the headers.
3. Parse information from each of the sections of the EML.
4. Display this information for ease of review in the console.

How it works...

We start by importing libraries for argument handling, EML processing, and decoding base64 encoded data. The email library provides classes and methods necessary to read EML files. We will use the message_from_file() function to parse data from the provided EML file. Quopri is a new library to this book which we use to decode the QP encoded values found in the HTML body and attachments. The base64 library, as one might expect, allows us to decode any base64 encoded data:

```
from __future__ import print_function
from argparse import ArgumentParser, FileType
from email import message_from_file
import os
import quopri
import base64
```

This recipe's command-line handler accepts one positional argument, EML_FILE, which represents the path to the EML file we will process. We use the FileType class to handle the opening of the file for us:

```
if __name__ == '__main__':
    parser = ArgumentParser(
        description=__description__,
        epilog="Developed by {} on {}".format(
            ", ".join(__authors__), __date__)
    )
    parser.add_argument("EML_FILE",
                        help="Path to EML File", type=FileType('r'))
    args = parser.parse_args()

    main(args.EML_FILE)
```

In the `main()` function, we read the file-like object into the `email` library using the `message_from_file()` function. We can now use the resulting variable, `emlfile`, to access the headers, body content, attachments, and other payload information. Reading the email headers is simply a matter of iterating through a dictionary provided by the library's `_headers` attribute. To handle the body content, we must check if this message contains multiple payloads and, if so, pass each to the designated processing function, `process_payload()`:

```
def main(input_file):
    emlfile = message_from_file(input_file)

    # Start with the headers
    for key, value in emlfile._headers:
        print("{}: {}".format(key, value))

    # Read payload
    print("\nBody\n")
    if emlfile.is_multipart():
        for part in emlfile.get_payload():
            process_payload(part)
    else:
        process_payload(emlfile[1])
```

The `process_payload()` function begins by extracting extracting the MIME type of the message using the `get_content_type()` method. We print this value to the console and, on a newline, we print a number of `"="` characters to distinguish between this and the remainder of the message.

In one line, we extract the message body content using the `get_payload()` method and decoding the QP encoded data with the `quopri.decodestring()` function. We then check the there is a character set of the data and, if we do identify a character set, use the `decode()` method on the content while specifying the character set. If the encoding is unknown, we will try to decode the object with UTF8, the default when leaving the `decode()` method empty, and Windows-1252:

```
def process_payload(payload):
    print(payload.get_content_type() + "\n" + "=" * len(
        payload.get_content_type()))
    body = quopri.decodestring(payload.get_payload())
    if payload.get_charset():
        body = body.decode(payload.get_charset())
    else:
        try:
            body = body.decode()
        except UnicodeDecodeError:
```

```
body = body.decode('cp1252')
```

With our decoded data, we check the content MIME type to properly handle the storage of the email. The first condition for HTML information, specified by the `text/html` MIME type, is written to an HTML document in the same directory as the input file. In the second condition, we handle binary data under the `Application` MIME type. This data is conveyed as `base64` encoded values, which we decode before writing to a file in the current directory using the `base64.b64decode()` function. The binary data has the `get_filename()` method, which we can use to accurately name the attachment. Note that the output file must be opened in `"w"` mode for the first type and `"wb"` mode for the second. If the MIME type is other than what we have covered here, we print the body to the console:

```python
if payload.get_content_type() == "text/html":
    outfile = os.path.basename(args.EML_FILE.name) + ".html"
    open(outfile, 'w').write(body)
elif payload.get_content_type().startswith('application'):
    outfile = open(payload.get_filename(), 'wb')
    body = base64.b64decode(payload.get_payload())
    outfile.write(body)
    outfile.close()
    print("Exported: {}\n".format(outfile.name))
else:
    print(body)
```

When we execute this code, we see the header information first printed to the console, followed by the various payloads. In this case, we have a `text/plain` MIME content first, containing a sample message, followed by an `application/vnd.ms-excel` attachment that we export, and another `text/plain` block showing the initial message:

```
Body

text/plain
==========
Hey Jim!

Yeah that looks similar to what I was looking at. Mine is a bit messier, but take
 a look and see what you think. I may have taken a couple of people from another
branch though… oops :D But I am fine with either, or a combo of the two, whatever
 works, just let me know!

~Michael

--Apple-Mail=_98E394A0-9A23-4009-907D-0E9D4469CD04
Content-Disposition: attachment;
        filename=Scranton-Master-1.xls
Content-Type: application/vnd.ms-excel;
        name="Scranton-Master-1.xls"
Content-Transfer-Encoding: base64

0M8R4KGxGuEAAAAAAAAAAAAAAAAAAAAAPgADAP7/CQAGAAAAAAAAAAAAAAABAAAAAQAAAAAAAAAA
EAAAXQAAAAEAAAD+////AAAAAAAAD////////////////////////////////////////////////
////////////////////////////////////////////////////////////////////////////
```

```
text/plain
==========

On Jun 18, 2012, at 10:26 AM, Jim Halpert wrote:

> Hi Michael!
> Here's my master for Scranton... don't know if you have any thoughts because I
can certainly switch it up. Just need to know soon so I can get next weeks schedu
le done. I have a couple of your guys (Stanley and Andy spring to mind) up at Buf
falo as well...
> --Jim
> <Master Schedule.xls>
```

Viewing MSG files

Recipe Difficulty: Easy

Python Version: 2.7 or 3.5

Operating System: Windows

Email messages can come in many different formats. The MSG format is another popular container for storing message content and attachments. In this example, we will learn to parse MSG files using the Outlook API.

Getting started

This recipe requires the installation of the third-party library `pywin32`. This means the script will only be compatible on Windows systems. We will also need to install `pywin32`, as we did in `Chapter 1`, *Essential Scripting and File Information Recipes*.

To install `pywin32`, we need to access its SourceForge page at `https://sourceforge.net/ projects/pywin32/` and download the version that matches your Python installation. To check our Python version, we can import the `sys` module and call `sys.version` within an interpreter. Both the version and the architecture are important when selecting the correct `pywin32` installer. We also want to confirm we have a valid installation of Outlook that has been setup on our machine, as the `pywin32` bindings rely on resources provided by Outlook. We are ready to create the script after running the `pywin32` installer.

How to do it...

To create an MSG parser, we must:

1. Accept an argument for an MSG file.
2. Print general metadata about the MSG file to the console.
3. Print recipient-specific metadata to the console.
4. Export the message content to an output file.
5. Export any attachments embedded within the message to appropriate output files.

How it works...

We begin by importing libraries for argument handling, `argparse` and `os`, followed by the `win32com` library from `pywin32`. We also import the `pywintypes` library to properly catch and handle `pywin32` errors:

```
from __future__ import print_function
from argparse import ArgumentParser
import os
import win32com.client
import pywintypes
```

This recipe's command-line handler accepts two positional arguments, `MSG_FILE` and `OUTPUT_DIR`, which represent the path to the MSG file to process and the desired output folder, respectively. We check if the desired output folder exists and create it if it does not. Afterwards, we pass the two inputs to the `main()` function:

```
if __name__ == '__main__':
    parser = ArgumentParser(
        description=__description__,
        epilog="Developed by {} on {}".format(
            ", ".join(__authors__), __date__)
    )
    parser.add_argument("MSG_FILE", help="Path to MSG file")
    parser.add_argument("OUTPUT_DIR", help="Path to output folder")
    args = parser.parse_args()
    out_dir = args.OUTPUT_DIR
    if not os.path.exists(out_dir):
        os.makedirs(out_dir)
    main(args.MSG_FILE, args.OUTPUT_DIR)
```

In the `main()` function we call the `win32com` library to set up the Outlook API configuring it in such a way that allows access to the `MAPI` namespace. Using this `mapi` variable, we can open an `MSG` file with the `OpenSharedItem()` method and create an object we will use for the other functions in this recipe. These functions include: `display_msg_attribs()`, `display_msg_recipients()`, `extract_msg_body()`, and `extract_attachments()`. Let's now turn our attention to each of these functions, in turn, to see how they work:

```
def main(msg_file, output_dir):
    mapi = win32com.client.Dispatch(
        "Outlook.Application").GetNamespace("MAPI")
    msg = mapi.OpenSharedItem(os.path.abspath(args.MSG_FILE))
    display_msg_attribs(msg)
    display_msg_recipients(msg)
    extract_msg_body(msg, output_dir)
    extract_attachments(msg, output_dir)
```

The `display_msg_attribs()` function allows us to display the various attributes of a message (subject, to, BCC, size, and so on). Some of these attributes may not be present in the message we are parsing, however, we attempt to export all values regardless. The `attribs` list shows, in order, the attributes we try to access from the message. As we iterate through each attribute, we use the built-in `getattr()` method on the `msg` object and attempt to extract the relevant value, if present, and `"N/A"` if not. We then print the attribute and its determined value to the console. As a word of caution, some of these values may be present but only set to a default value, such as the year `4501` for some dates:

```
def display_msg_attribs(msg):
    # Display Message Attributes
    attribs = [
        'Application', 'AutoForwarded', 'BCC', 'CC', 'Class',
        'ConversationID', 'ConversationTopic', 'CreationTime',
        'ExpiryTime', 'Importance', 'InternetCodePage', 'IsMarkedAsTask',
        'LastModificationTime', 'Links', 'OriginalDeliveryReportRequested',
        'ReadReceiptRequested', 'ReceivedTime', 'ReminderSet',
        'ReminderTime', 'ReplyRecipientNames', 'Saved', 'Sender',
        'SenderEmailAddress', 'SenderEmailType', 'SenderName', 'Sent',
        'SentOn', 'SentOnBehalfOfName', 'Size', 'Subject',
        'TaskCompletedDate', 'TaskDueDate', 'To', 'UnRead'
    ]
    print("\nMessage Attributes")
    print("==================")
    for entry in attribs:
        print("{}: {}".format(entry, getattr(msg, entry, 'N/A')))
```

The `display_msg_recipients()` function iterates through the message and displays recipient details. The `msg` object provides a `Recipients()` method, which accepts an integer argument to access recipients by index. Using a `while` loop, we try to load and display values for available recipients. For each recipient found, as in the prior function, we use of `getattr()` method with a list of attributes, called `recipient_attrib`, to extract and print the relevant values or, if they are not present, assign them the value `"N/A"`. Though most Python iterables use zero as the first index, the `Recipients()` method starts at `1`. For this reason, the variable `i` will start at `1` and be incremented until no further recipients are found. We will continue to try and read these values until we receive a `pywin32` error:

```
def display_msg_recipients(msg):
    # Display Recipient Information
    recipient_attrib = [
        'Address', 'AutoResponse', 'Name', 'Resolved', 'Sendable'
    ]
    i = 1
    while True:
```

```
try:
    recipient = msg.Recipients(i)
except pywintypes.com_error:
    break

print("\nRecipient {}".format(i))
print("=" * 15)
for entry in recipient_attrib:
    print("{}: {}".format(entry, getattr(recipient, entry, 'N/A')))
i += 1
```

The `extract_msg_body()` function is designed to extract the body content from the message. The `msg` object exposes the body content in a few different formats; in this recipe, we will export the HTML, using the `HTMLBody()` method, and plaintext, using the `Body()` method, versions of the body. Since these objects are byte strings, we must first decode them, which we do with the `cp1252` code page. With the decoded content, we open the output file for writing, in the user-specified directory, and create the respective `*.body.html` and `*.body.txt` files:

```
def extract_msg_body(msg, out_dir):
    # Extract HTML Data
    html_data = msg.HTMLBody.encode('cp1252')
    outfile = os.path.join(out_dir, os.path.basename(args.MSG_FILE))
    open(outfile + ".body.html", 'wb').write(html_data)
    print("Exported: {}".format(outfile + ".body.html"))

    # Extract plain text
    body_data = msg.Body.encode('cp1252')
    open(outfile + ".body.txt", 'wb').write(body_data)
    print("Exported: {}".format(outfile + ".body.txt"))
```

Lastly, the `extract_attachments()` function exports attachment data from the MSG file to the desired output directory. Using the `msg` object, we again create a list, `attachment_attribs`, representing a series of attributes about an attachment. Similar to the recipient function, we use a `while` loop and the `Attachments()` method, which accepts an integer as an argument to select an attachment by index, to iterate through each attachment. As we saw before with the `Recipients()` method, the `Attachments()` method starts its index at 1. For this reason, the variable `i` will start at 1 and be incremented until no further attachments are found:

```
def extract_attachments(msg, out_dir):
    attachment_attribs = [
        'DisplayName', 'FileName', 'PathName', 'Position', 'Size'
    ]
    i = 1 # Attachments start at 1
    while True:
```

```
try:
    attachment = msg.Attachments(i)
except pywintypes.com_error:
    break
```

For each attachment, we print its attributes to the console. The attributes we extract and print are defined in the `attachment_attrib` list at the beginning of this function. After printing available attachment details, we write its content using the `SaveAsFile()` method and supplying it with a string containing the output path and desired name of the output attachment (which is obtained using the `FileName` attribute). After this, we are ready to move onto the next attachment and so we increment variable `i` and try to access the next attachment.

```
print("\nAttachment {}".format(i))
print("=" * 15)
for entry in attachment_attribs:
    print('{}: {}'.format(entry, getattr(attachment, entry,
                                         "N/A")))
outfile = os.path.join(os.path.abspath(out_dir),
                       os.path.split(args.MSG_FILE)[-1])
if not os.path.exists(outfile):
    os.makedirs(outfile)
outfile = os.path.join(outfile, attachment.FileName)
attachment.SaveAsFile(outfile)
print("Exported: {}".format(outfile))
i += 1
```

When we execute this code, we see the following output, along with several files in the output directory. This includes the body as text and HTML, along with any discovered attachments. The attributes of the message and its attachments are displayed in the console window.

```
Message Attributes
==================
Application: Outlook
AutoForwarded: False
BCC:
CC:
Class: 43
ConversationID:
ConversationTopic: Quick Tips for the UBSWE migration
CreationTime: 2017-05-31 21:10:59+00:00
ExpiryTime: 4501-01-01 00:00:00+00:00
Importance: 0
InternetCodePage: 28591
IsMarkedAsTask: False
LastModificationTime: 2017-05-31 21:10:59+00:00
Links: None
OriginalDeliveryReportRequested: N/A
ReadReceiptRequested: False
ReceivedTime: 2002-02-05 21:40:23+00:00
ReminderSet: False
ReminderTime: 4501-01-01 00:00:00+00:00
ReplyRecipientNames:
Saved: True
Sender: mbx_ubswGlobalInf@ENRON.com
SenderEmailAddress: mbx_ubswGlobalInf@ENRON.com
SenderEmailType: SMTP
SenderName: UBSW Energy Global Infrastructure
Sent: True
SentOn: 2002-02-05 21:40:23+00:00
SentOnBehalfOfName: UBSW Energy Global Infrastructure
Size: 0
Subject: Quick Tips for the UBSWE migration
TaskCompletedDate: 4501-01-01 00:00:00+00:00
TaskDueDate: 4501-01-01 00:00:00+00:00
To: DL-UBSW Energy Canada; DL-UBSW Energy Houston
UnRead: False

Recipient 1
===============
Address: DL-UBSWEnergyCanada@ENRON.com
AutoResponse:
Name: DL-UBSW Energy Canada
Resolved: True
Sendable: True
Recipient 2
===============
Address: DL-UBSW Energy Houston
AutoResponse:
Name: DL-UBSW Energy Houston
Resolved: True
Sendable: True
Exported: MSG_Output\Quick Tips for the UBSWE migration.msg.body.html
Exported: MSG_Output\Quick Tips for the UBSWE migration.msg.body.txt
```

There's more...

This script can be further improved. We have provided one or more recommendations as follows:

- Consider adding more fields to the parser by referencing the properties of an MSG object on MSDN at `https://msdn.microsoft.com/en-us/library/microsoft.office.interop.outlook.mailitem_properties.aspx`

See also

Other libraries for accessing MSG files exist, including the `Redemption` library. This library provides handlers to access header information, along with many of the same attributes shown in this example.

Ordering Takeout

Recipe Difficulty: Easy

Python Version: N/A

Operating System: Any

Google Mail, popularly known as Gmail, is one of the more widely-used webmail services. Gmail accounts not only function as email addresses, but a gateway into the slew of other services that Google offers. In addition to providing access to mail through the web or **Internet Message Access Protocol** (**IMAP**) and **Post Office Protocol** (**POP**) mail protocols, Google has developed a system for the archival and acquisition of mail and other associated data stored in a Gmail account.

Getting started

This recipe, believe it or not, actually does not involve any Python and instead requires a browser and access to a Google account instead. The purpose of this recipe is to acquire the Google account mailbox in the MBOX format which we parse in the next recipe.

How to do it...

To initiate a Google Takeout, we follow these steps:

1. Login to the Google account in question.
2. Navigate to account settings and the Create Archive feature.
3. Select desired Google products to archive and begin the process.
4. Download the archived data.

How it works...

We start the Google Takeout process by logging into the account and selecting the **My Account** option. We can also navigate to `https://myaccount.google.com` if the **My Account** option is not present:

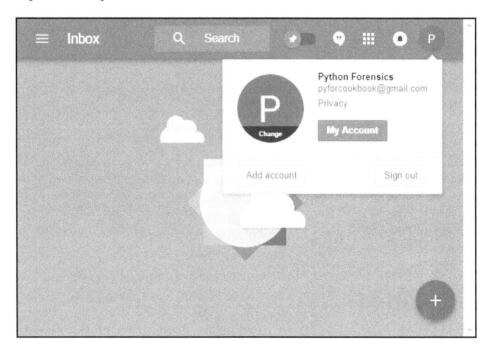

On the **My Account** dashboard, we select the **Control your content** link under the **Personal info & privacy** section:

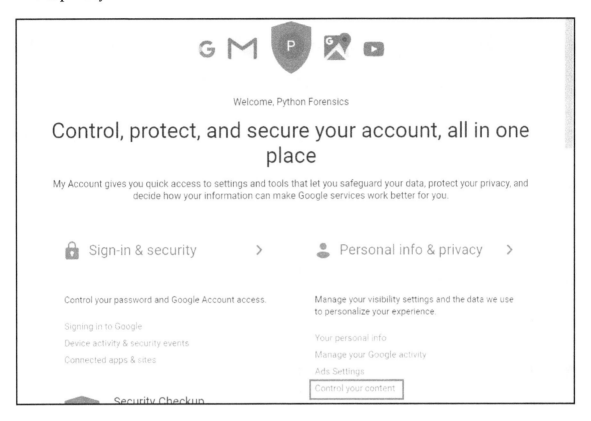

Within the **Control your content** section, we are presented with an option to **CREATE ARCHIVE**. This is where we start the Google Takeout collection:

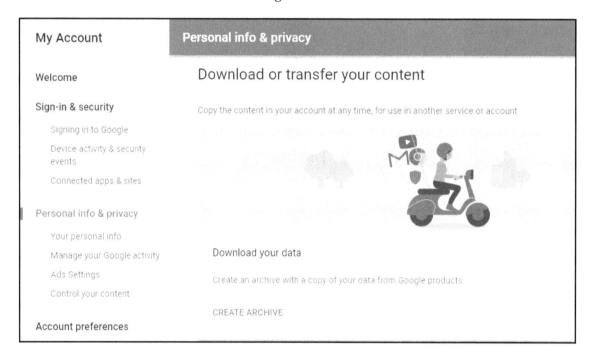

When selecting this option, we are presented with an option to manage existing archives or generate a new one. When generating a new one, we are presented with check boxes for each Google product we wish to include. Drop-down arrows provide sub-menus altering the export format or content. For example, we can choose how Google Drive Documents are exported as Microsoft Word, PDF, or plaintext formats. In this instance, we will leave the options as defaults, ensuring the Mail option is set to collect **All mail**:

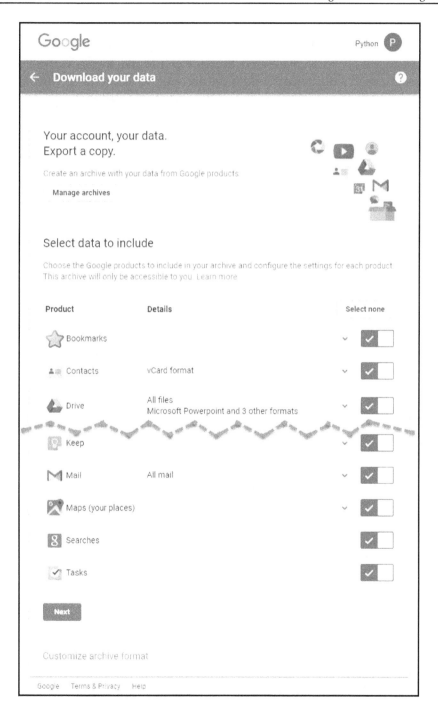

With the desired content selected, we can configure the format of the archive. Google Takeout allows us to select both an archive file type and a maximum segment size for ease of download and access. We can also select how we would like to access the Takeout. This option can be set to send a download link to the account being archived (the default option) or upload the archive to the account's Google Drive or other third-party cloud services, which may modify more information than necessary to preserve this data. We elect to receive the email and then select **Create archive** to start the process!

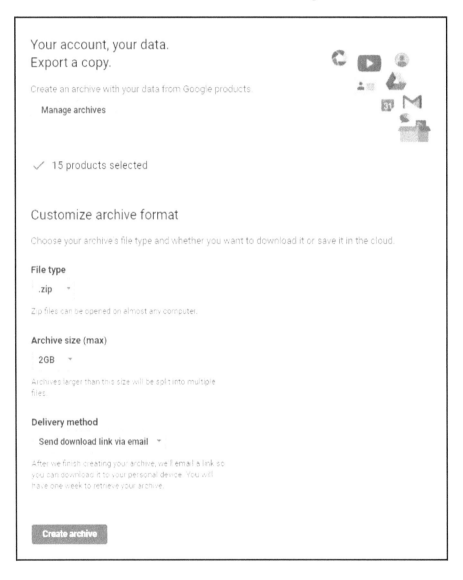

And now we must wait. Depending on the size of the data being preserved this can take a considerable amount of time, as Google has to gather, convert, and compress all of the data for you.

When you receive the notification email, select the provided link to download the archive. This archive is only available for a limited time, so it is important to collect it as soon as you are notified.

After downloading the data, extract the archive's contents and look at the internal folder structure and provided data. Each of the products selected is given a folder containing the relevant content or folder structure for the product. In this instance, we are most interested in mail, provided in the MBOX format. In the next recipe, we will show how to parse this MBOX data using Python.

There's more...

If you prefer a more direct route for this acquisition, you can navigate to `https://takeout.google.com/settings/takeout` after logging into the account. From here you can choose the products for export.

What's in the box?!

Recipe Difficulty: Medium

Python Version: 3.5

Operating System: Any

MBOX files are often found in association with UNIX systems, Thunderbird, and Google Takeouts. These MBOX containers are text files with special formatting that split messages stored within. Since there are several formats for structuring MBOX files, our script will focus on those from Google Takeout, using the output from the prior recipe.

Getting started

All libraries used in this script are present in Python's standard library. We use the built-in `mailbox` library to parse the Google Takeout structured MBOX file.

 To learn more about the `mailbox` library, visit `https://docs.python.org/3/library/mailbox.html`.

How to do it...

To implement this script, we must:

1. Design arguments to accept a file path to the MBOX file and an output the report its contents.
2. Develop a custom MBOX reader that handles encoded data.
3. Extract message metadata including attachment names.
4. Write attachments to the output directory.
5. Create an MBOX metadata report.

How it works...

We start by importing libraries for argument handling, followed by the `os`, `time`, and `csv` libraries required for creating the script's output. Next, we import the `mailbox` library to parse the MBOX message format and `base64` to decode binary data in attachments. Lastly, we bring in the `tqdm` library to provide a progress bar related to the message parsing status:

```
from __future__ import print_function
from argparse import ArgumentParser
import mailbox
import os
import time
import csv
from tqdm import tqdm
import base64
```

This recipe's command-line handler accepts two positional arguments, MBOX and OUTPUT_DIR, which represent the path to the MBOX file to process and the desired output folder, respectively. Both of these arguments are passed to the main() function to kick off the script:

```
if __name__ == '__main__':
    parser = ArgumentParser(
        description=__description__,
        epilog="Developed by {} on {}".format(
            ", ".join(__authors__), __date__)
    )
    parser.add_argument("MBOX", help="Path to mbox file")
    parser.add_argument("OUTPUT_DIR",
                        help="Path to output directory to write report "
                        "and exported content")
    args = parser.parse_args()

    main(args.MBOX, args.OUTPUT_DIR)
```

The main() function starts with a call to the mailbox library's mbox class. Using this class, we can parse a MBOX file by providing the path to the file and an optional argument for the factory, which in our case, is a custom reader function. Using this library, we now have an iterable object containing message objects we can interact with. We use the built-in len() method to print the number of messages contained within the MBOX file. Let's first look at how the custom_reader() function works:

```
def main(mbox_file, output_dir):
    # Read in the MBOX File
    print("Reading mbox file...")
    mbox = mailbox.mbox(mbox_file, factory=custom_reader)
    print("{} messages to parse".format(len(mbox)))
```

This recipe requires a number of functions to function (see what we did there...), but the custom_reader() method is a bit different than the others. This function is a reader method for the mailbox library. We need to create this function due to the fact that the default reader does not handle encoding such as cp1252. We can add other encodings into this reader, though ASCII and cp1252 are the two most common encodings for MBOX files.

After using the `read()` method on the input data stream, it tries to decode the data using the ASCII codepage. If this is unsuccessful, it instead relies on the `cp1252` codepage to get the job done. Any errors that are encountered when decoding with the `cp1252` codepage are replaced by the replacement character U+FFFD by supplying the `decode()` method with the `errors` keyword setting it to `"replace"`. We use the `mailbox.mboxMessage()` function to return the decoded content in the appropriate format:

```
def custom_reader(data_stream):
    data = data_stream.read()
    try:
        content = data.decode("ascii")
    except (UnicodeDecodeError, UnicodeEncodeError) as e:
        content = data.decode("cp1252", errors="replace")
    return mailbox.mboxMessage(content)
```

Back in the `main()` function, we prepare a few variables before we begin processing the messages. Namely, we set up the `parsed_data` results list, create an output directory for attachments, and define the `columns` for the MBOX metadata report. These columns will also be used to extract information from the message using the `get()` method. Two of these columns will not extract information from the message object and, instead, will contain data we assign after processing attachments. For consistency, we will keep these values in the `columns` list, as they will default to an `"N/A"` value anyways:

```
parsed_data = []
attachments_dir = os.path.join(output_dir, "attachments")
if not os.path.exists(attachments_dir):
    os.makedirs(attachments_dir)
columns = ["Date", "From", "To", "Subject", "X-Gmail-Labels",
          "Return-Path", "Received", "Content-Type", "Message-ID",
          "X-GM-THRID", "num_attachments_exported", "export_path"]
```

As we begin to iterate through the messages, we implement a `tqdm` progress bar to track the iteration process. Since the `mbox` object has a length property, we do not need to provide any additional arguments to `tqdm`. Inside of the loop, we define the `msg_data` dictionary to store message results and then try to assign message properties through a second `for` loop using the `get()` method to query for `columns` keys in the `header_data` dictionary:

```
for message in tqdm(mbox):
    # Preserve header information
    msg_data = dict()
    header_data = dict(message._headers)
    for hdr in columns:
        msg_data[hdr] = header_data.get(hdr, "N/A")
```

Next, in an `if` statement, we check if the `message` has a payload and, if it does, we use the `write_payload()` method supplying it the `message` object and the output attachments directory as its inputs. If no payloads exist for the `message`, the two attachment-related columns will remain with the default `"N/A"` values. Otherwise, we count the number of attachments found and join a list of their paths together into a comma-separated list:

```
if len(message.get_payload()):
    export_path = write_payload(message, attachments_dir)
    msg_data['num_attachments_exported'] = len(export_path)
    msg_data['export_path'] = ", ".join(export_path)
```

After each message is processed, its data is appended to the `parsed_data` list. After every message has been processed, the `create_report()` method is called and passed the `parsed_data` list and the desired output CSV name. Let's backtrack a bit and look at the `write_payload()` method first:

```
parsed_data.append(msg_data)

# Create CSV report
create_report(
    parsed_data, os.path.join(output_dir, "mbox_report.csv"), columns
)
```

Since messages can have a wide variety of payloads, we need to craft a dedicated function to handle the various MIME types. The `write_payload()` method is such a function. This function begins by extracting the payload with the `get_payload()` method and performing a quick check to see if the payload content consists of multiple parts. If it does, we call this function recursively to handle each subsection, by iterating through the payloads and appending the output to the `export_path` variable:

```
def write_payload(msg, out_dir):
    pyld = msg.get_payload()
    export_path = []
    if msg.is_multipart():
        for entry in pyld:
            export_path += write_payload(entry, out_dir)
```

If the payload is not multi-part, we determine its MIME type using the `get_content_type()` method and creating logic to handle the data source appropriately by category. Data types, including application, image, and video, are generally represented as `base64`-encoded data, allowing binary information to be transmitted as ASCII characters. For this reason, the majority of the formats, including some within the text category, require us to decode the data before providing it for writing. In other instances, the data already exists as a string and can be written as-is to the file. Regardless, the method is generally the same, the data is decoded (if necessary) and its contents are written to the filesystem using the `export_content()` method. Lastly, a string representing the path to the exported item is appended to the `export_path` list:

```
else:
    content_type = msg.get_content_type()
    if "application/" in content_type.lower():
        content = base64.b64decode(msg.get_payload())
        export_path.append(export_content(msg, out_dir, content))
    elif "image/" in content_type.lower():
        content = base64.b64decode(msg.get_payload())
        export_path.append(export_content(msg, out_dir, content))
    elif "video/" in content_type.lower():
        content = base64.b64decode(msg.get_payload())
        export_path.append(export_content(msg, out_dir, content))
    elif "audio/" in content_type.lower():
        content = base64.b64decode(msg.get_payload())
        export_path.append(export_content(msg, out_dir, content))
    elif "text/csv" in content_type.lower():
        content = base64.b64decode(msg.get_payload())
        export_path.append(export_content(msg, out_dir, content))
    elif "info/" in content_type.lower():
        export_path.append(export_content(msg, out_dir,
                                        msg.get_payload()))
    elif "text/calendar" in content_type.lower():
        export_path.append(export_content(msg, out_dir,
                                        msg.get_payload()))
    elif "text/rtf" in content_type.lower():
        export_path.append(export_content(msg, out_dir,
                                        msg.get_payload()))
```

The `else` statement adds an additional `if-elif` statement to the payload to determine if the export contains a filename. If it does, we treat it as the others, however, if it does not, it is likely a message body stored as HTML or text. While we could export each message body by modifying this section, it would generate a large amount of data for this example and so we choose not to. Once we have finished exporting data from the message, we return the list of paths for the data exported to the `main()` function:

```
    else:
        if "name=" in msg.get('Content-Disposition', "N/A"):
            content = base64.b64decode(msg.get_payload())
            export_path.append(export_content(msg, out_dir, content))
        elif "name=" in msg.get('Content-Type', "N/A"):
            content = base64.b64decode(msg.get_payload())
            export_path.append(export_content(msg, out_dir, content))

    return export_path
```

The `export_content()` function starts by calling the `get_filename()` function, a method that extracts the filename from the `msg` object. Additional processing is performed on the filename to extract an extension, if present, though the generic `.FILE` extension is used if none is found:

```
def export_content(msg, out_dir, content_data):
    file_name = get_filename(msg)
    file_ext = "FILE"
    if "." in file_name:
        file_ext = file_name.rsplit(".", 1)[-1]
```

Next, we perform additional formatting to create a unique filename by integrating the time, represented as a Unix time integer, followed by the determined file extension. This filename is then joined to the output directory to form a full path for writing the output. This unique filename ensures that we do not mistakenly overwrite already present attachments in the output directory:

```
    file_name = "{}_{:.4f}.{}".format(
        file_name.rsplit(".", 1)[0], time.time(), file_ext)
    file_name = os.path.join(out_dir, file_name)
```

The last segment of code in this function handles the actual export of file content. This `if` statement handles the different file modes (`"w"` or `"wb"`), based on the source type. After writing the data, we return the file path used in the export. This path will be added to our metadata report:

```
if isinstance(content_data, str):
    open(file_name, 'w').write(content_data)
else:
    open(file_name, 'wb').write(content_data)

return file_name
```

The next function, `get_filename()`, extracts filenames from the message to accurately represent the names of these files. The filenames can be found within the `"Content-Disposition"` or `"Content-Type"` properties and are generally found prepended with a `"name="` or `"filename="` string. For both properties, the logic is largely the same. The function first replaces any newline characters with one space and then splits the string on a semicolon and space. This delimiter generally separates the values within these properties. Using list comprehension, we identify which element contains a `name=` substring and use that as the filename:

```
def get_filename(msg):
    if 'name=' in msg.get("Content-Disposition", "N/A"):
        fname_data = msg["Content-Disposition"].replace("\r\n", " ")
        fname = [x for x in fname_data.split("; ") if 'name=' in x]
        file_name = fname[0].split("=", 1)[-1]

    elif 'name=' in msg.get("Content-Type", "N/A"):
        fname_data = msg["Content-Type"].replace("\r\n", " ")
        fname = [x for x in fname_data.split("; ") if 'name=' in x]
        file_name = fname[0].split("=", 1)[-1]
```

If the two content properties are empty, we assign a generic `NO_FILENAME` and continue preparing the filename. After we extract the potential filename, we remove any characters that are not alphanumeric, a space, or a period to prevent errors with writing the file to the system. With our filesystem-safe filename ready, we return it for use in the previously discussed `export_content()` method:

```
    else:
        file_name = "NO_FILENAME"

    fchars = [x for x in file_name if x.isalnum() or x.isspace() or
            x == "."]
    return "".join(fchars)
```

Lastly, we have reached the point where we are ready to discuss the CSV metadata report. The `create_report()` function, is similar to what we have seen variations of throughout this book, it creates a CSV report from a list of dictionaries using the `DictWriter` class. Tada!

```
def create_report(output_data, output_file, columns):
    with open(output_file, 'w', newline="") as outfile:
        csvfile = csv.DictWriter(outfile, columns)
        csvfile.writeheader()
        csvfile.writerows(output_data)
```

This script creates a CSV report and directory full of attachments. The first screenshot shows the first few columns and rows of the CSV report and how the data is displayed to the user:

Date	From	To	Subject	X-Gmail-Labels
Fri, 01 Jun 2012 14:15:34 +0000	example@gmail.com	pyfordev@gmail.com	Analytics For Your Website 201205 (Site Hits)	Important,Sent,AOL_Mail,AOL-mail
Fri, 10 Jun 2011 09:16:35 -0400 (EDT)	example@aol.com	pyfordev@gmail.com	Fwd: Please check this out and save to your H drive	Important,Sent
Fri, 01 Apr 2011 22:05:52 +0000	example@gmail.com	pyfordev@gmail.com	Analytics For Your Website 201103 (Site Hits)	Sent,AOL_Mail,AOL-mail

This second screenshot displays the last few columns of these same rows and reflects how attachment information is reported. These file paths can be followed to access the corresponding attachments:

Content-Type	Message-ID	X-GM-THRID	num_attachments_exported	export_path
multipart/mixed	14dae93412727034cf04c169d14e@google.com	1403582031247190000	1	output_folder\attachments\Analyticswww.example.com201205SiteHits_1496830769.7924.pdf
multipart/mixed	N/A	1371245213549610000	1	output_folder\attachments\CASH_FLOW_1496830270.0917.xlsx
multipart/mixed	000e0cd35695858e2d140fe29d09@google.com	1365026716022730000	1	output_folder\attachments\Analyticswww.example.com201103SiteHits_1496830774.7371.pdf

Parsing PST and OST mailboxes

Recipe Difficulty: Hard

Python Version: 2.7

Operating System: Linux

The **Personal Storage Table** (**PST**) file is commonly found on many systems and provides access to archived email. These files, generally associated with the Outlook application, contain message and attachment data. These files are commonly found in the corporate setting, as many business environments continue to leverage Outlook for internal and external email management.

Getting started

This recipe requires the installation of the `libpff`, and its Python bindings, `pypff`, to function. Available on GitHub, this library provides tools, and Python bindings, to handle and extract data from PST files. We will set up this library in Ubuntu 16.04 with bindings for Python 2 for ease of development. This library can be built for Python 3 as well, though we will use the Python 2 bindings for this section.

We must install a number of dependencies before installing the required library. Using the Ubuntu `apt` package manager, we will install the following eight packages. You may want to keep this Ubuntu environment handy as we will use it extensively Chapter 8, *Working with Forensic Evidence Container Recipes* and onwards:

```
sudo apt-get install automake autoconf libtool pkg-config autopoint git python-dev
```

With the dependencies installed, navigate to the GitHub repository and download the desired release for the library. This recipe was developed using the `libpff-experimental-20161119` release of the `pypff` library. Next, once the contents of the release are extracted, open a terminal and navigate to the extracted directory and execute the following commands for the release:

```
./synclibs.sh
./autogen.sh
sudo python setup.py install
```

 To learn more about the `pypff` library, visit `https://github.com/libyal/libpff`.

Lastly, we can check the library installation by opening a Python interpreter, importing `pypff`, and running the `pypff.get_version()` method to ensure we have the correct release version.

How to do it...

We extract PST message content following these steps:

1. Create a handle for the PST file using `pypff`.
2. Iterate through all folders and messages within the PST.

3. Store relevant metadata for each message.
4. Create a metadata report based on the contents of the PST.

How it works...

This script begins by importing libraries for argument handling, writing spreadsheets, performing regular expression searches, and processing PST files:

```
from __future__ import print_function
from argparse import ArgumentParser
import csv
import pypff
import re
```

This recipe's command-line handler accepts two positional arguments, PFF_FILE and CSV_REPORT, which represent the path to the PST file to process and the desired output CSV path, respectively. We forego a main() function in this recipe and immediately begin by using the pypff.file() object to instantiate the pff_obj variable. Following that, we use the open() method and attempt to access the user-supplied PST. We pass this PST to the process_folders() method and store the returned list of dictionaries in the parsed_data variable. After using the close() method on the pff_obj variable, we write the PST metadata report using the write_data() function by passing it the desired output CSV path and processed data dictionary:

```
if __name__ == '__main__':
    parser = ArgumentParser(
        description=__description__,
        epilog="Developed by {} on {}".format(
            ", ".join(__authors__), __date__)
    )
    parser.add_argument("PFF_FILE", help="Path to PST or OST File")
    parser.add_argument("CSV_REPORT", help="Path to CSV report location")
    args = parser.parse_args()

    # Open file
    pff_obj = pypff.file()
    pff_obj.open(args.PFF_FILE)

    # Parse and close file
    parsed_data = process_folders(pff_obj.root_folder)
    pff_obj.close()

    # Write CSV report
    write_data(args.CSV_REPORT, parsed_data)
```

This recipe consists of several functions that handle different elements of the PST file. The `process_folders()` function handles the folder processing and iteration. As we process these folders, we print their names, the number of subfolders, and the number of messages within that folder to the console. This can be accomplished by calling the `number_of_sub_folders` and `number_of_sub_messages` attributes on the `pff_folder` object:

```
def process_folders(pff_folder):
    folder_name = pff_folder.name if pff_folder.name else "N/A"
    print("Folder: {} (sub-dir: {}/sub-msg: {})".format(folder_name,
        pff_folder.number_of_sub_folders,
        pff_folder.number_of_sub_messages))
```

Following these print messages, we setup up the `data_list` which is responsible for storing processed message data. As we iterate through the messages within the folder, we call the `process_message()` method to create the dictionary object with the processed message data. Immediately afterward, we add the folder name to the dictionary before appending it to the list of results.

The second loop iterates through subfolders, recursively calling the `process_folders()` function and passing it the subfolder to process and appending the resulting list of dictionaries to the `data_list`. This allows us to walk through the PST and extract all of the data before we return the `data_list` and write the CSV report:

```
# Process messages within a folder
data_list = []
for msg in pff_folder.sub_messages:
    data_dict = process_message(msg)
    data_dict['folder'] = folder_name
    data_list.append(data_dict)

# Process folders within a folder
for folder in pff_folder.sub_folders:
    data_list += process_folders(folder)

return data_list
```

The `process_message()` function is responsible for accessing the various attributes of the message, including the email header information. As seen in previous recipes, we use a list of object attributes to build a dictionary of results. We then iterate through the `attribs` dictionary and, using the `getattr()` method, append the appropriate key-value pairs to the `data_dict` dictionary. Lastly, if email headers are present, which we determine by using the `transport_headers` attribute, we update the `data_dict` dictionary with additional values extracted from the `process_headers()` function:

```
def process_message(msg):
    # Extract attributes
    attribs = ['conversation_topic', 'number_of_attachments',
                'sender_name', 'subject']
    data_dict = {}
    for attrib in attribs:
        data_dict[attrib] = getattr(msg, attrib, "N/A")

    if msg.transport_headers is not None:
        data_dict.update(process_headers(msg.transport_headers))

    return data_dict
```

The `process_headers()` function ultimately returns a dictionary containing extracted email header data. This data is displayed as key-value pairs, delimited by a colon and space. Since content within a header may be stored on a new line, we use regular expression to check that there is a key at the start of the line followed by a value. If we do not find a key matching the pattern (any number of letters or a dash character followed by a colon), we will append the new value to the prior key, as the header displays information in a sequential fashion. At the end of this function, we have some specific lines of code, using `isinstance()`, to handle the dictionary value assignments. This code checks the key type to ensure that values are assigned to keys in a manner that will not overwrite any data already associated with a given key:

```
def process_headers(header):
    # Read and process header information
    key_pattern = re.compile("^([A-Za-z\-]+:)(.*)$")
    header_data = {}
    for line in header.split("\r\n"):
        if len(line) == 0:
            continue

        reg_result = key_pattern.match(line)
        if reg_result:
            key = reg_result.group(1).strip(":").strip()
            value = reg_result.group(2).strip()
        else:
```

```
                    value = line

            if key.lower() in header_data:
                if isinstance(header_data[key.lower()], list):
                    header_data[key.lower()].append(value)
                else:
                    header_data[key.lower()] = [header_data[key.lower()],
                                                value]
            else:
                header_data[key.lower()] = value
        return header_data
```

Lastly, the `write_data()` method is responsible for creating the metadata report. Since we may have a great number column names from the email header parsing, we iterate through the data and extract distinct column names if they are not already defined in the list. Using this method, we ensure that dynamic information from the PST is not excluded. In the `for` loop, we are also reassigning values from `data_list` into `formatted_data_list`, primarily to convert list values into a string to more easily write the data to the spreadsheet. The `csv` library does a nice job ensuring that commas within a cell are escaped and handled appropriately by our spreadsheet application:

```
def write_data(outfile, data_list):
    # Build out additional columns
    print("Writing Report: ", outfile)
    columns = ['folder', 'conversation_topic', 'number_of_attachments',
               'sender_name', 'subject']
    formatted_data_list = []
    for entry in data_list:
        tmp_entry = {}

        for k, v in entry.items():
            if k not in columns:
                columns.append(k)

            if isinstance(v, list):
                tmp_entry[k] = ", ".join(v)
            else:
                tmp_entry[k] = v
        formatted_data_list.append(tmp_entry)
```

Using the `csv.DictWriter` class, we open the file, write the header, and each of the rows to the output file:

```
    # Write CSV report
    with open(outfile, 'wb') as openfile:
        csvfile = csv.DictWriter(openfile, columns)
        csvfile.writeheader()
```

```
csvfile.writerows(formatted_data_list)
```

When this script runs, a CSV report is generated which should look similar to the one shown as shown in the following screenshot. While scrolling horizontally, we can see the columns specified at the top in the header row; especially with the email header columns, the majority of these columns only containing a handful of values. As you run this code against more email containers in your environment, make note of the columns that are most useful and commonly found in the PSTs you process to expedite analysis:

folder	conversation_topic	number_of_attachments	sender_name	subject
Sent Items	FW: Laid-Off A No Nothing Production	0	Meyers	FW: FW: Laid-Off A No Nothing Production
Sent Items	EPE Schedules for the past two days	0	Meyers	EPE Schedules for the past two days
Sent Items	How are you doing (plus a little about me)?	0	Meyers	How are you doing (plus a little about me)?
Sent Items	ADS Machine	0	Meyers	ADS Machine
Sent Items	How are you doing (plus a little about me)?	0	Meyers	RE: How are you doing (plus a little about me)?
Sent Items	Breakfast on Tuesday	0	Meyers	Breakfast on Tuesday
Sent Items	epe model for 01/25/02	1	Meyers	epe model for 01/25/02
Sent Items	EPE Schedules for Saturday 02/02/02	0	Meyers	EPE Schedules for Saturday 02/02/02
Sent Items	EPE model for 01/29/02	1	Meyers	EPE model for 01/29/02
Sent Items	Tuesday Morning	0	Meyers	Tuesday Morning
Sent Items	Buffalo Gap	0	Meyers	Buffalo Gap
Sent Items	Trader Assistant	0	Meyers	Trader Assistant
Inbox	Suz, Katie and Kourtney's Housewarming Party	0	Suz Warjone Kourtney Nelson and Katie Sullivan	Suz, Katie and Kourtney's Housewarming Party
Inbox	Profile Error Again	0	Oh John	RE: Profile Error Again

There's more...

This process can be further improved. We have provided one or more recommendations as follows:

- This library also handles **Offline Storage Table** (**OST**) files, which are generally associated with Outlook's offline storage of mail content. Find and test this script on an OST file and, if necessary, modify it to support this other common mail format.

See also

In this instance, we could also leverage the `Redemtion` library for accessing information within Outlook.

7
Log-Based Artifact Recipes

The following recipes are covered in this chapter:

- About time
- Parsing IIS weblogs with RegEx
- Going spelunking
- Interpreting the daily out log
- Adding `daily.out` parsing to Axiom
- Scanning for indicators with YARA

Introduction

These days it is not uncommon to encounter modern systems equipped with some form of event or activity monitoring software. This software may be implemented to assist with security, debugging, or compliance requirements. Whatever the situation, this veritable treasure trove of information can be, and commonly is, leveraged in all types of cyber investigations. A common issue with log analysis can be the huge amount of data one is required to sift through for the subset of interest. Through the recipes in this chapter, we will explore various logs with great evidentiary value and demonstrate ways to quickly process and review them. Specifically, we will cover:

- Converting different timestamp formats (UNIX, FILETIME, and so on) to human-readable formats
- Parsing web server access logs from an IIS platform
- Ingesting, querying, and exporting logs with Splunk's Python API

- Extracting drive usage information from macOS `daily.out` logs
- Executing our `daily.out` log parser from Axiom
- A bonus recipe for identifying files of interest with YARA rules

 Visit `www.packtpub.com/books/content/support` to download the code bundle for this chapter.

About time

Recipe Difficulty: Easy

Python Version: 2.7 or 3.5

Operating System: Any

One important element of any good log file is the timestamp. This value conveys the date and time of the activity or event noted in the log. These date values can come in many formats and may be represented as numbers or hexadecimal values. Outside of logs, different files and artifacts store dates in different manners, even if the data type remains the same. A common differentiating factor is the epoch value, which is the date that the format counts time from. A common epoch is January 1, 1970, though other formats count from January 1, 1601. Another factor that differs between formats is the interval used for counting. While it is common to see formats that count seconds or milliseconds, some formats count blocks of time, such as the number of 100-nanoseconds since the epoch. Because of this, the recipe developed here can take the raw datetime input and provide a formatted timestamp as its output.

Getting started

All libraries used in this script are present in Python's standard library.

How to do it...

To interpret common date formats in Python, we perform the following:

1. Set up arguments to take the raw date value, the source of the date, and the data type.
2. Develop a class that provides a common interface for data across different date formats.
3. Support processing of Unix epoch values and Microsoft `FILETIME` dates.

How it works...

We begin by importing libraries for argument handling and parsing dates. Specifically, we need the `datetime` class from the `datetime` library to read the raw date values and the `timedelta` class to specify timestamp offsets.

```
from __future__ import print_function
from argparse import ArgumentParser, ArgumentDefaultsHelpFormatter
from datetime import datetime as dt
from datetime import timedelta
```

This recipe's command-line handler takes three positional arguments, `date_value`, `source`, and `type`, which represent the date value to process, the source of date value (UNIX, FILETIME, and so on), and the type (integer or hexadecimal value), respectively. We use the choices keyword for the source and type arguments to limit the options the user can supply. Notice, that the source argument uses a custom `get_supported_formats()` function rather than a predefined list of supported date formats. We then take these arguments and initiate an instance of the `ParseDate` class and call the `run()` method to handle the conversion process before printing its `timestamp` attribute to the console.

```
if __name__ == '__main__':
    parser = ArgumentParser(
        description=__description__,
        formatter_class=ArgumentDefaultsHelpFormatter,
        epilog="Developed by {} on {}".format(
            ", ".join(__authors__), __date__)
    )
    parser.add_argument("date_value", help="Raw date value to parse")
    parser.add_argument("source", help="Source format of date",
                        choices=ParseDate.get_supported_formats())
    parser.add_argument("type", help="Data type of input value",
                        choices=('number', 'hex'), default='int')
    args = parser.parse_args()
```

```
date_parser = ParseDate(args.date_value, args.source, args.type)
date_parser.run()
print(date_parser.timestamp)
```

Let's look at how the `ParseDate` class works. By using a class, we can easily extend and implement this code in other scripts. From the command-line arguments, we accept arguments for the date value, date source, and the value type. These values and the output variable, `timestamp`, are defined in the __init__ method:

```
class ParseDate(object):
    def __init__(self, date_value, source, data_type):
        self.date_value = date_value
        self.source = source
        self.data_type = data_type
        self.timestamp = None
```

The `run()` method is the controller, much like the `main()` function of many of our recipes, and selects the correct method to call based on the date source. This allows us to easily extend the class and add new support with ease. In this version, we only support three date types: Unix epoch second, Unix epoch millisecond, and Microsoft's FILETIME. To reduce the number of methods we would need to write, we will design the Unix epoch method to handle both second - and millisecond - formatted timestamps.

```
    def run(self):
        if self.source == 'unix-epoch':
            self.parse_unix_epoch()
        elif self.source == 'unix-epoch-ms':
            self.parse_unix_epoch(True)
        elif self.source == 'windows-filetime':
            self.parse_windows_filetime()
```

To help those wanting to use this library in the future, we add a method for viewing what formats are supported. By using the `@classmethod` decorator, we expose this function without needing to initialize the class first. This is the reason we can use the `get_supported_formats()` method in the command-line handler. Just remember to update this as new features are added!

```
    @classmethod
    def get_supported_formats(cls):
        return ['unix-epoch', 'unix-epoch-ms', 'windows-filetime']
```

The `parse_unix_epoch()` method handles processing Unix epoch time. We specify an optional argument, `milliseconds`, to switch this method between processing second and millisecond values. First we must determine if the data type is `"hex"` or `"number"`. If it is `"hex"`, we convert it to an integer and if it is a `"number"` we convert it to a float. If we do not recognize or support the data type for this method, such as a `string`, we throw an error to the user and exit the script.

After converting the value, we evaluate if this should be treated as a millisecond value and, if so, divide it by $1,000$ before handling it further. Following this, we use the `fromtimestamp()` method of the `datetime` class to convert the number to a `datetime` object. Lastly, we format this date to a human-readable format and store this string in the `timestamp` property.

```
def parse_unix_epoch(self, milliseconds=False):
    if self.data_type == 'hex':
        conv_value = int(self.date_value)
        if milliseconds:
            conv_value = conv_value / 1000.0
    elif self.data_type == 'number':
        conv_value = float(self.date_value)
        if milliseconds:
            conv_value = conv_value / 1000.0
    else:
        print("Unsupported data type '{}' provided".format(
            self.data_type))
        sys.exit('1')

    ts = dt.fromtimestamp(conv_value)
    self.timestamp = ts.strftime('%Y-%m-%d %H:%M:%S.%f')
```

The `parse_windows_filetime()` class method handles the `FILETIME` format, commonly stored as a hex value. Using a similar block of code as before, we convert the `"hex"` or `"number"` value into a Python object and raise an error for any other provided formats. The one difference is that we divide the date value by 10 rather than $1,000$ before processing them further.

While in the previous method the `datetime` library handled the epoch offset, we need to handle this offset separately this time. Using the `timedelta` class, we specify the millisecond value and add that to a `datetime` object representing the FILETIME format's epoch. The resulting `datetime` object is now ready for us to format and output for the user:

```
def parse_windows_filetime(self):
    if self.data_type == 'hex':
        microseconds = int(self.date_value, 16) / 10.0
    elif self.data_type == 'number':
        microseconds = float(self.date_value) / 10
    else:
        print("Unsupported data type '{}' provided".format(
            self.data_type))
        sys.exit('1')

    ts = dt(1601, 1, 1) + timedelta(microseconds=microseconds)
    self.timestamp = ts.strftime('%Y-%m-%d %H:%M:%S.%f')
```

When we run this script, we can provide a timestamp and see the converted value in an easy-to-read format, as shown here:

```
(venv2) pyforcookbook@dev-vm$ python date_parser.py 1504633427 unix-epoch number
2017-09-05 13:43:47.000000
(venv2) pyforcookbook@dev-vm$ python date_parser.py 1504633427154 unix-epoch-ms
number
2017-09-05 13:43:47.154000
(venv2) pytorcookbook@dev-vm$ python date_parser.py 1D3266EEA1E7900 windows-file
time hex
2017-09-05 17:46:34.000000
```

There's more...

This script can be further improved. We have provided one or more recommendations as follows:

- Add support for other types of timestamps (OLE, WebKit, and so on)
- Add time zone support through `pytz`
- Handle the formatting of hard-to-read dates with `dateutil`

Parsing IIS web logs with RegEx

Recipe Difficulty: Medium

Python Version: 3.5

Operating System: Any

Logs from web servers are very useful for generating user statistics, providing us with insightful information about the devices used and the geographical locations of the visitors. They also provide clarification to examiners looking for users attempting to exploit the web server or otherwise unauthorized use. While these logs store important details, they do so in a manner inconvenient to analyze efficiently. If you were to attempt to do so manually, the field names are specified at the top of the file and would require you to remember the order of the fields as you read through the text file. Fortunately, there is a better way. Using the following script, we show how to iterate through each line, map the values to the fields, and create a spreadsheet of properly displayed results - making it much easier to quickly analyze the dataset.

Getting started

All libraries used in this script are present in Python's standard library.

How to do it...

To properly form this recipe, we need to take the following steps:

1. Accept arguments for an input log file and output CSV file.
2. Define regular expression patterns for each of the log's columns.
3. Iterate through each line in the log and prepare each line in a manner that we can parse individual elements and handle quoted space characters.
4. Validate and map each value to its respective column.
5. Write mapped columns and values to a spreadsheet report.

How it works...

We begin with by importing libraries for argument handling and logging, followed by the built-in libraries we need to parse and validate the log information. These include the `re` regular expression library and `shlex` lexical analyzer library. We also include `sys` and `csv` for handling the output of log messages and reports. We initialize the recipe's logging object by calling the `getLogger()` method.

```
from __future__ import print_function
from argparse import ArgumentParser, FileType
import re
import shlex
import logging
import sys
import csv

logger = logging.getLogger(__file__)
```

Following the imports, we define patterns for the fields we will parse from the logs. This information may vary a bit between logs, though the patterns expressed here should cover most elements in a log.

 You may need to add, remove, or reorder some of the patterns defined as follows to properly parse the IIS log you are working with. These patterns should cover the common elements found in IIS logs.

We build these patterns as a list of tuples called `iis_log_format`, where the first tuple element is the column name and the second is the regular expression pattern to validate the expected content. By using a regular expression pattern, we can define a set of rules that the data must follow in order to be valid. It is critical that these columns are expressed in the order they appear in the log; otherwise, the code won't be able to properly map values to columns.

```
iis_log_format = [
    ("date", re.compile(r"\d{4}-\d{2}-\d{2}")),
    ("time", re.compile(r"\d\d:\d\d:\d\d")),
    ("s-ip", re.compile(
        r"((25[0-5]|2[0-4][0-9]|[01]?[0-9][0-9]?)(\.|$)){4}")),
    ("cs-method", re.compile(
        r"(GET)|(POST)|(PUT)|(DELETE)|(OPTIONS)|(HEAD)|(CONNECT)")),
    ("cs-uri-stem", re.compile(r"([A-Za-z0-1/\.-]*)")),
    ("cs-uri-query", re.compile(r"([A-Za-z0-1/\.-]*)")),
    ("s-port", re.compile(r"\d*")),
    ("cs-username", re.compile(r"([A-Za-z0-1/\.-]*)")),
```

```
    ("c-ip", re.compile(
        r"((25[0-5]|2[0-4][0-9]|[01]?[0-9][0-9]?)(\.|$)){4}")),
    ("cs(User-Agent)", re.compile(r".*")),
    ("sc-status", re.compile(r"\d*")),
    ("sc-substatus", re.compile(r"\d*")),
    ("sc-win32-status", re.compile(r"\d*")),
    ("time-taken", re.compile(r"\d*"))
]
```

This recipe's command-line handler takes two positional arguments, `iis_log` and `csv_report`, which represent the IIS log to process and the desired CSV path, respectively. Additionally, this recipe also accepts an optional argument, `l`, specifying the output path for the recipe's log file.

Next, we initialize the recipe's logging utility and configure it for console and file-based logging. This is important as we should note in a formal manner when we fail to parse a line for the user. In this manner, if something fails they shouldn't be working under the mistaken assumption that all lines were parsed successfully and are displayed in the resulting CSV spreadsheet. We also want to record runtime messages, including the version of the script and the supplied arguments. At this point, we are ready to call the `main()` function and kick off the script. Refer to the logging recipe in Chapter 1, *Essential Scripting and File Information Recipes* for a more detailed explanation of setting up a logging object.

```
if __name__ == '__main__':
    parser = ArgumentParser(
        description=__description__,
        epilog="Developed by {} on {}".format(
            ", ".join(__authors__), __date__)
    )
    parser.add_argument('iis_log', help="Path to IIS Log",
                        type=FileType('r'))
    parser.add_argument('csv_report', help="Path to CSV report")
    parser.add_argument('-l', help="Path to processing log",
                        default=__name__ + '.log')
    args = parser.parse_args()

    logger.setLevel(logging.DEBUG)
    msg_fmt = logging.Formatter("%(asctime)-15s %(funcName)-10s "
                                "%(levelname)-8s %(message)s")

    strhndl = logging.StreamHandler(sys.stdout)
    strhndl.setFormatter(fmt=msg_fmt)
    fhndl = logging.FileHandler(args.log, mode='a')
    fhndl.setFormatter(fmt=msg_fmt)

    logger.addHandler(strhndl)
```

```
logger.addHandler(fhndl)

logger.info("Starting IIS Parsing ")
logger.debug("Supplied arguments: {}".format(", ".join(sys.argv[1:])))
logger.debug("System " + sys.platform)
logger.debug("Version " + sys.version)
main(args.iis_log, args.csv_report, logger)
logger.info("IIS Parsing Complete")
```

The `main()` function handles the bulk of the logic in this script. We create a list, `parsed_logs`, to store the parsed lines before iterating over the lines in the log file. Inside the `for` loop, we strip the line and create a storage dictionary, `log_entry`, for the record. We speed up our processing, and prevent errors in column matching, by skipping lines beginning with the comment (or pound) character or if the line is empty.

While IIS logs are stored as space-delimited values, they use double quotes to escape strings that contain spaces. For example, a `useragent` string is a single value but generally, contains one or more spaces. Using the `shlex` module, we can parse the line with the `shlex()` method, and handle quote escaped spaces automatically by delimiting the data correctly on space values. This library can slow down processing, so we only use it on lines containing a double-quote character.

```
def main(iis_log, report_file, logger):
    parsed_logs = []
    for raw_line in iis_log:
        line = raw_line.strip()
        log_entry = {}
        if line.startswith("#") or len(line) == 0:
            continue
        if '\"' in line:
            line_iter = shlex.shlex(line_iter)
        else:
            line_iter = line.split(" ")
```

With the line properly delimited, we use the `enumerate` function to step through each element in the record and extract the corresponding column name and pattern. Using the pattern, we call the `match()` method on the value and, if it matches, create an entry in the `log_entry` dictionary. If the value doesn't match the pattern, we log an error and provide the whole line in the log file. After iterating through each of the columns, we append the record dictionary to the initial list of parsed log records and repeat this process for the remaining lines.

```
for count, split_entry in enumerate(line_iter):
    col_name, col_pattern = iis_log_format[count]
    if col_pattern.match(split_entry):
```

```
                    log_entry[col_name] = split_entry
              else:
                    logger.error("Unknown column pattern discovered. "
                                 "Line preserved in full below")
                    logger.error("Unparsed Line: {}".format(line))

        parsed_logs.append(log_entry)
```

Once all lines have been processed, we print a status message to the console prior to preparing for the `write_csv()` method. We use a simple list comprehension expression to extract the first element of each tuple, which represents a column name, within the `iis_log_format` list. With the columns extracted, let's look at the report writer.

```
    logger.info("Parsed {} lines".format(len(parsed_logs)))

    cols = [x[0] for x in iis_log_format]
    logger.info("Creating report file: {}".format(report_file))
    write_csv(report_file, cols, parsed_logs)
    logger.info("Report created")
```

The report writer creates a CSV file using the methods we have previously explored. Since we stored the lines as a list of dictionaries, we can easily create the report with four lines of code using the `csv.DictWriter` class.

```
def write_csv(outfile, fieldnames, data):
    with open(outfile, 'w', newline="") as open_outfile:
        csvfile = csv.DictWriter(open_outfile, fieldnames)
        csvfile.writeheader()
        csvfile.writerows(data)
```

When we look at the CSV report generated by the script, we see the following fields in the sample output:

date	time	s-ip	cs-method	cs-uri-stem	cs-uri-query	s-port	cs-username	c-ip
2012-03-02	03:55:53 PM	10.3.58.4	GET	/CertEnroll/RootCA-1+.crl	-	80	-	10.3.58.4
2012-03-02	05:34:06 PM	10.3.58.4	GET	/	-	80	-	220.181.108.168
2012-03-02	05:40:23 PM	10.3.58.4	GET	/robots.txt	-	80	-	66.249.71.225
2012-03-02	05:40:23 PM	10.3.58.4	GET	/	-	80	-	66.249.71.225
2012-03-02	06:22:52 PM	10.3.58.4	GET	/robots.txt	-	80	-	180.76.5.168
2012-03-02	06:22:57 PM	10.3.58.4	GET	/	-	80	-	123.125.71.113
2012-03-02	06:22:57 PM	10.3.58.4	GET	/robots.txt	-	80	-	180.76.5.56
2012-03-02	07:57:44 PM	10.3.58.4	GET	/style.css	-	80	-	96.255.98.154
2012-03-02	07:57:44 PM	10.3.58.4	GET	/topbar1.jpg	-	80	-	96.255.98.154
2012-03-02	07:57:45 PM	10.3.58.4	GET	/templogo.jpg	-	80	-	96.255.98.154
2012-03-02	07:57:45 PM	10.3.58.4	GET	/tempbuttons/button1.jpg	-	80	-	96.255.98.154
2012-03-02	07:57:45 PM	10.3.58.4	GET	/3buttonarea.jpg	-	80	-	96.255.98.154
2012-03-02	07:57:45 PM	10.3.58.4	GET	/tempbuttons/button4.jpg	-	80	-	96.255.98.154
2012-03-02	07:57:45 PM	10.3.58.4	GET	/tempbuttons/button5.jpg	-	80	-	96.255.98.154
2012-03-02	07:57:45 PM	10.3.58.4	GET	/tempbuttons/button6.jpg	-	80	-	96.255.98.154
2012-03-02	07:57:45 PM	10.3.58.4	GET	/tempbuttons/button7.jpg	-	80	-	96.255.98.154

cs(User-Agent)	sc-status	sc-substatus	sc-win32-status	time-taken
Microsoft-CryptoAPI/6.1	404	11	0	45711
Mozilla/5.0+(compatible;+Baiduspider/2.0;++http://www.baidu.com/search/spider.html)	200	0	64	273
Mozilla/5.0+(compatible;+Googlebot/2.1;++http://www.google.com/bot.html)	404	0	2	44
Mozilla/5.0+(compatible;+Googlebot/2.1;++http://www.google.com/bot.html)	304	0	0	60
Baiduspider+(+http://www.baidu.com/search/spider.htm)	404	0	64	365
Mozilla/5.0+(compatible;+Baiduspider/2.0;++http://www.baidu.com/search/spider.html)	200	0	64	528
Baiduspider+(+http://www.baidu.com/search/spider.htm)	404	0	64	250
Mozilla/5.0+(Windows+NT+6.1;+WOW64;+rv:10.0.2)+Gecko/20100101+Firefox/10.0.2	200	0	0	19
Mozilla/5.0+(Windows+NT+6.1;+WOW64;+rv:10.0.2)+Gecko/20100101+Firefox/10.0.2	200	0	0	134
Mozilla/5.0+(Windows+NT+6.1;+WOW64;+rv:10.0.2)+Gecko/20100101+Firefox/10.0.2	200	0	0	189
Mozilla/5.0+(Windows+NT+6.1;+WOW64;+rv:10.0.2)+Gecko/20100101+Firefox/10.0.2	200	0	0	196
Mozilla/5.0+(Windows+NT+6.1;+WOW64;+rv:10.0.2)+Gecko/20100101+Firefox/10.0.2	200	0	0	199
Mozilla/5.0+(Windows+NT+6.1;+WOW64;+rv:10.0.2)+Gecko/20100101+Firefox/10.0.2	200	0	0	8
Mozilla/5.0+(Windows+NT+6.1;+WOW64;+rv:10.0.2)+Gecko/20100101+Firefox/10.0.2	200	0	0	64
Mozilla/5.0+(Windows+NT+6.1;+WOW64;+rv:10.0.2)+Gecko/20100101+Firefox/10.0.2	200	0	0	60

There's more...

This script can be further improved. Here is a recommendation:

- While we can define regex patterns as seen at the start of the script, we can make our lives easier using regular expression management libraries instead. One example is the `grok` library, which is used to create variable names for patterns. This allows us to organize and extend patterns with ease, as we can express them by name instead of a string value. This library is used by other platforms, such as the ELK stack, for management and implementation of regular expressions.

Going spelunking

Recipe Difficulty: Medium

Python Version: 2.7

Operating System: Any

Log files can quickly become quite sizable due to the level of detail and time frame preserved. As you may have noticed, the CSV report from the prior recipe can easily become too large for our spreadsheet application to open or browse efficiently. Rather than analyzing this data in a spreadsheet, one alternative would be to load the data into a database.

Splunk is a platform that incorporates a NoSQL database with an ingestion and query engine, making it a powerful analysis tool. Its database operates in a manner like Elasticsearch or MongoDB, permitting the storage of documents or structured records. Because of this, we do not need to provide records with a consistent key-value mapping to store them in the database. This is what makes NoSQL databases so useful for log analysis, as log formats can be variable depending on the event type.

In this recipe, we learn to index the CSV report from the previous recipe into Splunk, allowing us to interact with the data inside the platform. We also design the script to run queries against the dataset and to export the resulting subset of data responsive to the query to a CSV file. These processes are handled in separate stages so we can independently query and export data as needed.

Getting started

This recipe requires the installation of the third-party library `splunk-sdk`. All other libraries used in this script are present in Python's standard library. Additionally, we must install Splunk on the host operating system and, due to limitations of the `splunk-sdk` library, run the script using Python 2.

To install Splunk, we need to navigate to `Splunk.com`, fill out the form, and select the Splunk Enterprise free trial download. This enterprise trial allows us to practice with the API and gives us the ability to upload 500 MB per day. Once we have downloaded the application, we need to launch it to configure the application. While there are a lot of configurations we could change, launch it with the defaults, for now, to keep things simple and focus on the API. In doing so, the default address for the server will be `localhost:8000`. By navigating to this address in a browser, we can log in for the first time, set up accounts and (*please do this*) change the administrator password.

 The default username and password for a new Splunk install is *admin* and *changeme*.

With the Splunk instance active, we can now install the API library. This library handles the conversion from the REST API into Python objects. At the time of writing of this book, the Splunk API is only available in Python 2. The `splunk-sdk` library can be installed with `pip`:

```
pip install splunk-sdk==1.6.2
```

> To learn more about the `splunk-sdk` library, visit `http://dev.splunk.com/python`.

How to do it...

Now that the environment is properly configured, we can begin to develop the code. This script will index new data to Splunk, run queries on that data, and export subsets of data responsive to our queries to a CSV file. To accomplish this, we need to:

1. Develop a robust argument-handling interface allowing the user to specify these options.
2. Build a class to handle operations with the various properties' methods.
3. Create methods to handle the process of indexing new data and creating the index for data storage.
4. Set up methods for running Splunk queries in a manner that allows for informative reports.
5. Provide a mechanism for exporting reports to a CSV format.

How it works...

We begin by importing the required libraries for this script, including the newly installed `splunklib`. To prevent unnecessary errors arising due to user ignorance, we use the `sys` library to determine the version of Python executing the script and raise an error if it is not Python 2.

```
from __future__ import print_function
from argparse import ArgumentParser, ArgumentError
from argparse import ArgumentDefaultsHelpFormatter
import splunklib.client as client
import splunklib.results as results
import os
import sys
```

```
import csv

if sys.version_info.major != 2:
    print("Invalid python version. Must use Python 2 due to splunk api "
        "library")
```

The next logical block to develop is the recipe's command-line argument handler. As we have many options and operations to execute in this code, we need to spend some extra time on this section. And because this code is class based, we must set up some additional logic in this section.

This recipe's command-line handler takes one positional input, `action`, which represents the action to run (index, query, or export). This recipe also supports seven optional arguments: `index`, `config`, `file`, `query`, `cols`, `host`, and `port`. Let's start looking at what all of these options do.

The `index` argument, which is actually a required argument, is used to specify the name of the Splunk index to ingest, query, or export the data from. This can be an existing or new `index` name. The `config` parameter refers to the configuration file containing your username and password for the Splunk instance. This file, as described in the argument's help, should be protected and stored outside of the location where the code is executed. In an enterprise environment, you may need to further protect these credentials.

```
if __name__ == '__main__':
    parser = ArgumentParser(
        description=__description__,
        formatter_class=ArgumentDefaultsHelpFormatter,
        epilog="Developed by {} on {}".format(
            ", ".join(__authors__), __date__)
    )
    parser.add_argument('action', help="Action to run",
                        choices=['index', 'query', 'export'])
    parser.add_argument('--index-name', help="Name of splunk index",
                        required=True)
    parser.add_argument('--config',
                        help="Place where login details are stored."
                        " Should have the username on the first line and"
                        " the password on the second."
                        " Please Protect this file!",
                        default=os.path.expanduser("~/.splunk_py.ini"))
```

The `file` parameter will be used to provide a path to the `file` to `index` into the platform or be used to specify the filename to write the exported `query` data to. For example, we will use the `file` parameter to point to the CSV spreadsheet we wish to ingest from the previous recipe. The `query` parameter also serves a dual purpose, it can be used to run a query from Splunk or to specify a query ID to export as CSV. This means that the `index` and `query` actions require only one of these parameters, but the `export` action requires both.

```
parser.add_argument('--file', help="Path to file")
parser.add_argument('--query', help="Splunk query to run or sid of "
                    "existing query to export")
```

The last block of arguments allows the user to modify default properties of the recipe. The `cols` argument, for example, can be used to specify what columns from the source data to export and in what order. As we will be querying and exporting IIS logs, we already know what columns are available and are of interest to us. You may want to specify alternative default columns based on what type of data is being explored. Our last two arguments include the `host` and `port` parameters, each defaulting to a local server but can be configured to allow you to interact with alternate instances.

```
parser.add_argument(
    '--cols',
    help="Speficy columns to export. comma seperated list",
    default='_time,date,time,sc_status,c_ip,s_ip,cs_User_Agent')
parser.add_argument('--host', help="hostname of server",
                    default="localhost")
parser.add_argument('--port', help="help", default="8089")
args = parser.parse_args()
```

With our arguments specified, we can parse them and verify that all requirements are met prior to executing the recipe. First, we must open and read the `config` file containing the authentication credentials, where the `username` is on the first line and the `password` is on the second line. Using this information, we create a dictionary, `conn_dict`, containing the login details and server location. This dictionary is passed to the `splunklib` `client.connect()` method. Notice how we delete, using the `del()` method, the variables containing this sensitive information. While the username and password are still accessible through the `service` object, we want to limit the number of areas in which those details are stored. Following the creation of the `service` variable, we test if any applications are installed in Splunk, as by default there is at least one, and use that as a test of successful authentication.

```
with open(args.config, 'r') as open_conf:
    username, password = [x.strip() for x in open_conf.readlines()]
conn_dict = {'host': args.host, 'port': int(args.port),
```

```
                    'username': username, 'password': password}
    del(username)
    del(password)
    service = client.connect(**conn_dict)
    del(conn_dict)

    if len(service.apps) == 0:
        print("Login likely unsuccessful, cannot find any applications")
        sys.exit()
```

We continue processing the supplied arguments by converting the columns into a list and creating the Spelunking class instance. To initialize the class, we must supply it the service variable, the action to take, the index name, and the columns. Using this, our class instance is now ready for use.

```
    cols = args.cols.split(",")
    spelunking = Spelunking(service, args.action, args.index_name, cols)
```

Next, we use a series of if-elif-else statements to handle the three various actions we expect to encounter. If the user supplied the index action, we first confirm that the optional file parameter is present, raising an error if it is not. If we do find it, we assign the value to the corresponding property of the Spelunking class instance. This type of logic is repeated for the query and export actions, confirming that they also were used with the correct optional arguments. Notice how we assign the absolute path of the file for the class using the os.path.abspath() function. This allows splunklib to find the correct file on the system. And, in what perhaps may be the longest argument handling section in the book, we have completed the requisite logic and can now call the class run() method to kick off the processing for the specific action requested.

```
    if spelunking.action == 'index':
        if 'file' not in vars(args):
            ArgumentError('--file parameter required')
            sys.exit()
        else:
            spelunking.file = os.path.abspath(args.file)

    elif spelunking.action == 'export':
        if 'file' not in vars(args):
            ArgumentError('--file parameter required')
            sys.exit()
        if 'query' not in vars(args):
            ArgumentError('--query parameter required')
            sys.exit()
        spelunking.file = os.path.abspath(args.file)
        spelunking.sid = args.query
```

```
        elif spelunking.action == 'query':
            if 'query' not in vars(args):
                ArgumentError('--query parameter required')
                sys.exit()
            else:
                spelunking.query = "search index={} {}".format(args.index_name,
                                                               args.query)

        else:
            ArgumentError('Unknown action required')
            sys.exit()

    spelunking.run()
```

With the arguments now behind us, let's dive into the class responsible for handling the operations requested by the user. This class takes four arguments, including the `service` variable, the `action` specified by the user, the Splunk index name, and the columns to use. All other properties are set to `None` and, as seen in the previous code block, will be appropriately initialized at the time of execution if they were supplied. This is done to limit the number of arguments required by the class and to handle the situations where certain properties are unused. All of these properties are initialized at the start of our class to ensure we have assigned default values.

```
    class Spelunking(object):
        def __init__(self, service, action, index_name, cols):
            self.service = service
            self.action = action
            self.index = index_name
            self.file = None
            self.query = None
            self.sid = None
            self.job = None
            self.cols = cols
```

The `run()` method is responsible for obtaining the `index` object from the Splunk instance using the `get_or_create_index()` method. It also checks which action was specified at the command-line and calls the corresponding class instance method.

```
        def run(self):
            index_obj = self.get_or_create_index()
            if self.action == 'index':
                self.index_data(index_obj)
            elif self.action == 'query':
                self.query_index()
            elif self.action == 'export':
                self.export_report()
            return
```

The `get_or_create_index()` method, as the name suggests, first tests whether the specified index exists and makes a connection to it, or creates a new index if none is found by that name. Since this information is stored in the `indexes` property of the `service` variable as a dictionary-like object, we can easily test for the existence of the index by name.

```
def get_or_create_index(self):
    # Create a new index
    if self.index not in self.service.indexes:
        return service.indexes.create(self.index)
    else:
        return self.service.indexes[self.index]
```

To ingest the data from a file, such as a CSV file, we can use a one-line statement to send information to the instance in the `index_data()` method. This method uses the `upload()` method of the `splunk_index` object to send the file to Splunk for ingestion. While a CSV file is a simplistic example of how we can import data, we could also use some of the logic from the previous recipe to read the raw log into the Splunk instance without the intermediate CSV step. For that, we would want to use a different method of the `index` object that would allow us to send each parsed event individually.

```
def index_data(self, splunk_index):
    splunk_index.upload(self.file)
```

The `query_index()` method is a little more involved, as we first need to modify the query provided from the user. As seen in the following snippet, we need to add the columns specified by the user to the initial query. This will make fields not used in the query available during the export stage. Following this modification, we create a new job in the Splunk system with the `service.jobs.create()` method and record the query SID. This SID will be used in the exporting phase to export the results of the specific query job. We print this information, along with the time before the job expires from the Splunk instance. By default, this time-to-live value is 300 seconds, or five minutes.

```
def query_index(self):
    self.query = self.query + "| fields + " + ", ".join(self.cols)
    self.job = self.service.jobs.create(self.query, rf=self.cols)
    self.sid = self.job.sid
    print("Query job {} created. will expire in {} seconds".format(
        self.sid, self.job['ttl']))
```

As previously alluded to, the `export_report()` method uses the SID mentioned in the prior method to check whether the job is complete and to retrieve the data for export. in order to do this, we iterate through the available jobs, and if ours is not present, raise a warning. If the job is found, but the `is_ready()` method returns `False`, the job is still processing and not ready to export results.

```
def export_report(self):
    job_obj = None
    for j in self.service.jobs:
        if j.sid == self.sid:
            job_obj = j

    if job_obj is None:
        print("Job SID {} not found. Did it expire?".format(self.sid))
        sys.exit()

    if not job_obj.is_ready():
        print("Job SID {} is still processing. "
            "Please wait to re-run".format(self.sir))
```

If the job passes these two tests, we extract the data from Splunk and write it to a CSV file using the `write_csv()` method. Before we can do that, we need to initialize a list to store the job results. Next, we retrieve the results, specifying the columns of interest, and read this raw data into the `job_results` variable. Luckily, `splunklib` provides a `ResultsReader` that converts the `job_results` variable into a list of dictionaries. We iterate through this list and append each of these dictionaries to the `export_data` list. Finally, we provide the file path, column names, and dataset to export to the CSV writer.

```
export_data = []
job_results = job_obj.results(rf=self.cols)
for result in results.ResultsReader(job_results):
    export_data.append(result)

self.write_csv(self.file, self.cols, export_data)
```

The `write_csv()` method in this class is a `@staticmethod`. This decorator allows us to use a generalized method in the class without needing to specify an instance. This method will no doubt look familiar to those used elsewhere in the book, where we open the output file, create a `DictWriter` object, then write the column headers and data to file.

```
@staticmethod
def write_csv(outfile, fieldnames, data):
    with open(outfile, 'wb') as open_outfile:
        csvfile = csv.DictWriter(open_outfile, fieldnames,
                                    extrasaction="ignore")
        csvfile.writeheader()
```

```
csvfile.writerows(data)
```

In our hypothetical use case, the first stage will be to index the data contained in the CSV spreadsheet from the previous recipe. As seen in the following snippet, we supply the CSV file from our previous recipe and add it to the Splunk index. Next, we look for all entries where the user agent is an iPhone. Finally, the last stage involves taking the output from the query and creating a CSV report.

```
(venv2) pyforcookbook@dev-vm$ python splunk_connector.py index --index-name iis-
data --file /media/working/iis.csv
(venv2) pyforcookbook@dev-vm$ python splunk_connector.py query --index-name iis-
data --query "cs_User_Agent=*iPhone*"
Query job 1505090221.12 created. will expire in 600 seconds
(venv2) pyforcookbook@dev-vm$ python splunk_connector.py export --index-name iis
-data --query 1505090221.12 --file /media/working/splunk_export.csv
```

With these three commands successfully executed, we can open and review the filtered output:

date	time	sc_status	c_ip	s_ip	cs_User_Agent
2012-03-06	11:44:32 PM	200	90.198.159.52	10.3.58.4	Mozilla/5.0+(iPhone;+CPU+iPhone+OS+5_0_1+like+Mac+OS+X)
2012-03-06	11:44:31 PM	200	90.198.159.52	10.3.58.4	Mozilla/5.0+(iPhone;+CPU+iPhone+OS+5_0_1+like+Mac+OS+X)
2012-03-06	11:44:31 PM	200	90.198.159.52	10.3.58.4	Mozilla/5.0+(iPhone;+CPU+iPhone+OS+5_0_1+like+Mac+OS+X)
2012-03-06	11:44:31 PM	200	90.198.159.52	10.3.58.4	Mozilla/5.0+(iPhone;+CPU+iPhone+OS+5_0_1+like+Mac+OS+X)
2012-03-06	11:44:31 PM	200	90.198.159.52	10.3.58.4	Mozilla/5.0+(iPhone;+CPU+iPhone+OS+5_0_1+like+Mac+OS+X)
2012-03-06	11:44:31 PM	200	90.198.159.52	10.3.58.4	Mozilla/5.0+(iPhone;+CPU+iPhone+OS+5_0_1+like+Mac+OS+X)
2012-03-06	11:44:31 PM	200	90.198.159.52	10.3.58.4	Mozilla/5.0+(iPhone;+CPU+iPhone+OS+5_0_1+like+Mac+OS+X)
2012-03-06	11:44:31 PM	200	90.198.159.52	10.3.58.4	Mozilla/5.0+(iPhone;+CPU+iPhone+OS+5_0_1+like+Mac+OS+X)
2012-03-06	11:44:31 PM	200	90.198.159.52	10.3.58.4	Mozilla/5.0+(iPhone;+CPU+iPhone+OS+5_0_1+like+Mac+OS+X)
2012-03-06	11:44:31 PM	200	90.198.159.52	10.3.58.4	Mozilla/5.0+(iPhone;+CPU+iPhone+OS+5_0_1+like+Mac+OS+X)
2012-03-06	11:44:31 PM	200	90.198.159.52	10.3.58.4	Mozilla/5.0+(iPhone;+CPU+iPhone+OS+5_0_1+like+Mac+OS+X)
2012-03-06	11:44:30 PM	200	90.198.159.52	10.3.58.4	Mozilla/5.0+(iPhone;+CPU+iPhone+OS+5_0_1+like+Mac+OS+X)
2012-03-06	11:44:30 PM	200	90.198.159.52	10.3.58.4	Mozilla/5.0+(iPhone;+CPU+iPhone+OS+5_0_1+like+Mac+OS+X)
2012-03-06	11:44:30 PM	200	90.198.159.52	10.3.58.4	Mozilla/5.0+(iPhone;+CPU+iPhone+OS+5_0_1+like+Mac+OS+X)
2012-03-06	11:44:30 PM	200	90.198.159.52	10.3.58.4	Mozilla/5.0+(iPhone;+CPU+iPhone+OS+5_0_1+like+Mac+OS+X)

There's more...

This script can be further improved. We have provided one or more recommendations as shown here:

- The Splunk API for Python (and in general) has many other features. Additionally, more advanced querying techniques can be used to generate data that we can manipulate into graphics for technical and non-technical end users alike. Learn more about the many features that the Splunk API affords you.

Interpreting the daily.out log

Recipe Difficulty: Medium

Python Version: 3.5

Operating System: Any

Operating system logs generally reflect events for software, hardware, and services on the system. These details can assist us in our investigations as we look into an event, such as the use of removable devices. One example of a log that can prove useful in identifying this activity is `daily.out` log found on macOS systems. This log records a lot of information, including what drives are connected to the machine and the amount of storage available and used daily. While we can also learn about shutdown times, network states, and other information from this log, we will focus on drive usage over time.

Getting started

All libraries used in this script are present in Python's standard library.

How to do it...

This script will leverage the following steps:

1. Set up arguments to accept the log file and a path to write the report.
2. Build a class that handles the parsing of the log's various sections.
3. Create a method to extract the relevant section and pass it for further processing.
4. Extract disk information from these sections.
5. Create a CSV writer to export the extracted details.

How it works...

We begin by importing libraries necessary for argument handling, date interpretation, and the writing spreadsheets. One of the great things about processing text files in Python is that you rarely need a third-party library.

```
from __future__ import print_function
from argparse import ArgumentParser, FileType
from datetime import datetime
import csv
```

This recipe's command-line handler accepts two positional arguments, `daily_out` and `output_report`, which represent the path to the daily.out log file and the desired output path for the CSV spreadsheet, respectively. Notice how we pass an open file object for processing through the `argparse.FileType` class. Following this, we initialize the `ProcessDailyOut` class with the log file and call the `run()` method and store the returned results in the `parsed_events` variable. We then call the `write_csv()` method to write the results to a spreadsheet in the desired output directory using defined columns from the `processor` class object.

```
if __name__ == '__main__':
    parser = ArgumentParser(
        description=__description__,
        epilog="Developed by {} on {}".format(
            ", ".join(__authors__), __date__)
    )
    parser.add_argument("daily_out", help="Path to daily.out file",
                        type=FileType('r'))
    parser.add_argument("output_report", help="Path to csv report")
    args = parser.parse_args()

    processor = ProcessDailyOut(args.daily_out)
    parsed_events = processor.run()
    write_csv(args.output_report, processor.report_columns, parsed_events)
```

In the `ProcessDailyOut` class, we set up the properties supplied by the user and define the columns used for the report. Notice how we add two different sets of columns: the `disk_status_columns` and the `report_columns`. The `report_columns` are simply the `disk_status_columns` with two additional fields to identify the entry date and time zone.

```
class ProcessDailyOut(object):
    def __init__(self, daily_out):
        self.daily_out = daily_out
        self.disk_status_columns = [
            'Filesystem', 'Size', 'Used', 'Avail', 'Capacity', 'iused',
            'ifree', '%iused', 'Mounted on']
        self.report_columns = ['event_date', 'event_tz'] + \
            self.disk_status_columns
```

The `run()` method begins by iterating over the provided log file. After stripping whitespace characters from the start and end of each line, we validate the content to identify breaks in sections. The "`-- End of daily output --`" string breaks each entry in the log file. Each entry contains several sections of data broken up by new lines. For this reason, we must use several blocks of code to split and process each section separately.

In this loop, we gather all lines from a single event and pass it to the `process_event()` method and append the processed results to the `parsed_events` list that is eventually returned.

```
def run(self):
    event_lines = []
    parsed_events = []
    for raw_line in self.daily_out:
        line = raw_line.strip()
        if line == '-- End of daily output --':
            parsed_events += self.process_event(event_lines)
            event_lines = []
        else:
            event_lines.append(line)
    return parsed_events
```

In the `process_event()` method, we will define variables that will allow us to split sections of an event for further processing. To better understand this next segment of code, please take a moment to review the following example of an event:

```
Sat Nov  5 12:17:54 EDT 2016

Removing old temporary files:
  /tmp/dumps/Discarded=1.dmp
  /tmp/dumps/uploads.log
  /tmp/CrashUpload-KmfyV

Cleaning out old system announcements:

Removing stale files from /var/rwho:

Disk status:
Filesystem    Size   Used  Avail Capacity iused       ifree %iused  Mounted on
/dev/disk1    465Gi  402Gi  63Gi    87% 1865625 4293101654    0%   /
/dev/disk2s1  120Gi   26Gi  94Gi    22%  212193     769559   22%   /Volumes/SDCard

Network interface status:
Name  Mtu   Network       Address           Ipkts Ierrs    Opkts Oerrs  Coll
lo0   16384 <Link#1>                       880974     0   880974     0     0
lo0   16384 127           localhost        880974     -   880974     -     -
lo0   16384 localhost     ::1              880974     -   880974     -     -
lo0   16384 fe80::1%lo0   fe80:1::1        880974     -   880974     -     -
en2   1500  <Link#5>      d2:07:14:20:96:40     0     0        0     0     0
en1   1500  <Link#6>      60:02:06:fe:4d:70 2751219    0  1220839     0     0
en1   1500  192.168.0     192.168.0.100    2751219    -  1220839     -     -

Local system status:
12:18  up 5 days, 21:22, 2 users, load averages: 1.87 1.65 1.72

-- End of daily output --
```

Within this event, we can see that the first element is the date value and time zone, followed by a series of subsections. Each of the subsection headers is a line that ends with a colon; we use this to split the various data elements within this file, as seen in the following code. We create a dictionary, `event_data`, using the section headers as a key and their content, if present, as the value before further processing each subsection.

```
def process_event(self, event_lines):
    section_header = ""
    section_data = []
    event_data = {}
    for line in event_lines:
        if line.endswith(":"):
            if len(section_data) > 0:
                event_data[section_header] = section_data
                section_data = []
                section_header = ""

            section_header = line.strip(":")
```

If the section header line does not end with a colon, we check if there are exactly two colons in the line. If so, we try to validate this line as a date value. To handle this date format with built-in libraries, we need to extract the time zone separately from the rest of the date as there is a known bug in versions of Python 3 with parsing time zones with the %Z formatter. For the curious, more information on this bug can be found at https://bugs.python.org/ issue22377.

To separate the time zone from the date value, we delimit the string on the space value, place the time zone value (element 4 in this example) in its own variable, then join the remaining time values into a new string that we can parse with the datetime library. This may raise an IndexError if the string does not have a minimum of 5 elements or a ValueError if the datetime format string is invalid. If either of these error types are not raised, we assign the date to the event_data dictionary. If we do receive either of these errors, the line will be appended to the section_data list and the next loop iteration will continue. This is important as a line may contain two colons and not be a date value, and so we wouldn't want to then disregard the line by removing it from the script's consideration.

```
elif line.count(":") == 2:
    try:
        split_line = line.split()
        timezone = split_line[4]
        date_str = " ".join(split_line[:4] + [split_line[-1]])
        try:
            date_val = datetime.strptime(
                date_str, "%a %b %d %H:%M:%S %Y")
        except ValueError:
            date_val = datetime.strptime(
                date_str, "%a %b %d %H:%M:%S %Y")
        event_data["event_date"] = [date_val, timezone]
        section_data = []
        section_header = ""
    except ValueError:
        section_data.append(line)
    except IndexError:
        section_data.append(line)
```

The last piece of this conditional appends any line that has content to the section_data variable for further processing as needed. This prevents blank lines from finding their way in and allows us to capture all information between two section headers.

```
else:
    if len(line):
        section_data.append(line)
```

We close this function by calling to any subsection processors. At this time, we only handle the disk information subsection, with the `process_disk()` method, though one could develop code to extract other values of interest. This method accepts as its input the event information and the event date. The disk information is returned as a list of processed disk information elements which we return to the `run()` method and add the values to the processed event list.

```
return self.process_disk(event_data.get("Disk status", []),
                         event_data.get("event_date", []))
```

To process a disk subsection, we iterate through each of the lines, if there are any, and extract the relevant event information. The `for` loop starts by checking the iteration number and skipping row zero as it contains the data's column headers. For any other line, we use list comprehension and split the line on a single space, strip whitespace, and filter out any fields that are blank.

```
def process_disk(self, disk_lines, event_dates):
    if len(disk_lines) == 0:
        return {}

    processed_data = []
    for line_count, line in enumerate(disk_lines):
        if line_count == 0:
            continue
        prepped_lines = [x for x in line.split(" ")
                         if len(x.strip()) != 0]
```

Next, we initialize a dictionary, `disk_info`, that holds the event information with the date and time zone details for this snapshot. The `for` loop uses the `enumerate()` function to map values to their column names. If the column name contains `"/Volumes/"` (the standard mount point for drive volumes), we will join the remainder of the split items. This ensures that volumes with spaces in their names are preserved appropriately.

```
disk_info = {
    "event_date": event_dates[0],
    "event_tz": event_dates[1]
}
for col_count, entry in enumerate(prepped_lines):
    curr_col = self.disk_status_columns[col_count]
    if "/Volumes/" in entry:
        disk_info[curr_col] = " ".join(
            prepped_lines[col_count:])
        break
    disk_info[curr_col] = entry.strip()
```

The innermost `for` loop ends by appending the disk information to the `processed_data` list. Once all lines in the disk section have been processed, we return the `processed_data` list to the parent function.

```
        processed_data.append(disk_info)
    return processed_data
```

Lastly, we briefly touch on the `write_csv()` method, which uses the `DictWriter` class to open the file and write the header rows and the content to the CSV file.

```
def write_csv(outfile, fieldnames, data):
    with open(outfile, 'w', newline="") as open_outfile:
        csvfile = csv.DictWriter(open_outfile, fieldnames)
        csvfile.writeheader()
        csvfile.writerows(data)
```

When we run this script, we can see the extracted details in the CSV report. An example of this output is shown here:

event_date	event_tz	Filesystem	Size	Used	Avail	Capacity	iused	ifree	%iused	Mounted on
11/05/16 12:17 PM	EDT	/dev/disk1	465Gi	402Gi	63Gi	87.00%	1865625	4293101654	0.00%	/
11/05/16 12:17 PM	EDT	/dev/disk2s1	120Gi	26Gi	94Gi	22.00%	212193	769559	22.00%	/Volumes/SDCard
11/05/16 12:18 PM	EDT	/dev/disk1	465Gi	402Gi	63Gi	87.00%	1865837	4293101442	0.00%	/
11/05/16 12:18 PM	EDT	/dev/disk2s1	120Gi	26Gi	94Gi	22.00%	212193	769559	22.00%	/Volumes/SDCard
11/12/16 08:14 AM	EST	/dev/disk1	465Gi	403Gi	61Gi	87.00%	2010736	4292956543	0.00%	/
11/14/16 07:59 PM	EST	/dev/disk1	465Gi	403Gi	62Gi	87.00%	1848693	4293118586	0.00%	/
11/14/16 07:59 PM	EST	/dev/disk1	465Gi	403Gi	62Gi	87.00%	1848678	4293118601	0.00%	/
11/20/16 01:05 PM	EST	/dev/disk1	465Gi	402Gi	62Gi	87.00%	1848189	4293119090	0.00%	/
11/20/16 01:05 PM	EST	/dev/disk2s1	120Gi	26Gi	94Gi	22.00%	212193	769559	22.00%	/Volumes/SDCard
11/20/16 01:05 PM	EST	/dev/disk1	465Gi	402Gi	62Gi	87.00%	1848068	4293119211	0.00%	/
11/20/16 01:05 PM	EST	/dev/disk2s1	120Gi	26Gi	94Gi	22.00%	212193	769559	22.00%	/Volumes/SDCard
11/23/16 07:02 PM	EST	/dev/disk1	465Gi	404Gi	61Gi	87.00%	1856552	4293110727	0.00%	/
11/23/16 07:02 PM	EST	/dev/disk2s1	120Gi	26Gi	94Gi	22.00%	212193	769559	22.00%	/Volumes/SDCard
11/23/16 07:02 PM	EST	/dev/disk1	465Gi	404Gi	61Gi	87.00%	1856540	4293110739	0.00%	/
11/23/16 07:02 PM	EST	/dev/disk2s1	120Gi	26Gi	94Gi	22.00%	212193	769559	22.00%	/Volumes/SDCard
11/26/16 11:34 AM	EST	/dev/disk1	465Gi	446Gi	18Gi	97.00%	1879317	4293087962	0.00%	/
11/26/16 11:34 AM	EST	/dev/disk2s1	120Gi	26Gi	94Gi	22.00%	212193	769559	22.00%	/Volumes/SDCard
11/26/16 11:34 AM	EST	/dev/disk1	465Gi	446Gi	18Gi	97.00%	1879350	4293087929	0.00%	/
11/26/16 11:34 AM	EST	/dev/disk2s1	120Gi	26Gi	94Gi	22.00%	212193	769559	22.00%	/Volumes/SDCard
11/30/16 07:51 PM	EST	/dev/disk1	465Gi	448Gi	17Gi	97.00%	1881277	4293086002	0.00%	/
11/30/16 07:51 PM	EST	/dev/disk2s1	120Gi	26Gi	94Gi	22.00%	212193	769559	22.00%	/Volumes/SDCard
11/30/16 07:51 PM	EST	/dev/disk1	465Gi	448Gi	17Gi	97.00%	1880967	4293086312	0.00%	/
11/30/16 07:51 PM	EST	/dev/disk2s1	120Gi	26Gi	94Gi	22.00%	212193	769559	22.00%	/Volumes/SDCard
12/04/16 01:28 PM	EST	/dev/disk1	465Gi	448Gi	16Gi	97.00%	1928399	4293038880	0.00%	/
12/04/16 01:28 PM	EST	/dev/disk2s1	120Gi	26Gi	94Gi	22.00%	212193	769559	22.00%	/Volumes/SDCard
12/04/16 01:28 PM	EST	/dev/disk1	465Gi	448Gi	16Gi	97.00%	1928403	4293038876	0.00%	/
12/04/16 01:28 PM	EST	/dev/disk2s1	120Gi	26Gi	94Gi	22.00%	212193	769559	22.00%	/Volumes/SDCard
12/06/16 09:43 PM	EST	/dev/disk1	465Gi	449Gi	15Gi	97.00%	1917706	4293049573	0.00%	/
12/06/16 09:43 PM	EST	/dev/disk2s1	120Gi	26Gi	94Gi	22.00%	212193	769559	22.00%	/Volumes/SDCard

Adding daily.out parsing to Axiom

Recipe Difficulty: Easy

Python Version: 2.7

Operating System: Any

Using the code we just developed to parse macOS `daily.out` logs, we add this functionality into Axiom, developed by *Magnet Forensics*, for the automatic extraction of these events. As Axiom supports the processing of forensic images and loose files, we can either provide it a full acquisition or just an export of the `daily.out` log for this example. Through the API made available by this tool, we can access and process files found by its engine and return results for review directly within Axiom.

Getting started

The Magnet Forensics team developed an API for both Python and XML to add support for creating custom artifacts within Axiom. The Python API, at of the writing of this book, is only available through `IronPython` running Python version 2.7. While we have developed our code outside of this platform, we can easily integrate it into Axiom following the steps laid out in this recipe. We used Axiom version 1.1.3.5726 to test and develop this recipe.

We first need to install Axiom in a Windows instance and ensure that our code is stable and portable. Additionally, our code needs to be sandbox friendly. The Axiom sandbox limits the use of third-party libraries and access to some Python modules and functions that could cause code to interact with the system outside of the application. For this reason, we designed our `daily.out` parser to only use built-in libraries that are safe in the sandbox to demonstrate the ease of develop with these custom artifacts.

How to do it...

To develop and implement a custom artifact, we will need to:

1. Install Axiom in on a Windows machine.
2. Import the script we developed.
3. Create the `Artifact` class and define the parser metadata and columns.
4. Develop the `Hunter` class to handle the artifact processing and result reporting.

How it works...

For this script, we import the `axiom` library and the datetime library. Notice, we have removed the previous `argparse` and `csv` imports are they are unnecessary here.

```
from __future__ import print_function
from axiom import *
from datetime import datetime
```

Next, we must paste in the `ProcessDailyOut` class from the prior recipe, not including the `write_csv` or argument handling code, to use in this script. Since the current version of the API does not allow imports, we have to bundle all the code we need into a single script. To save pages and avoid redundancy, we will omit the code block in this section (though it exists as you'd expect in the code file bundled with this chapter).

The next class is the `DailyOutArtifact`, a subclass of the `Artifact` class provided by the Axiom API. We call the `AddHunter()` method, providing our (not yet shown) `hHunter` class, before defining the plugin's name within the `GetName()` method.

```
class DailyOutArtifact(Artifact):
    def __init__(self):
        self.AddHunter(DailyOutHunter())

    def GetName(self):
        return 'daily.out parser'
```

The last method of this class, `CreateFragments()`, specifies how to handle a single entry of the processed daily.out log results. A fragment, with respect to the Axiom API, is the term used to describe a single entry of an artifact. This code block allows us to add custom column names and assign the proper categories and data types for those columns. The categories include date, location, and other special values defined by the tool. The majority of columns for our artifact will be in the `None` category, as they don't display a specific kind of information.

One important categorical difference is `DateTimeLocal` versus `DateTime`: the `DateTime` will present the date as a UTC value to the user, so we need to be conscious about selecting the proper date category. Because we extracted the time zone from the daily.out log entries, we use the `DateTimeLocal` category in this recipe. The `FragmentType` property is a string for all of the values, as the class does not convert values from strings into another data type.

```
    def CreateFragments(self):
        self.AddFragment('Snapshot Date - LocalTime (yyyy-mm-dd)',
                        Category.DateTimeLocal, FragmentType.DateTime)
        self.AddFragment('Snapshot Timezone', Category.None,
                        FragmentType.String)
```

```
        self.AddFragment('Volume Name',
                            Category.None, FragmentType.String)
        self.AddFragment('Filesystem Mount',
                            Category.None, FragmentType.String)
        self.AddFragment('Volume Size',
                            Category.None, FragmentType.String)
        self.AddFragment('Volume Used',
                            Category.None, FragmentType.String)
        self.AddFragment('Percentage Used',
                            Category.None, FragmentType.String)
```

The next class is our `Hunter`. This parent class is used to run the processing code and, as you will see, specifies the platform and content that will be provided to the plugin by the Axiom engine. In this instance, we only want to run this against the computer platform and a file that goes by a single name. The `RegisterFileName()` method is one of several options for specifying what files will be requested by the plugin. We can also use regular expressions or file extensions to select the files we would like to process.

```
class DailyOutHunter(Hunter):
    def __init__(self):
        self.Platform = Platform.Computer

    def Register(self, registrar):
        registrar.RegisterFileName('daily.out')
```

The `Hunt()` method is where the magic happens. To start, we get a temporary path where the file can be read within the sandbox and assign it to the `temp_daily_out` variable. With this open file, we hand the file object to the `ProcessDailyOut` class and use the `run()` method to parse the file, just like in the last recipe.

```
    def Hunt(self, context):
        temp_daily_out = open(context.Searchable.FileCopy, 'r')

        processor = ProcessDailyOut(temp_daily_out)
        parsed_events = processor.run()
```

After gathering the parsed event information, we are ready to "publish" the data to the software and display it to the user. In the `for` loop, we first initiate a `Hit()` object to add data to a new fragment using the `AddValue()` method. Once we have assigned the event values to a hit, we publish the hit to the platform with the `PublishHit()` method and continue the loop until all parsed events have been published:

```
        for entry in parsed_events:
            hit = Hit()
            hit.AddValue(
                "Snapshot Date - LocalTime (yyyy-mm-dd)",
```

```
                  entry['event_date'].strftime("%Y-%m-%d %H:%M:%S"))
            hit.AddValue("Snapshot Timezone", entry['event_tz'])
            hit.AddValue("Volume Name", entry['Mounted on'])
            hit.AddValue("Filesystem Mount", entry["Filesystem"])
            hit.AddValue("Volume Size", entry['Size'])
            hit.AddValue("Volume Used", entry['Used'])
            hit.AddValue("Percentage Used", entry['Capacity'])
            self.PublishHit(hit)
```

The last bit of code checks to see if the file is not `None` and will close it if so. This is the end of the processing code, which may be called again if another `daily.out` file is discovered on the system!

```
        if temp_daily_out is not None:
            temp_daily_out.close()
```

The last line registers our hard work with Axiom's engine to ensure it is included and called by the framework.

```
    RegisterArtifact(DailyOutArtifact())
```

To use the newly developed artifact in Axiom, we need to take a few more steps to import and run the code against an image. First, we need to launch Axiom Process. This is where we will load, select, and run the artifact against the provided evidence. Under the **Tools** menu, we select the **Manage custom artifacts** option:

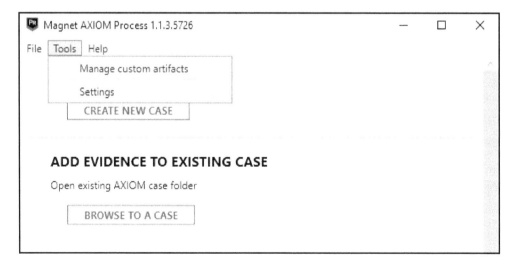

Within the **Manage custom artifacts** window, we will see any existing custom artifacts and can import new ones as seen here:

We will add our custom artifact and the updated **Manage custom artifacts** window should show the name of the artifact:

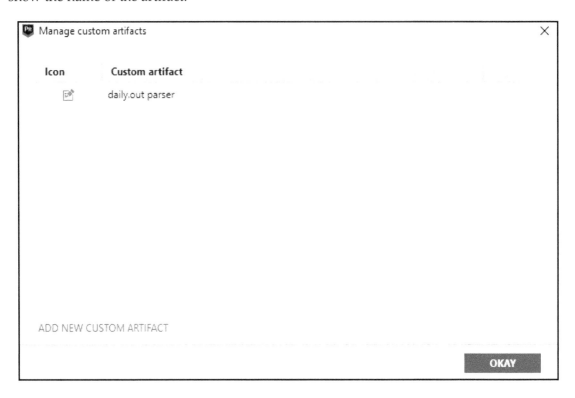

Now we can press **OKAY** and continue through Axiom, adding the evidence and configuring our processing options. When we reach the **COMPUTER ARTIFACTS** selection, we want to confirm that the custom artifact is selected to run. It probably goes without saying: we should only run this artifact if the machine is running macOS or has a macOS partition on it:

After completing the remaining configuration options, we can start processing the evidence. With processing complete, we run Axiom Examine to review the processed results. As seen in the following screenshot, we can navigate to the **CUSTOM** pane of the artifact review and see the parsed columns from the plugin! These columns can be sorted and exported using the standard options in Axiom, without any additional code on our part:

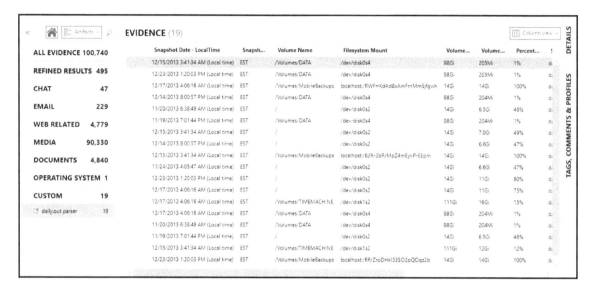

Scanning for indicators with YARA

Recipe Difficulty: Medium

Python Version: 3.5

Operating System: Any

As a bonus section, we will leverage the powerful **Yet Another Recursive Algorithm** (**YARA**) regular-expression engine to scan for files of interest and indicators of compromise. YARA is a pattern-matching utility designed for use in malware identification and incident response. Many tools use this engine as the backbone for identification of likely malicious files. Through this recipe, we learn how to take YARA rules, compile them, and match them across one or more folders or files. While we will not cover the steps required to form a YARA rule, one can learn more about the process from their documentation at `http://yara.readthedocs.io/en/latest/writingrules.html`.

Getting started

This recipe requires the installation of the third-party library `yara`. All other libraries used in this script are present in Python's standard library. This library can be installed with `pip`:

```
pip install yara-python==3.6.3
```

 To learn more about the `yara-python` library, visit `https://yara.readthedocs.io/en/latest/`.

We can also use projects such as YaraRules (`http://yararules.com`) and use pre-built rules from the industry and VirusShare (`http://virusshare.com`) to use real malware samples for analysis.

How to do it...

This script has four main developmental steps:

1. Set up and compile YARA rules.
2. Scan a single file.
3. Iterate through directories to process individual files.
4. Export results to CSV.

How it works...

This script imports the required libraries to handle argument parsing, file and folder iteration, writing CSV spreadsheets, and the `yara` library to compile and scan for the YARA rules.

```
from __future__ import print_function
from argparse import ArgumentParser, ArgumentDefaultsHelpFormatter
import os
import csv
import yara
```

This recipe's command-line handler accepts two positional arguments, `yara_rules` and `path_to_scan`, which represent the path to the YARA rules and the file or folder to scan, respectively. This recipe also accepts one optional argument, `output`, which, if supplied, writes the results of the scan to a spreadsheet as opposed to the console. Lastly, we pass these values to the `main()` method.

```
if __name__ == '__main__':
    parser = ArgumentParser(
        description=__description__,
        formatter_class=ArgumentDefaultsHelpFormatter,
        epilog="Developed by {} on {}".format(
            ", ".join(__authors__), __date__)
    )
    parser.add_argument(
        'yara_rules',
        help="Path to Yara rule to scan with. May be file or folder path.")
    parser.add_argument(
        'path_to_scan',
        help="Path to file or folder to scan")
    parser.add_argument(
        '--output',
        help="Path to output a CSV report of scan results")
    args = parser.parse_args()

    main(args.yara_rules, args.path_to_scan, args.output)
```

In the `main()` function, we accept the path to the `yara` rules, the files or folders to scan, and the output file (if any). Since the `yara` rules can be a file or directory, we use the `ios.isdir()` method to determine if we use the `compile()` method on a whole directory or, if the input is a file, pass it to the method using the `filepath` keyword. The `compile()` method reads the rule file or files and creates an object that we can match against objects we scan.

```
def main(yara_rules, path_to_scan, output):
    if os.path.isdir(yara_rules):
        yrules = yara.compile(yara_rules)
    else:
        yrules = yara.compile(filepath=yara_rules)
```

Once the rules are compiled, we perform a similar `if-else` statement to process the path to scan. If the input to scan is a directory, we pass it to the `process_directory()` function and, otherwise, we use the `process_file()` method. Both take the compiled YARA rules and the path to scan and return a list of dictionaries containing any matches.

```
if os.path.isdir(path_to_scan):
    match_info = process_directory(yrules, path_to_scan)
else:
    match_info = process_file(yrules, path_to_scan)
```

As you may guess, we will ultimately convert this list of dictionaries to a CSV report if the output path was specified, using the columns we define in the `columns` list. However, if the output argument is `None`, we write this data to the console in a different format instead.

```
columns = ['rule_name', 'hit_value', 'hit_offset', 'file_name',
           'rule_string', 'rule_tag']

if output is None:
    write_stdout(columns, match_info)
else:
    write_csv(output, columns, match_info)
```

The `process_directory()` function essentially iterates through a directory and passes each file to the `process_file()` function. This decreases the amount of redundant code in the script. Each processed entry that is returned is added to the `match_info` list, as the returned object is a list. Once we have processed each file, we return the complete list of results to the parent function.

```
def process_directory(yrules, folder_path):
    match_info = []
    for root, _, files in os.walk(folder_path):
        for entry in files:
            file_entry = os.path.join(root, entry)
            match_info += process_file(yrules, file_entry)
    return match_info
```

The `process_file()` method uses with the `match()` method of the `yrules` object. The returned match object is an iterable containing one or more hits against the rules. From the hit, we can extract the rule name, any tags, the offset in the file, the string value of the rule, and the string value of the hit. This information, plus the file path, will form an entry in the report. Collectively, this information is useful in identifying whether the hit is a false positive or is of significance. It can also be helpful when fine-tuning YARA rules to ensure only relevant results are presented for review.

```
def process_file(yrules, file_path):
    match = yrules.match(file_path)
    match_info = []
    for rule_set in match:
        for hit in rule_set.strings:
            match_info.append({
                'file_name': file_path,
                'rule_name': rule_set.rule,
                'rule_tag': ",".join(rule_set.tags),
                'hit_offset': hit[0],
                'rule_string': hit[1],
                'hit_value': hit[2]
            })
    return match_info
```

To `write_stdout()` function reports match information to the console if the user does not specify an output file. We iterate through each entry in the `match_info` list and print each column name and its value from the `match_info` dictionary in a colon-delimited, newline-separated format. After each entry, we print 30 equals signs to visually separate the entries from each other.

```
def write_stdout(columns, match_info):
    for entry in match_info:
        for col in columns:
            print("{}: {}".format(col, entry[col]))
        print("=" * 30)
```

The `write_csv()` method follows the standard convention, using the `DictWriter` class to write the headers and all of the data into the sheet. Notice how this function is adjusted to handle CSV writing in Python 3, using the `'w'` mode and `newline` parameter.

```
def write_csv(outfile, fieldnames, data):
    with open(outfile, 'w', newline="") as open_outfile:
        csvfile = csv.DictWriter(open_outfile, fieldnames)
        csvfile.writeheader()
        csvfile.writerows(data)
```

Using this code, we can provide the appropriate arguments at the command-line and generate a report of any matches. The following screenshot shows the custom rules for detecting Python files and keyloggers:

```
rule PythonFile : PY_CODE
{
    meta:
        description = "Python File"
    strings:
        $py0 = /def [A-Za-z0-9_\.]+\(\):/
        $py1 = /^import [A-Za-z0-9_\.]+/
        $py2 = /^from [A-Za-z0-9_\.]+ import
        [A-Za-z0-9_\.]+/
        $py3 = /elif /
        $py4 = /__name__/
        $py5 = /__main__/
    condition:
        2 of them
}

rule PythonKeyloggerFile : PY_KEYLOGGER
{
    meta:
        description = "Python Keylogger"
        version = "1"
    strings:
        $py0 =
        "compat_dc,'screenshot'+timestr+'.bmp'"
        $py1 =
        "GetClipboardData(win32con.CF_TEXT)"
        fullword
        $py2 = "OnKeyboardEvent(event)" fullword
        $py3 = "event.Ascii" fullword
        $py4 = "pyHook.HookManager()" fullword
        $py5 = "Win32_Process.watch_for" fullword
    condition:
        4 of them and PythonFile
}
```

These rules are shown in the output CSV report, or console if a report is not specified, as seen here:

rule_name	hit_value	hit_offset	file_name	rule_string	rule_tag
PythonFile	b'def take_screenshot():'	188	/media/working/mal/logger.pyw	$py0	PY_CODE
PythonFile	b'def get_clipboard():'	1167	/media/working/mal/logger.pyw	$py0	PY_CODE
PythonFile	b'def keylogger_main():'	2500	/media/working/mal/logger.pyw	$py0	PY_CODE
PythonFile	b'def process_logger_main():'	2800	/media/working/mal/logger.pyw	$py0	PY_CODE
PythonFile	b'def main():'	3179	/media/working/mal/logger.pyw	$py0	PY_CODE
PythonFile	b'import multiprocessing'	0	/media/working/mal/logger.pyw	$py1	PY_CODE
PythonFile	b'elif '	1840	/media/working/mal/logger.pyw	$py3	PY_CODE
PythonFile	b'elif '	2118	/media/working/mal/logger.pyw	$py3	PY_CODE
PythonFile	b'__name__'	3652	/media/working/mal/logger.pyw	$py4	PY_CODE
PythonFile	b'__main__'	3665	/media/working/mal/logger.pyw	$py5	PY_CODE
PythonKeyloggerFile	b"compat_dc,'screenshot'+timestr+'.bmp'"	934	/media/working/mal/logger.pyw	$py0	PY_KEYLOGGER
PythonKeyloggerFile	b'GetClipboardData(win32con.CF_TEXT)'	1310	/media/working/mal/logger.pyw	$py1	PY_KEYLOGGER
PythonKeyloggerFile	b'OnKeyboardEvent(event)'	1462	/media/working/mal/logger.pyw	$py2	PY_KEYLOGGER
PythonKeyloggerFile	b'event.Ascii'	1713	/media/working/mal/logger.pyw	$py3	PY_KEYLOGGER
PythonKeyloggerFile	b'event.Ascii'	1845	/media/working/mal/logger.pyw	$py3	PY_KEYLOGGER
PythonKeyloggerFile	b'event.Ascii'	1918	/media/working/mal/logger.pyw	$py3	PY_KEYLOGGER
PythonKeyloggerFile	b'event.Ascii'	2123	/media/working/mal/logger.pyw	$py3	PY_KEYLOGGER
PythonKeyloggerFile	b'event.Ascii'	2144	/media/working/mal/logger.pyw	$py3	PY_KEYLOGGER
PythonKeyloggerFile	b'event.Ascii'	2165	/media/working/mal/logger.pyw	$py3	PY_KEYLOGGER
PythonKeyloggerFile	b'event.Ascii'	2413	/media/working/mal/logger.pyw	$py3	PY_KEYLOGGER
PythonKeyloggerFile	b'pyHook.HookManager()'	2566	/media/working/mal/logger.pyw	$py4	PY_KEYLOGGER
PythonKeyloggerFile	b'Win32_Process.watch_for'	2863	/media/working/mal/logger.pyw	$py5	PY_KEYLOGGER

8

Working with Forensic Evidence Container Recipes

In this chapter, we will cover the following recipes:

- Opening acquisitions
- Gathering acquisition and media information
- Iterating through files
- Processing files within the container
- Searching for hashes

Introduction

The Sleuth Kit, and its Python bindings `pytsk3`, is perhaps the most well-known Python forensic library. This library offers rich support for accessing and manipulating filesystems. And with the help of supporting libraries, such as `pyewf`, they can be used to work with common forensic containers such as EnCase's popular `E01` format. Without these libraries (and many others), we would be inherently more limited by what can be accomplished with Python in forensics. Due to its lofty goal as an all-in-one filesystem analysis tool, `pytsk3` is perhaps the most complicated library we will work with in this book.

For this reason, we have dedicated a number of recipes exploring the fundamentals of this library. Up to this point, recipes have been mainly focused on loose file support. That convention ends here. We will routinely use this library going forward to interact with forensic evidence. Understanding how to interact with forensic containers will take your Python forensic capabilities to the next level.

In this chapter, we will learn how to install `pytsk3` and `pyewf`, two libraries that will allow us to leverage the Sleuth Kit and `E01` image support, respectively. Additionally, we will learn how to perform basic tasks, such as accessing and printing a partition table, iterating through a filesystem, exporting files by extension, and searching for known bad hashes in an evidence container. You will learn about:

- Installing and setting up `pytsk3` and `pyewf`
- Opening forensic acquisitions such as `raw` and `E01` files
- Extracting partition table data and `E01` metadata
- Recursing through active files and creating an active file listing spreadsheet
- Exporting files from the evidence container by file extension
- Searching for known bad hashes in an evidence container

 Visit `www.packtpub.com/books/content/support` to download the code bundle for this chapter.

Opening acquisitions

Recipe Difficulty: Medium

Python Version: 2.7

Operating System: Linux

With `pyewf` and `pytsk3` comes a whole new set of tools and operations we must first learn. In this recipe, we will start with the basics: opening an evidence container. This recipe supports `raw` and `E01` images. Note that unlike our previous scripts, these recipes will use Python 2.X due to some bugs found while working with the Python 3.X version of these libraries. That said, the main logic would not differ between the two versions and could easily be ported. Before we learn to open the container, we need to set up our environment. We will explore this in the next section.

Getting started

Excluding a few scripts, we have been OS agnostic for the majority of this cookbook. Here, however, we will specifically provide instructions for building on Ubuntu 16.04.2. With a fresh install of Ubuntu, execute the following commands to install necessary dependencies:

```
sudo apt-get update && sudo apt-get -y upgrade
sudo apt-get install python-pip git autoconf automake autopoint libtool
pkg-config
```

Beyond the two previously mentioned libraries (`pytsk3` and `pyewf`), we will also be using the third-party module `tabulate` to print tables to the console. As that is the easiest module to install, let's complete that task first by executing the following:

```
pip install tabulate==0.7.7
```

 To learn more about the tabulate library, visit `https://pypi.python.org/pypi/tabulate`.

Believe it or not, we can install `pytsk3` using `pip` as well:

```
pip install pytsk3==20170802
```

 To learn more about the `pytsk3` library, visit `https://github.com/py4n6/pytsk`.

Lastly, for `pyewf`, we must take a slightly more circuitous route and install it from its GitHub repository, `https://github.com/libyal/libewf/releases`. These recipes were written using the `libewf-experimental-20170605` release, and we recommend you install that version here. Once the package has been downloaded and extracted, open a Command Prompt in the extracted directory and execute the following:

```
./synclibs.sh
./autogen.sh
sudo python setup.py build
sudo python setup.py install
```

 To learn more about the `pyewf` library, visit : `https://github.com/libyal/libewf`.

It goes without saying that for this script you will need a `raw` or `E01` evidence file to run these recipes against. For the first script, we recommend using a logical image, such as `fat-img-kw.dd` from `http://dftt.sourceforge.net/test2/index.html`. The reason is that this first script will lack some necessary logic to handle physical disk images and their partitions. We will introduce this functionality in the *Gathering acquisition and media information* recipe.

How to do it...

We employ the following methodology to open forensic evidence containers:

1. Identify if the evidence container is a `raw` image or an `E01` container.
2. Access the image using `pytsk3`.
3. Print a table of the root-level folders and files to the console.

How it works...

We import a number of libraries to assist with argument parsing, handling evidence containers and filesystems, and creating tabular console data.

```
from __future__ import print_function
import argparse
import os
import pytsk3
import pyewf
import sys
from tabulate import tabulate
```

This recipe's command-line handler takes two positional arguments, `EVIDENCE_FILE` and `TYPE`, which represent the path to the evidence file and the type of evidence file (that is, `raw` or `ewf`). Note that for segmented `E01` files, you only need to supply the path to the first `E01` (with the assumption that the other splits are in the same directory). After performing some input validation on the evidence file, we supply the `main()` function with the two provided inputs and begin executing the script.

```
if __name__ == '__main__':
    parser = argparse.ArgumentParser(
        description=__description__,
        epilog="Developed by {} on {}".format(
            ", ".join(__authors__), __date__)
    )
```

```
parser.add_argument("EVIDENCE_FILE", help="Evidence file path")
parser.add_argument("TYPE",
                    help="Type of evidence: raw (dd) or EWF (E01)",
                    choices=("raw", "ewf"))
parser.add_argument("-o", "--offset",
                    help="Partition byte offset", type=int)
args = parser.parse_args()

if os.path.exists(args.EVIDENCE_FILE) and \
        os.path.isfile(args.EVIDENCE_FILE):
    main(args.EVIDENCE_FILE, args.TYPE, args.offset)
else:
    print("[-] Supplied input file {} does not exist or is not a "
          "file".format(args.EVIDENCE_FILE))
    sys.exit(1)
```

In the `main()` function, we first check what type of evidence file we are working with. If it is an `E01` container, we need to first use `pyewf` to create a handle before we can access its contents with `pytsk3`. With a `raw` image, we can directly access its contents with `pytsk3` without needing to perform this intermediate step first.

The `pyewf.glob()` method is used here to combine all segments of the `E01` container, if there are any, and store the segment names in a list. Once we have the list of filenames, we can create the `E01` handle object. We can then use this object to open the `filenames`.

```
def main(image, img_type, offset):
    print("[+] Opening {}".format(image))
    if img_type == "ewf":
        try:
            filenames = pyewf.glob(image)
        except IOError:
            _, e, _ = sys.exc_info()
            print("[-] Invalid EWF format:\n {}".format(e))
            sys.exit(2)
        ewf_handle = pyewf.handle()
        ewf_handle.open(filenames)
```

Next, we must pass the `ewf_handle` to the `EWFImgInfo` class, which will create the `pytsk3` object. The else statement here is for `raw` images that can use the `pytsk3.Img_Info` function to achieve the same task. Let's now look at the `EWFImgInfo` class to understand how EWF files are processed slightly differently.

```
        # Open PYTSK3 handle on EWF Image
        img_info = EWFImgInfo(ewf_handle)
    else:
        img_info = pytsk3.Img_Info(image)
```

The code for this component of the script is from the *Combining pyewf with pytsk3* section of the Python development page for `pyewf`.

 Learn more about `pyewf` functions, visit `https://github.com/libyal/libewf/wiki/Development`.

This `EWFImgInfo` class inherits from the `pytsk3.Img_Info` base class and is of the type `TSK_IMG_TYPE_EXTERNAL`. It is important to note that the three functions defined next, `close()`, `read()`, and `get_size()`, are all required by `pytsk3` to interact with the evidence container appropriately. With this simple class created, we can now use `pytsk3` with any supplied `E01` file.

```
class EWFImgInfo(pytsk3.Img_Info):
    def __init__(self, ewf_handle):
        self._ewf_handle = ewf_handle
        super(EWFImgInfo, self).__init__(url="",
                                type=pytsk3.TSK_IMG_TYPE_EXTERNAL)

    def close(self):
        self._ewf_handle.close()

    def read(self, offset, size):
        self._ewf_handle.seek(offset)
        return self._ewf_handle.read(size)

    def get_size(self):
        return self._ewf_handle.get_media_size()
```

Back in the `main()` function, we have successfully created our `pytsk3` handler for either `raw` or `E01` images. We can now begin accessing the filesystem. As mentioned, this script is designed to work with logical images and not physical images. We will introduce support for physical images in the next recipe. Accessing the filesystem is really simple; we do so by calling the `FS_Info()` function on the `pytsk3` handle.

```
# Get Filesystem Handle
try:
    fs = pytsk3.FS_Info(img_info, offset)
except IOError:
    _, e, _ = sys.exc_info()
    print("[-] Unable to open FS:\n {}".format(e))
    exit()
```

With access to the filesystem, we can iterate through the folders and files in the root directory. First, we access the root using the `open_dir()` method on the filesystem and specifying the root directory, **/**, as the input. Next, we create a nested list structure that will hold the table content, which we will later print to the console using `tabulate`. The first element of this list is the headers of that table.

Following that, we'll begin to iterate through the image as we would with any Python iterable object. There are a variety of attributes and functions for each object, and we begin to use them here. First, we extract the name of the object using the `f.info.name.name` attribute. We then check if we are dealing with a directory or a file using the `f.info.meta.type` attribute. If this is equal to the built-in `TSK_FS_META_TYPE_DIR` object, then we set the `f_type` variable to `DIR`; otherwise, to `FILE`.

Lastly, we use a few more attributes to extract the directory or file size and create and modify timestamps. Be aware that object timestamps are stored in `Unix` time and must be converted if you would like to display them in a human-readable format. With these attributes extracted, we append the data to the `table` list and continue on to the next object. Once we have finished processing all objects in the root folder, we use `tabulate` to print the data to the console. This is accomplished in one line by supplying the `tabulate()` method with the list and setting the `headers` keyword argument to `firstrow` to indicate that the first element in the list should be used as the table header.

```
root_dir = fs.open_dir(path="/")
table = [["Name", "Type", "Size", "Create Date", "Modify Date"]]
for f in root_dir:
    name = f.info.name.name
    if f.info.meta.type == pytsk3.TSK_FS_META_TYPE_DIR:
        f_type = "DIR"
    else:
        f_type = "FILE"
    size = f.info.meta.size
    create = f.info.meta.crtime
    modify = f.info.meta.mtime
    table.append([name, f_type, size, create, modify])
print(tabulate(table, headers="firstrow"))
```

When we run the script, we can learn about the files and folders at the root of the evidence container as seen in the following screenshot:

```
(venv2) pyforcookbook@dev-vm$ python open_evidence.py /media/evidence/tedmosby.E
01 ewf -o 1048576
[+] Opening /media/evidence/tedmosby.E01
Name                       Type         Size   Create Date    Modify Date
------------------------   ------   ----------   -------------   -------------
$AttrDef                   FILE         2560   1350505126     1350505126
$BadClus                   FILE            0   1350505126     1350505126
$Bitmap                    FILE      1966016   1350505126     1350505126
$Boot                      FILE         8192   1350505126     1350505126
$Extend                    DIR           552   1350505126     1350505126
$LogFile                   FILE     67108864   1350505126     1350505126
$MFT                       FILE     63963136   1350505126     1350505126
$MFTMirr                   FILE         4096   1350505126     1350505126
$Recycle.Bin               DIR           328   1247541536     1350491438
$Secure                    FILE            0   1350505126     1350505126
$UpCase                    FILE       131072   1350505126     1350505126
$Volume                    FILE            0   1350505126     1350505126
.                          DIR            56   1247539136     1350491616
Boot                       DIR            56   1350505491     1350505491
bootmgr                    FILE       383786   1350505491     1290309831
BOOTSECT.BAK               FILE         8192   1350505491     1350505491
Documents and Settings     DIR            48   1247548136     1247548136
pagefile.sys               FILE   1073741824   1350501938     1352130469
PerfLogs                   DIR           144   1247541608     1247541608
Program Files              DIR            56   1247541608     1350491504
Program Files (x86)        DIR           192   1247541608     1351708862
ProgramData                DIR            56   1247541608     1351708710
Recovery                   DIR           312   1350491406     1350491406
System Volume Information   DIR           56   1350501937     1350491496
Users                      DIR            56   1247541608     1350491412
```

Gathering acquisition and media information

Recipe Difficulty: Medium

Python Version: 2.7

Operating System: Linux

In this recipe, we learn how to view and print the partition table using `tabulate`. Additionally, for `E01` containers, we will print `E01` acquisition and container metadata stored in the evidence file. Oftentimes, we will be working with a physical disk image of a given machine. In pretty much any process going forward, we will need to iterate through the different partitions (or a user-selected partition) to get a handle on the filesystem and its files. Therefore, this recipe is of critical importance as we build upon our burgeoning understanding of the Sleuth Kit and its bevy of features.

Getting started

Refer to the *Getting started* section in the *Opening Acquisitions* recipe for information on the build environment and setup details for `pytsk3`, `pyewf`, and `tabulate`. All other libraries used in this script are present in Python's standard library.

How to do it...

The recipe follows these basic steps:

1. Identify if the evidence container is a `raw` image or an `E01` container.
2. Access the image using `pytsk3`.
3. If applicable, print `E01` metadata to the console.
4. Print partition table data to the console.

How it works...

We import a number of libraries to assist with argument parsing, handling evidence containers and filesystems, and creating tabular console data.

```
from __future__ import print_function
import argparse
import os
import pytsk3
import pyewf
import sys
from tabulate import tabulate
```

This recipe's command-line handler takes two positional arguments, EVIDENCE_FILE and TYPE, which represent the path to the evidence file and the type of evidence file. Additionally, if the user is experiencing difficulties with the evidence file, they can use the optional p switch to manually supply the partition. This switch should not be necessary for the most part but has been added as a precaution. After performing input validation checks, we pass the three arguments to the main() function.

```
if __name__ == '__main__':
    parser = argparse.ArgumentParser(
        description=__description__,
        epilog="Developed by {} on {}".format(
            ", ".join(__authors__), __date__)
    )
```

```
        parser.add_argument("EVIDENCE_FILE", help="Evidence file path")
        parser.add_argument("TYPE", help="Type of Evidence",
                            choices=("raw", "ewf"))
        parser.add_argument("-p", help="Partition Type",
                            choices=("DOS", "GPT", "MAC", "SUN"))
        args = parser.parse_args()

        if os.path.exists(args.EVIDENCE_FILE) and \
                os.path.isfile(args.EVIDENCE_FILE):
            main(args.EVIDENCE_FILE, args.TYPE, args.p)
        else:
            print("[-] Supplied input file {} does not exist or is not a "
                  "file".format(args.EVIDENCE_FILE))
            sys.exit(1)
```

The `main()` function is substantially similar, at least initially, to the previous recipe. We must first create the `pyewf` handle and then use the `EWFImgInfo` class to create, as shown previously in the `pytsk3` handle. If you would like to learn more about the `EWFImgInfo` class, refer to the *Opening Acquisitions* recipe. However, note that we have added an additional line calling the `e01_metadata()` function to print `E01` metadata to the console. Let's explore that function now.

```
    def main(image, img_type, part_type):
        print("[+] Opening {}".format(image))
        if img_type == "ewf":
            try:
                filenames = pyewf.glob(image)
            except IOError:
                print("[-] Invalid EWF format:\n {}".format(e))
                sys.exit(2)

            ewf_handle = pyewf.handle()
            ewf_handle.open(filenames)
            e01_metadata(ewf_handle)

            # Open PYTSK3 handle on EWF Image
            img_info = EWFImgInfo(ewf_handle)
        else:
            img_info = pytsk3.Img_Info(image)
```

The `e01_metadata()` function primarily relies on the `get_header_values()` and `get_hash_values()` methods to acquire `E01`-specific metadata. The `get_header_values()` method returns a dictionary of `key-value` pairs for various types of acquisition and media metadata. We use a loop to iterate through this dictionary and print the `key-value` pairs to the console.

Similarly, we use a loop with the `hashes` dictionary to print stored acquisition hashes of the image to the console. Lastly, we call an attribute and a few functions to print acquisition size metadata.

```
def e01_metadata(e01_image):
    print("\nEWF Acquisition Metadata")
    print("-" * 20)
    headers = e01_image.get_header_values()
    hashes = e01_image.get_hash_values()
    for k in headers:
        print("{}: {}".format(k, headers[k]))
    for h in hashes:
        print("Acquisition {}: {}".format(h, hashes[h]))
    print("Bytes per Sector: {}".format(e01_image.bytes_per_sector))
    print("Number of Sectors: {}".format(
        e01_image.get_number_of_sectors()))
    print("Total Size: {}".format(e01_image.get_media_size()))
```

With that covered, we can now return to the `main()` function. Recall that in the first recipe of this chapter, we did not create support for physical acquisitions (which was totally on purpose). Now, however, we add that support in using the `Volume_Info()` function. While `pytsk3` can be daunting at first, appreciate the consistency in naming conventions used in the major functions we have introduced so far: `Img_Info`, `FS_Info`, and `Volume_Info`. These three functions are vital in order to access the contents of the evidence container. In this recipe, we will not be using the `FS_Info()` function as the purpose here is to only print out the partition table.

We attempt to access the volume info in a `try-except` block. First, we check if the `p` switch was supplied by the user and, if so, assign the attribute for that partition type to a variable. Then we supply that, along with the `pytsk3` handle, in the `Volume_Info` method. Otherwise, if no partition was specified, we call the `Volume_Info` method and supply it with just the `pytsk3` handle object. If we receive an `IOError` attempting to do this, we catch the exception as `e` and print it to the console before exiting. If we are able to access the volume info, we pass this onto the `part_metadata()` function to print the partition data to the console.

```
    try:
        if part_type is not None:
            attr_id = getattr(pytsk3, "TSK_VS_TYPE_" + part_type)
            volume = pytsk3.Volume_Info(img_info, attr_id)
        else:
            volume = pytsk3.Volume_Info(img_info)
    except IOError:
        _, e, _ = sys.exc_info()
        print("[-] Unable to read partition table:\n {}".format(e))
```

```
            sys.exit(3)
    part_metadata(volume)
```

The `part_metadata()` function is relatively light on logic. We create a nested list structure, as seen in the previous recipe, with the first element representing the eventual table header. Next, we iterate through the volume object and append the partition address, type, offset, and length to the `table` list. Once we have iterated through the partitions, we use `tabulate` to print a table of this data to the console using `firstrow` as the table header.

```python
def part_metadata(vol):
    table = [["Index", "Type", "Offset Start (Sectors)",
              "Length (Sectors)"]]
    for part in vol:
        table.append([part.addr, part.desc.decode("utf-8"), part.start,
                      part.len])
    print("\n Partition Metadata")
    print("-" * 20)
    print(tabulate(table, headers="firstrow"))
```

When running this code, we can review information about the acquisition and partition information in the console, if present:

```
(venv2) pyforcookbook@dev-vm$ python evidence_metadata.py \
> /media/evidence/tedmosby.E01 ewf
[+] Opening /media/evidence/tedmosby.E01

EWF Acquisition Metadata
--------------------
system_date: Wed Nov  7 15:50:58 2012
description: untitled
evidence_number:
acquiry_date: Wed Nov  7 15:50:58 2012
notes:
compression_level: f
examiner_name:
acquiry_software_version: ADI3.0.1.14
case_number:
acquiry_operating_system: Windows 7
Acquisition SHA1: 38f8b69e7f3b7d0a7a50c9c1dc91f9204bff2d99
Acquisition MD5: 4a90f93278dea2d230030014bc54521c
Bytes per Sector: 512
Number of Sectors: 125829120
Total Size: 64424509440

 Partition Metadata
--------------------
  Index  Type                    Offset Start (Sectors)    Length (Sectors)
-------  --------------------    ----------------------    -----------------
      0  Primary Table (#0)                           0                    1
      1  Unallocated                                  0                 2048
      2  NTFS / exFAT (0x07)                       2048            125825024
      3  Unallocated                          125827072                 2048
```

Iterating through files

Recipe Difficulty: Medium

Python Version: 2.7

Operating System: Linux

In this recipe, we learn how to recurse through the filesystem and create an active file listing. Oftentimes, one of the first questions we, as the forensic examiner, are often asked is "What data is on the device?". An active file listing comes in handy here. Creating a file listing of loose files is a very straightforward task in Python. However, this will be slightly more complicated because we are working with a forensic image rather than loose files. This recipe will be a cornerstone for future scripts as it will allow us to recursively access and process every file in the image. As you may have noticed, this chapter's recipes are building upon each other as each function we develop it becomes necessary to explore the image further. In a similar way, this recipe will become integral in future recipes to iterate through directories and process files.

Getting started

Refer to the *Getting started* section in the *Opening Acquisitions* recipe for information on the build environment and setup details for `pytsk3` and `pyewf`. All other libraries used in this script are present in Python's standard library.

How to do it...

We perform the following steps in this recipe:

1. Identify if the evidence container is a `raw` image or an `E01` container.
2. Access the forensic image using `pytsk3`.
3. Recurse through all directories in each partition.
4. Store file metadata in a list.
5. Write the `active` file list to CSV.

How it works...

We import a number of libraries to assist with argument parsing, parsing dates, creating CSV spreadsheets, and handling evidence containers and filesystems.

```
from __future__ import print_function
import argparse
import csv
from datetime import datetime
import os
import pytsk3
import pyewf
import sys
```

This recipe's command-line handler takes three positional arguments, EVIDENCE_FILE, TYPE, and OUTPUT_CSV, which represent the path to the evidence file, the type of evidence file, and the output CSV file, respectively. Similar to the previous recipe, the optional p switch can be supplied to specify a partition type. We use the os.path.dirname() method to extract the desired output directory path for the CSV file and, with the os.makedirs() function, create the necessary output directories if they do not exist.

```
if __name__ == '__main__':
    parser = argparse.ArgumentParser(
        description=__description__,
        epilog="Developed by {} on {}".format(
            ", ".join(__authors__), __date__)
    )
    parser.add_argument("EVIDENCE_FILE", help="Evidence file path")
    parser.add_argument("TYPE", help="Type of Evidence",
                        choices=("raw", "ewf"))
    parser.add_argument("OUTPUT_CSV",
                        help="Output CSV with lookup results")
    parser.add_argument("-p", help="Partition Type",
                        choices=("DOS", "GPT", "MAC", "SUN"))
    args = parser.parse_args()

    directory = os.path.dirname(args.OUTPUT_CSV)
    if not os.path.exists(directory) and directory != "":
        os.makedirs(directory)
```

Once we have validated the input evidence file by checking that it exists and is a file, the four arguments are passed to the main() function. If there is an issue with initial validation of the input, an error is printed to the console before the script exits.

```
    if os.path.exists(args.EVIDENCE_FILE) and \
            os.path.isfile(args.EVIDENCE_FILE):
```

```
            main(args.EVIDENCE_FILE, args.TYPE, args.OUTPUT_CSV, args.p)
        else:
            print("[-] Supplied input file {} does not exist or is not a "
                  "file".format(args.EVIDENCE_FILE))
            sys.exit(1)
```

In the `main()` function, we instantiate the volume variable with `None` to avoid errors referencing it later in the script. After printing a status message to the console, we check if the evidence type is an `E01` to properly process it and create a valid `pyewf` handle, as demonstrated in more detail in the *Opening Acquisitions* recipe. Refer to that recipe for more details as this part of the function is identical. The end result is the creation of the `pytsk3` handle, `img_info`, for the user-supplied evidence file.

```
def main(image, img_type, output, part_type):
    volume = None
    print("[+] Opening {}".format(image))
    if img_type == "ewf":
        try:
            filenames = pyewf.glob(image)
        except IOError:
            _, e, _ = sys.exc_info()
            print("[-] Invalid EWF format:\n {}".format(e))
            sys.exit(2)

        ewf_handle = pyewf.handle()
        ewf_handle.open(filenames)

        # Open PYTSK3 handle on EWF Image
        img_info = EWFImgInfo(ewf_handle)
    else:
        img_info = pytsk3.Img_Info(image)
```

Next, we attempt to access the volume of the image using the `pytsk3.Volume_Info()` method by supplying it with the image handle. If the partition type argument was supplied, we add its attribute ID as the second argument. If we receive an `IOError` when attempting to access the volume, we catch the exception as `e` and print it to the console. Notice, however, that we do not exit the script as we often do when we receive an error. We'll explain why in the next function. Ultimately, we pass the `volume`, `img_info`, and `output` variables to the `open_fs()` method.

```
    try:
        if part_type is not None:
            attr_id = getattr(pytsk3, "TSK_VS_TYPE_" + part_type)
            volume = pytsk3.Volume_Info(img_info, attr_id)
        else:
            volume = pytsk3.Volume_Info(img_info)
```

```
except IOError:
    _, e, _ = sys.exc_info()
    print("[-] Unable to read partition table:\n {}".format(e))

open_fs(volume, img_info, output)
```

The `open_fs()` method tries to access the filesystem of the container in two ways. If the `volume` variable is not `None`, it iterates through each partition and, if that partition meets certain criteria, attempts to open it. If, however, the `volume` variable is `None`, it instead tries to directly call the `pytsk3.FS_Info()` method on the image handle, `img`. As we saw, this latter method will work and give us filesystem access for logical images, whereas the former works for physical images. Let's look at the differences between these two methods.

Regardless of the method, we create a `recursed_data` list to hold our active file metadata. In the first instance, where we have a physical image, we iterate through each partition and check whether it is greater than `2,048` sectors and does not contain the words `Unallocated`, `Extended`, or `Primary Table` in its description. For partitions meeting these criteria, we attempt to access their filesystem using the `FS_Info()` function by supplying the `pytsk3 img` object and the offset of the partition in bytes.

If we are able to access the filesystem, we use the `open_dir()` method to get the root directory and pass that, along with the partition address ID, the filesystem object, two empty lists, and an empty string, to the `recurse_files()` method. These empty lists and string will come into play in recursive calls to this function, as we will see shortly. Once the `recurse_files()` method returns, we append the active file metadata to the `recursed_data` list. We repeat this process for each partition.

```
def open_fs(vol, img, output):
    print("[+] Recursing through files..")
    recursed_data = []
    # Open FS and Recurse
    if vol is not None:
        for part in vol:
            if part.len > 2048 and "Unallocated" not in part.desc and \
                    "Extended" not in part.desc and \
                    "Primary Table" not in part.desc:
                try:
                    fs = pytsk3.FS_Info(
                        img, offset=part.start * vol.info.block_size)
                except IOError:
                    _, e, _ = sys.exc_info()
                    print("[-] Unable to open FS:\n {}".format(e))
                root = fs.open_dir(path="/")
                data = recurse_files(part.addr, fs, root, [], [], [""])
                recursed_data.append(data)
```

We employ a similar method for the second instance, where we have a logical image, where the volume is None. In this case, we attempt to directly access the filesystem and, if successful, we pass that to the recurseFiles() method and append the returned data to our recursed_data list. Once we have our active file list, we send it and the user-supplied output file path to the csvWriter() method. Let's dive into the recurseFiles() method, which is the meat of this recipe.

```
        else:
            try:
                fs = pytsk3.FS_Info(img)
            except IOError:
                _, e, _ = sys.exc_info()
                print("[-] Unable to open FS:\n {}".format(e))
            root = fs.open_dir(path="/")
            data = recurse_files(1, fs, root, [], [], [""])
            recursed_data.append(data)
        write_csv(recursed_data, output)
```

The recurse_files() function is based on an example of the *FLS* tool (https://github.com/py4n6/pytsk/blob/master/examples/fls.py) and David Cowen's tool DFIR Wizard (https://github.com/dlcowen/dfirwizard/blob/master/dfirwizard-v9.py). To start this function, we append the root directory inode to the dirs list. This list is used later to avoid unending loops. Next, we begin to loop through each object in the root directory and check whether it has certain attributes we would expect and that its name is not either "." or "..".

```
    def recurse_files(part, fs, root_dir, dirs, data, parent):
        dirs.append(root_dir.info.fs_file.meta.addr)
        for fs_object in root_dir:
            # Skip ".", ".." or directory entries without a name.
            if not hasattr(fs_object, "info") or \
                    not hasattr(fs_object.info, "name") or \
                    not hasattr(fs_object.info.name, "name") or \
                    fs_object.info.name.name in [".", ".."]:
                continue
```

If the object passes that test, we extract its name using the info.name.name attribute. Next, we use the parent variable, which was supplied as one of the function's inputs, to manually create the file path for this object. There is no built-in method or attribute to do this automatically for us.

We then check if the file is a directory or not and set the `f_type` variable to the appropriate type. If the object is a file, and it has an extension, we extract it and store it in the `file_ext` variable. If we encounter an `AttributeError` when attempting to extract this data, we continue onto the next object.

```
try:
    file_name = fs_object.info.name.name
    file_path = "{}/{}".format(
        "/".join(parent), fs_object.info.name.name)
    try:
        if fs_object.info.meta.type == pytsk3.TSK_FS_META_TYPE_DIR:
            f_type = "DIR"
            file_ext = ""
        else:
            f_type = "FILE"
            if "." in file_name:
                file_ext = file_name.rsplit(".")[-1].lower()
            else:
                file_ext = ""
    except AttributeError:
        continue
```

Similar to the first recipe in this chapter, we create variables for the object size and timestamps. However, notice that we pass the dates to a `convert_time()` method. This function exists to convert the `Unix` timestamps into a human-readable format. With these attributes extracted, we append them to the data list using the partition address ID to ensure we keep track of which partition the object is from.

```
size = fs_object.info.meta.size
create = convert_time(fs_object.info.meta.crtime)
change = convert_time(fs_object.info.meta.ctime)
modify = convert_time(fs_object.info.meta.mtime)
data.append(["PARTITION {}".format(part), file_name, file_ext,
            f_type, create, change, modify, size, file_path])
```

If the object is a directory, we need to recurse through it to access all of its subdirectories and files. To accomplish this, we append the directory name to the `parent` list. Then, we create a directory object using the `as_directory()` method. We use the `inode` here, which is for all intents and purposes a unique number, and check that the `inode` is not already in the `dirs` list. If that were the case, then we would not process this directory as it would have already been processed.

If the directory needs to be processed, we call the `recurse_files()` method on the new `sub_directory` and pass it current `dirs`, `data`, and `parent` variables. Once we have processed a given directory, we pop that directory from the `parent` list. Failing to do this will result in false file path details as all of the former directories will continue to be referenced in the path unless removed.

Most of this function was in a large `try-except` block. We pass on any `IOError` exception generated during this process. Once we have iterated through all of the subdirectories, we return the data list to the `open_fs()` function.

```
            if f_type == "DIR":
                parent.append(fs_object.info.name.name)
                sub_directory = fs_object.as_directory()
                inode = fs_object.info.meta.addr

                # This ensures that we don't recurse into a directory
                # above the current level and thus avoid circular loops.
                if inode not in dirs:
                    recurse_files(part, fs, sub_directory, dirs, data,
                                  parent)
                parent.pop(-1)

    except IOError:
        pass
    dirs.pop(-1)
    return data
```

Let's briefly look at the `convert_time()` function. We've seen this type of function before: if the `Unix` timestamp is not 0, we use the `datetime.utcfromtimestamp()` method to convert the timestamp into a human-readable format.

```
def convert_time(ts):
    if str(ts) == "0":
        return ""
    return datetime.utcfromtimestamp(ts)
```

With the active file listing data in hand, we are now ready to write it to a CSV file using the `write_csv()` method. If we did find data (that is, the list is not empty), we open the output CSV file, write the headers, and loop through each list in the `data` variable. We use the `csvwriterows()` method to write each nested list structure to the CSV file.

```
def write_csv(data, output):
    if data == []:
        print("[-] No output results to write")
        sys.exit(3)
```

```
print("[+] Writing output to {}".format(output))
with open(output, "wb") as csvfile:
    csv_writer = csv.writer(csvfile)
    headers = ["Partition", "File", "File Ext", "File Type",
               "Create Date", "Modify Date", "Change Date", "Size",
               "File Path"]
    csv_writer.writerow(headers)
    for result_list in data:
        csv_writer.writerows(result_list)
```

The following screenshot demonstrates the type of data this recipe extracts from forensic images:

Partition	File	File Ext	File Type	Create Date	Modify Date	Change Date	Size	File Path
PARTITION 2	pePIRes[1].dll	dll	FILE	10/31/12 06:38 PM	06/14/72 09:13 PM	10/31/12 06:38 PM	103320	/Users/Admin/AppData
PARTITION 2	catalog[1].xml	xml	FILE	10/31/12 06:38 PM	06/14/72 09:13 PM	10/31/12 06:38 PM	689	/Users/Admin/AppData
PARTITION 2	imagesCAO0OXQM.jpg	jpg	FILE	10/29/12 02:15 PM	06/12/73 04:08 AM	10/29/12 02:15 PM	11106	/Users/Admin/AppData
PARTITION 2	google_com[1].txt	txt	FILE	11/05/12 02:42 PM	06/12/73 07:00 AM	11/05/12 02:42 PM	108435	/Users/Admin/AppData
PARTITION 2	imagesCAAR54O4.jpg	jpg	FILE	11/05/12 02:45 PM	03/23/84 09:14 AM	11/05/12 02:45 PM	7249	/Users/Admin/AppData
PARTITION 2	imagesCAUANMII.jpg	jpg	FILE	11/05/12 02:45 PM	03/28/84 08:57 PM	11/05/12 02:45 PM	5259	/Users/Admin/AppData
PARTITION 2	imagesCAXHWQL4.jpg	jpg	FILE	11/05/12 02:45 PM	03/28/84 08:57 PM	11/05/12 02:45 PM	8063	/Users/Admin/AppData
PARTITION 2	imagesCAYJ73VM.jpg	jpg	FILE	11/05/12 02:45 PM	03/28/84 08:57 PM	11/05/12 02:45 PM	6333	/Users/Admin/AppData
PARTITION 2	imagesCA4EC4XD.jpg	jpg	FILE	11/05/12 02:45 PM	03/28/84 08:57 PM	11/05/12 02:45 PM	5244	/Users/Admin/AppData
PARTITION 2	imagesCAEGV9W1.jpg	jpg	FILE	11/05/12 02:45 PM	03/28/84 08:57 PM	11/05/12 02:45 PM	5793	/Users/Admin/AppData
PARTITION 2	imagesCAH8Y5BJ.jpg	jpg	FILE	11/05/12 02:45 PM	03/28/84 08:57 PM	11/05/12 02:45 PM	8282	/Users/Admin/AppData
PARTITION 2	imagesCAKJZD3U.jpg	jpg	FILE	11/05/12 02:45 PM	03/28/84 08:57 PM	11/05/12 02:45 PM	4185	/Users/Admin/AppData
PARTITION 2	imagesCALDWQEN.jpg	jpg	FILE	11/05/12 02:45 PM	03/28/84 08:57 PM	11/05/12 02:45 PM	5668	/Users/Admin/AppData
PARTITION 2	imagesCAEDFU2B.jpg	jpg	FILE	11/05/12 02:45 PM	03/28/84 08:57 PM	11/05/12 02:45 PM	5043	/Users/Admin/AppData
PARTITION 2	imagesCAGQE8AG.jpg	jpg	FILE	11/05/12 02:45 PM	03/28/84 08:57 PM	11/05/12 02:45 PM	5916	/Users/Admin/AppData
PARTITION 2	imagesCAH06NJF.jpg	jpg	FILE	11/05/12 02:45 PM	03/28/84 08:57 PM	11/05/12 02:45 PM	6251	/Users/Admin/AppData
PARTITION 2	imagesCAHC7ZZC.jpg	jpg	FILE	11/05/12 02:45 PM	03/28/84 08:57 PM	11/05/12 02:45 PM	5165	/Users/Admin/AppData
PARTITION 2	imagesCAJMNTK3.jpg	jpg	FILE	11/05/12 02:45 PM	03/28/84 08:57 PM	11/05/12 02:45 PM	6772	/Users/Admin/AppData
PARTITION 2	imagesCAQE196N.jpg	jpg	FILE	11/05/12 02:45 PM	03/28/84 08:57 PM	11/05/12 02:45 PM	5134	/Users/Admin/AppData

There's more...

This script can be further improved. We have provided one or more recommendations as follows:

- Use `tqdm`, or another library, to create a progress bar to inform the user of the current execution progress
- Learn about the additional metadata values that can be extracted from filesystem objects using `pytsk3` and add them to the output CSV file

Processing files within the container

Recipe Difficulty: Medium

Python Version: 2.7

Operating System: Linux

Now that we can iterate through a filesystem, let's look at how we can create file objects as we have been accustomed to doing. In this recipe, we create a simple triage script that extracts files matching specified file extensions and copies them to an output directory while preserving their original file path.

Getting started

Refer to the *Getting started* section in the *Opening Acquisitions* recipe for information on the build environment and setup details for `pytsk3` and `pyewf`. All other libraries used in this script are present in Python's standard library.

How to do it...

We will perform the following steps in this recipe:

1. Identify if the evidence container is a `raw` image or an `E01` container.
2. Access the image using `pytsk3`.
3. Recurse through all directories in each partition.
4. Check if the file extension matches those supplied.
5. Write responsive files with the preserved folder structure to the output directory.

How it works...

We import a number of libraries to assist with argument parsing, creating CSV spreadsheets, and handling evidence containers and filesystems.

```
from __future__ import print_function
import argparse
import csv
import os
import pytsk3
```

```
import pyewf
import sys
```

This recipe's command-line handler takes four positional arguments: EVIDENCE_FILE, TYPE, EXT, and OUTPUT_DIR. These are the evidence file itself, the type of evidence file, a comma-delimited list of extensions to extract, and the desired output directory, respectively. We also have the optional p switch to manually specify the partition type.

```
if __name__ == '__main__':
    parser = argparse.ArgumentParser(
        description=__description__,
        epilog="Developed by {} on {}".format(
            ", ".join(__authors__), __date__)
    )
    parser.add_argument("EVIDENCE_FILE", help="Evidence file path")
    parser.add_argument("TYPE", help="Type of Evidence",
                        choices=("raw", "ewf"))
    parser.add_argument("EXT",
                        help="Comma-delimited file extensions to extract")
    parser.add_argument("OUTPUT_DIR", help="Output Directory")
    parser.add_argument("-p", help="Partition Type",
                        choices=("DOS", "GPT", "MAC", "SUN"))
    args = parser.parse_args()
```

Before calling the main() function, we create any necessary output directories and perform our standard input-validation steps. Once we have validated the input, we pass the supplied arguments onto the main() function.

```
    if not os.path.exists(args.OUTPUT_DIR):
        os.makedirs(args.OUTPUT_DIR)

    if os.path.exists(args.EVIDENCE_FILE) and \
            os.path.isfile(args.EVIDENCE_FILE):
        main(args.EVIDENCE_FILE, args.TYPE, args.EXT, args.OUTPUT_DIR,
             args.p)
    else:
        print("[-] Supplied input file {} does not exist or is not a "
              "file".format(args.EVIDENCE_FILE))
        sys.exit(1)
```

The main() function, EWFImgInfo class, and the open_fs() function, have been covered in previous recipes. Recall that this chapter takes a more iterative approach to our recipes as we build upon the previous ones. Refer to those previous recipes for a more detailed description of each function and the EWFImgInfo class. Let's briefly show the two functions again so as to avoid jumping around logically.

In the `main()` function, we check whether the evidence file is a `raw` file or an `E01` file. Then, we perform the necessary steps to ultimately create a `pytsk3` handle on the evidence file. With this handle, we attempt to access the volume, using the manually supplied partition type if supplied. If we are able to open the volume, we pass `pytsk3` handle and volume to the `open_fs()` method.

```
def main(image, img_type, ext, output, part_type):
    volume = None
    print("[+] Opening {}".format(image))
    if img_type == "ewf":
        try:
            filenames = pyewf.glob(image)
        except IOError:
            _, e, _ = sys.exc_info()
            print("[-] Invalid EWF format:\n {}".format(e))
            sys.exit(2)

        ewf_handle = pyewf.handle()
        ewf_handle.open(filenames)

        # Open PYTSK3 handle on EWF Image
        img_info = EWFImgInfo(ewf_handle)
    else:
        img_info = pytsk3.Img_Info(image)

    try:
        if part_type is not None:
            attr_id = getattr(pytsk3, "TSK_VS_TYPE_" + part_type)
            volume = pytsk3.Volume_Info(img_info, attr_id)
        else:
            volume = pytsk3.Volume_Info(img_info)
    except IOError:
        _, e, _ = sys.exc_info()
        print("[-] Unable to read partition table:\n {}".format(e))

    open_fs(volume, img_info, ext, output)
```

In the `open_fs()` function, we use logic to support accessing the filesystem for both logical and physical acquisitions. For logical acquisitions, we can simply attempt to access the root of the filesystem on the `pytsk3` handle. On the other hand, for physical acquisitions, we must iterate through each partition and attempt to access the filesystem for those meeting certain criteria. Once we have access to the filesystem, we call the `recurse_files()` method to iterate through all of the files in the filesystem.

```
def open_fs(vol, img, ext, output):
    # Open FS and Recurse
```

```
            print("[+] Recursing through files and writing file extension matches "
                "to output directory")
        if vol is not None:
            for part in vol:
                if part.len > 2048 and "Unallocated" not in part.desc \
                        and "Extended" not in part.desc \
                        and "Primary Table" not in part.desc:
                    try:
                        fs = pytsk3.FS_Info(
                            img, offset=part.start * vol.info.block_size)
                    except IOError:
                        _, e, _ = sys.exc_info()
                        print("[-] Unable to open FS:\n {}".format(e))
                    root = fs.open_dir(path="/")
                    recurse_files(part.addr, fs, root, [], [""], ext, output)
        else:
            try:
                fs = pytsk3.FS_Info(img)
            except IOError:
                _, e, _ = sys.exc_info()
                print("[-] Unable to open FS:\n {}".format(e))
            root = fs.open_dir(path="/")
            recurse_files(1, fs, root, [], [""], ext, output)
```

Stop skimming here! The new logic for this recipe is contained in the `recurse_files()` method. This is sort of a blink-and-you'll-miss-it recipe. We've done the heavy lifting with the previous recipes, and we can now essentially treat these files like we would any other file with Python. Let's look at how this works.

Admittedly, the first part of this function is still the same as before, with one exception. On the first line of the function, we use list comprehension to split each comma-delimited extension supplied by the user and remove any white spaces and normalize the string to lowercase. As we iterate through each object, we check whether the object is a directory or a file. If it is a file, we separate and normalize the file's extension to lower case and store it in a `file_ext` variable.

```
def recurse_files(part, fs, root_dir, dirs, parent, ext, output):
    extensions = [x.strip().lower() for x in ext.split(',')]
    dirs.append(root_dir.info.fs_file.meta.addr)
    for fs_object in root_dir:
        # Skip ".", ".." or directory entries without a name.
        if not hasattr(fs_object, "info") or \
                not hasattr(fs_object.info, "name") or \
                not hasattr(fs_object.info.name, "name") or \
                fs_object.info.name.name in [".", ".."]:
            continue
        try:
```

```
file_name = fs_object.info.name.name
file_path = "{}/{}".format("/".join(parent),
                    fs_object.info.name.name)
try:
    if fs_object.info.meta.type == pytsk3.TSK_FS_META_TYPE_DIR:
        f_type = "DIR"
        file_ext = ""
    else:
        f_type = "FILE"
        if "." in file_name:
            file_ext = file_name.rsplit(".")[-1].lower()
        else:
            file_ext = ""
except AttributeError:
    continue
```

Next, we check if the extracted file's extension is in our user supplied list. If it is, we pass the file object itself and its name, extension, path, and the desired output directory to the file_writer() method to output. Notice that this operation, we have logic, discussed in the previous recipe, to recursively process any subdirectories to identify more potential files matching the extension criteria. So far, so good; let's now take a look at this last function.

```
if file_ext.strip() in extensions:
    print("{}".format(file_path))
    file_writer(fs_object, file_name, file_ext, file_path,
                output)
if f_type == "DIR":
    parent.append(fs_object.info.name.name)
    sub_directory = fs_object.as_directory()
    inode = fs_object.info.meta.addr
    if inode not in dirs:
        recurse_files(part, fs, sub_directory, dirs,
                    parent, ext, output)
        parent.pop(-1)
except IOError:
    pass
dirs.pop(-1)
```

The file_writer() method relies on the file object's read_random() method to access the file content. Before we do that, however, we first set up the output path for the file by combining the user-supplied output with the extension and the path of the file. We then create these directories if they do not already exist. Next, we open the output file in "w" mode and are now ready to write the file's content to the output file. As used here, the read_random() function takes two inputs: the byte offset within the file to start reading from and the number of bytes to read. In this case, since we want to read the entire file, we use the integer 0 as the first argument and the file's size as the second argument.

We supply this directly to the `write()` method, although note that going forward, if we were to perform any processing to this file, we could instead read it into a variable and work with the file from there. Also, note that for evidence containers with large files, this process of reading the entire file into memory may not be ideal. In that scenario, you would want to read and write to this file in chunks rather than all at once.

```
def file_writer(fs_object, name, ext, path, output):
    output_dir = os.path.join(output, ext,
                              os.path.dirname(path.lstrip("//")))
    if not os.path.exists(output_dir):
        os.makedirs(output_dir)
    with open(os.path.join(output_dir, name), "w") as outfile:
        outfile.write(fs_object.read_random(0, fs_object.info.meta.size))
```

When we run this script, we see responsive files based on the supplied extensions:

```
(venv2) pyforcookbook@dev-vm$ python extract_file_type.py /media/evidence/tedmos
by.E01 ewf jpg,png,gif /media/scratch/tm_001
[+] Opening /media/evidence/tedmosby.E01
[+] Recursing through files and writing file extension matches to output directo
ry
/Program Files/Common Files/Microsoft Shared/Stationery/Bears.jpg
/Program Files/Common Files/Microsoft Shared/Stationery/Garden.jpg
/Program Files/Common Files/Microsoft Shared/Stationery/GreenBubbles.jpg
/Program Files/Common Files/Microsoft Shared/Stationery/HandPrints.jpg
/Program Files/Common Files/Microsoft Shared/Stationery/OrangeCircles.jpg
/Program Files/Common Files/Microsoft Shared/Stationery/Peacock.jpg
/Program Files/Common Files/Microsoft Shared/Stationery/Roses.jpg
/Program Files/Common Files/Microsoft Shared/Stationery/ShadesOfBlue.jpg
/Program Files/Common Files/Microsoft Shared/Stationery/SoftBlue.jpg
/Program Files/Common Files/Microsoft Shared/Stationery/Stars.jpg
/Program Files/DVD Maker/Shared/DissolveAnother.png
/Program Files/DVD Maker/Shared/DissolveNoise.png
/Program Files/Microsoft Games/FreeCell/FreeCellMCE.png
```

Additionally, we can review these files within the defined structure as shown in the following screenshot:

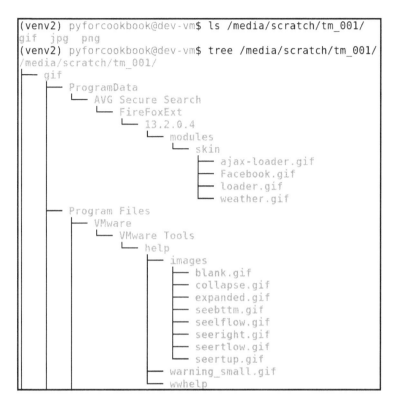

Searching for hashes

Recipe Difficulty: Hard

Python Version: 2.7

Operating System: Linux

In this recipe, we create another triage script, this time focused on identifying files matching provided hash values. This script takes a text file containing MD5, SHA-1, or SHA-256 hashes, separated by a newline, and searches for those hashes within the evidence container. With this recipe, we will be able to quickly process evidence files, locate files of interest, and alert the user by printing the file path to the console.

Getting started

Refer to the *Getting started* section in the *Opening Acquisitions* recipe for information on the `build` environment and setup details for `pytsk3` and `pyewf`. All other libraries used in this script are present in Python's standard library.

How to do it...

We use the following methodology to accomplish our objective:

1. Identify if the evidence container is a `raw` image or an `E01` container.
2. Access the image using `pytsk3`.
3. Recurse through all directories in each partition.
4. Send each file to be hashed using the appropriate hashing algorithm.
5. Check if the hash matches one of those provided and if so, print to the console.

How it works...

We import a number of libraries to assist with argument parsing, creating CSV spreadsheets, hashing files, handling evidence containers and filesystems, and creating progress bars.

```
from __future__ import print_function
import argparse
import csv
import hashlib
import os
import pytsk3
import pyewf
import sys
from tqdm import tqdm
```

This recipe's command-line handler takes three positional arguments, `EVIDENCE_FILE`, `TYPE`, and `HASH_LIST`, which represent the evidence file, the type of evidence file, and the newline delimited list of hashes to search for, respectively. As always, the user can also manually supply the partition type using the `p` switch if necessary.

```
if __name__ == '__main__':
    parser = argparse.ArgumentParser(
        description=__description__,
        epilog="Developed by {} on {}".format(
```

```
            ", ".join(__authors__), __date__)
    )
    parser.add_argument("EVIDENCE_FILE", help="Evidence file path")
    parser.add_argument("TYPE", help="Type of Evidence",
                        choices=("raw", "ewf"))
    parser.add_argument("HASH_LIST",
                        help="Filepath to Newline-delimited list of "
                             "hashes (either MD5, SHA1, or SHA-256)")
    parser.add_argument("-p", help="Partition Type",
                        choices=("DOS", "GPT", "MAC", "SUN"))
    parser.add_argument("-t", type=int,
                        help="Total number of files, for the progress bar")
    args = parser.parse_args()
```

After we parse the inputs, we perform our typical input-validation checks on both the evidence file and the hash list. If those pass, we call the main() function and supply it with the user-supplied inputs.

```
    if os.path.exists(args.EVIDENCE_FILE) and \
            os.path.isfile(args.EVIDENCE_FILE) and \
            os.path.exists(args.HASH_LIST) and \
            os.path.isfile(args.HASH_LIST):
        main(args.EVIDENCE_FILE, args.TYPE, args.HASH_LIST, args.p, args.t)
    else:
        print("[-] Supplied input file {} does not exist or is not a "
              "file".format(args.EVIDENCE_FILE))
        sys.exit(1)
```

As in the previous recipe, the main() function, EWFImgInfo class, and the open_fs() function are nearly identical to the previous recipes. For a more detailed explanation of these functions, refer to the previous recipes. One new addition to the main() function is the first line, where we call the read_hashes() method. This method reads the input hash list and returns a list of hashes and the type of hash (that is, MD5, SHA-1, or SHA-256).

Other than that, the main() function proceeds as we are accustomed to seeing it. First, it determines what type of evidence file it is working with in order to create a pytsk3 handle on the image. Then, it uses that handle and attempts to access the image volume. Once this process has completed, the variables are sent to the open_fs() function for further processing.

```
def main(image, img_type, hashes, part_type, pbar_total=0):
    hash_list, hash_type = read_hashes(hashes)
    volume = None
    print("[+] Opening {}".format(image))
    if img_type == "ewf":
        try:
```

```
            filenames = pyewf.glob(image)
        except IOError:
            _, e, _ = sys.exc_info()
            print("[-] Invalid EWF format:\n {}".format(e))
            sys.exit(2)

        ewf_handle = pyewf.handle()
        ewf_handle.open(filenames)

        # Open PYTSK3 handle on EWF Image
        img_info = EWFImgInfo(ewf_handle)
    else:
        img_info = pytsk3.Img_Info(image)

    try:
        if part_type is not None:
            attr_id = getattr(pytsk3, "TSK_VS_TYPE_" + part_type)
            volume = pytsk3.Volume_Info(img_info, attr_id)
        else:
            volume = pytsk3.Volume_Info(img_info)
    except IOError:
        _, e, _ = sys.exc_info()
        print("[-] Unable to read partition table:\n {}".format(e))

    open_fs(volume, img_info, hash_list, hash_type, pbar_total)
```

Let's quickly look at one of the new functions, the `read_hashes()` method. First, we instantiate the `hash_list` and `hash_type` variables as an empty list and `None` object, respectively. Next, we open and iterate through the input hash list and add each hash to our list. As we do this, if the `hash_type` variable is still `None`, we check the length of the line as a means of identifying the type of hash algorithm we should use.

At the end of this process, if for whatever reason the `hash_type` variable is still `None`, then the hash list must be made up of hashes we do not support, and so we exit the script after printing the error to the console.

```
def read_hashes(hashes):
    hash_list = []
    hash_type = None
    with open(hashes) as infile:
        for line in infile:
            if hash_type is None:
                if len(line.strip()) == 32:
                    hash_type = "md5"
                elif len(line.strip()) == 40:
                    hash_type == "sha1"
                elif len(line.strip()) == 64:
```

```
                hash_type == "sha256"
            hash_list.append(line.strip().lower())
    if hash_type is None:
        print("[-] No valid hashes identified in {}".format(hashes))
        sys.exit(3)

    return hash_list, hash_type
```

The `open_fs()` method function is identical to that of previous recipes. It tries to use two different methods to access both physical and logical filesystems. Once successful, it passes these filesystems onto the `recurse_files()` method. As with the previous recipe, the magic happens within this function. We are also incorporating a progress bar with `tqdm` to provide feedback to the user, as it may take a while to hash all of the files within an image.

```
def open_fs(vol, img, hashes, hash_type, pbar_total=0):
    # Open FS and Recurse
    print("[+] Recursing through and hashing files")
    pbar = tqdm(desc="Hashing", unit=" files",
                unit_scale=True, total=pbar_total)
    if vol is not None:
        for part in vol:
            if part.len > 2048 and "Unallocated" not in part.desc and \
                    "Extended" not in part.desc and \
                    "Primary Table" not in part.desc:
                try:
                    fs = pytsk3.FS_Info(
                        img, offset=part.start * vol.info.block_size)
                except IOError:
                    _, e, _ = sys.exc_info()
                    print("[-] Unable to open FS:\n {}".format(e))
                root = fs.open_dir(path="/")
                recurse_files(part.addr, fs, root, [], [""], hashes,
                        hash_type, pbar)
    else:
        try:
            fs = pytsk3.FS_Info(img)
        except IOError:
            _, e, _ = sys.exc_info()
            print("[-] Unable to open FS:\n {}".format(e))
        root = fs.open_dir(path="/")
        recurse_files(1, fs, root, [], [""], hashes, hash_type, pbar)
    pbar.close()
```

Within the `recurse_files()` method, we iterate through all subdirectories and hash each file. We skip the . and .. directory entries and check that the `fs_object` has the correct properties. If so, we build the file path for use in our output.

```
def recurse_files(part, fs, root_dir, dirs, parent, hashes,
                  hash_type, pbar):
    dirs.append(root_dir.info.fs_file.meta.addr)
    for fs_object in root_dir:
        # Skip ".", ".." or directory entries without a name.
        if not hasattr(fs_object, "info") or \
                not hasattr(fs_object.info, "name") or \
                not hasattr(fs_object.info.name, "name") or \
                fs_object.info.name.name in [".", ".."]:
            continue
        try:
            file_path = "{}/{}".format("/".join(parent),
                                       fs_object.info.name.name)
```

As we perform each iteration, we determine which objects are files versus directories. For each file discovered, we send it to the `hash_file()` method along with its path, the list of hashes, and the hash algorithm. The remainder of the `recurse_files()` function logic is specifically designed to handle directories and makes recursive calls to this function for any sub-directories to ensure the whole tree is walked and files are not missed.

```
            if getattr(fs_object.info.meta, "type", None) == \
                    pytsk3.TSK_FS_META_TYPE_DIR:
                parent.append(fs_object.info.name.name)
                sub_directory = fs_object.as_directory()
                inode = fs_object.info.meta.addr

                # This ensures that we don't recurse into a directory
                # above the current level and thus avoid circular loops.
                if inode not in dirs:
                    recurse_files(part, fs, sub_directory, dirs,
                                  parent, hashes, hash_type, pbar)
                    parent.pop(-1)
            else:
                hash_file(fs_object, file_path, hashes, hash_type, pbar)

        except IOError:
            pass
    dirs.pop(-1)
```

The `hash_file()` method first checks which type of hash algorithm instance to create based on the `hash_type` variable. With that decided and an update of the file size to the progress bar, we read the file's data into the hash object using the `read_random()` method. Again, we read the entire file's contents by starting our read at the first byte and reading the entire file's size. We generate the hash of the file using the `hexdigest()` function on the hash object and then check whether that hash is in our list of supplied hashes. If it is, we alert the user by printing the file path, using `pbar.write()` to prevent progress bar display issues, and name to the console.

```
def hash_file(fs_object, path, hashes, hash_type, pbar):
    if hash_type == "md5":
        hash_obj = hashlib.md5()
    elif hash_type == "sha1":
        hash_obj = hashlib.sha1()
    elif hash_type == "sha256":
        hash_obj = hashlib.sha256()
    f_size = getattr(fs_object.info.meta, "size", 0)
    pbar.set_postfix(File_Size="{:.2f}MB".format(f_size / 1024.0 / 1024))
    hash_obj.update(fs_object.read_random(0, f_size))
    hash_digest = hash_obj.hexdigest()
    pbar.update()

    if hash_digest in hashes:
        pbar.write("[*] MATCH: {}\n{}".format(path, hash_digest))
```

By running the script we are presented with a nice progress bar showing the hashing status and a list of files that match the list of provided hashes, as seen in the following screenshot:

```
(venv2) pyforcookbook@dev-vm$ python search_evidence_hashes.py /media/evidence/t
edmosby.E01 ewf /media/scratch/tm_00001/tm_md5_hashlist.txt -t 67100
[+] Opening /media/evidence/tedmosby.E01
[+] Recursing through and hashing files
[*] MATCH: /Users/Admin/AppData/Local/Microsoft/Windows/Temporary Internet Files
/Content.IE5/L9AMIRWL/download_bar[1].png
7e5cc3327bce5408958b88a6ee7ee865
[*] MATCH: /Users/Admin/AppData/Local/Microsoft/Windows/Temporary Internet Files
/Low/Content.IE5/JL6083YE/images[7].jpg
f877a2751cd8a6df9463438768e63001
[*] MATCH: /Users/Admin/AppData/Local/Microsoft/Windows/Temporary Internet Files
/Low/Content.IE5/JL6083YE/Ziw39zQjoop[1].png
258e535d0aaf7c79f0ae5a6d41c68e4a
[*] MATCH: /Users/Admin/AppData/Local/Microsoft/Windows/Temporary Internet Files
/Low/Content.IE5/WJGTKNR0/printer_0[1].gif
abb9d805a04180c8272e1c1c37d592d0
[*] MATCH: /Users/Admin/AppData/Local/Microsoft/Windows/Temporary Internet Files
/Low/Content.IE5/WJGTKNR0/imagesCAT4T8XX.jpg
786ebe353e1b6684abe1e40214be753b
[*] MATCH: /Users/Admin/AppData/Local/Microsoft/Windows/Temporary Internet Files
/Low/Content.IE5/WJGTKNR0/images[1].jpg
f877a2751cd8a6df9463438768e63001
Hashing: 100%|██████████| 67.1K/67.1K [05:19<00:00, 210 files/s, File_Size=0.01MB]
```

There's more...

This script can be further improved. We have provided one or more recommendations as follows:

- Rather than printing matches, create a CSV of matching files with metadata for review
- Add an optional switch to dump matching files to an output directory (with the folder path preserved)

9
Exploring Windows Forensic Artifacts Recipes - Part I

The following recipes will be covered in this chapter:

- One man's trash is a forensic examiner's treasure
- A sticky situation
- Reading the registry
- Gathering user activity
- The missing link
- Searching high and low

Introduction

Windows has long reigned supreme as the operating system of choice in the PC market. In fact, Windows makes up approximately 47 percent of the users visiting government websites, with the second most popular PC operating system, macOS, making up only 8.5 percentage. There is no reason to suspect that this will be changing anytime soon, especially with the warm reception that Windows 10 has received. Therefore, it is exceedingly likely that future investigations will continue to require the analysis of Windows artifacts.

This chapter covers many types of artifacts and how to interpret them with Python, using various first and third-party libraries, directly from forensic evidence containers. We will leverage the framework we developed in `Chapter 8`, *Working with Forensic Evidence Container Recipes* to process these artifacts directly from forensic acquisitions. In this manner, we can provide captured raw or EWF images to our code and not worry about the process of extracting the required files or mounting the image prior to processing the data. Specifically, we will cover:

- Interpreting `$I` files to learn more about files sent to the Recycle Bin
- Reading content and metadata from Sticky Notes on Window 7 systems
- Extracting values from the registry to learn about the operating system version and other configuration details
- Revealing user activity related to searches, typed paths, and run commands
- Parsing LNK files to learn about historical and recent file access
- Examining `Windows.edb` for information about indexed files, folders, and messages

 To view more interesting metrics, visit `https://analytics.usa.gov/`. Visit `www.packtpub.com/books/content/support` to download the code bundle for this chapter.

One man's trash is a forensic examiner's treasure

Recipe difficulty: Medium

Python version: 2.7

Operating system: Linux

While that may not be the exact saying, forensic examination of deleted files residing in the Recycle Bin is an important step in most investigations. The non-technical custodian likely does not understand that these files sent to the Recycle Bin are still present and that we can learn a good deal about the original file, such as its original file path and the time that it was sent to the Recycle Bin. While the specific artifacts vary between versions of Windows, this recipe focuses on the Windows 7 version of the Recycle Bin's `$I` and `$R` files.

Getting started

This recipe requires the installation of three third-party modules to function: `pytsk3`, `pyewf`, and `unicodecsv`. *Refer to* `Chapter 8`, *Working with Forensic Evidence Container Recipes* for a detailed explanation of installing the `pytsk3` and `pyewf` modules. All other libraries used in this script are present in Python's standard library

Because we are developing these recipes in Python 2.x, we are likely to encounter Unicode encode and decode errors. To account for that, we use the `unicodecsv` library to write all CSV output in this chapter. This third-party module takes care of Unicode support, unlike Python 2.x's standard `csv` module, and will be put to great use here. As usual, we can use `pip` to install `unicodecsv`:

```
pip install unicodecsv==0.14.1
```

 To learn more about the `unicodecsv` library, visit `https://github.com/jdunck/python-unicodecsv`.

In addition to these, we'll continue to use the `pytskutil` module developed from `Chapter 8`, *Working with Forensic Evidence Container recipes,* to allow interaction with forensic acquisitions. This module is largely similar to what we previously wrote, with some minor changes to better suit our purposes. You can review the code by navigating to the utility directory within the code package.

How to do it...

To parse the `$I` and `$R` files from a Windows 7 machine, we will need to:

1. Recurse through the `$Recycle.bin` folder in the evidence file, selecting all files starting with `$I`.
2. Read the contents of the files and parse the available metadata structures.
3. Search for the associated `$R` file and check if it is a file or folder.
4. Write the results into a CSV file for review.

How it works...

We import the `argparse`, `datetime`, `os`, and `struct` built-in libraries to assist with running the script and interpreting the binary data within these files. We also bring in our Sleuth Kit utilities for handling the evidence files, reading the content, and iterating through folders and files. Lastly, we import the `unicodecsv` library to assist with writing the CSV report:

```
from __future__ import print_function
from argparse import ArgumentParser
import datetime
import os
import struct

from utility.pytskutil import TSKUtil
import unicodecsv as csv
```

This recipe's command-line handler takes three positional arguments, `EVIDENCE_FILE`, `IMAGE_TYPE`, and `CSV_REPORT`, which represent the path to the evidence file, the type of evidence file, and the desired output path to the CSV report, respectively. These three arguments are passed to the `main()` function.

```
if __name__ == '__main__':
    parser = argparse.ArgumentParser(
        description=__description__,
        epilog="Developed by {} on {}".format(
            ", ".join(__authors__), __date__)
    )
    parser.add_argument('EVIDENCE_FILE', help="Path to evidence file")
    parser.add_argument('IMAGE_TYPE', help="Evidence file format",
                        choices=('ewf', 'raw'))
    parser.add_argument('CSV_REPORT', help="Path to CSV report")
    args = parser.parse_args()
    main(args.EVIDENCE_FILE, args.IMAGE_TYPE, args.CSV_REPORT)
```

The `main()` function handles the necessary interactions with the evidence file to identify and provide any `$I` files for processing. To access the evidence file, one must provide the path to the container and the image type. This initiates the `TSKUtil` instance, which we use to search for files and folders within the image. To find the `$I` files, we call the `recurse_files()` method on the `tsk_util` instance, specifying the file name pattern to look for, the `path` to start the search in, and the string `logic` used to find the filename. The `logic` keyword argument accepts the following values which correspond to string operations: `startswith`, `endswith`, `contains`, and `equals`. These dictate the string operation used to search for our `$I` pattern within the scanned file and folder names.

If any $I files are found, we pass this list to the `process_dollar_i()` function along with the `tsk_util` object. After they are all processed, we write the extracted metadata to a CSV report with the `write_csv()` method:

```
def main(evidence, image_type, report_file):
    tsk_util = TSKUtil(evidence, image_type)

    dollar_i_files = tsk_util.recurse_files("$I", path='/$Recycle.bin',
                                            logic="startswith")

    if dollar_i_files is not None:
        processed_files = process_dollar_i(tsk_util, dollar_i_files)

        write_csv(report_file,
                  ['file_path', 'file_size', 'deleted_time',
                   'dollar_i_file', 'dollar_r_file', 'is_directory'],
                  processed_files)
    else:
        print("No $I files found")
```

The `process_dollar_i()` function accepts as its input, the `tsk_util` object and the list of discovered $I files. We iterate through this list and inspect each of these files. Each element within the `dollar_i_files` list is itself a list of tuples, where each tuple element contains (in order) the file's name, relative path, handle to access the file's content, and filesystem identifier. With these available attributes, we will call our `read_dollar_i()` function and provide it the third tuple, the file object handle. If this is a valid $I file, this method returns a dictionary of extracted metadata from the raw file, otherwise, it returns None. If the file is valid, we continue processing it by adding the file path to the $I file to the `file_attribs` dictionary:

```
def process_dollar_i(tsk_util, dollar_i_files):
    processed_files = []
    for dollar_i in dollar_i_files:
        # Interpret file metadata
        file_attribs = read_dollar_i(dollar_i[2])
        if file_attribs is None:
            continue  # Invalid $I file
        file_attribs['dollar_i_file'] = os.path.join(
            '/$Recycle.bin', dollar_i[1][1:])
```

Next, we search for the associated $R file within the image. In preparation of this, we join base path to the $I file (including the $Recycle.bin and the SID folders) to reduce the amount of time required to search for the corresponding $R file. On Windows 7, the $I and $R files have a similar file name, where the first two letters are $I and $R, respectively, followed by a shared identifier. By using that identifier in our search and specifying the specific folder we expect to find the $R file, we have reduced the likelihood of false positives. Using these patterns, we query our evidence file again with the startswith logic:

```
# Get the $R file
recycle_file_path = os.path.join(
    '/$Recycle.bin',
    dollar_i[1].rsplit("/", 1)[0][1:]
)
dollar_r_files = tsk_util.recurse_files(
    "$R" + dollar_i[0][2:],
    path=recycle_file_path, logic="startswith"
)
```

If the search for the $R files is unsuccessful, we try to query for a directory with the same information. If this query is also unsuccessful, we append dictionary values that the $R file was not found and that we are unsure if it was a file or directory. If, however, we do find a matching directory, we log the path of the directory and set the is_directory attribute to True:

```
if dollar_r_files is None:
    dollar_r_dir = os.path.join(recycle_file_path,
                                "$R" + dollar_i[0][2:])
    dollar_r_dirs = tsk_util.query_directory(dollar_r_dir)
    if dollar_r_dirs is None:
        file_attribs['dollar_r_file'] = "Not Found"
        file_attribs['is_directory'] = 'Unknown'
    else:
        file_attribs['dollar_r_file'] = dollar_r_dir
        file_attribs['is_directory'] = True
```

If the search for the $R file returned one or more hits, we create a list of the matched files, using list comprehension, to store in the CSV, delimited by semicolons, and mark the is_directory attribute as False.

```
    else:
        dollar_r = [os.path.join(recycle_file_path, r[1][1:])
                    for r in dollar_r_files]
        file_attribs['dollar_r_file'] = ";".join(dollar_r)
        file_attribs['is_directory'] = False
```

Prior to exiting the loop, we append the `file_attribs` dictionary to the `processed_files` list which stores all $I processed dictionaries. This list of dictionaries is returned to the `main()` function where it is used in the reporting process.

```
        processed_files.append(file_attribs)
    return processed_files
```

Let's briefly look at the `read_dollar_i()` method, used to parse metadata from the binary file with `struct`. We start by checking the file header, using the Sleuth Kit's `read_random()` method to read the signature's first eight bytes. If the signature does not match, we return `None` to alert that the $I failed validation and is an invalid file format.

```
def read_dollar_i(file_obj):
    if file_obj.read_random(0, 8) != '\x01\x00\x00\x00\x00\x00\x00\x00':
        return None # Invalid file
```

If we detect a valid file, we continue to read and unpack values from the $I file. The first is the file size attribute, which is located at byte offset 8 and is 8 bytes long. We unpack this with `struct` and store the integer in a temporary variable. The next attribute, deletion time, is stored at byte offset 16 and 8 bytes long. This is a Windows `FILETIME` object and we will borrow some old code to later process it into a human-readable timestamp. The last attribute is the former file path, which we read from byte 24 to the end of the file:

```
    raw_file_size = struct.unpack('<q', file_obj.read_random(8, 8))
    raw_deleted_time = struct.unpack('<q', file_obj.read_random(16, 8))
    raw_file_path = file_obj.read_random(24, 520)
```

With these values extracted, we interpret the integers into human-readable values. We use the `sizeof_fmt()` function to convert the file size integer into a human-readable size, containing size prefixes such as MB or GB. Next, we interpret the timestamp using the logic from our date parsing recipe from Chapter 7, *Log-Based Artifact Recipes* (after adapting the function to work only with integers). Lastly, we decode the path as UTF-16 and remove null-byte values. These refined details are then returned as a dictionary to the calling function:

```
    file_size = sizeof_fmt(raw_file_size[0])
    deleted_time = parse_windows_filetime(raw_deleted_time[0])
    file_path = raw_file_path.decode("utf16").strip("\x00")
    return {'file_size': file_size, 'file_path': file_path,
            'deleted_time': deleted_time}
```

Our `sizeof_fmt()` function is borrowed from StackOverflow.com, a site filled with many solutions to programming problems. While we could have drafted our own, this code is well formed for our purpose. It takes the integer `num` and iterates through the listed unit suffixes. If the number is less than `1024`, the number, unit, and suffix are joined into a string and returned; otherwise, the number is divided by `1024` and run through the next iteration. If the number is larger than a zettabyte, it returns the information in terms of yottabytes. For your sake, we hope the number is never that large.

```
def sizeof_fmt(num, suffix='B'):
    # From https://stackoverflow.com/a/1094933/3194812
    for unit in ['', 'Ki', 'Mi', 'Gi', 'Ti', 'Pi', 'Ei', 'Zi']:
        if abs(num) < 1024.0:
            return "%3.1f%s%s" % (num, unit, suffix)
        num /= 1024.0
    return "%.1f%s%s" % (num, 'Yi', suffix)
```

Our next support function is `parse_windows_filetime()`, adapted from the previous date-parsing recipe in Chapter 7, *Log-Based Artifact Recipes*. We borrow the logic and condense the code to only interpret integers into a formatted date that is then returned to the calling function. Generic functions, like the two we just discussed, are handy to keep in your arsenal as you never know when you may need this logic.

```
def parse_windows_filetime(date_value):
    microseconds = float(date_value) / 10
    ts = datetime.datetime(1601, 1, 1) + datetime.timedelta(
        microseconds=microseconds)
    return ts.strftime('%Y-%m-%d %H:%M:%S.%f')
```

Finally, we are ready to write the processed results to a CSV file. As you have no doubt come to expect, this function is similar to all of our other CSV functions. The only difference is that it is using the `unicodecsv` library under the hood, though the method and function names used here are the same:

```
def write_csv(outfile, fieldnames, data):
    with open(outfile, 'wb') as open_outfile:
        csvfile = csv.DictWriter(open_outfile, fieldnames)
        csvfile.writeheader()
        csvfile.writerows(data)
```

In the following two screenshots, we can see examples of the type of data this recipe extracts from $I and $R files:

file_path	file_size	deleted_time
C:\Users\Admin\AppData\Roaming\Microsoft\Windows\Libraries\Music.library-ms	3.4KiB	04/01/12 01:35 PM
C:\Users\Public\Temp\è‡ªè¿°	64.0B	04/06/12 06:39 PM
C:\Users\Admin\Documents\Stardust\Stardust	0.0B	03/16/12 07:39 PM
C:\Users\Admin\Documents\Research\Stardust.zip	707.9KiB	03/12/12 08:49 PM
C:\Users\Admin\AppData\Roaming\Microsoft\Windows\Libraries\Videos.library-ms	3.4KiB	04/01/12 01:35 PM
C:\Windows\System32\dllhost	100.3KiB	04/06/12 06:42 PM
C:\Windows\System32\malware.exe	3.8MiB	04/06/12 06:43 PM
C:\Windows\System32\malwarez.exe	2.9MiB	04/06/12 06:43 PM

dollar_i_file	dollar_r_file	is_directory
/$Recycle.bin/S-1-5-21-2036804247-3058324640-2116585241-1503/$I3TPCIK.library-ms	/$Recycle.bin/S-1-5-21-2036804247-3058324640-2116585241-1503/$R3TPCIK.library-ms	FALSE
/$Recycle.bin/S-1-5-21-2036804247-3058324640-2116585241-1503/$I6MHA5W	/$Recycle.bin/S-1-5-21-2036804247-3058324640-2116585241-1503/$R6MHA5W	FALSE
/$Recycle.bin/S-1-5-21-2036804247-3058324640-2116585241-1503/$I8XLAY7	/$Recycle.bin/S-1-5-21-2036804247-3058324640-2116585241-1503/$R8XLAY7	TRUE
/$Recycle.bin/S-1-5-21-2036804247-3058324640-2116585241-1503/$II3DF3L.zip	/$Recycle.bin/S-1-5-21-2036804247-3058324640-2116585241-1503/$RI3DF3L.zip	FALSE
/$Recycle.bin/S-1-5-21-2036804247-3058324640-2116585241-1503/$IUUH4BS.library-ms	/$Recycle.bin/S-1-5-21-2036804247-3058324640-2116585241-1503/$RUUH4BS.library-ms	FALSE
/$Recycle.bin/S-1-5-21-2036804247-3058324640-2116585241-1590/$I6SODDB	/$Recycle.bin/S-1-5-21-2036804247-3058324640-2116585241-1590/$R6SODDB	TRUE
/$Recycle.bin/S-1-5-21-2036804247-3058324640-2116585241-1590/$ID5HSV3.exe	/$Recycle.bin/S-1-5-21-2036804247-3058324640-2116585241-1590/$RD5HSV3.exe	FALSE
/$Recycle.bin/S-1-5-21-2036804247-3058324640-2116585241-1590/$IZI9VH9.exe	/$Recycle.bin/S-1-5-21-2036804247-3058324640-2116585241-1590/$RZI9VH9.exe	FALSE

A sticky situation

Recipe difficulty: Medium

Python version: 2.7

Operating system: Linux

Computers have replaced pen and paper. We have transferred many processes and habits, one relegated solely to the confines of paper, to these machines, including taking notes and making lists. One feature that replicates a real-world habit is Windows Sticky Notes. These sticky notes allow persistent notes to float on the desktop, with options for color, fonts, and more. This recipe will allow us to explore these sticky notes and add them to our investigative workflow.

Getting started

This recipe requires the installation of four third-party modules to function: `olefile`, `pytsk3`, `pyewf`, and `unicodecsv`. Refer to `Chapter 8`, *Working with Forensic Evidence Container Recipes* for a detailed explanation of installing the `pytsk3` and `pyewf` modules. Likewise, refer to the *Getting started* section in the *One man's trash is a forensic examiner's treasure* recipe for details on installing `unicodecsv`. All other libraries used in this script are present in Python's standard library.

The Windows Sticky Note file is stored as an `OLE` file. Therefore, we will leverage the `olefile` library to interact with and extract data from Windows Sticky Notes. The `olefile` library can be installed with `pip`:

```
pip install olefile==0.44
```

 To learn more about the `olefile` library, visit `https://olefile.readthedocs.io/en/latest/index.html`.

How to do it...

To properly form this recipe, we need to take the following steps:

1. Open the evidence file and find all `StickyNote.snt` files across the user profiles.
2. Parse metadata and content from the OLE streams.
3. Write the RTF content to files.
4. Create a CSV report of the metadata.

How it works...

This script, like the others, begins with import statements of the libraries required for its execution. The two new libraries here are `olefile` which, as we discussed, parses the Windows Sticky Note OLE streams and `StringIO`, a built-in library used to interpret a string of data as a file-like object. This library will be used to convert the `pytsk` file object into a stream the `olefile` library can interpret:

```
from __future__ import print_function
from argparse import ArgumentParser
```

```
import unicodecsv as csv
import os
import StringIO

from utility.pytskutil import TSKUtil
import olefile
```

We specify a global variable, REPORT_COLS, which represent the report columns. These static columns will be used across several functions.

```
REPORT_COLS = ['note_id', 'created', 'modified', 'note_text', 'note_file']
```

This recipe's command-line handler takes three positional arguments, EVIDENCE_FILE, IMAGE_TYPE, and REPORT_FOLDER, which represent the path to the evidence file, the type of evidence file, and the desired output directory path, respectively. This is similar to the previous recipe, with the exception of the REPORT_FOLDER, which is a directory that we will write the Sticky Note RTF files to:

```
if __name__ == '__main__':
    parser = argparse.ArgumentParser(
        description=__description__,
        epilog="Developed by {} on {}".format(
            ", ".join(__authors__), __date__)
    )
    parser.add_argument('EVIDENCE_FILE', help="Path to evidence file")
    parser.add_argument('IMAGE_TYPE', help="Evidence file format",
                        choices=('ewf', 'raw'))
    parser.add_argument('REPORT_FOLDER', help="Path to report folder")
    args = parser.parse_args()
    main(args.EVIDENCE_FILE, args.IMAGE_TYPE, args.REPORT_FOLDER)
```

Our main function starts similarly to the last, by handling the evidence file and searching for the files we seek to parse. In this case, we are looking for the StickyNotes.snt file, which is found within each user's AppData directory. For this reason, we limit the search to the /Users folder and look for a file matching the exact name:

```
def main(evidence, image_type, report_folder):
    tsk_util = TSKUtil(evidence, image_type)
    note_files = tsk_util.recurse_files('StickyNotes.snt', '/Users',
                                        'equals')
```

We then iterate through the resulting files, splitting out the user's home directory name and setting up the file-like object required for processing by the `olefile` library. Next, we call the `parse_snt_file()` function to process the file and return a list of results to iterate through. At this point, if the `note_data` is not `None`, we write the RTF file with the `write_note_rtf()` method. Additionally, we append the processed the processed data from the `prep_note_report()` to the `report_details` list. Once the `for` loop completes, we write the CSV report with the `write_csv()` method by providing the report name, report columns, and the list we have built of the sticky note information.

```
report_details = []
for note_file in note_files:
    user_dir = note_file[1].split("/")[1]
    file_like_obj = create_file_like_obj(note_file[2])
    note_data = parse_snt_file(file_like_obj)
    if note_data is None:
        continue
    write_note_rtf(note_data, os.path.join(report_folder, user_dir))
    report_details += prep_note_report(note_data, REPORT_COLS,
                                       "/Users" + note_file[1])
write_csv(os.path.join(report_folder, 'sticky_notes.csv'), REPORT_COLS,
          report_details)
```

The `create_file_like_obj()` function takes our `pytsk` file object and reads the size of the file. This size is used in the `read_random()` function to read the entire sticky note content into memory. We feed the `file_content` into the `StringIO()` class to convert it into a file-like object the `olefile` library can read before returning it to the parent function:

```
def create_file_like_obj(note_file):
    file_size = note_file.info.meta.size
    file_content = note_file.read_random(0, file_size)
    return StringIO.StringIO(file_content)
```

The `parse_snt_file()` function accepts the file-like object as its input and is used to read and interpret the sticky note file. We begin by validating that the file-like object is an OLE file, returning `None` if it is not. If it is, we open the file-like object using the `OleFileIO()` method. This provides a list of streams, allowing us to iterate through each element of each sticky note. As we iterate over the list, we check if the stream contains three dashes, as this suggests that the stream contains a unique identifier for a sticky note. This file can contain one or more sticky notes, each identified by the unique IDs. The sticky note data is either read directly as RTF data or UTF-16 encoded data based on the value of the element in the first index of the stream.

We also read the created and modified information from the stream using the `getctime()` and `getmtime()` functions, respectively. Next, we extract the sticky note RTF or UTF-16 encoded data to the `content` variable. Note, we must decode the UTF-16 encoded data prior to storing it. If there is content to save, we add it to the `note` dictionary and continue processing all remaining streams. Once all streams are processed, the `note` dictionary is returned to the parent function:

```python
def parse_snt_file(snt_file):
    if not olefile.isOleFile(snt_file):
        print("This is not an OLE file")
        return None
    ole = olefile.OleFileIO(snt_file)
    note = {}
    for stream in ole.listdir():
        if stream[0].count("-") == 3:
            if stream[0] not in note:
                note[stream[0]] = {
                    # Read timestamps
                    "created": ole.getctime(stream[0]),
                    "modified": ole.getmtime(stream[0])
                }

            content = None
            if stream[1] == '0':
                # Parse RTF text
                content = ole.openstream(stream).read()
            elif stream[1] == '3':
                # Parse UTF text
                content = ole.openstream(stream).read().decode("utf-16")

            if content:
                note[stream[0]][stream[1]] = content

    return note
```

To create the RTF files, we pass the dictionary of note data to the `write_note_rtf()` function. If the report folder does not exist, we use the `os` library to create it. At this point, we iterate through the `note_data` dictionary, splitting the `note_id` keys from `stream_data` values. The `note_id` is used to create the output RTF filename prior to opening it.

The data stored in stream zero is then written to the ouput RTF file before it is closed and the next sticky note is handled:

```
def write_note_rtf(note_data, report_folder):
    if not os.path.exists(report_folder):
        os.makedirs(report_folder)
    for note_id, stream_data in note_data.items():
        fname = os.path.join(report_folder, note_id + ".rtf")
        with open(fname, 'w') as open_file:
            open_file.write(stream_data['0'])
```

With the content of the sticky notes written, we now move onto the CSV report itself which is handled a little differently by the `prep_note_report()` function. This translates the nested dictionary into a flat list of dictionaries that are more conducive and appropriate for a CSV spreadsheet. We flatten it by including the `note_id` key and naming the fields using the keys specified in the global `REPORT_COLS` list.

```
def prep_note_report(note_data, report_cols, note_file):
    report_details = []
    for note_id, stream_data in note_data.items():
        report_details.append({
            "note_id": note_id,
            "created": stream_data['created'],
            "modified": stream_data['modified'],
            "note_text": stream_data['3'].strip("\x00"),
            "note_file": note_file
        })
    return report_details
```

Lastly, in the `write_csv()` method, we create a `csv.Dictwriter` object to create an overview report of the sticky note data. This CSV writer also uses the `unicodecsv` library and writes the list of dictionaries to the file, using the `REPORT_COLS` list of columns as the `fieldnames`.

```
def write_csv(outfile, fieldnames, data):
    with open(outfile, 'wb') as open_outfile:
        csvfile = csv.DictWriter(open_outfile, fieldnames)
        csvfile.writeheader()
        csvfile.writerows(data)
```

We can then view the output as we have a new directory containing the exported sticky notes and report:

```
(venv2) pyforcookbook@dev-vm$ tree ~/Desktop/sticky_notes/
/home/pyforcookbook/Desktop/sticky_notes/
├── Admin
│   ├── 0a2f853e-7aab-11e7-8.rtf
│   ├── 22c8be82-7ab3-11e7-8.rtf
│   ├── 22c8be83-7ab3-11e7-8.rtf
│   ├── 4d893415-7ab4-11e7-8.rtf
│   ├── 4d893416-7ab4-11e7-8.rtf
│   ├── 5c80970b-7ab4-11e7-8.rtf
│   └── 5c80970c-7ab4-11e7-8.rtf
└── sticky_notes.csv

1 directory, 8 files
```

Opening our report, we can view the note metadata and gather some of the internal content, though most spreadsheet viewers have difficulty with non-ASCII character interpretations:

note_id	created	modified	note_text
			ālohā Ĉ yshjgs☒
22c8be83-7ab3-11e7-8	08/06/17 02:28 PM	08/06/17 02:33 PM	ᴖ·⋖êç떺⊠
			Hello World!
0a2f853e-7aab-11e7-8	08/06/17 01:27 PM	08/06/17 02:34 PM	This is a sticky note!
5c80970c-7ab4-11e7-8	08/06/17 02:34 PM	08/06/17 02:34 PM	this one is purple
22c8be82-7ab3-11e7-8	08/06/17 02:28 PM	08/06/17 02:28 PM	Whats up!!!???
4d893415-7ab4-11e7-8	08/06/17 02:34 PM	08/06/17 02:34 PM	Blank Note
4d893416-7ab4-11e7-8	08/06/17 02:34 PM	08/06/17 02:34 PM	Lorem ipsum dolor sit amet, consectetur adipiscing
5c80970b-7ab4-11e7-8	08/06/17 02:34 PM	08/06/17 02:34 PM	green man

Lastly, we can open the output RTF files and view the raw content:

```
{\rtf1\ansi\ansicpg1252\deff0
\deflang1033{\fonttbl{\f0\fnil
\fcharset0 Segoe Print;}{\f1\fnil Segoe
Print;}}
{\*\generator Msftedit 5.41.21.2510;}
\viewkind4\uc1\pard\tx360\tx720\tx1080
\tx1440\tx1800\tx2160\tx2520\tx2880
\tx3240\tx3600\tx3960\tx4320\tx4680
\tx5040\tx5400\tx5760\tx6120\tx6480
\tx6840\tx7200\tx7560\tx7920\tx8280
\tx8640\tx9000\tx9360\tx9720\tx10080
\tx10440\tx10800\tx11160\tx11520\f0
\fs22 Hello World!\par
This is a sticky note!\lang9\f1\par
}
```

Reading the registry

Recipe Difficulty: Medium

Python Version: 2.7

Operating System: Linux

The Windows registry contains many important details related to the operating system configuration, user activity, software installation and usage, and so much more. These files are often heavily scrutinized and researched due to the number of artifacts they contain and their relevance to Windows systems. Parsing registry files gives us access to the keys and values that can reveal basic operating system information, access to folders and files, application usage, USB devices, and more. In this recipe, we focus on accessing common baseline information from the SYSTEM and SOFTWARE hives.

Getting started

This recipe requires the installation of three third-party modules to function: pytsk3, pyewf, and Registry. Refer to Chapter 8, *Working with Forensic Evidence Container Recipes*, for a detailed explanation of installing the pytsk3 and pyewf modules. All other libraries used in this script are present in Python's standard library.

In this recipe, we use the Registry module to interact with registry hives in an object-oriented manner. Critically, this module can be used to interact with external and standalone registry files. The Registry module can be installed with pip:

```
pip install python-registry==1.0.4
```

 To learn more about the Registry library, visit https://github.com/williballenthin/python-registry.

How to do it...

To build our registry system overview script, we will need to:

1. Find the registry hives to process by name and path.
2. Open these files using the `StringIO` and `Registry` modules.
3. Process each hive, printing the parsed values to the console for interpretation.

How it works...

The imports overlap with the other recipes in this chapter. These modules allow us to handle argument parsing, date manipulation, read our files into memory for the `Registry` library, and unpack and interpret binary data we extract from registry values. We also import the `TSKUtil()` class and the `Registry` module to process registry files.

```
from __future__ import print_function
from argparse import ArgumentParser
import datetime
import StringIO
import struct

from utility.pytskutil import TSKUtil
from Registry import Registry
```

This recipe's command-line handler takes two positional arguments, `EVIDENCE_FILE` and `IMAGE_TYPE`, which represent the path to the evidence file and the type of evidence file, respectively:

```
if __name__ == '__main__':
    parser = argparse.ArgumentParser(
        description=__description__,
        epilog="Developed by {} on {}".format(
            ", ".join(__authors__), __date__)
    )
    parser.add_argument('EVIDENCE_FILE', help="Path to evidence file")
    parser.add_argument('IMAGE_TYPE', help="Evidence file format",
                        choices=('ewf', 'raw'))
    args = parser.parse_args()
    main(args.EVIDENCE_FILE, args.IMAGE_TYPE)
```

The `main()` function starts by creating a `TSKUtil` object from the evidence and searches for the `SYSTEM` and `SOFTWARE` hives within the `/Windows/System32/config` folder. We create `Registry()` class instances of these hives with the `open_file_as_reg()` function before they are passed to their respective processing functions.

```
def main(evidence, image_type):
    tsk_util = TSKUtil(evidence, image_type)
    tsk_system_hive = tsk_util.recurse_files(
        'system', '/Windows/system32/config', 'equals')
    tsk_software_hive = tsk_util.recurse_files(
        'software', '/Windows/system32/config', 'equals')

    system_hive = open_file_as_reg(tsk_system_hive[0][2])
    software_hive = open_file_as_reg(tsk_software_hive[0][2])

    process_system_hive(system_hive)
    process_software_hive(software_hive)
```

To open the registry files, we need to gather the size of the file from the `pytsk` metadata and read the entire file, from byte zero to the end of the file into a variable. We then provide this variable to a `StringIO()` instance which allows us to open the file-like object with the `Registry()` class. We return the `Registry` class instance to the calling function for further processing:

```
def open_file_as_reg(reg_file):
    file_size = reg_file.info.meta.size
    file_content = reg_file.read_random(0, file_size)
    file_like_obj = StringIO.StringIO(file_content)
    return Registry.Registry(file_like_obj)
```

Let's start with the `SYSTEM` hive processing. This hive holds the majority of its information within control sets. The `SYSTEM` hive generally has two or more control sets that act as a backup system for the configurations they store. For simplicity, we will only read the current control set. To identify the current control set, we get our foothold within the hive with the `root` key and use the `find_key()` method to get the `Select` key. Within this key, we read the `Current` value, using the `value()` method to select it and the `value()` method on the `value` object to present the content of the value. While the method naming is a little ambiguous, the values within a key are named, so we first need to select them by name before then calling out the content that they hold. Using this information, we select the current control set key, passing an appropriately padded integer for the current control set (such as `ControlSet0001`). This object will be used through the remainder of the function to navigate to specific `subkeys` and `values`:

```
def process_system_hive(hive):
    root = hive.root()
```

```
current_control_set = root.find_key("Select").value("Current").value()
control_set = root.find_key("ControlSet{:03d}".format(
    current_control_set))
```

The first piece of information we will extract from the SYSTEM hive is the shutdown time. We read the `Control\Windows\ShutdownTime` value from the current control set and pass the hexadecimal value into `struct` to convert it to a `64-bit` integer. We then provide this integer to the Windows `FILETIME` parser to obtain a human-readable date string which we print to the console.

```
raw_shutdown_time = struct.unpack(
    '<Q', control_set.find_key("Control").find_key("Windows").value(
        "ShutdownTime").value()
)
shutdown_time = parse_windows_filetime(raw_shutdown_time[0])
print("Last Shutdown Time: {}".format(shutdown_time))
```

Next, we will ascertain the time zone information for the machine. This is found within the `Control\TimeZoneInformation\TimeZoneKeyName` value. This returns a string value that we can print directly to the console:

```
time_zone = control_set.find_key("Control").find_key(
    "TimeZoneInformation").value("TimeZoneKeyName").value()
print("Machine Time Zone: {}".format(time_zone))
```

Following that, we gather the machine's hostname. This is found under the `Control\ComputerName\ComputerName` key in the `ComputerName` value. The extracted value is a string that we can print to the console:

```
computer_name = control_set.find_key(
    "Control").find_key("ComputerName").find_key(
        "ComputerName").value("ComputerName").value()
print("Machine Name: {}".format(computer_name))
```

Pretty easy so far, right? Lastly, for the System hive, we parse information about the last access timestamp configuration. This `registry` key determines if the NTFS volume's last access timestamp is maintained, and is generally disabled by default on systems. To confirm this, we look for the `NtfsDisableLastAccessUpdate` value in the `Control\FileSystem` key and see if it is equal to 1. If it is, the last access timestamp is not maintained and marked as disabled before printing to the console. Notice the one-liner `if-else` statement, while perhaps a little more difficult to read it does have its uses:

```
last_access = control_set.find_key("Control").find_key(
    "FileSystem").value("NtfsDisableLastAccessUpdate").value()
last_access = "Disabled" if last_access == 1 else "enabled"
print("Last Access Updates: {}".format(last_access))
```

Our Windows FILETIME parser borrows logic from our former date-parsing recipe, accepting an integer that we convert into a human-readable date string. We also borrowed the logic for the Unix epoch date parser from the same date-parsing recipe and will use it to interpret dates from the Software hive.

```
def parse_windows_filetime(date_value):
    microseconds = float(date_value) / 10
    ts = datetime.datetime(1601, 1, 1) + datetime.timedelta(
        microseconds=microseconds)
    return ts.strftime('%Y-%m-%d %H:%M:%S.%f')


def parse_unix_epoch(date_value):
    ts = datetime.datetime.fromtimestamp(date_value)
    return ts.strftime('%Y-%m-%d %H:%M:%S.%f')
```

Our last function processes the SOFTWARE hive, presenting information to users in the console window. This function also begins by gathering the root of the hive and then selecting the Microsoft\Windows NT\CurrentVersion key. This key contains values about OS installation metadata and other useful subkeys. In this function, we will extract the ProductName, CSDVersion, CurrentBuild number, RegisteredOwner, RegisteredOrganization, and InstallDate values. While most of these values are strings we can print directly to the console, we need to use the Unix epoch converter to interpret the installation date value prior to printing it.

```
def process_software_hive(hive):
    root = hive.root()
    nt_curr_ver = root.find_key("Microsoft").find_key(
        "Windows NT").find_key("CurrentVersion")

    print("Product name: {}".format(nt_curr_ver.value(
        "ProductName").value()))
    print("CSD Version: {}".format(nt_curr_ver.value(
        "CSDVersion").value()))
    print("Current Build: {}".format(nt_curr_ver.value(
        "CurrentBuild").value()))
    print("Registered Owner: {}".format(nt_curr_ver.value(
        "RegisteredOwner").value()))
    print("Registered Org: {}".format(nt_curr_ver.value(
        "RegisteredOrganization").value()))

    raw_install_date = nt_curr_ver.value("InstallDate").value()
    install_date = parse_unix_epoch(raw_install_date)
    print("Installation Date: {}".format(install_date))
```

When we run this script, we can learn about the information stored in the keys we interpreted:

```
(venv2) pyforcookbook@dev-vm$ python registry_overview.py /media/evidence/Ev0001
.E01
[+] Opening /media/evidence/Ev0001.E01
Last Shutdown Time: 2017-08-06 13:24:36.644434
Machine Time Zone: Pacific Standard Time
Machine Name: WIN-178961236
Last Access Updates: Disabled
Product name: Windows 7 Enterprise
CSD Version: Service Pack 1
Current Build: 7601
Registered Owner:  Admin
Registered Org:
Installation Date: 2014-11-02 10:27:00.000000
```

There's more...

This script can be further improved. We have provided one or more recommendations as follows:

- Add logic to handle the situation where the SYSTEM or SOFTWARE hives are not found in the initial search
- Consider adding support for NTUSER.DAT files, pulling basic information about mount points and shell bags queries
- List basic USB device information from the System hive
- Parse the SAM hive to show user and group information

Gathering user activity

Recipe Difficulty: Medium

Python Version: 2.7

Operating System: Linux

Windows stores a plethora of information about user activity, and like other registry hives, the NTUSER.DAT file is a great resource to be relied upon during an investigation. This hive lives within each user's profile and stores information and configurations as they relate to the specific user's on the system.

In this recipe, we cover multiple keys within NTUSER.DAT that throw light on the actions of a user on a system. This includes the prior searches run in Windows Explorer, paths typed into Explorer's navigation bar, and the recently used statements in the Windows run command. These artifacts better illustrate how the user interacted with the system and may give insight into what normal, or abnormal, usage of the system looked like for the user.

Getting started

This recipe requires the installation of four third-party modules to function: jinja2, pytsk3, pyewf, and Registry. Refer to Chapter 8, *Working with Forensic Evidence Container Recipes,* for a detailed explanation of installing the pytsk3 and pyewf modules. Likewise, refer to the *Getting started* section in the *Reading the registry* recipe for details on installing Registry. All other libraries used in this script are present in Python's standard library.

We will reintroduce jinja2, first introduced in Chapter 2, *Creating Artifact Report Recipes,* to build an HTML report. This library is a template language that allows us to build text files programmatically using a Pythonic syntax. As a reminder, we can use pip to install this library:

```
pip install jinja2==2.9.6
```

How to do it...

To extract these values from NTUSER.DAT files within the image, we must:

1. Search for all NTUSER.DAT files across the system.
2. Parse the WordWheelQuery key for each NTUSER.DAT file.
3. Read the TypedPath key for each NTUSER.DAT file.
4. Extract the RunMRU key for each NTUSER.DAT file.
5. Write each of the processed artifacts to an HTML report.

How it works...

Our imports start in the same manner as our prior recipe, adding in the `jinja2` module:

```
from __future__ import print_function
from argparse import ArgumentParser
import os
import StringIO
import struct

from utility.pytskutil import TSKUtil
from Registry import Registry
import jinja2
```

This recipe's command-line handler takes three positional arguments, EVIDENCE_FILE, IMAGE_TYPE, and REPORT, which represent the path to the evidence file, the type of evidence file, and the desired output path to the HTML report, respectively. These three arguments are passed to the main() function.

```
if __name__ == '__main__':
    parser = argparse.ArgumentParser(
        description=__description__,
        epilog="Developed by {} on {}".format(
            ", ".join(__authors__), __date__)
    )
    parser.add_argument('EVIDENCE_FILE',
                        help="Path to evidence file")
    parser.add_argument('IMAGE_TYPE',
                        help="Evidence file format",
                        choices=('ewf', 'raw'))
    parser.add_argument('REPORT',
                        help="Path to report file")
    args = parser.parse_args()
    main(args.EVIDENCE_FILE, args.IMAGE_TYPE, args.REPORT)
```

The main() function begins by reading the evidence file and searching for all NTUSER.DAT files. Following this, we set up a dictionary object, nt_rec, which, while complex, is designed in a manner that eases the HTML report generation process. We then begin iterating through the discovered hives and parse out the username from the path for reference in the processing functions.

```
def main(evidence, image_type, report):
    tsk_util = TSKUtil(evidence, image_type)
    tsk_ntuser_hives = tsk_util.recurse_files('ntuser.dat',
                                              '/Users', 'equals')

    nt_rec = {
```

```
        'wordwheel': {'data': [], 'title': 'WordWheel Query'},
        'typed_path': {'data': [], 'title': 'Typed Paths'},
        'run_mru': {'data': [], 'title': 'Run MRU'}
    }
    for ntuser in tsk_ntuser_hives:
        uname = ntuser[1].split("/")[1]
```

Next, we pass the `pytsk` file handle to be opened as a `Registry` object. This resulting object is used to gather the `root` key in common with all of the desired values (`Software\Microsoft\Windows\CurrentVersion\Explorer`). If this key path is not found, we continue to the next `NTUSER.DAT` file.

```
        open_ntuser = open_file_as_reg(ntuser[2])
        try:
            explorer_key = open_ntuser.root().find_key(
                "Software").find_key("Microsoft").find_key(
                    "Windows").find_key("CurrentVersion").find_key(
                        "Explorer")
        except Registry.RegistryKeyNotFoundException:
            continue # Required registry key not found for user
```

If they key is found, we call the three processing functions responsible for each artifact and provide the shared key object and username. The returned data is stored in the respective data key within the dictionary. We can easily extend the number of artifacts parsed by the code by expanding the storage object definition and adding a new function with the same profile as the others shown here:

```
        nt_rec['wordwheel']['data'] += parse_wordwheel(
            explorer_key, uname)
        nt_rec['typed_path']['data'] += parse_typed_paths(
            explorer_key, uname)
        nt_rec['run_mru']['data'] += parse_run_mru(
            explorer_key, uname)
```

After iterating through the `NTUSER.DAT` files, we set up the headers for each of the record types by extracting the key list of the first item on our data list. Since all of the dictionary objects in our data list have uniform keys, we can use this method to reduce the number of arguments or variables passed around. These statements are also easily extensible.

```
    nt_rec['wordwheel']['headers'] = \
        nt_rec['wordwheel']['data'][0].keys()

    nt_rec['typed_path']['headers'] = \
        nt_rec['typed_path']['data'][0].keys()

    nt_rec['run_mru']['headers'] = \
        nt_rec['run_mru']['data'][0].keys()
```

Lastly, we take our completed dictionary object and pass it, along with the path to the report file, to our `write_html()` method:

```
write_html(report, nt_rec)
```

We've seen the `open_file_as_reg()` method before in the previous recipe. As a reminder, it takes the `pytsk` file handle and reads it into the `Registry` class via the `StringIO` class. The returned `Registry` object allows us to interact and read the registry in an object-oriented manner.

```
def open_file_as_reg(reg_file):
    file_size = reg_file.info.meta.size
    file_content = reg_file.read_random(0, file_size)
    file_like_obj = StringIO.StringIO(file_content)
    return Registry.Registry(file_like_obj)
```

The first processing function handles the `WordWheelQuery` key, which stores information about searches run by a user within Windows Explorer. We can parse this artifact by accessing the key by name from our `explorer_key` object. If the key does not exist, we will return an empty list as we do not have any values to extract.

```
def parse_wordwheel(explorer_key, username):
    try:
        wwq = explorer_key.find_key("WordWheelQuery")
    except Registry.RegistryKeyNotFoundException:
        return []
```

On the other hand, should the key exist, we iterate through the `MRUListEx` value, which holds a list of integers that contain the order of the searches. Each number in the list matches a value of the same number in the key. For this reason, we read the order of the list and interpret the remaining values in the order they appear. Each value name is stored as a two-byte integer, and so we split this list into two-byte chunks and read the integers with `struct`. We then append this value to the list after checking that it does not exist. If it does exist in the list, and is `\x00` or `\xFF`, we have reached the end of the `MRUListEx` data and break out of the loop:

```
mru_list = wwq.value("MRUListEx").value()
mru_order = []
for i in xrange(0, len(mru_list), 2):
    order_val = struct.unpack('h', mru_list[i:i + 2])[0]
    if order_val in mru_order and order_val in (0, -1):
        break
    else:
        mru_order.append(order_val)
```

Using our ordered value list, we iterate through it to extract the search terms in the order they were run. Since we know the order of use, we can associate the last write time of the WordWheelQuery key as the timestamp for the search term. This timestamp is only associated with the most recently run search. All other searches are given the value of N/A.

```
search_list = []
for count, val in enumerate(mru_order):
    ts = "N/A"
    if count == 0:
        ts = wwq.timestamp()
```

Afterwards, we build out the dictionary within the append statement, adding the time value, username, order (as the count integer), the value's name, and the search content. To properly display the search content, we will need to provide the key name as a string and decode the text as UTF-16. This text, once stripped of null termination, is ready for the report. The list is built out until all values are processed and then ultimately returned.

```
search_list.append({
    'timestamp': ts,
    'username': username,
    'order': count,
    'value_name': str(val),
    'search': wwq.value(str(val)).value().decode(
        "UTF-16").strip("\x00")
})
return search_list
```

The next processing function handles the typed paths key, taking the same arguments as the prior processing function. We access the key in the same manner and return the empty list in case the TypedPaths subkey is not found.

```
def parse_typed_paths(explorer_key, username):
    try:
        typed_paths = explorer_key.find_key("TypedPaths")
    except Registry.RegistryKeyNotFoundException:
        return []
```

This key does not have an MRU value ordering the typed paths, so we read all of its values and add them directly to the list. We can gather the value's name and path from this key, adding the username value for additional context. We finish this function by returning the list of dictionary values to the main() function.

```
typed_path_details = []
for val in typed_paths.values():
    typed_path_details.append({
        "username": username,
```

```
                "value_name": val.name(),
                "path": val.value()
        })
    return typed_path_details
```

Our last processing function handles the RunMRU key. If it does not exist in the
explorer_key, we return an empty list as seen before.

```
def parse_run_mru(explorer_key, username):
    try:
        run_mru = explorer_key.find_key("RunMRU")
    except Registry.RegistryKeyNotFoundException:
        return []
```

Since this key can be empty, we first check if there are values for us to parse and, if there are
not, return an empty list to prevent any unnecessary processing.

```
        if len(run_mru.values()) == 0:
            return []
```

Similar to the WordWheelQuery, this key also has an MRU value, which we process to learn
the correct order of the other values. This list stores items differently, as its values are letters
as opposed to integers. This makes our job quite simple as we directly query for the
necessary values using these characters without additional processing. We append the
order of values to a list and move on.

```
    mru_list = run_mru.value("MRUList").value()
    mru_order = []
    for i in mru_list:
        mru_order.append(i)
```

As we iterate through the order of values, we begin to build out our dictionary of results.
First, we handle the timestamps in the same manner as our WordWheelQuery processor, by
assigning a default N/A value and updating it with the key's last written time if it is the first
entry in our ordered list. Following this, we append a dictionary containing the relevant
entries, such as the username, the value order, value name, and value content. This list of
dictionaries is returned once we have processed all remaining values in the Run key.

```
    mru_details = []
    for count, val in enumerate(mru_order):
        ts = "N/A"
        if count == 0:
            ts = run_mru.timestamp()
        mru_details.append({
            "username": username,
            "timestamp": ts,
            "order": count,
```

```
            "value_name": val,
            "run_statement": run_mru.value(val).value()
        })

    return mru_details
```

The last function handles the creation of the HTML report. This function starts by preparing the path of the code and the `jinja2` environment class. This class is used to store shared resources within the library, and we use it to point the library to the directory it should search for template files. In our case, we want it to look for template HTML files in the current directory, so we use the `os` library to get the current working directory and provide it to the `FileSystemLoader()` class.

```
def write_html(outfile, data_dict):
    cwd = os.path.dirname(os.path.abspath(__file__))
    env = jinja2.Environment(loader=jinja2.FileSystemLoader(cwd))
```

With the environment configured, we call the template we would like to use and then the `render()` method to create an HTML file with our passed dictionary. The `render` function returns a string representing the rendered HTML output with the results of the processed data inserted which we write to the output file.

```
    template = env.get_template("user_activity.html")
    rendering = template.render(nt_data=data_dict)
    with open(outfile, 'w') as open_outfile:
        open_outfile.write(rendering)
```

Let's look at the template file, it starts as any HTML document with the `html`, `head`, and `body` tags. While we've included scripts and style sheets in our `head` tag, we have omitted the unrelated material here. This information is available for review in full in the code bundle.

We start the HTML document with a `div` that holds the processed data tables and section headers. To simplify the amount of HTML we need to write, we use a `for` loop to gather each of the nested dictionaries from the `nt_data` values. The `jinja2` template language allows us to still use Python loops as long as they are wrapped in curly brackets, a percentage symbol, and a space character. We can also reference properties and methods of objects, allowing us to iterate through the values of the `nt_data` dictionary without extra code.

The other commonly used template syntax is shown within the `h2` tag, where we access the title attribute we set in the `main()` function. Variables we would like the `jinja2` engine to interpret (versus show as literal strings) need to be enclosed in double curly brackets and a space character. This will now print the section header for each section in our `nt_data` dictionary.

```
<html>
<head>...</head>
<body>
    <div class="container">
        {% for nt_content in nt_data.values() %}
            <h2>{{ nt_content['title'] }}</h2>
```

Within this loop, we set up our data table using the `data` tag and create a new row to hold the table headers. To generate the headers, we step through each of the headers we gathered and assign the value in a nested `for` loop. Notice how we need to specify the end of the loop with the `endfor` statement; this is required by the templating engine, as (unlike Python) it is not sensitive to indents:

```
<table class="table table-hover table-condensed">
    <tr>
        {% for header in nt_content['headers'] %}
            <th>{{ header }}</th>
        {% endfor %}
    <tr/>
```

Following the table headers, we enter a separate loop to iterate through each dictionary in our data list. Inside each table row, we use similar logic as the table headers to create another `for` loop to write each value into a cell in the row:

```
{% for entry in nt_content['data'] %}
    <tr>
        {% for header in nt_content['headers'] %}
            <td>{{ entry[header] }}</td>
        {% endfor %}
    </tr>
```

Now that the HTML data table is populated, we close the `for` loop for the current data point: we draw a horizontal line and start writing the next artifact's data table. Once we completely iterate through those, we close the outer `for` loop and the tags we opened at the start of the HTML report.

```
    {% endfor %}
</table>
<br />
<hr />
```

```
            <br />
        {% endfor %}
    </div>
  </body>
  </html>
```

Our generated report is as follows:

Typed Paths

username	value_name	path
Admin	url1	\\controller

Run MRU

username	timestamp	run_statement	order	value_name
Admin	2015-11-10 07:59:46.499125	\\controller\WebDevShare\1	0	a

WordWheel Query

username	timestamp	search	order	value_name
Admin	2015-04-06 18:44:16.075672	malwarez.exe	0	1
Admin	N/A	secrets	1	0

There's more...

This script can be further improved. We have provided one or more recommendations as follows:

- Add additional `NTUser` or other easy to review artifacts to the dashboard to provide more useful information at a glance

- Add charts, a timeline, or other interactive elements to this dashboard using various JavaScript and CSS elements
- Provide export options from the dashboard into CSV or Excel spreadsheets with additional JavaScript

The missing link

Recipe Difficulty: Medium

Python Version: 2.7

Operating System: Linux

Shortcut files, also known as link files, are common across operating system platforms. They enable the user to use one file to reference another, located elsewhere on the system. On the Windows platform, these link files also record historical access to the files they reference. Generally, the creation time of a link file represents the first access time of a file with that name, and the modification time represents the most recent access time of the file with that name. Using this, we can extrapolate a window of activity and learn about how, and where, these files were accessed.

Getting started

This recipe requires the installation of three third-party modules to function: `pytsk3`, `pyewf`, and `pylnk`. Refer to `Chapter 8`, *Working with Forensic Evidence Container Recipes* for a detailed explanation of installing the `pytsk3` and `pyewf` modules. All other libraries used in this script are present in Python's standard library.

Navigate to the GitHub repository and download the desired release of the `pylnk` library. This recipe was developed using the `pylnk-alpha-20170111` release. Next, once the contents of the release are extracted, open a terminal and navigate to the extracted directory and execute the following commands:

```
./synclibs.sh
./autogen.sh
sudo python setup.py install
```

To learn more about the `pylnk` library, visit `https://github.com/libyal/liblnk`.

Lastly, we can check our library's installation by opening a Python interpreter, importing `pylnk`, and running the `gpylnk.get_version()` method to ensure we have the correct release version.

How to do it...

This script will leverage the following steps:

1. Search for all `lnk` files within the system.
2. Iterate through discovered `lnk` files and extract relevant attributes.
3. Write all artifacts to a CSV report.

How it works...

Starting with the imports, we bring in the Sleuth Kit utilities and `pylnk` library. We also bring in libraries for argument parsing, writing the CSV reports, and `StringIO` to read the Sleuth Kit objects as files:

```
from __future__ import print_function
from argparse import ArgumentParser
import csv
import StringIO

from utility.pytskutil import TSKUtil
import pylnk
```

This recipe's command-line handler takes three positional arguments, `EVIDENCE_FILE`, `IMAGE_TYPE`, and `CSV_REPORT`, which represent the path to the evidence file, the type of evidence file, and the desired output path to the CSV report, respectively. These three arguments are passed to the `main()` function.

```
if __name__ == '__main__':
    parser = argparse.ArgumentParser(
        description=__description__,
        epilog="Developed by {} on {}".format(
            ", ".join(__authors__), __date__)
    )
```

```
parser.add_argument('EVIDENCE_FILE', help="Path to evidence file")
parser.add_argument('IMAGE_TYPE', help="Evidence file format",
                    choices=('ewf', 'raw'))
parser.add_argument('CSV_REPORT', help="Path to CSV report")
args = parser.parse_args()
main(args.EVIDENCE_FILE, args.IMAGE_TYPE, args.CSV_REPORT)
```

The `main()` function begins with creating the `TSKUtil` object used to interpret the evidence file and iterate through the filesystem to find files ending in `lnk`. If there are not any `lnk` files found on the system, the script alerts the user and exits. Otherwise, we specify columns representing the data attributes we want to store for each of the `lnk` files. While there are other attributes available, these are some of the more relevant ones we extract in this recipe:

```
def main(evidence, image_type, report):
    tsk_util = TSKUtil(evidence, image_type)
    lnk_files = tsk_util.recurse_files("lnk", path="/", logic="endswith")
    if lnk_files is None:
        print("No lnk files found")
        exit(0)

    columns = [
        'command_line_arguments', 'description', 'drive_serial_number',
        'drive_type', 'file_access_time', 'file_attribute_flags',
        'file_creation_time', 'file_modification_time', 'file_size',
        'environmental_variables_location', 'volume_label',
        'machine_identifier', 'local_path', 'network_path',
        'relative_path', 'working_directory'
    ]
```

Next, we iterate through the discovered `lnk` files, opening each as a file using the `open_file_as_lnk()` function. The returned object is an instance of the `pylnk` library, ready for us to read the attributes from. We initialize the attribute dictionary with the file's name and path and then iterate through the columns we specified in the `main()` function. For each of the columns, we try to read the specified attribute value, and, if we are unable to, store an "N/A" value otherwise. These attributes are stored in the `lnk_data` dictionary which is appended to the `parsed_lnks` list once all attributes are extracted. After this process completes for each `lnk` file, we pass this list, along with the output path, and column names, to the `write_csv()` method.

```
    parsed_lnks = []
    for entry in lnk_files:
        lnk = open_file_as_lnk(entry[2])
        lnk_data = {'lnk_path': entry[1], 'lnk_name': entry[0]}
        for col in columns:
            lnk_data[col] = getattr(lnk, col, "N/A")
        lnk.close()
```

```
                parsed_lnks.append(lnk_data)

        write_csv(report, columns + ['lnk_path', 'lnk_name'], parsed_lnks)
```

To open our `pytsk` file object as a `pylink` object, we use the `open_file_as_lnk()` function which operates like other similarly named functions throughout this chapter. This function reads the entire file, using the `read_random()` method and file size property, into a `StringIO` buffer that is then passed into a `pylnk` file object. Reading in this manner allows us to read the data as a file without needing to cache it to the disk. Once we have loaded the file into our `lnk` object, we return it to the `main()` function:

```python
def open_file_as_lnk(lnk_file):
    file_size = lnk_file.info.meta.size
    file_content = lnk_file.read_random(0, file_size)
    file_like_obj = StringIO.StringIO(file_content)
    lnk = pylnk.file()
    lnk.open_file_object(file_like_obj)
    return lnk
```

The last function is the common CSV writer, which uses the `csv.DictWriter` class to iterate through the data structure and write the relevant fields to a spreadsheet. The order of the columns list defined in the `main()` function determines their order here as the `fieldnames` argument. One could change that order, if desired, to modify the order in which they are displayed in the resulting spreadsheet.

```python
def write_csv(outfile, fieldnames, data):
    with open(outfile, 'wb') as open_outfile:
        csvfile = csv.DictWriter(open_outfile, fieldnames)
        csvfile.writeheader()
        csvfile.writerows(data)
```

After running the script, we can view the results in a single CSV report as seen in the following two screenshots. Since there are many visible columns, we have elected to display only a few for the readability sake:

local_path	file_creation_time	file_modification_time	file_access_time
C:\Program Files\Internet Explorer\IEXPLORE.EXE	07/25/07 01:12 AM	08/23/01 12:00 PM	07/25/07 01:12 AM
C:\Documents and Settings\All Users\Documents\My Music\Sample Music	07/25/07 01:12 AM	07/25/07 01:13 AM	07/25/07 01:13 AM
C:\Documents and Settings\All Users\Documents\My Pictures\Sample Pictures	07/25/07 01:12 AM	07/25/07 01:13 AM	07/25/07 01:13 AM
E:\Old Images\Really Old Images\07-09-very-old-man.jpg	07/24/07 06:34 AM	07/24/07 06:34 AM	02/12/08 04:00 PM
C:\Documents and Settings\Administrator\My Documents\My Pictures\bad day.jpg	01/01/01 12:00 AM	01/01/01 12:00 AM	01/01/01 12:00 AM
C:\Documents and Settings\Administrator\Desktop\Stuff\blocks_image_0_1.png	01/01/01 12:00 AM	01/01/01 12:00 AM	01/01/01 12:00 AM
C:\Documents and Settings\Administrator\My Documents\My Pictures\cancer.jpg	01/01/01 12:00 AM	01/01/01 12:00 AM	01/01/01 12:00 AM
E:\Old Images\Really Old Images\chinamanbeard.jpg	07/24/07 06:33 AM	07/24/07 06:33 AM	02/12/08 04:00 PM
C:\Documents and Settings\Administrator\Desktop\cht.htm	07/25/07 01:51 AM	07/25/07 01:51 AM	07/25/07 06:09 PM
C:\Documents and Settings\Administrator\Desktop\Dc6.JPG	08/04/07 01:31 AM	10/06/03 05:24 AM	02/13/08 01:25 AM

machine_identifier	network_path	drive_serial_number	volume_label	drive_type	file_size	lnk_name
dryer1		1491926564		3	91136	Launch Internet Explorer Browser.lnk
dryer1		1491926564		3	0	Sample Music.lnk
dryer1		1491926564		3	0	Sample Pictures.lnk
		1280030948	FAMILY PIX	2	42725	07-09-very-old-man.jpg.lnk
		1491926564	dryer	3	0	bad day.jpg.lnk
	\\dryer1\Stuff\blocks _image_0_1.png	1491926564	dryer	3	0	blocks_image_0_1.png.lnk
		1491926564	dryer	3	0	cancer.jpg.lnk
		1280030948	FAMILY PIX	2	39605	chinamanbeard.jpg.lnk
dryer1		1491926564		3	4448	cht.lnk
dryer1		1491926564	dryer	3	386922	Dc6.JPG.lnk

There's more...

This script can be further improved. We have provided one or more recommendations as follows:

- Add checks to see if the target file still exists
- Identify target locations on remote or removable volumes
- Add support for parsing jumplists

Searching high and low

Recipe difficulty: Hard

Python version: 2.7

Operating system: Linux

Most modern operating systems maintain an index of files and other data content stored on the system. These indexes allow for more efficient searches across file formats, emails, and other content found on the system's volumes. On Windows, such an index is found in the `Windows.edb` file. This database is stored in the **Extensible Storage Engine** (**ESE**) file format and found within the `ProgramData` directory. We will leverage another library from the `libyal` project to parse this file to extract information about the indexed content on the system.

Getting started

This recipe requires the installation of four third-party modules to function: `pytsk3`, `pyewf`, `pyesedb`, and `unicodecsv`. Refer to `Chapter 8`, *Working with Forensic Evidence Container Recipes* for a detailed explanation on installing the `pytsk3` and `pyewf` modules. Likewise, refer to the *Getting started* section in the *One man's trash is a forensic examiner's treasure* recipe for details on installing `unicodecsv`. All other libraries used in this script are present in Python's standard library.

Navigate to the GitHub repository and download the desired release for each library. This recipe was developed using the `libesedb-experimental-20170121` release. Once the contents of the release are extracted, open a terminal, navigate to the extracted directory, and execute the following commands:

```
./synclibs.sh
./autogen.sh
sudo python setup.py install
```

 To learn more about the `pyesedb` library, visit
https://github.com/libyal/libesedb.

Lastly, we can check our library's installation by opening a Python interpreter, importing `pyesedb`, and running the `epyesedb.get_version()` method to ensure we have the correct release version.

How to do it...

To draft this script we will need to:

1. Recurse the `ProgramData` directory to search for the `Windows.edb` file.
2. Iterate through discovered `Windows.edb` files (though there should really only be one) and open the files using the `pyesedb` library.
3. Process each of the files to extract key columns and attributes.
4. Write these key columns and attributes to the report.

How it works...

The imports here include those libraries we've used for most recipes in the chapter for argument parsing, string buffer file-like objects, and the TSK utilities. We also import the unicodecsv library to handle any Unicode objects in the CSV report, the datetime library to assist with timestamp parsing, and the struct module to help make sense of the binary data we read. Additionally, we define a global variable, COL_TYPES, that aliases the column types from the pyesedb library, used to help identify the types of data that we will extract later in the code:

```python
from __future__ import print_function
from argparse import ArgumentParser
import unicodecsv as csv
import datetime
import StringIO
import struct

from utility.pytskutil import TSKUtil
import pyesedb

COL_TYPES = pyesedb.column_types
```

This recipe's command-line handler takes three positional arguments, EVIDENCE_FILE, IMAGE_TYPE, and CSV_REPORT, which represent the path to the evidence file, the type of evidence file, and the desired output path to the CSV report, respectively. These three arguments are passed to the main() function.

```python
if __name__ == '__main__':
    parser = argparse.ArgumentParser(
        description=__description__,
        epilog="Developed by {} on {}".format(
            ", ".join(__authors__), __date__)
    )
    parser.add_argument('EVIDENCE_FILE', help="Path to evidence file")
    parser.add_argument('IMAGE_TYPE', help="Evidence file format",
                        choices=('ewf', 'raw'))
    parser.add_argument('CSV_REPORT', help="Path to CSV report")
    args = parser.parse_args()
    main(args.EVIDENCE_FILE, args.IMAGE_TYPE, args.CSV_REPORT)
```

The `main()` function opens the evidence and searches for the `Windows.edb` file within the `ProgramData` directory. If one or more files are found, we iterate through the list and open each ESE database for further processing with the `process_windows_search()` function. This function returns the spreadsheet column headers to use and a list of dictionaries containing the data to include in the report. This information is then written to the output CSV for review by the `write_csv()` method:

```
def main(evidence, image_type, report):
    tsk_util = TSKUtil(evidence, image_type)
    esedb_files = tsk_util.recurse_files(
        "Windows.edb",
        path="/ProgramData/Microsoft/Search/Data/Applications/Windows",
        logic="equals"
    )
    if esedb_files is None:
        print("No Windows.edb file found")
        exit(0)

    for entry in esedb_files:
        ese = open_file_as_esedb(entry[2])
        if ese is None:
            continue # Invalid ESEDB
        report_cols, ese_data = process_windows_search(ese)

    write_csv(report, report_cols, ese_data)
```

Reading the responsive ESE database requires the `open_file_as_esedb()` function. This code block uses similar logic to the previous recipes to read the file into a `StringIO` object and open the file-like object with the library. Note, this could cause errors on your system if the file is rather large or your machine has lower amounts of memory. You can use the built-in `tempfile` library to cache the file to a temporary location on disk, reading from there if you would prefer.

```
def open_file_as_esedb(esedb):
    file_size = esedb.info.meta.size
    file_content = esedb.read_random(0, file_size)
    file_like_obj = StringIO.StringIO(file_content)
    esedb = pyesedb.file()
    try:
        esedb.open_file_object(file_like_obj)
    except IOError:
        return None
    return esedb
```

Our `process_windows_search()` function starts with column definitions. While our previous recipe used a simple list of columns, the `pyesedb` library takes a column index as an input to retrieve a value from a row within a table. For this reason, our column list must consist of tuples, where the first element is a number (the index) and the second is the string description. Since the description isn't used in the function to select columns, we name these in the manner we would like them displayed in the report. For this recipe, we have defined the following column indexes and names:

```
def process_windows_search(ese):
    report_cols = [
        (0, "DocID"), (286, "System_KindText"),
        (35, "System_ItemUrl"), (5, "System_DateModified"),
        (6, "System_DateCreated"), (7, "System_DateAccessed"),
        (3, "System_Size"), (19, "System_IsFolder"),
        (2, "System_Search_GatherTime"), (22, "System_IsDeleted"),
        (61, "System_FileOwner"), (31, "System_ItemPathDisplay"),
        (150, "System_Link_TargetParsingPath"),
        (265, "System_FileExtension"), (348, "System_ComputerName"),
        (34, "System_Communication_AccountName"),
        (44, "System_Message_FromName"),
        (43, "System_Message_FromAddress"), (49, "System_Message_ToName"),
        (47, "System_Message_ToAddress"),
        (62, "System_Message_SenderName"),
        (189, "System_Message_SenderAddress"),
        (52, "System_Message_DateSent"),
        (54, "System_Message_DateReceived")
    ]
```

After we define the columns of interest, we access the `SystemIndex_0A` table, which contains the indexed file, mail, and other entries. We iterate through the records within the table, building a `record_info` dictionary of the column values for each record that will eventually be appended to the `table_data` list. A second loop iterates through the columns we defined earlier and attempts to extract the value and value type for each column in the record.

```
table = ese.get_table_by_name("SystemIndex_0A")
table_data = []
for record in table.records:
    record_info = {}
    for col_id, col_name in report_cols:
        rec_val = record.get_value_data(col_id)
        col_type = record.get_column_type(col_id)
```

Using the COL_TYPES global variable we defined earlier, we can reference the various data types and ensure we are interpreting the values correctly. The logic in the following code block focuses on interpreting the values correctly based on their data type. First, we handle dates, which may be stored as Windows FILETIME values. We attempt to convert the FILETIME value, if possible, or present the date value in hexadecimal if not. The next statement checks for text values, interpreting the value with the pyesedb get_value_data_as_string() function or as a UTF-16 big-endian and replacing any unrecognized character for completeness.

We then individually handle integer and Boolean data type interpretation using the pyesedb get_value_data_as_integer() function and a simple comparison statement, respectively. Specifically, we check if the rec_val is equal to "\x01" and allow rec_val to be set True or False based on that comparison. If none of these data types are valid, we interpret the value as hex and store it with the associated column name before appending the value to the table:

```
if col_type in (COL_TYPES.DATE_TIME, COL_TYPES.BINARY_DATA):
    try:
        raw_val = struct.unpack('>q', rec_val)[0]
        rec_val = parse_windows_filetime(raw_val)
    except Exception:
        if rec_val is not None:
            rec_val = rec_val.encode('hex')

elif col_type in (COL_TYPES.TEXT, COL_TYPES.LARGE_TEXT):
    try:
        rec_val = record.get_value_data_as_string(col_id)
    except Exception:
        rec_val = rec_val.decode("utf-16-be", "replace")

elif col_type == COL_TYPES.INTEGER_32BIT_SIGNED:
    rec_val = record.get_value_data_as_integer(col_id)

elif col_type == COL_TYPES.BOOLEAN:
    rec_val = rec_val == '\x01'

else:
    if rec_val is not None:
        rec_val = rec_val.encode('hex')

record_info[col_name] = rec_val
table_data.append(record_info)
```

We then return a tuple to our calling function, where the first element is the list of names of the columns in the `report_cols` dictionary and the second is a list of data dictionaries.

```
    return [x[1] for x in report_cols], table_data
```

Borrowing our logic from our date-parsing recipe in Chapter 7, *Log-Based Artifact Recipes*, we implement a function to parse the Windows `FILETIME` value into a human-readable state. This accepts an integer value as input and returns a human-readable string:

```
def parse_windows_filetime(date_value):
    microseconds = float(date_value) / 10
    ts = datetime.datetime(1601, 1, 1) + datetime.timedelta(
        microseconds=microseconds)
    return ts.strftime('%Y-%m-%d %H:%M:%S.%f')
```

The last function is the CSV report writer, which writes the columns and the rows of collected information to the open CSV spreadsheet using the `DictWriter` class. While we selected a subset of the available columns at the outset, there are many more to choose from that may be useful in varying case types. Therefore, we recommend taking a look at all available columns to better understand this recipe and what columns may or may not be useful for you.

```
def write_csv(outfile, fieldnames, data):
    with open(outfile, 'wb') as open_outfile:
        csvfile = csv.DictWriter(open_outfile, fieldnames)
        csvfile.writeheader()
        csvfile.writerows(data)
```

After running the recipe, we can review the output CSV shown here. As there are many columns to this report, we have highlighted a few interesting ones in the following two screenshots:

DocID	System_ItemUrl	System_DateModified	System_DateCreated	System_DateAccessed	System_IsFolder
0	file:C:/Users/Admin/Searches/Indexed Locations.search-ms	10/17/12 04:30 PM	10/17/12 04:30 PM	10/17/12 04:30 PM	FALSE
1	file:C:/Users/Admin/Searches/Everywhere.search-ms	10/17/12 04:30 PM	10/17/12 04:30 PM	10/17/12 04:30 PM	FALSE
2	file:C:/Users/Admin/Links	10/17/12 04:31 PM	10/17/12 04:30 PM	10/17/12 04:30 PM	TRUE
3	file:C:/Users/Admin/Links/RecentPlaces.lnk	10/17/12 04:31 PM	10/17/12 04:30 PM	10/17/12 04:30 PM	FALSE
4	file:C:/Users/Admin/Desktop	10/17/12 04:31 PM	10/17/12 04:30 PM	10/17/12 04:30 PM	TRUE
5	file:C:/Users/Admin/Links/Desktop.lnk	10/17/12 04:31 PM	10/17/12 04:30 PM	10/17/12 04:30 PM	FALSE
6	file:C:/Users/Admin/Downloads	10/17/12 04:31 PM	10/17/12 04:30 PM	10/17/12 04:30 PM	TRUE
7	file:C:/Users/Admin/Links/Downloads.lnk	10/17/12 04:31 PM	10/17/12 04:30 PM	10/17/12 04:30 PM	FALSE
8	file:C:/Users/Admin/Favorites/Microsoft Websites	10/17/12 04:30 PM	10/17/12 04:30 PM	10/17/12 04:30 PM	TRUE
9	file:C:/Users/Admin/Favorites/Microsoft Websites/IE site on Microsoft.com.url	10/29/12 01:48 PM	10/17/12 04:30 PM	10/29/12 01:48 PM	FALSE
10	file:C:/Users/Admin/Favorites/Microsoft Websites/IE Add-on site.url	10/29/12 01:48 PM	10/17/12 04:30 PM	10/29/12 01:48 PM	FALSE
11	file:C:/Users/Admin/Favorites/Microsoft Websites/Microsoft At Home.url	10/29/12 01:48 PM	10/17/12 04:30 PM	10/29/12 01:48 PM	FALSE
12	file:C:/Users/Admin/Favorites/Microsoft Websites/Microsoft At Work.url	10/29/12 01:48 PM	10/17/12 04:30 PM	10/29/12 01:48 PM	FALSE
13	file:C:/Users/Admin/Favorites/MSN Websites	10/17/12 04:30 PM	10/17/12 04:30 PM	10/17/12 04:30 PM	TRUE
14	file:C:/Users/Admin/Favorites/MSN Websites/MSN.url	10/29/12 01:48 PM	10/17/12 04:30 PM	10/29/12 01:48 PM	FALSE
15	file:C:/Users/Admin/Favorites/MSN Websites/MSN Sports.url	10/29/12 01:48 PM	10/17/12 04:30 PM	10/29/12 01:48 PM	FALSE

System_Search_GatherTime	System_IsDeleted	System_FileOwner	System_ItemPathDisplay	System_Link_TargetParsingPath
10/29/12 01:51 PM	FALSE	WIN-O3EOD5MV6UQ\Admin	C:\Users\Admin\Searches\Indexed Locations.search-ms	
10/29/12 01:51 PM	FALSE	WIN-O3EOD5MV6UQ\Admin	C:\Users\Admin\Searches\Everywhere.search-ms	
10/29/12 01:51 PM	FALSE		C:\Users\Admin\Links	
10/29/12 01:51 PM	FALSE	WIN-O3EOD5MV6UQ\Admin	C:\Users\Admin\Links\Recent Places.lnk	Recent Places
10/29/12 01:51 PM	FALSE		C:\Users\Admin\Desktop	
10/29/12 01:51 PM	FALSE	WIN-O3EOD5MV6UQ\Admin	C:\Users\Admin\Links\Desktop.lnk	Desktop
10/29/12 01:51 PM	FALSE		C:\Users\Admin\Downloads	
10/29/12 01:51 PM	FALSE	WIN-O3EOD5MV6UQ\Admin	C:\Users\Admin\Links\Downloads.lnk	
10/29/12 01:51 PM	FALSE		C:\Users\Admin\Favorites\Microsoft Websites	
10/31/12 06:14 PM	FALSE	WIN-O3EOD5MV6UQ\Admin	C:\Users\Admin\Favorites\Microsoft Websites\IE site on Microsoft.com.url	http://go.microsoft.com/fwlink/?linkid=44661
10/31/12 06:14 PM	FALSE	WIN-O3EOD5MV6UQ\Admin	C:\Users\Admin\Favorites\Microsoft Websites\IE Add-on site.url	http://go.microsoft.com/fwlink/?LinkId=50893
10/31/12 06:14 PM	FALSE	WIN-O3EOD5MV6UQ\Admin	C:\Users\Admin\Favorites\Microsoft Websites\Microsoft At Home.url	http://go.microsoft.com/fwlink/?linkid=55424
10/31/12 06:14 PM	FALSE	WIN-O3EOD5MV6UQ\Admin	C:\Users\Admin\Favorites\Microsoft Websites\Microsoft At Work.url	http://go.microsoft.com/fwlink/?linkid=68920
10/29/12 01:51 PM	FALSE		C:\Users\Admin\Favorites\MSN Websites	
10/31/12 06:14 PM	FALSE	WIN-O3EOD5MV6UQ\Admin	C:\Users\Admin\Favorites\MSN Websites\MSN.url	http://go.microsoft.com/fwlink/?LinkId=54729
10/31/12 06:14 PM	FALSE	WIN-O3EOD5MV6UQ\Admin	C:\Users\Admin\Favorites\MSN Websites\MSN Sports.url	http://go.microsoft.com/fwlink/?LinkId=68921

There's more...

This script can be further improved. We have provided one or more recommendations as follows:

- Add support to check for the existence of referenced files and folders
- Write our `Windows.edb` file to a temporary location to relieve memory pressure when parsing large databases with the Python `tempfile` library
- Add more columns or create separate (targeted) reports using more of the over 300 available columns in the table

10
Exploring Windows Forensic Artifacts Recipes - Part II

In this chapter, the following recipes will be covered:

- Parsing prefetch files
- A series of fortunate events
- Indexing internet history
- Shadow of a former self
- Dissecting the SRUM database

Introduction

Microsoft Windows is one of the most common operating systems found on machines during forensic analysis. This has led to a large effort in the community over the past two decades to develop, share, and document artifacts deposited by this operating system for use in forensic casework.

In this chapter, we continue to look at various Windows artifacts and how to process them using Python. We will leverage the framework we developed in Chapter 8, *Working with Forensic Evidence Container Recipes* to process these artifacts directly from forensic acquisitions. We'll use various libyal libraries to handle the underlying processing of various files, including pyevt, pyevtx, pymsiecf, pyvshadow, and pyesedb. We'll also explore how to process prefetch files using struct and a file format table of offsets and data types of interest. Here's what we'll learn to do in this chapter:

- Parsing prefetch files for application execution information
- Searching for event logs and extract events to a spreadsheet
- Extracting internet history from index.dat files
- Enumerating and creating file listings of volume shadow copies
- Dissecting the Windows 10 SRUM database

For a full listing of libyal repositories, visit https://github.com/libyal. Visit www.packtpub.com/books/content/support to download the code bundle for this chapter.

Parsing prefetch files

Recipe difficulty: Medium

Python version: 2.7

Operating system: Linux

Prefetch files are a common artifact to rely on for information about application execution. While they may not always be present, they are undoubtedly worth reviewing in scenarios where they exist. Recall that prefetching can be enabled to various degrees or disabled based upon the value of the PrefetchParameters subkey in the SYSTEM hive. This recipe searches for files with the prefetch extension (.pf) and processes them for valuable application information. We will only demonstrate this process for Windows XP prefetch files; however, be aware that the underlying process we use is similar to other iterations of Windows.

Getting started

Because we have decided to build out the Sleuth Kit and its dependencies on an Ubuntu environment, we continue development on that operating system for ease of use. This script will require the installation, if they are not already present, of three additional libraries: `pytsk3`, `pyewf`, and `unicodecsv`. All other libraries used in this script are present in Python's standard library.

Refer to `Chapter 8`, *Working with Forensic Evidence Container Recipes* for a detailed explanation of installing the `pytsk3` and `pyewf` modules. Because we are developing these recipes in Python 2.x, we are likely to encounter Unicode encode and decode errors. To account for that, we use the `unicodecsv` library to write all CSV output in this chapter. This third-party module takes care of Unicode support, unlike Python 2.x's standard `csv` module, and will be put to great use here. As usual, we can use `pip` to install `unicodecsv`:

```
pip install unicodecsv==0.14.1
```

In addition to these, we'll continue to use the `pytskutil` module developed from `Chapter 8`, *Working with Forensic Evidence Container Recipes,* to allow interaction with forensic acquisitions. This module is largely similar to what we previously wrote, with some minor changes to better suit our purposes. You can review the code by navigating to the utility directory within the code package.

How to do it...

We process prefetch files following these basic principles:

1. Scan for files ending with the `.pf` extension.
2. Eliminate false positives through signature verification.
3. Parse the Windows XP prefetch file format.
4. Create a spreadsheet of parsed results to the current working directory.

How it works...

We import a number of libraries to assist with argument parsing, parsing dates, interpreting binary data, writing CSVs, and the custom `pytskutil` module.

```
from __future__ import print_function
import argparse
from datetime import datetime, timedelta
```

```
import os
import pytsk3
import pyewf
import struct
import sys
import unicodecsv as csv
from utility.pytskutil import TSKUtil
```

This recipe's command-line handler takes two positional arguments, EVIDENCE_FILE and TYPE, which represent the path to the evidence file and the type of evidence file (that is, raw or ewf). Most of the recipes featured in this chapter will only feature the two positional inputs. The output from these recipes will be spreadsheets created in the current working directory. This recipe has an optional argument, d, which specifies the path to scan for prefetch files. By default, this is set to the /Windows/Prefetch directory, although users can elect to scan the entire image or a separate directory if desired. After performing some input validation on the evidence file, we supply the main() function with the three inputs and begin executing the script:

```
if __name__ == "__main__":
    parser = argparse.ArgumentParser(
        description=__description__,
        epilog="Developed by {} on {}".format(
            ", ".join(__authors__), __date__)
    )
    parser.add_argument("EVIDENCE_FILE", help="Evidence file path")
    parser.add_argument("TYPE", help="Type of Evidence",
                        choices=("raw", "ewf"))
    parser.add_argument("OUTPUT_CSV", help="Path to write output csv")
    parser.add_argument("-d", help="Prefetch directory to scan",
                        default="/WINDOWS/PREFETCH")
    args = parser.parse_args()

    if os.path.exists(args.EVIDENCE_FILE) and \
            os.path.isfile(args.EVIDENCE_FILE):
        main(args.EVIDENCE_FILE, args.TYPE, args.OUTPUT_CSV, args.d)
    else:
        print("[-] Supplied input file {} does not exist or is not a "
              "file".format(args.EVIDENCE_FILE))
        sys.exit(1)
```

In the main() function, we first create the TSKUtil object, tsk_util, which represents the pytsk3 image object. With the TSKUtil object, we can call a number of helper functions to directly interact with the evidence file. We use the TSKUtil.query_directory() function to confirm that the specified directory exists. If it does, we use the TSKUtil.recurse_files() method to recurse through the specified directory and identify any file that ends with the .pf extension. This method returns a list of tuples, where each tuple contains a number of potentially useful objects, including the filename, path, and object itself. If no such files are found, None is returned instead.

```
def main(evidence, image_type, output_csv, path):
    # Create TSK object and query path for prefetch files
    tsk_util = TSKUtil(evidence, image_type)
    prefetch_dir = tsk_util.query_directory(path)
    prefetch_files = None
    if prefetch_dir is not None:
        prefetch_files = tsk_util.recurse_files(
            ".pf", path=path, logic="endswith")
```

If we do find files matching the search criteria, we print a status message to the console with the number of files found. Next, we set up the prefetch_data list, which will be used to store the parsed prefetch data from each valid file. As we iterate through each hit in the search, we extract the file object, the second index of the tuple, for further processing.

Before we do anything with the file object, we validate the file signature of the potential prefetch file with the check_signature() method. If the file does not match the known prefetch file signature, None is returned as the pf_version variable, preventing further processing from occurring for this particular file. Before we delve any further into the actual processing of the file, let's look at how this check_signature() method functions.

```
    if prefetch_files is None:
        print("[-] No .pf files found")
        sys.exit(2)

    print("[+] Identified {} potential prefetch files".format(
        len(prefetch_files)))
    prefetch_data = []
    for hit in prefetch_files:
        prefetch_file = hit[2]
        pf_version = check_signature(prefetch_file)
```

The `check_signature()` method takes the file object as its input and returns either the prefetch version or, if the file is not a valid prefetch file, returns `None`. We use `struct` to extract two little-endian `32-bit` integers from the first `8` bytes of the potential prefetch file. The first integer represents the file version, while the second integer is the file's signature. The file signature should be `0x53434341`, whose decimal representation is `1,094,927,187`. We compare the value we extracted from the file to that number to determine whether the file signatures match. If they do match, we return the prefetch version to the `main()` function. The prefetch version tells us what type of prefetch file we are working with (Windows XP, 7, 10, and so on). We return this value back to dictate how to process the file as prefetch files have changed slightly in different versions of Windows. Now, back to the `main()` function!

 To learn more about prefetch versions and file formats, visit `http://www.forensicswiki.org/wiki/Windows_Prefetch_File_Format`.

```
def check_signature(prefetch_file):
    version, signature = struct.unpack(
        "<2i", prefetch_file.read_random(0, 8))

    if signature == 1094927187:
        return version
    else:
        return None
```

Back in the `main()` function, we check that the `pf_version` variable is not `None`, indicating it was successfully validated. Following that, we extract the name of the file to the `pf_name` variable, which is stored at the zero index of the tuple. Next, we check which version of prefetch file we are working with. A breakdown of prefetch versions and their related operating systems can be viewed here:

Prefetch version	Windows desktop operating system
17	Windows XP
23	Windows Vista, Windows 7
26	Windows 8.1
30	Windows 10

This recipe has only been developed to process Windows XP prefetch files using the file format as recorded on the previously referenced forensics wiki page. However, there are placeholders to add in the logic to support the other prefetch formats. They are largely similar, with the exception of Windows 10, and can be parsed by following the same basic methodology used for Windows XP. Windows 10 prefetch files are MAM compressed and must be decompressed first before they can be processed--other than that, they can be handled in a similar manner. For version 17 (Windows XP format), we call the parsing function, providing the TSK file object and name of the prefetch file:

```
if pf_version is None:
    continue

pf_name = hit[0]
if pf_version == 17:
    parsed_data = parse_pf_17(prefetch_file, pf_name)
    parsed_data.append(os.path.join(path, hit[1].lstrip("//")))
    prefetch_data.append(parsed_data)
```

We begin processing the Windows XP prefetch file by storing the `create` and `modify` timestamps of the file itself into local variables. These `Unix` timestamps are converted using the `convertUnix()` method, which we have worked with before. Besides `Unix` timestamps, we also encounter `FILETIME` timestamps embedded within the prefetch file themselves. Let's look at these functions briefly to get them out of the way before continuing our discussion of the `main()` method:

```
def parse_pf_17(prefetch_file, pf_name):
    # Parse Windows XP, 2003 Prefetch File
    create = convert_unix(prefetch_file.info.meta.crtime)
    modify = convert_unix(prefetch_file.info.meta.mtime)
```

Both functions rely on the `datetime` module to appropriately convert the timestamps into a human-readable format. Both functions check whether the supplied timestamp string is equal to `"0"` and return an empty string if that is the case. Otherwise, for the `convert_unix()` method, we use the `utcfromtimestamp()` method to convert the `Unix` timestamp to a `datetime` object and return that. For the `FILETIME` timestamp, we add the number of 100 nanoseconds elapsed since January 1, 1601, and return the resulting `datetime` object. With our brief dalliance with time complete, let's get back to the `main()` function.

```
def convert_unix(ts):
    if int(ts) == 0:
        return ""
    return datetime.utcfromtimestamp(ts)
```

```
def convert_filetime(ts):
    if int(ts) == 0:
        return ""
    return datetime(1601, 1, 1) + timedelta(microseconds=ts / 10)
```

Now that we have extracted the file metadata, we start using `struct` to extract the data embedded within the prefetch file itself. We read in `136` bytes from the file using the `pytsk3.read_random()` method and `struct` and unpack that data into Python variables. Specifically, in those `136` bytes, we extract five `32-bit` integers (`i`), one `64-bit` integer (`q`), and a 60-character string (`s`). In parentheses in the preceding sentence are the `struct` format characters related to those data types. This can also be seen in the `struct` format string `"<i60s32x3iq16xi"`, where the number preceding the `struct` format character instructs `struct` how many there are (for example, `60s` tells `struct` to interpret the next `60` bytes as a string). Likewise, the `"x"` `struct` format character is a null value. If `struct` receives `136` bytes to read, it must also receive format characters accounting for each of those `136` bytes. Therefore, we must supply these null values to ensure we appropriately account for the data we are reading in and ensure we are interpreting the values at the appropriate offsets. The `"<"` character at the beginning of the string ensures all values are interpreted as little-endian.

Right, that was maybe a bit much, but we probably all have a better understanding of `struct` now. After `struct` interprets the data, it returns a tuple of unpacked data types in the order in which they were unpacked. We assign these to a series of local variables including the prefetch file size, application name, last executed `FILETIME`, and the execution count. The application's `name` variable, the 60-character string we extracted, needs to be UTF-16 decoded, and we need to remove all `x00` values padding the string. Notice that one of the values we extracted, `vol_info`, is the pointer to where volume information is stored within the prefetch file. We extract this information next:

```
pf_size, name, vol_info, vol_entries, vol_size, filetime, \
    count = struct.unpack("<i60s32x3iq16xi",
                          prefetch_file.read_random(12, 136))

name = name.decode("utf-16", "ignore").strip("/x00").split("/x00")[0]
```

Let's look at a simpler example with `struct`. We read `20` bytes, starting from the `vol_info` pointer, and extract three `32-bit` integers and one `64-bit` integer. These are the volume name offset and length, the volume serial number, and the volume creation date. Most forensic programs display the volume serial number as two four-character hex values separated by a dash. We do the same by converting the integer to hex and removing the prepended `"0x"` value to isolate just the eight-character hex value. Next, we append a dash halfway between the volume serial number using string slicing and concatenation.

Finally, we use the volume name offset and length we extracted to pull out the volume name. We use string formatting to insert the volume name length in the `struct` format string. We must multiply the length by two to extract the full string. Similar to the application name, we must decode the string as UTF-16 and remove any `"/x00"` values present. We append the extracted elements from the prefetch file to the list. Notice how we perform a few last-minute operations while doing so, including converting two `FILETIME` timestamps and joining the prefetch path with the name of the file. Note that if we do not remove the prepended `"/"` character from the `filename`, the `os.path.join()` method will not combine these two strings correctly. Therefore, we use `lstrip()` to remove it from the beginning of the string:

```
vol_name_offset, vol_name_length, vol_create, \
    vol_serial = struct.unpack("<2iqi",
                            prefetch_file.read_random(vol_info, 20))

vol_serial = hex(vol_serial).lstrip("0x")
vol_serial = vol_serial[:4] + "-" + vol_serial[4:]

vol_name = struct.unpack(
    "<{}s".format(2 * vol_name_length),
    prefetch_file.read_random(vol_info + vol_name_offset,
                            vol_name_length * 2)
)[0]

vol_name = vol_name.decode("utf-16", "ignore").strip("/x00").split(
    "/x00")[0]

return [
    pf_name, name, pf_size, create,
    modify, convert_filetime(filetime), count, vol_name,
    convert_filetime(vol_create), vol_serial
]
```

As we discussed at the beginning of this recipe, we currently only support Windows XP-format prefetch files. We have left placeholders to support the other format types. Currently, however, if these formats are encountered, an unsupported message is printed to the console and we continue onto the next prefetch file:

```
elif pf_version == 23:
    print("[-] Windows Vista / 7 PF file {} -- unsupported".format(
        pf_name))
    continue
elif pf_version == 26:
    print("[-] Windows 8 PF file {} -- unsupported".format(
        pf_name))
    continue
```

```
        elif pf_version == 30:
            print("[-] Windows 10 PF file {} -- unsupported".format(
                pf_name))
            continue
```

Recall back to the beginning of this recipe how we checked if the `pf_version` variable was `None`. If that is the case, the prefetch file does not pass signature verification, and so we print a message to that effect and continue onto the next file. Once we have finished processing all prefetch files, we send the list containing the parsed data to the `write_output()` method:

```
    else:
        print("[-] Signature mismatch - Name: {}\nPath: {}".format(
            hit[0], hit[1]))
        continue

write_output(prefetch_data, output_csv)
```

The `write_output()` method takes the data list we created and writes that data out to a CSV file. We use the `os.getcwd()` method to identify the current working directory, where we write the CSV file. After printing a status message to the console, we create our CSV file, write the names of our columns, and then use the `writerows()` method to write all of the lists of parsed prefetch data within the data list.

```
def write_output(data, output_csv):
    print("[+] Writing csv report")
    with open(output_csv, "wb") as outfile:
        writer = csv.writer(outfile)
        writer.writerow([
            "File Name", "Prefetch Name", "File Size (bytes)",
            "File Create Date (UTC)", "File Modify Date (UTC)",
            "Prefetch Last Execution Date (UTC)",
            "Prefetch Execution Count", "Volume", "Volume Create Date",
            "Volume Serial", "File Path"
        ])
        writer.writerows(data)
```

When we run this script, we generate a CSV document with the following columns:

File Name	Prefetch Name	File Size (bytes)	File Create Date (UTC)	File Modify Date (UTC)
JAVA.EXE-0C263507.pf	JAVA.EXE	53776	04/02/12 10:25 PM	04/06/12 07:12 PM
JAVAW.EXE-2DC32ABC.pf	JAVAW.EXE	89938	04/02/12 12:47 PM	04/06/12 07:12 PM
JAVAWS.EXE-021AC9A9.pf	JAVAWS.EXE	11824	04/02/12 12:47 PM	04/06/12 07:12 PM
JQS.EXE-1D781F77.pf	JQS.EXE	19098	04/02/12 12:47 PM	04/02/12 12:47 PM
JUSCHED.EXE-0F4A509D.pf	JUSCHED.EXE	13542	04/03/12 01:03 AM	04/06/12 07:07 PM
JXPIINSTALL.EXE-377602ED.pf	JXPIINSTALL.EXE	30820	04/02/12 12:46 PM	04/02/12 12:46 PM
LOGON.SCR-151EFAEA.pf	LOGON.SCR	8808	09/09/11 06:40 PM	04/06/12 07:16 PM
MCSCRIPT_INUSE.EXE-396579E3.pf	MCSCRIPT_INUSE.EXE	90470	09/16/11 09:55 PM	04/06/12 09:24 PM
SETUP.EXE-0541E6D6.pf	SETUP.EXE	28704	04/06/12 03:58 AM	04/06/12 03:58 AM
SETUP.EXE-15046A0E.pf	SETUP.EXE	56830	04/06/12 03:58 AM	04/06/12 03:58 AM
SETUP50.EXE-362FF7C9.pf	SETUP50.EXE	32784	04/04/12 12:25 PM	04/04/12 04:41 PM
SHMGRATE.EXE-1BA69E68.pf	SHMGRATE.EXE	23792	04/04/12 12:25 PM	04/04/12 04:41 PM
SHSTAT.EXE-29A2BE4E.pf	SHSTAT.EXE	25732	04/03/12 01:03 AM	04/06/12 07:07 PM
SLLAUNCHER.EXE-0E3D1802.pf	SLLAUNCHER.EXE	62860	03/05/12 01:21 PM	04/03/12 02:44 PM
SOFTWAREUPDATE.EXE-1415D1B8.pf	SOFTWAREUPDATE.EXE	58428	03/09/12 02:16 PM	03/31/12 10:35 PM

Scrolling left, we can see the following columns for the same entries (the file path column is not shown due to its size).

Prefetch Last Execution Date (UTC)	Prefetch Execution Count	Volume	Volume Create Date	Volume Serial
04/06/12 07:12 PM	8	\DEVICE\HARDDISKVOLUME1	11/10/10 05:38 PM	2017-4c22
04/06/12 07:12 PM	9	\DEVICE\HARDDISKVOLUME1	11/10/10 05:38 PM	2017-4c22
04/06/12 07:12 PM	4	\DEVICE\HARDDISKVOLUME1	11/10/10 05:38 PM	2017-4c22
04/02/12 12:47 PM	2	\DEVICE\HARDDISKVOLUME1	11/10/10 05:38 PM	2017-4c22
04/06/12 07:07 PM	6	\DEVICE\HARDDISKVOLUME1	11/10/10 05:38 PM	2017-4c22
04/02/12 12:46 PM	1	\DEVICE\HARDDISKVOLUME1	11/10/10 05:38 PM	2017-4c22
04/06/12 07:16 PM	40	\DEVICE\HARDDISKVOLUME1	11/10/10 05:38 PM	2017-4c22
04/06/12 09:24 PM	403	\DEVICE\HARDDISKVOLUME1	11/10/10 05:38 PM	2017-4c22
04/06/12 03:58 AM	1	\DEVICE\HARDDISKVOLUME1	11/10/10 05:38 PM	2017-4c22
04/06/12 03:58 AM	1	\DEVICE\HARDDISKVOLUME1	11/10/10 05:38 PM	2017-4c22
04/04/12 04:41 PM	4	\DEVICE\HARDDISKVOLUME1	11/10/10 05:38 PM	2017-4c22
04/04/12 04:41 PM	8	\DEVICE\HARDDISKVOLUME1	11/10/10 05:38 PM	2017-4c22
04/06/12 07:07 PM	7	\DEVICE\HARDDISKVOLUME1	11/10/10 05:38 PM	2017-4c22
04/03/12 02:44 PM	18	\DEVICE\HARDDISKVOLUME1	11/10/10 05:38 PM	2017-4c22
03/31/12 10:35 PM	9	\DEVICE\HARDDISKVOLUME1	11/10/10 05:38 PM	2017-4c22
04/02/12 12:49 PM	1	\DEVICE\HARDDISKVOLUME1	11/10/10 05:38 PM	2017-4c22
04/04/12 12:16 PM	242	\DEVICE\HARDDISKVOLUME1	11/10/10 05:38 PM	2017-4c22
04/02/12 12:46 PM	1	\DEVICE\HARDDISKVOLUME1	11/10/10 05:38 PM	2017-4c22

There's more...

This script can be further improved. We have provided one or more recommendations here:

- Add support for other Windows prefetch file formats. Starting with Windows 10, prefetch files now have MAM compression and must first be decompressed prior to parsing the data with `struct`
- Check out the `libscca` (https://github.com/libyal/libscca) library and its Python bindings, `pyscca`, which was developed to process prefetch files

A series of fortunate events

Recipe Difficulty: Hard

Python Version: 2.7

Operating System: Linux

Event logs, if configured appropriately, contain a wealth of information useful in any cyber investigation. These logs retain historical user activity information, such as logons, RDP access, Microsoft Office file access, system changes, and application-specific events. In this recipe, we use the `pyevt` and `pyevtx` libraries to process both legacy and current Windows event log formats.

Getting started

This recipe requires the installation of five third-party modules to function: `pytsk3`, `pyewf`, `pyevt`, `pyevtx`, and `unicodecsv`. Refer to `Chapter 8`, *Working with Forensic Evidence Container Recipes* for a detailed explanation of installing the `pytsk3` and `pyewf` modules. Likewise, refer to the *Getting started* section in the *Parsing prefetch files* recipe, for details on installing `unicodecsv`. All other libraries used in this script are present in Python's standard library. When it comes to installing the Python bindings of most `libyal` libraries, they follow a very similar path.

Navigate to the GitHub repository and download the desired release for each library. This recipe was developed using the `libevt-alpha-20170120` and `libevtx-alpha-20170122` releases of the `pyevt` and `pyevtx` libraries, respectively. Next, once the contents of the release are extracted, open a terminal and navigate to the extracted directory and execute the following commands for each release:

```
./synclibs.sh
./autogen.sh
sudo python setup.py install
```

 To learn more about the `pyevt` library, visit `https://github.com/libyal/libevt`.
To learn more about the `pyevtx` library, visit `https://github.com/libyal/libevtx`.

Lastly, we can check the libraries installation by opening a Python interpreter, importing `pyevt` and `pyevtx`, and running their respective `get_version()` methods to ensure we have the correct release versions.

How to do it...

We extract event logs with these basic steps:

1. Search for all event logs matching the input argument.
2. Eliminate false positives with file signature verification.
3. Process each event log found with the appropriate library.
4. Output a spreadsheet of all discovered events to the current working directory.

How it works...

We import a number of libraries to assist with argument parsing, writing CSVs, processing event logs, and the custom `pytskutil` module.

```
from __future__ import print_function
import argparse
import unicodecsv as csv
import os
import pytsk3
import pyewf
import pyevt
import pyevtx
import sys
from utility.pytskutil import TSKUtil
```

This recipe's command-line handler takes three positional arguments, `EVIDENCE_FILE`, `TYPE`, and `LOG_NAME`, which represents the path to the evidence file, the type of evidence file, and the name of the event log to process. Additionally, the user may specify the directory within the image to scan with the `"d"` switch and enable fuzzy searching with the `"f"` switch. If the user does not supply a directory to scan, the script defaults to the `"/Windows/System32/winevt"` directory. The fuzzy search, when comparing file names, will check whether the suppled `LOG_NAME` is a substring of the `filename` rather than equal to the filename. This capability allows a user to search for a very specific event log or any file with an `.evt` or `.evtx` extension, and anything in between. After performing input validation checks, we pass the five arguments to the `main()` function:

```
if __name__ == "__main__":
    parser = argparse.ArgumentParser(
        description=__description__,
        epilog="Developed by {} on {}".format(
            ", ".join(__authors__), __date__)
    )
    parser.add_argument("EVIDENCE_FILE", help="Evidence file path")
```

```
        parser.add_argument("TYPE", help="Type of Evidence",
                            choices=("raw", "ewf"))
        parser.add_argument("LOG_NAME",
                            help="Event Log Name (SecEvent.Evt, SysEvent.Evt, "
                                 "etc.)")
        parser.add_argument("-d", help="Event log directory to scan",
                            default="/WINDOWS/SYSTEM32/WINEVT")
        parser.add_argument("-f", help="Enable fuzzy search for either evt or"
                            " evtx extension", action="store_true")
        args = parser.parse_args()

        if os.path.exists(args.EVIDENCE_FILE) and \
                os.path.isfile(args.EVIDENCE_FILE):
            main(args.EVIDENCE_FILE, args.TYPE, args.LOG_NAME, args.d, args.f)
        else:
            print("[-] Supplied input file {} does not exist or is not a "
                  "file".format(args.EVIDENCE_FILE))
            sys.exit(1)
```

In the `main()` function, we create our `TSKUtil` object, which we will be interacting with to query the existence of the user-supplied path. If the path exists and is not `None`, we then check whether fuzzy searching has been enabled. Regardless, we call the same function, `recurse_files()`, and pass it the log to search for and the directory to scan. If fuzzy searching was enabled, we supply the `recurse_files()` method an additional optional argument by setting logic to `"equal"`. Without specifying this optional argument, the function will check whether the log is a substring of a given file rather than an exact match. We store any resulting hits in the `event_log` variable.

```
    def main(evidence, image_type, log, win_event, fuzzy):
        # Create TSK object and query event log directory for Windows XP
        tsk_util = TSKUtil(evidence, image_type)
        event_dir = tsk_util.query_directory(win_event)
        if event_dir is not None:
            if fuzzy is True:
                event_log = tsk_util.recurse_files(log, path=win_event)
            else:
                event_log = tsk_util.recurse_files(
                    log, path=win_event, logic="equal")
```

If we do have hits for the log, we set up the `event_data` list, which will hold the parsed event log data. Next, we begin iterating through each discovered event log. For each hit, we extract its file object, which is the second index of the tuple returned by the `recurse_files()` method, and send that to be temporarily written to the host filesystem with the `write_file()` method. This will be a common practice in further recipes so that these third-party libraries can more easily interact with the file.

```
if event_log is not None:
    event_data = []
    for hit in event_log:
        event_file = hit[2]
        temp_evt = write_file(event_file)
```

The `write_file()` method is rather simplistic. All it does is open a Python `File` object in `"w"` mode with the same name and write the entire contents of the input file to the current working directory. We return the name of this output file back to the `main()` method.

```
def write_file(event_file):
    with open(event_file.info.name.name, "w") as outfile:
        outfile.write(event_file.read_random(0, event_file.info.meta.size))
    return event_file.info.name.name
```

Back in the `main()` method, we use the `pyevt.check_file_signature()` method to check whether the file we just cached is a valid `evt` file. If it is, we use the `pyevt.open()` method to create our `evt` object. After printing a status message to the console, we iterate through all of the records within the event log. The record can have a number of strings, and so we iterate through those and ensure they are added to the `strings` variable. We then append a number of event log attributes to the `event_data` list, including the computer name, the SID, the creation and written time, the category, source name, event ID, event type, the strings, and the file path.

You may notice the empty string added as the second-to-last item in the list. This empty string is there due to a lack of an equivalent counterpart found in `.evtx` files and is necessary to maintain proper spacing as the output spreadsheet is designed to accommodate both `.evt` and `.evtx` results. That's all we need to do to process the legacy event log format. Let's now move on to the scenario where the log file is an `.evtx` file.

```
if pyevt.check_file_signature(temp_evt):
    evt_log = pyevt.open(temp_evt)
    print("[+] Identified {} records in {}".format(
        evt_log.number_of_records, temp_evt))
    for i, record in enumerate(evt_log.records):
        strings = ""
        for s in record.strings:
            if s is not None:
```

```
                                    strings += s + "\n"

                    event_data.append([
                        i, hit[0], record.computer_name,
                        record.user_security_identifier,
                        record.creation_time, record.written_time,
                        record.event_category, record.source_name,
                        record.event_identifier, record.event_type,
                        strings, "",
                        os.path.join(win_event, hit[1].lstrip("//"))
                    ])
```

Thankfully, both `pyevt` and `pyevtx` libraries handle similarly. We start by validating the file signature of the log search hit using the `pyevtx.check_file_signature()` method. As with its `pyevt` counterpart, this method returns a Boolean `True` or `False` depending on the results of the file signature check. If the file's signature checks out, we use the `pyevtx.open()` method to create an `evtx` object, write a status message to the console, and begin iterating through the records present in the event log:

After storing all strings into the `strings` variable, we append a number of event log record attributes to the event log list. These include the computer name, SID, written time, event level, source, event ID, strings, any XML strings, and the event log path. Note there are a number of empty strings, which are present to maintain spacing and fill gaps where an `.evt` equivalent is not fount. For example, there is no `creation_time` timestamp as seen in the legacy `.evt` logs, and therefore, an empty string replaced it instead.

```
        elif pyevtx.check_file_signature(temp_evt):
            evtx_log = pyevtx.open(temp_evt)
            print("[+] Identified {} records in {}".format(
                evtx_log.number_of_records, temp_evt))
            for i, record in enumerate(evtx_log.records):
                strings = ""
                for s in record.strings:
                    if s is not None:
                        strings += s + "\n"

                event_data.append([
                    i, hit[0], record.computer_name,
                    record.user_security_identifier, "",
                    record.written_time, record.event_level,
                    record.source_name, record.event_identifier,
                    "", strings, record.xml_string,
                    os.path.join(win_event, hit[1].lstrip("//"))
                ])
```

If the given log hit from the search cannot be validated as either a `.evt` or `.evtx` log, we print a status message to the console, remove the cached file with the `os.remove()` method, and continue onto the next hit. Note that we only remove cached event logs if they could not be validated. Otherwise, we leave them in the current working directory so as to allow the user the opportunity to process them further with other tools if desired. After we have finished processing all of the event logs, we write the parsed list of lists to a CSV with the `write_output()` method. The two remaining `else` statements handle situations where there are either no event log hits from our search or the directory we scanned for does not exist in the evidence file:

```
                else:
                    print("[-] {} not a valid event log. Removing temp "
                        "file...".format(temp_evt))
                    os.remove(temp_evt)
                    continue
            write_output(event_data)
        else:
            print("[-] {} Event log not found in {} directory".format(
                log, win_event))
            sys.exit(3)

    else:
        print("[-] Win XP Event Log Directory {} not found".format(
            win_event))
        sys.exit(2)
```

The `write_output()` method behaves similarly to that discussed in the previous recipe. We create a CSV in the current working directory and write all of the parsed results to it using the `writerows()` method.

```
def write_output(data):
    output_name = "parsed_event_logs.csv"
    print("[+] Writing {} to current working directory: {}".format(
        output_name, os.getcwd()))
    with open(output_name, "wb") as outfile:
        writer = csv.writer(outfile)

        writer.writerow([
            "Index", "File name", "Computer Name", "SID",
            "Event Create Date", "Event Written Date",
            "Event Category/Level", "Event Source", "Event ID",
            "Event Type", "Data", "XML Data", "File Path"
        ])

        writer.writerows(data)
```

The following screenshot shows basic information about events in the specified log files:

Index	File name	Computer Name	SID	Event Create Date	Event Written Date	Event Category/Level	Event Source
0	System.evtx	WIN-O3EOD5MV6UQ			10/17/12 04:30 PM		4 Service Control Manager
1	System.evtx	WIN-O3EOD5MV6UQ			10/17/12 04:30 PM		4 Service Control Manager
2	System.evtx	WIN-O3EOD5MV6UQ	S-1-5-18 S-1-5-21-2101393550-2846089865-3711467980-1000		10/17/12 04:30 PM		4 Microsoft-Windows-Winlogon
3	System.evtx	WIN-O3EOD5MV6UQ			10/17/12 04:30 PM		4 Microsoft-Windows-GroupPolicy
4	System.evtx	WIN-O3EOD5MV6UQ			10/17/12 04:30 PM		4 Service Control Manager
5	System.evtx	WIN-O3EOD5MV6UQ	S-1-5-18		10/17/12 04:30 PM		4 Microsoft-Windows-UserPnp

The second screenshot shows additional columns for these rows:

Event ID	Event Type	Data	XML Data
7036		WinHTTP Web Proxy Auto-Discovery Service running 570069006E00480074007400700040100750074006F00500072006F00780079005	80079005300760063002F0034000000</Binary> </EventData> </Event>
7036		Portable Device Enumerator Service running 57005000440042007500730045006E0075006D002F0034000000	ry> </EventData> </Event>
7001		1 S-1-5-21-2101393550-2846089865-3711467980-1000	1000</Data> </EventData> </Event>
1501		3182 1 421	<Data Name="DCName"/> </EventData> </Event>
7036		Application Information running 41007000700069006E0066006F002F0034000000	<Binary>41007000700069006E0066006F002F00340000 </EventData> </Event>
20003		AsyncMac system32\DRIVERS\asyncmac.sys SW\{EEAB7790-C514-11D1-B42B-00805FC1270E}\ASYNCMAC true true 0	<PrimaryService>true</PrimaryService> <UpdateService>true</UpdateService> <AddServiceStatus>0</AddServiceStatus> </AddServiceID> </UserData> </Event>

There's more...

This script can be further improved. We have provided one or more recommendations here:

- Enable loose file support
- Add an event ID argument to selectively extract events only matching the given event ID

Indexing internet history

Recipe Difficulty: Medium

Python Version: 2.7

Operating System: Linux

Internet history can be invaluable during an investigation. These records can give insight into a user's thought process and provide context around other user activity occurring on the system. Microsoft has been persistent in getting users to use Internet Explorer as their browser of choice. As a result, it is not uncommon to see internet history information present in `index.dat` files used by Internet Explorer. In this recipe, we scour the evidence file for these `index.dat` files and attempt to process them using `pymsiecf`.

Getting started

This recipe requires the installation of four third-party modules to function: `pytsk3`, `pyewf`, `pymsiecf`, and `unicodecsv`. Refer to `Chapter 8`, *Working with Forensic Evidence Container Recipes,* for a detailed explanation on installing the `pytsk3` and `pyewf` modules. Likewise, refer to the *Getting started* section in the *Parsing prefetch files* recipe for details on installing `unicodecsv`. All other libraries used in this script are present in Python's standard library

Navigate to the GitHub repository and download the desired release of the `pymsiecf` library. This recipe was developed using the `libmsiecf-alpha-20170116` release. Once the contents of the release are extracted, open a terminal and navigate to the extracted directory and execute the following commands:

```
./synclibs.sh
./autogen.sh
sudo python setup.py install
```

To learn more about the `pymsiecf` library, visit `https://github.com/libyal/libmsiecf`.

Lastly, we can check our library's installation by opening a Python interpreter, importing `pymsiecf`, and running the `gpymsiecf.get_version()` method to ensure we have the correct release version.

How to do it...

We follow these steps to extract Internet Explorer history:

1. Find and verify all `index.dat` files within the image.
2. Process the files for internet history.
3. Output a spreadsheet of the results to the current working directory.

How it works...

We import a number of libraries to assist with argument parsing, writing CSVs, processing `index.dat` files, and the custom `pytskutil` module:

```
from __future__ import print_function
import argparse
from datetime import datetime, timedelta
import os
import pytsk3
import pyewf
import pymsiecf
import sys
import unicodecsv as csv
from utility.pytskutil import TSKUtil
```

This recipe's command-line handler takes two positional arguments, `EVIDENCE_FILE` and `TYPE`, which represent the path to the evidence file and the type of evidence file, respectively. Similar to the previous recipe, the optional `d` switch can be supplied to specify a directory to scan. Otherwise, the recipe starts scanning at the `"/Users"` directory. After performing input validation checks, we pass the three arguments to the `main()` function.

```
if __name__ == "__main__":
    parser = argparse.ArgumentParser(
        description=__description__,
```

```
            epilog="Developed by {} on {}".format(
                ", ".join(__authors__), __date__)
        )
    parser.add_argument("EVIDENCE_FILE", help="Evidence file path")
    parser.add_argument("TYPE", help="Type of Evidence",
                        choices=("raw", "ewf"))
    parser.add_argument("-d", help="Index.dat directory to scan",
                        default="/USERS")
    args = parser.parse_args()

    if os.path.exists(args.EVIDENCE_FILE) and os.path.isfile(
            args.EVIDENCE_FILE):
        main(args.EVIDENCE_FILE, args.TYPE, args.d)
    else:
        print("[-] Supplied input file {} does not exist or is not a "
              "file".format(args.EVIDENCE_FILE))
        sys.exit(1)
```

The `main()` function starts by creating the now-familiar `TSKUtil` object and scans the specified directory to confirm it exists within the evidence file. If it does exist, we recursively scan from the specified directory for any file that is equal to the string `"index.dat"`. These files are returned from the `recurse_files()` method as a list of tuples, where each tuple represents a particular file matching the search criteria.

```
def main(evidence, image_type, path):
    # Create TSK object and query for Internet Explorer index.dat files
    tsk_util = TSKUtil(evidence, image_type)
    index_dir = tsk_util.query_directory(path)
    if index_dir is not None:
        index_files = tsk_util.recurse_files("index.dat", path=path,
                                             logic="equal")
```

If we do find potential `index.dat` files to process, we print a status message to the console and set up a list to retain the parsed results of the said files. We begin to iterate through hits; extract the `index.dat` file object, which is the second index of the tuple; and write it out to the host filesystem using the `write_file()` method:

```
        if index_files is not None:
            print("[+] Identified {} potential index.dat files".format(
                len(index_files)))
            index_data = []
            for hit in index_files:
                index_file = hit[2]
                temp_index = write_file(index_file)
```

The `write_file()` method was discussed in more detail in the previous recipe. It is identical to what we previously discussed. In essence, this function copies out the `index.dat` file in the evidence container to the current working directory to allow processing by the third-party module. Once that output is created, we return the name of the output file, which in this case is going to always be `index.dat`, back to the `main()` function:

```
def write_file(index_file):
    with open(index_file.info.name.name, "w") as outfile:
        outfile.write(index_file.read_random(0, index_file.info.meta.size))
    return index_file.info.name.name
```

Similar to the other `libyal` libraries before, the `pymsiecf` module has a built-in method, `check_file_signature()`, which we use to determine if the search hit is a valid `index.dat` file. If it is, we use the `pymsiecf.open()` method to create an object we can manipulate with the library. We print a status message to the console and begin iterating through the items present in the `.dat` file. The very first thing we attempt is to access the `data` attribute. This contains the bulk of information we will be interested in but is not necessarily always available. If the attribute is present, however, and is not `None`, we remove an appended `"\x00"` value:

```
if pymsiecf.check_file_signature(temp_index):
    index_dat = pymsiecf.open(temp_index)
    print("[+] Identified {} records in {}".format(
        index_dat.number_of_items, temp_index))
    for i, record in enumerate(index_dat.items):
        try:
            data = record.data
            if data is not None:
                data = data.rstrip("\x00")
```

As alluded to before, there are scenarios where there will be no `data` attribute. Two examples are the `pymsiecf.redirected` and `pymsiecf.leak` objects. These objects, however, still have data that may potentially be relevant. Therefore, in the exception, we check if the record is an instance of one of those two objects and append what data is available to our list of parsed `index.dat` data. We continue on to the next `record` after we have appended this data to our list or if the record is not an instance of either of those types, except `AttributeError`:

```
except AttributeError:
    if isinstance(record, pymsiecf.redirected):
        index_data.append([
            i, temp_index, "", "", "", "", "",
            record.location, "", "", record.offset,
            os.path.join(path, hit[1].lstrip("//"))
```

```
                                       ])

               elif isinstance(record, pymsiecf.leak):
                   index_data.append([
                       i, temp_index, record.filename, "",
                       "", "", "", "", "", "", record.offset,
                       os.path.join(path, hit[1].lstrip("//"))
                   ])

               continue
```

In most scenarios, the `data` attribute is present and we can extract a number of potentially relevant information points from the record. This includes the filename, the type, a number of timestamps, the location, number of hits, and the data itself. To be clear, the `data` attribute is often a URL of some sort recorded as a result of browsing activity on the system:

```
           index_data.append([
               i, temp_index, record.filename,
               record.type, record.primary_time,
               record.secondary_time,
               record.last_checked_time, record.location,
               record.number_of_hits, data, record.offset,
               os.path.join(path, hit[1].lstrip("//"))
           ])
```

If the `index.dat` file cannot be validated, we remove the offending cached file and continue iterating through all other search results. Likewise, this time we elect to remove the `index.dat` cached file regardless of whether it was valid or not after we finish processing the final one. Because all of these files will have the same name, they will overwrite each other as they are being processed. Therefore, it did mot make sense to keep only one in the current working directory for further processing. If desired, however, one could do something a bit more elaborate and cache each file to the host filesystem while preserving its path. The remaining two `else` statements are reserved for situations where no `index.dat` files are found and the directory to scan for does not exist in the evidence file, respectively:

```
           else:
               print("[-] {} not a valid index.dat file. Removing "
                   "temp file..".format(temp_index))
               os.remove("index.dat")
               continue

       os.remove("index.dat")
       write_output(index_data)
   else:
       print("[-] Index.dat files not found in {} directory".format(
```

```
                path))
        sys.exit(3)

    else:
        print("[-] Directory {} not found".format(win_event))
        sys.exit(2)
```

The `write_output()` method behaves like the other methods of the same name in the previous recipes. We create a mildly descriptive output name, create the output CSV in the current working directory, and then write the headers and data to the file. With that, we have completed this recipe and can now add processed `index.dat` files to our toolbox:

```
def write_output(data):
    output_name = "Internet_Indexdat_Summary_Report.csv"
    print("[+] Writing {} with {} parsed index.dat files to current "
            "working directory: {}".format(output_name, len(data),
                                            os.getcwd()))
    with open(output_name, "wb") as outfile:
        writer = csv.writer(outfile)
        writer.writerow(["Index", "File Name", "Record Name",
                        "Record Type", "Primary Date", "Secondary Date",
                        "Last Checked Date", "Location", "No. of Hits",
                        "Record Data", "Record Offset", "File Path"])
        writer.writerows(data)
```

When we execute the script, we can review a spreadsheet containing data such as the one shown here:

Index	File Name	Record Name	Record Type	Primary Date	Secondary Date	Last Checked Date	Location
0	index.dat	noie9[1].aspx	cache	08/15/11 03:03 AM	01/01/01 12:00 AM	08/15/11 03:03 AM	http://iegallery.com/en/ie9slice/noie9.aspx
1	index.dat						http://go.microsoft.com/fwlink/?LinkId=121315
2	index.dat	rss[1].xml	cache	08/15/11 01:15 AM	01/01/01 12:00 AM	08/15/11 01:15 AM	http://www.microsoft.com/athome/community/rss.xml
3	index.dat	updates[1].xml	cache	08/15/11 01:15 AM	07/22/11 09:28 PM	08/15/11 01:15 AM	http://www.usa.gov/rss/updates.xml?WT.rss_f=USA.gov+Updates+News+and+Features&WT.rss_ev=s
4	index.dat	FAQs[1].xml	cache	08/15/11 01:15 AM	08/03/11 11:56 PM	08/15/11 01:15 AM	http://www.usa.gov/rss/FAQs.xml?WT.rss_f=FAQs&WT.rss_ev=s
5	index.dat	administrator@usa[2].txt	cookie	08/15/11 01:15 AM	08/15/11 01:15 AM	08/15/11 01:15 AM	Cookie:administrator@usa.gov/

While this report has many columns, the following screenshot shows a snippet of a few additional columns for the same rows:

No. of Hits	Record Data	Record Offset	File Path
2	HTTP/1.1 200 OK X-Powered-By: ASP.NET X-AspNet-Version: 2.0.50727 Content-Type: text/html; charset=utf-8 Content-Length: 3562 ~U:administrator	29184 29568	/USERS/Administrator/AppData/Local/Microsoft/Windows/Temporary Internet Files/Content.IE5/index.dat /USERS/Administrator/AppData/Local/Microsoft/Windows/Temporary Internet Files/Content.IE5/index.dat
2	HTTP/1.0 200 OK Pragma: no-cache Refresh: 0.1 Content-Type: text/html; charset=iso-8859-1 ~U:administrator	30080	/USERS/Administrator/AppData/Local/Microsoft/Windows/Temporary Internet Files/Content.IE5/index.dat
2	HTTP/1.1 200 OK ETag: "84adbc7c79616b98bf763b747380e7cd:1311370859" Content-Length: 9381 Content-Type: application/xml ~U:administrator	30464	/USERS/Administrator/AppData/Local/Microsoft/Windows/Temporary Internet Files/Content.IE5/index.dat
2	HTTP/1.1 200 OK ETag: "8dc7f855ea1de493347087e3b9ce8962:1312416075" Content-Length: 3160 Content-Type: application/xml ~U:administrator	30848	/USERS/Administrator/AppData/Local/Microsoft/Windows/Temporary Internet Files/Content.IE5/index.dat
3		20736	/USERS/Administrator/AppData/Roaming/Microsoft/Windows/Cookies/index.dat

There's more...

This script can be further improved. We have provided one or more recommendations here:

- Create summary metrics of available data (most and least popular domain visited, average time-frame of internet usage, and so on)

Shadow of a former self

Recipe Difficulty: Hard

Python Version: 2.7

Operating System: Linux

Volume shadow copies can contain data from files that are no longer present on the active system. This can give an examiner some historical information about how the system changed over time and what files used to exist on the computer. In this recipe, we will use the pyvshadow library to enumerate and access any volume shadow copies present in the forensic image.

Getting started

This recipe requires the installation of five third-party modules to function: pytsk3, pyewf, pyvshadow, unicodecsv, and vss. Refer to Chapter 8, *Working with Forensic Evidence Container Recipes* for a detailed explanation on installing the pytsk3 and pyewf modules. Likewise, refer to the *Getting started* section in the *Parsing prefetch files* recipe for details on installing unicodecsv. All other libraries used in this script are present in Python's standard library.

Navigate to the GitHub repository and download the desired release for the pyvshadow library. This recipe was developed using the libvshadow-alpha-20170715 release. Once the contents of the release are extracted, open a terminal, navigate to the extracted directory, and execute the following commands:

```
./synclibs.sh
./autogen.sh
sudo python setup.py install
```

 Learn more about the pyvshadow library at https://github.com/libyal/libvshadow.

The pyvshadow module is designed to work only with raw images and does not support other forensic image types out of the box. As noted in a blog post by *David Cowen* at http://www.hecfblog.com/2015/05/automating-dfir-how-to-series-on_25.html, the plaso project has created a helper library, vss, that can be integrated with pyvshadow, which we will use here. The vss code can be found in the same blog post.

Lastly, we can check our library's installation by opening a Python interpreter, importing `pyvshadow`, and running the `pyvshadow.get_version()` method to ensure we have the correct release version.

How to do it...

We access volume shadow copies using the following steps:

1. Access the volume of the raw image and identify all NTFS partitions.
2. Enumerate over each volume shadow copy found on valid NTFS partitions.
3. Create a file listing of data within the snapshots.

How it works...

We import a number of libraries to assist with argument parsing, date parsing, writing CSVs, processing volume shadow copies, and the custom `pytskutil` module.

```
from __future__ import print_function
import argparse
from datetime import datetime, timedelta
import os
import pytsk3
import pyewf
import pyvshadow
import sys
import unicodecsv as csv
from utility import vss
from utility.pytskutil import TSKUtil
from utility import pytskutil
```

This recipe's command-line handler takes two positional arguments: `EVIDENCE_FILE` and `OUTPUT_CSV`. These represent the path to the evidence file and the file path for the output spreadsheet, respectively. Notice the conspicuous absence of the evidence type argument. This script only supports raw image files and does not work with `E01s`. To prepare an EWF image for use with the script you may either convert it to a raw image or mount it with `ewfmount`, a tool associated with `libewf`, and provide the mount point as the input.

```
if __name__ == "__main__":
    parser = argparse.ArgumentParser(
        description=__description__,
        epilog="Developed by {} on {}".format(
            ", ".join(__authors__), __date__)
```

```
    )
    parser.add_argument("EVIDENCE_FILE", help="Evidence file path")
    parser.add_argument("OUTPUT_CSV",
                        help="Output CSV with VSS file listing")
    args = parser.parse_args()
```

After parsing the input arguments, we separate the directory from the OUTPUT_CSV input and confirm that it exists or create it if it is not present. We also validate the input file path's existence before passing the two positional arguments to the main() function.

```
    directory = os.path.dirname(args.OUTPUT_CSV)
    if not os.path.exists(directory) and directory != "":
        os.makedirs(directory)

    if os.path.exists(args.EVIDENCE_FILE) and \
            os.path.isfile(args.EVIDENCE_FILE):
        main(args.EVIDENCE_FILE, args.OUTPUT_CSV)
    else:
        print("[-] Supplied input file {} does not exist or is not a "
              "file".format(args.EVIDENCE_FILE))
        sys.exit(1)
```

The main() function calls a few new functions within the TSKUtil object that we have not explored yet. After we create our TSKUtil object, we extract its volume using the return_vol() method. Interacting with an evidence file's volume, as we have seen in previous recipes, is one of the requisite steps before we can interact with the filesystem. However, this process has been previously performed in the background when necessary. This time, however, we need access to the pytsk3 volume object to iterate through each partition to identify NTFS filesystems. The detect_ntfs() method returns a Boolean value if the specific partition has an NTFS filesystem.

For each NTFS filesystem we encounter, we pass the evidence file, the offset of the discovered NTFS partition, and the output CSV file to the explore_vss() function. If the volume object is None, we print a status message to the console to remind users that the evidence file must be a physical device image as opposed to only a logical image of a specific partition.

```
def main(evidence, output):
    # Create TSK object and query path for prefetch files
    tsk_util = TSKUtil(evidence, "raw")
    img_vol = tsk_util.return_vol()
    if img_vol is not None:
        for part in img_vol:
            if tsk_util.detect_ntfs(img_vol, part):
                print("Exploring NTFS Partition for VSS")
                explore_vss(evidence, part.start * img_vol.info.block_size,
```

```
                                        output)
            else:
                print("[-] Must be a physical preservation to be compatible "
                    "with this script")
                sys.exit(2)
```

The `explore_vss()` method starts by creating a `pyvshadow.volume()` object. We use this volume to open the `vss_handle` object created from the `vss.VShadowVolume()` method. The `vss.VShadowVolume()` method takes the evidence file and the partition offset value and exposes a volume-like object that is compatible with the `pyvshadow` library, which does not natively support physical disk images. The `GetVssStoreCount()` function returns the number of volume shadow copies found in the evidence.

If there are volume shadows, we open our `vss_handle` object with the `pyvshadow` `vss_volume` and instantiate a list to hold our data. We create a `for` loop to iterate through each volume shadow copy present and perform the same series of steps. First, we use the `pyvshadow` `get_store()` method to access the particular volume shadow copy of interest. Then, we use the `vss` helper library `VShadowImgInfo` to create a `pytsk3` image handle. Lastly, we pass the image handle to the `openVSSFS()` method and append the returned data to our list. The `openVSSFS()` method uses similar methods as discussed before to create a `pytsk3` filesystem object and then recurse through the directories present to return an active file listing. After we have performed these steps on all of the volume shadow copies, we pass the data and the output CSV file path to our `csvWriter()` method.

```
    def explore_vss(evidence, part_offset, output):
        vss_volume = pyvshadow.volume()
        vss_handle = vss.VShadowVolume(evidence, part_offset)
        vss_count = vss.GetVssStoreCount(evidence, part_offset)
        if vss_count > 0:
            vss_volume.open_file_object(vss_handle)
            vss_data = []
            for x in range(vss_count):
                print("Gathering data for VSC {} of {}".format(x, vss_count))
                vss_store = vss_volume.get_store(x)
                image = vss.VShadowImgInfo(vss_store)
                vss_data.append(pytskutil.openVSSFS(image, x))

            write_csv(vss_data, output)
```

The `write_csv()` method functions as you would expect it to. It first checks if there is any data to write. If there isn't, it prints a status message to the console before exiting the script. Alternatively, it creates a CSV file using the user-provided input, writes the spreadsheet headers, and iterates through each list, calling `writerows()` for each volume shadow copy. To prevent the headers from ending up several times in the CSV output, we will check to see if the CSV already exists and add new data in for review. This allows us to dump information after each volume is processed for volume shadow copies.

```
def write_csv(data, output):
    if data == []:
        print("[-] No output results to write")
        sys.exit(3)

    print("[+] Writing output to {}".format(output))
    if os.path.exists(output):
        append = True
    with open(output, "ab") as csvfile:
        csv_writer = csv.writer(csvfile)
        headers = ["VSS", "File", "File Ext", "File Type", "Create Date",
                   "Modify Date", "Change Date", "Size", "File Path"]
        if not append:
            csv_writer.writerow(headers)
        for result_list in data:
            csv_writer.writerows(result_list)
```

After running this script, we can review the files found within each volume shadow copy and learn about the metadata of each item:

VSS	File	File Ext	File Type	Create Date	Modify Date	Change Date	Size	File Path
VSS 0	Config.Msi		DIR	11/23/12 01:48 AM	09/07/17 10:38 AM	09/07/17 10:38 AM	56	/Config.Msi
VSS 0	19170ea7.rbs	rbs	FILE	12/26/14 07:07 PM	12/26/14 07:07 PM	12/26/14 07:07 PM	2446	/Config.Msi/19170ea7.rbs
VSS 0	cd12b.rbf	rbf	FILE	08/19/14 09:07 PM	08/19/14 09:07 PM	06/01/11 09:57 PM	225600	/Config.Msi/cd12b.rbf
VSS 0	278467d.rbf	rbf	FILE	08/06/17 12:17 PM	08/06/17 12:18 PM	07/14/17 09:42 PM	38135248	/Config.Msi/278467d.rbf
VSS 0	Perl64		DIR	10/07/14 01:00 AM	02/12/17 12:54 AM	02/12/17 12:54 AM	56	/Perl64
VSS 0	bin		DIR	10/07/14 01:00 AM	04/27/15 09:57 AM	10/07/14 01:02 AM	56	/Perl64/bin
VSS 0	a2p.exe	exe	FILE	04/14/14 08:06 PM	04/27/15 09:57 AM	04/14/14 08:06 PM	123904	/Perl64/bin/a2p.exe
VSS 0	ap-iis-config		FILE	01/05/10 10:45 PM	04/27/15 09:57 AM	01/05/10 10:45 PM	24435	/Perl64/bin/ap-iis-config
VSS 0	ap-iis-config.bat	bat	FILE	04/14/14 08:36 PM	04/27/15 09:57 AM	04/14/14 08:36 PM	24853	/Perl64/bin/ap-iis-config.bat

There's more...

This script can be further improved. We have provided one or more recommendations here:

- Add support for logical acquisitions and additional forensic acquisition types
- Add support to process artifacts found within snapshots using previously written recipes

Dissecting the SRUM database

Recipe Difficulty: Hard

Python Version: 2.7

Operating System: Linux

With the major release of popular operating systems, everyone in the cyber community gets excited (or worried) about the potential new artifacts and changes to existing artifacts. With the advent of Windows 10, we saw a few changes (such as the MAM compression of prefetch files) and new artifacts as well. One of these artifacts is the **System Resource Usage Monitor** (**SRUM**), which can retain execution and network activity for applications. This includes information such as when a connection was established by a given application and how many bytes were sent and received by this application. Obviously, this can be very useful in a number of different scenarios. Imagine having this information on hand with a disgruntled employee who uploads many gigabytes of data on their last day using the Dropbox desktop application.

In this recipe, we leverage the `pyesedb` library to extract data from the database. We will also implement logic to interpret this data as the appropriate type. With this accomplished, we will be able to view historical application information stored within the `SRUM.dat` file found on Windows 10 machines.

 To learn more about the SRUM database, visit `https://www.sans.org/summit-archives/file/summit-archive-1492184583.pdf`.

Getting started

This recipe requires the installation of four third-party modules to function: `pytsk3`, `pyewf`, `pyesedb`, and `unicodecsv`. Refer to `Chapter 8`, *Working with Forensic Evidence Container Recipes,* for a detailed explanation on installing the `pytsk3` and `pyewf` modules. Likewise, refer to the *Getting started* section in the *Parsing prefetch files* recipe for details on installing `unicodecsv`. All other libraries used in this script are present in Python's standard library.

Navigate to the GitHub repository and download the desired release for each library. This recipe was developed using the `libesedb-experimental-20170121` release. Once the contents of the release are extracted, open a terminal, navigate to the extracted directory, and execute the following commands:

```
./synclibs.sh
./autogen.sh
sudo python setup.py install
```

To learn more about the `pyesedb` library, visit
https://github.com/libyal/libesedb.

Lastly, we can check our library's installation by opening a Python interpreter, importing `pyesedb`, and running the `gpyesedb.get_version()` method to ensure we have the correct release version.

How to do it...

We use the following methodology to accomplish our objective:

1. Determine if the `SRUDB.dat` file exists and perform a file signature verification.
2. Extract tables and table data using `pyesedb`.
3. Interpret extracted table data as appropriate data types.
4. Create multiple spreadsheets for each table present within the database.

How it works...

We import a number of libraries to assist with argument parsing, date parsing, writing CSVs, processing the ESE database, and the custom `pytskutil` module:

```
from __future__ import print_function
import argparse
from datetime import datetime, timedelta
import os
import pytsk3
import pyewf
import pyesedb
import struct
import sys
import unicodecsv as csv
from utility.pytskutil import TSKUtil
```

This script uses two global variables during its execution. The `TABLE_LOOKUP` variable is a lookup table matching various SRUM table names to a more human-friendly description. These descriptions were pulled from *Yogesh Khatri's* presentation, referenced at the beginning of the recipe. The `APP_ID_LOOKUP` dictionary will store data from the SRUM `SruDbIdMapTable` table, which assigns applications to an integer value referenced in other tables.

```
TABLE_LOOKUP = {
    "{973F5D5C-1D90-4944-BE8E-24B94231A174}": "Network Data Usage",
    "{D10CA2FE-6FCF-4F6D-848E-B2E99266FA86}": "Push Notifications",
    "{D10CA2FE-6FCF-4F6D-848E-B2E99266FA89}": "Application Resource Usage",
    "{DD6636C4-8929-4683-974E-22C046A43763}": "Network Connectivity Usage",
    "{FEE4E14F-02A9-4550-B5CE-5FA2DA202E37}": "Energy Usage"}

APP_ID_LOOKUP = {}
```

This recipe's command-line handler takes two positional arguments, `EVIDENCE_FILE` and `TYPE`, which represent the evidence file and the type of evidence file, respectively. After validating the provided arguments, we pass these two inputs to the `main()` method, where the action kicks off.

```
if __name__ == "__main__":
    parser = argparse.ArgumentParser(
        description=__description__,
        epilog="Developed by {} on {}".format(
            ", ".join(__authors__), __date__)
    )
    parser.add_argument("EVIDENCE_FILE", help="Evidence file path")
    parser.add_argument("TYPE", help="Type of Evidence",
                        choices=("raw", "ewf"))
    args = parser.parse_args()

    if os.path.exists(args.EVIDENCE_FILE) and os.path.isfile(
            args.EVIDENCE_FILE):
        main(args.EVIDENCE_FILE, args.TYPE)
    else:
        print("[-] Supplied input file {} does not exist or is not a "
              "file".format(args.EVIDENCE_FILE))
        sys.exit(1)
```

The `main()` method starts by creating a `TSKUtil` object and creating a variable to reference the folder which contains the SRUM database on Windows 10 systems. Then, we use the `query_directory()` method to determine if the directory exist. If it does, we use the `recurse_files()` method to return the SRUM database from the evidence (if present):

```
def main(evidence, image_type):
    # Create TSK object and query for Internet Explorer index.dat files
    tsk_util = TSKUtil(evidence, image_type)
    path = "/Windows/System32/sru"
    srum_dir = tsk_util.query_directory(path)
    if srum_dir is not None:
        srum_files = tsk_util.recurse_files("SRUDB.dat", path=path,
                                            logic="equal")
```

If we do find the SRUM database, we print a status message to the console and iterate through each hit. For each hit, we extract the file object stored in the second index of the tuple returned by the `recurse_files()` method and use the `write_file()` method to cache the file to the host filesystem for further processing:

```
    if srum_files is not None:
        print("[+] Identified {} potential SRUDB.dat file(s)".format(
            len(srum_files)))
        for hit in srum_files:
            srum_file = hit[2]
            srum_tables = {}
            temp_srum = write_file(srum_file)
```

The `write_file()` method, as seen before, simply creates a file of the same name on the host filesystem. This method reads the entire contents of the file in the evidence container and writes it to the temporary file. After this has completed, it returns the name of the file to the parent function.

```
def write_file(srum_file):
    with open(srum_file.info.name.name, "w") as outfile:
        outfile.write(srum_file.read_random(0, srum_file.info.meta.size))
    return srum_file.info.name.name
```

Back in the `main()` method, we use the `pyesedb.check_file_signature()` method to validate the file hit before proceeding with any further processing. After the file is validated, we use the `pyesedb.open()` method to create the `pyesedb` object and print a status message to the console with the number of tables contained within the file. Next, we create a `for` loop to iterate through all of the tables within the database. Specifically, we look for the `SruDbIdMapTable` as we first need to populate the `APP_ID_LOOKUP` dictionary with the integer-to-application name pairings before processing any other table.

Once that table is found, we read each record within the table. The integer value of interest is stored in the first index while the application name is stored in the second index. We use the `get_value_data_as_integer()` method to extract and interpret the integer appropriately. Using the `get_value_data()` method instead, we can extract the application name from the record and attempt to replace any padding bytes from the string. Finally, we store both of these values in the global `APP_ID_LOOKUP` dictionary, using the integer as a key and the application name as the value.

```
if pyesedb.check_file_signature(temp_srum):
    srum_dat = pyesedb.open(temp_srum)
    print("[+] Process {} tables within database".format(
        srum_dat.number_of_tables))
    for table in srum_dat.tables:
        if table.name != "SruDbIdMapTable":
            continue
        global APP_ID_LOOKUP
        for entry in table.records:
            app_id = entry.get_value_data_as_integer(1)
            try:
                app = entry.get_value_data(2).replace(
                    "\x00", "")
            except AttributeError:
                app = ""
            APP_ID_LOOKUP[app_id] = app
```

After creating the `app lookup` dictionary, we are ready to iterate over each table (again) and this time actually extract the data. For each table, we assign its name to a local variable and print a status message to the console regarding execution progress. Then, within the dictionary that will hold our processed data, we create a key using the table's name and a dictionary containing column and data lists. The column list represents the actual column names from the table itself. These are extracted using list comprehension and then assigned to the column's key within our dictionary structure.

```
for table in srum_dat.tables:
    t_name = table.name
    print("[+] Processing {} table with {} records"
        .format(t_name, table.number_of_records))
    srum_tables[t_name] = {"columns": [], "data": []}
    columns = [x.name for x in table.columns]
    srum_tables[t_name]["columns"] = columns
```

With the columns handle, we turn our attention to the data itself. As we iterate through each row in the table, we use the `number_of_values()` method to create a loop to iterate through each value in the row. As we do this, we append the interpreted value to a list, which itself is later assigned to the data key within the dictionary. The SRUM database stores a number of different types of data (`32-bit` integers, `64-bit` integers, strings, and so on). The `pyesedb` library does not necessarily support each data type present using the various `get_value_as` methods. We must interpret the data for ourselves and have created a new function, `convert_data()`, to do just that. This function needs the value's raw data, the column name, and the column's type (which correlates to the type of data present). Let's focus on this method now.

If the search hit fails the file signature verification, we print a status message to the console, delete the temporary file, and continue onto the next hit. The remaining `else` statements handle scenarios where there are no SRUM databases found and where the SRUM database directory does not exist, respectively.

```
                    for entry in table.records:
                        data = []
                        for x in range(entry.number_of_values):
                            data.append(convert_data(
                                entry.get_value_data(x), columns[x],
                                entry.get_column_type(x))
                            )
                        srum_tables[t_name]["data"].append(data)
                    write_output(t_name, srum_tables)

            else:
                print("[-] {} not a valid SRUDB.dat file. Removing "
                    "temp file...".format(temp_srum))
                os.remove(temp_srum)
                continue

    else:
        print("[-] SRUDB.dat files not found in {} "
            "directory".format(path))
        sys.exit(3)

else:
    print("[-] Directory {} not found".format(path))
    sys.exit(2)
```

The `convert_data()` method relies on the column type to dictate how the data should be interpreted. For the most part, we use `struct` to unpack the data as the appropriate data types. This function is one large `if-elif-else` statement. In the first scenario, we check if the data is `None`, and if it is, return an empty string. In the first `elif` statement, we check if the column name is `"AppId"`; if it is, we unpack the `32-bit` integer representing the value from the `SruDbIdMapTable`, which correlates to an application name. We return the proper application name using the global `APP_ID_LOOKUP` dictionary created previously. Next, we create cases for various column values to return the appropriate data types, such as `8-bit` unsigned integers, `16-` and `32-bit` signed integers, `32-bit` floats, and `64-bit` doubles.

```
def convert_data(data, column, col_type):
    if data is None:
        return ""
    elif column == "AppId":
        return APP_ID_LOOKUP[struct.unpack("<i", data)[0]]
    elif col_type == 0:
        return ""
    elif col_type == 1:
        if data == "*":
            return True
        else:
            return False
    elif col_type == 2:
        return struct.unpack("<B", data)[0]
    elif col_type == 3:
        return struct.unpack("<h", data)[0]
    elif col_type == 4:
        return struct.unpack("<i", data)[0]
    elif col_type == 6:
        return struct.unpack("<f", data)[0]
    elif col_type == 7:
        return struct.unpack("<d", data)[0]
```

Continuing where the other paragraph left off, we have an `OLE` timestamp when the column type is equal to `8`. We must unpack the value as a `64-bit` integer and then use the `convert_ole()` method to convert this to a `datetime` object. Column types 5, 9, 10, 12, 13, and 16 are returned as is without any additional processing. Most of the other `elif` statements use different `struct` format characters to interpret the data appropriately. Column type 15 can also be a timestamp or a `64-bit` integer. Therefore, specific to the SRUM database, we check if the column name is either `"EventTimestamp"` or `"ConnectStartTime"`, in which case the value is a `FILETIME` timestamp and must be converted. Regardless of the column type, suffice to say that it is handled here and returned to the `main()` method as the appropriate type.

Enough of this; let's go look at these timestamp conversion methods:

```
elif col_type == 8:
    return convert_ole(struct.unpack("<q", data)[0])
elif col_type in [5, 9, 10, 12, 13, 16]:
    return data
elif col_type == 11:
    return data.replace("\x00", "")
elif col_type == 14:
    return struct.unpack("<I", data)[0]
elif col_type == 15:
    if column in ["EventTimestamp", "ConnectStartTime"]:
        return convert_filetime(struct.unpack("<q", data)[0])
    else:
        return struct.unpack("<q", data)[0]
elif col_type == 17:
    return struct.unpack("<H", data)[0]
else:
    return data
```

 To learn more about the ESE database column types, visit `https://github.com/libyal/libesedb/blob/b5abe2d05d5342ae02929c26475774dbb3c3aa5d/include/libesedb/definitions.h.in`.

The `convert_filetime()` method takes an integer and attempts to convert it using the tried-and-true method shown before. We have observed scenarios where the input integer can be too large for the `datetime` method and have added some error handling for that scenario. Otherwise, this method is similar to what has been previously discussed.

```
def convert_filetime(ts):
    if str(ts) == "0":
        return ""
    try:
        dt = datetime(1601, 1, 1) + timedelta(microseconds=ts / 10)
    except OverflowError:
        return ts
    return dt
```

New to any of our recipes is the `convert_ole()` method. The `OLE` timestamp format is a floating point number representing the number of days since midnight of December 30, 1899. We take the `64-bit` integer supplied to the function and pack and unpack it into the appropriate format required for the date conversion. Then, we use the familiar process, with `datetime` specifying our epoch and `timedelta` to provide the appropriate offset. If we find this value to be too large, we catch the `OverflowError` and return the `64-bit` integer as is.

```
def convert_ole(ts):
    ole = struct.unpack(">d", struct.pack(">Q", ts))[0]
    try:
        dt = datetime(1899, 12, 30, 0, 0, 0) + timedelta(days=ole)
    except OverflowError:
        return ts
    return dt
```

 To learn more about common timestamp formats (including `ole`), visit `https://blogs.msdn.microsoft.com/oldnewthing/20030905-02/?p=42653`.

The `write_output()` method is called for every table in the database. We check the dictionary and return the function if there are no results for the given table. As long as we do have results, we create an output name to distinguish the SRUM table and create it in the current working directory. We then open the spreadsheet, create the CSV writer, and then write the columns and data to the spreadsheet using the `writerow()` and `writerows()` methods, respectively.

```
def write_output(table, data):
    if len(data[table]["data"]) == 0:
        return
    if table in TABLE_LOOKUP:
        output_name = TABLE_LOOKUP[table] + ".csv"
    else:
        output_name = "SRUM_Table_{}.csv".format(table)
    print("[+] Writing {} to current working directory: {}".format(
        output_name, os.getcwd()))
    with open(output_name, "wb") as outfile:
        writer = csv.writer(outfile)
        writer.writerow(data[table]["columns"])
        writer.writerows(data[table]["data"])
```

After running the code, we can review the extracted values in the spreadsheets. The following two screenshots display the first few values found in our application resource usage report:

AutoIncId	TimeStamp	AppId	UserId	ForegroundCycleTime	BackgroundCycleTime	FaceTime
0	08/05/17 12:05 AM	\Device\HarddiskVolume1\Windows\System32\svchost.exe [appmodel]	6	546539600	0	517030000
1	08/05/17 01:17 AM	\Device\HarddiskVolume1\Program Files\Windows Defender\NisSrv.exe	4	847086737	0	35997500000
2	08/05/17 01:17 AM	\Device\HarddiskVolume1\Program Files\OpenSSH\bin\cygrunsrv.exe	603	60252227	0	36486720000
3	08/05/17 01:17 AM	\Device\HarddiskVolume1\Windows\System32\conhost.exe	603	3681988831	0	36486720000
4	08/05/17 01:17 AM	\Device\HarddiskVolume1\Program Files\OpenSSH\usr\sbin\sshd.exe	603	8213957743	0	72973440000
5	08/05/17 01:40 AM	\Device\HarddiskVolume1\Windows\explorer.exe	191	1877901905	0	13800000000
6	08/05/17 01:40 AM	\Device\HarddiskVolume1\Windows\System32\dllhost.exe	191	1019687523	0	13800000000
7	08/05/17 01:40 AM	\Device\HarddiskVolume1\Windows\System32\smartscreen.exe	191	1560414	0	13800000000
8	08/05/17 01:40 AM	\Device\HarddiskVolume1\Windows\System32\ctfmon.exe	191	2573282	0	13800000000
9	08/05/17 01:40 AM	\Device\HarddiskVolume1\Program Files\OpenSSH\bin\sh.exe	191	659411	0	13800000000
10	08/05/17 01:40 AM	\Device\HarddiskVolume1\Windows\System32\cmd.exe	191	1014174	0	27600000000
11	08/05/17 01:40 AM	\Device\HarddiskVolume1\Program Files\Windows Defender\MSASCuiL.exe	191	992524	0	13800000000
12	08/05/17 01:40 AM	\Device\HarddiskVolume1\Windows\SysWOW64\OneDriveSetup.exe	191	74403033264	0	27600000000
13	08/05/17 01:40 AM	svc.svchost.s1.uc24595.host3b_1.0.0.0_neutral__1234567890abc	191	1679022	0	13800003936
14	08/05/17 01:40 AM	\Device\HarddiskVolume1\Windows\Temp\sdelete.exe	191	1058316719781	0	13800000000
15	08/05/17 01:40 AM	Microsoft.WindowsAlarms_10.1706.1742.0_x64__8wekyb3d8bbwe	191	0	262385557	0
16	08/05/17 01:40 AM	Microsoft.SkypeApp_11.18.596.0_x64__kzf8qxf38zg5c	191	0	273520285	0

BackgroundContextSwitches	ForegroundBytesRead	ForegroundBytesWritten	ForegroundNumReadOperations	ForegroundNumWriteOperations
0	6983168	811008	34	198
0	0	40960	0	10
0	1458176	0	60	0
0	49152	0	2	0
0	1231872	16384	60	4
0	353792	0	18	0
0	0	2498560	0	148
0	0	0	0	0
0	0	0	0	0
0	0	0	0	0
0	0	0	0	0
0	0	0	0	0
0	7006208	8851456	135	757
0	0	0	0	0
0	0	7961796608	0	1943798
868	0	0	0	0
812	0	0	0	0

There's more...

This script can be further improved. We have provided one or more recommendations here:

- Further research the file format and extend support for other information of interest via this recipe
- Check out `srum-dump` by Mark Baggett (`https://github.com/MarkBaggett/srum-dump`)

Conclusion

Whether this was your first time using Python, or you have employed it numerous times before, you can see how the correct code can make all the difference in your investigative process. Python gives you the ability to effectively sift through large datasets and more effectively find that proverbial smoking gun in an investigation. As you continue developing, you'll find automation becomes second nature and you're many times more productive because of it.

The quote "While we teach, we learn", attributed to Roman philosopher Seneca, is fitting here, even if a computer was not originally thought of as the subject being taught at the quote's conception. But it is apropos, writing code helps refine your knowledge of a given artifact by requiring you to understand its structure and content at a deeper level.

We hope you have learned a lot and continue to do so. There are a plethora of freely available resources worth checking out and open source projects to work on to better hone your skills. If there's one thing you should have learned from this book: how to write an amazing CSV writer. But, really, we hope through these examples you've developed a better feel for when and how to use Python to your advantage. Good luck cookin'.

Index

www.ingramcontent.com/pod-product-compliance
Lightning Source LLC
Chambersburg PA
CBHW060651060326
40690CB00020B/4591